Animals and Capital

Animalities

Series Editor
Matthew Chrulew, Curtin University

Editorial Advisory Board
Brett Buchanan, Concordia University of Edmonton
Vinciane Despret, Université de Liège
Donna Haraway, University of California, Santa Cruz
Jean Langford, University of Minnesota
Dominique Lestel, École normale supérieure
Stephen Muecke, University of New South Wales
Stephanie Posthumus, McGill University
Isabelle Stengers, Université libre de Bruxelles
Thom van Dooren, University of Sydney
Cary Wolfe, Rice University

Books available
Robert Briggs, *The Animal-to-Come: Zoopolitics in Deconstruction*
Deborah Bird Rose, *Shimmer: Flying Fox Exuberance in Worlds of Peril*
Dinesh Joseph Wadiwel, *Animals and Capital*

Forthcoming books
Dominique Lestel, *Animality: An Essay on the Status of the Human*, together
    with *Animalities* by Matthew Chrulew
Felice Cimatti and Carlo Salzani (eds), *The Biopolitical Animal*
Visit the series website at edinburghuniversitypress.com/series-animalities

Animals and Capital

Dinesh Joseph Wadiwel

Edinburgh University Press is one of the leading university presses in the UK. We publish academic books and journals in our selected subject areas across the humanities and social sciences, combining cutting-edge scholarship with high editorial and production values to produce academic works of lasting importance. For more information visit our website: edinburghuniversitypress.com

© Dinesh Joseph Wadiwel, 2023

Edinburgh University Press Ltd
The Tun – Holyrood Road
12(2f) Jackson's Entry
Edinburgh EH8 8PJ

Typeset in 10/14pt Warnock Pro and Gill Sans
by Cheshire Typesetting Ltd, Cuddington, Cheshire, and
printed and bound in Great Britain.

A CIP record for this book is available from the British Library

ISBN 978 1 3995 1806 2 (hardback)
ISBN 978 1 3995 1808 6 (webready PDF)
ISBN 978 1 3995 1809 3 (epub)

The right of Dinesh Joseph Wadiwel to be identified as the author of this work has been asserted in accordance with the Copyright, Designs and Patents Act 1988, and the Copyright and Related Rights Regulations 2003 (SI No. 2498).

Contents

Preface and Acknowledgements		vi
1.	Value	1
2.	Material	35
3.	Commodity	59
4.	Labour	91
5.	Circulation	130
6.	Resistance	161
7.	Dreams	192
Notes		216
Index		309

Preface and Acknowledgements

The phrase 'factory farm' is a canny hybrid of two different words, with two contrasting images conjured. On one hand, in the word 'farm' there is the popular imagination of a benign pastoral landscape which, if the nostalgia's memory is correct (which it rarely is), was the site of free-ranging, happy domesticated animals. This image is contrasted with its antithesis: in the word 'factory' we find the cold brutality and efficient workings of industrial production. Animal advocates spent decades forging the meaning of this phrase in order to inform the public of the conditions under which their food was produced. Over this period, pro-animal movements worked relentlessly to describe the meticulous and calculating ways in which, in modern farming, cruelty is multiplied and set to the marching rhythm of commercial production. And it wasn't just producers that were targets of the message, but consumers too. Advocates argued that the existence of these factory farms said something about humanity itself and its failed ethical values; that is our 'speciesism'.

Unfortunately, as morally and logically compelling as their message was, pro-animal movements have by and large been unable to stand in the way of the tide which arrived in the twentieth century and radically altered food systems across the globe. Today, the industrialised and commercialised production of animal-sourced foods is a prominent contributor to global food supplies. But while animal advocates have demonstrably failed to stop the rise of the factory farm, we should at least note one area of success. Despite the ongoing efforts of industries and governments to sequester these facilities, and even criminalise those who expose their internality, the efforts of pro-animal movements have made it clear that within these facilities lurk some of the worst horrors devised. Today, while almost nobody wants to look, almost nobody can pretend not to know.

To an extent, this book is also about the factory farm. But it differs from the tradition of animal advocacy above. While this book will traverse many sites of violence, my goal is not to 'reveal' to the reader the horrors within the factory farm; you should already know. Nor is the aim of this book to outline in philosophical terms whether our treatment of animals constitutes a moral wrong or says something about 'us' as humans. There are now many excellent texts in moral philosophy available to address the issues of conscience that might afflict us when we ponder our food systems; please consult these. Instead, my goal is to provide a new description of how intensive animal agriculture works within a global system of domination. In this book I want to understand the specific location of the factory farm within our prevailing economic system: that is, to describe the factory farm in its relationship to capitalism.

There are three ways in which this book provides a different understanding of the factory farm as a concept from those advanced previously. Firstly, in my view the factory farm is not simply about our so-called 'speciesism'. Instead, I believe we must understand the factory farm as the meeting point – or 'handshake' – between a prevailing hierarchical anthropocentrism and the capitalist production process. The former – hierarchical anthropocentrism – describes a set of knowledge relations associated with the European Enlightenment, which categorised and ranked humans and animals into a 'great chain of being' and provided a rationale for downwards violence and exploitation. The latter – capitalism, an economic system founded upon an endless cycle of production and exchange – overproduces commodities with the aim of generating surplus money. These two forces – hierarchical anthropocentrism and capitalism – come together in modern agriculture; they produce the factory farm, an apparatus that is perhaps without historical precedent.

Secondly, the factory farm is not simply the outcome of growing consumer demand for meat. This book is not only about the politics of consumption. Instead, my focus is on the site of production. From this standpoint, intensive animal agriculture has two functional purposes within capitalism. In one sense, the factory farm is a concentrated mechanism for extracting the labour and energies of those engaged within productive processes; not just human labour, but also the labour of animals. It is through this process that a surplus is derived: the promise of this value motivates production, and motivates a continual 'over-production'. In this case, this 'over-production' comprises a surplus of animals who must be born into the horror of intensive facilities through coerced gestational labour, 'processed' through a lifetime of containment, alienation and discomfort; and then, when it is economical to do so, these lives are extinguished. This calculating process of production

– life, death, then life again – creates, almost miraculously for consumers, animal-sourced foods as its result. It is here that the factory farm can be said to produce humanity itself. The factory farm as a site of production finds itself today deeply embedded within the 'biopolitics' of human population survival. The effect of the exponential expansion of animal-sourced foods globally is that today, more and more, animal populations have been functionally sewn into the biological sustenance of human populations. Humans have come to rely on animal-sourced foods as an energy source in order to survive, to labour, to care, to reproduce themselves; that is, as a means of 'social reproduction'. In so far as it would seem that animal-sourced foods appear today as fundamental to human survival, we might say that under capitalism, factory farms have been the instrument that has enabled an explosion in animal populations, which in turn has enabled the reproduction of humanity. Given this context, should we be surprised that humanity's addiction to industrial animal agriculture shows no sign of abating? This is, after all, not merely a moral problem but also a structural one.

Thirdly, animal advocates have argued that the factory farm turns animals into 'mere commodities'. This is certainly true. But our analysis should not just stop at the apparent wrong of commodification, which after all is central to most relations under capitalism. Here, a deeper analysis beckons on the distinct characteristics of the factory farm as a unique outcome of capitalist agriculture. There are a number of features to take note of here. We know that capitalism always seeks efficiencies in order to expand profits, and we might certainly observe that within animal agriculture, as in other industries, cost-cutting happens by reducing human labour time and replacing this with automated processes: machines, enclosures and facilities (or fixed capital). Of course, human labour remains in place in many animal agriculture systems, and as we know, it is often low paid (or occasionally forced) and is frequently dangerous. However, in arguing that human labour time is reduced, the process I am highlighting is the expansion of the mass of 'commodities' relative to the volume of human labour required to produce these. Today we see the continuing progression of this process of capitalist industrialisation on full display in agricultural facilities such as robotic dairy farms, which almost completely remove human labour from the scene of production. We also know that capitalism seeks the continual expansion of production for profit. No surprise, then, that as animal agriculture intensifies, the animal populations within expand in order for more commodities to be produced. Capitalism demands more production; more animals are bred and 'processed'; and more animal-sourced foods are produced. But this reveals a curious 'law' of capitalist animal agriculture. As I argue in this book, it means that the mass of animal labour expands as human labour time is diminished: a simple formula, but one we see materialised everywhere globally. Note here what we discover when we assemble together these observations and break down capitalist animal agriculture into its core characteristics. In a technical sense we could describe the factory farm as an apparatus of production where human labour time is minimised or eliminated; large quantities of fixed capital are deployed; the mass of animal labour time is expanded; and production becomes largely a process of interaction between animals and fixed capital to produce value. Perhaps a different way to describe all of this would be as follows. Humans start to disappear from the scene of production. Fixed capital, in the forms of terrifying machines and constraining, all-encompassing enclosures, is deployed and massified. Through forced reproduction, animal populations expand exponentially. Animals then face fixed capital in a horrific, brutalising, antagonistic and inherently deadly relation in order to produce surplus money and surplus food. This is the factory farm.

The above narrative allows us to see the factory farm in a new light. This space remains a site for concentrated cruelty, and animal advocates should certainly continue to spotlight that reality. But in line with the goals of this book, I want to also highlight how the factory farm is situated within the circuits of the capitalist economic relation. For those who are concerned about the injustice of the latter, the factory farm is worthy of attention. Indeed, my hope is that the lessons from this book are as compelling for anti-capitalists as they are for animal advocates. My explicit goal in writing the book is to bring together the concerns of two different movements – animal advocates and anti-capitalists – which, as I suggest, are operating on structurally overlapping terrain.

This book is the product of more than a decade of research. The origins of the text began with a set of questions I grappled with when drafting Chapter 4 of *The War against Animals*, on animals as property and commodities. Those familiar with that text will know that I began to interrogate the work of Karl Marx in that chapter, but only partially resolved the problems raised there; *Animals and Capital* attempts to finalise this analysis. Indeed, in some respects, reflecting on the relationship between the two texts, *Animals and Capital* could reasonably be considered the second volume of *The War against Animals* – though I cannot claim an unfailing coherence between these two works, since many of my ideas presented here have evolved and taken on different framings.

Over the last decade I have published work that has tried to refine some of these ideas, and this book contains writing that has previously been published elsewhere. Sections of the text Dinesh Joseph Wadiwel, "'Like One Who is Bringing his Own Hide to Market'": Marx, Irigaray, Derrida and Animal

Commodification', *Angelaki* 21, no. 2 (2016), 65–82, are reprinted with permission of the publisher Taylor & Francis Ltd. Sections of the text Dinesh Joseph Wadiwel, 'Chicken Harvesting Machine: Animal Labor, Resistance, and the Time of Production', *SAQ: The South Atlantic Quarterly* 117, no. 3 (2018), 527–49, are republished with the permission of the copyright holder, Duke University Press. Finally, sections of the essay Dinesh Joseph Wadiwel, 'Do Fish Resist?' *Cultural Studies Review* 22, no. 1 (2016), 196–242, are reproduced in this book; this work is available under a Creative Commons Attribution License 4.0, and I acknowledge UTS e-Press as the publisher.

This book was supported by a number of important fellowships and networks, which I wish to acknowledge. Some of my perspectives were shaped by important research conducted in 2015 as part of a Wissenschaftszentrum Berlin für Sozialforschung (WZB) Staff exchange fellowship, supported by the Sydney Democracy Network (SDN). This was an immensely valuable experience, and I extend my thanks in particular to Martin Krzywdzinski, Ulrich Jürgens and John Keane. Thanks are also owed to Animals' Angels in Germany for providing vital information on research related to live animal transport within the European Union. In 2016, I attended the Race and Animals Summer Institute at Wesleyan University, organised by three generous and influential scholars whom I admire greatly and wish to thank: Lori Gruen, Claire Jean Kim and Timothy Pachirat. The institute substantially reoriented my thinking, and thanks are owed in particular to the guest interlocutors: Colin Dayan, Maria Elena Garcia and Jared Sexton. In 2017 I was fortunate to speak about my ideas at events at the Sheffield Animal Studies Research Centre, University of Sheffield, and at the Institute of Geography, University of Edinburgh; my thanks to Alasdair Cochrane, Robert McKay, John Miller and Krithika Srinivasan for hosting me and supporting the development of my ideas. I attended a workshop on animal labour at Queen's University; thanks are owed Charlotte Blattner, Kendra Coulter and Will Kymlicka for hosting the conversations at that amazing event. I was fortunate to present in 2018 at the Humanities & Social Change Center at the University of California, Santa Barbara; my thanks to Thomas A. Carlson and Jan Dutkiewicz for making this event possible. And my thanks are owed to Maneesha Deckha, Kelly Struthers Montford and Chloë Taylor for hosting visits to the University of Victoria, the University of British Columbia and the University of Alberta respectively, where important in-progress work was presented and tested. At the University of Sydney, the Past & Present Reading Group in the discipline of Political Economy provided a wonderful space to think through ideas; while the Multispecies Justice collective at the Sydney Environment Institute provided a welcoming home. The Australasian Animal Studies Association continues to be one of the most dynamic studies associations I am aware of, and I am pleased to be actively involved with it.

Of course, aside from the generous scholars and interlocutors named above, there are many other people to thank for facilitating the emergence of this text. My thanks to Matthew Chrulew for investing deep faith and trust in the work, and for his ongoing friendship; and Carol Macdonald at Edinburgh University Press for ushering the text through reviews and approvals in the midst of all the uncertainty of a global pandemic. Thanks are also owed to Sarah Foyle, Judith Mackenzie, Camilla Rockwood and Rob Gibson for all their assistance during the production, copy-editing, proofing and indexing stages. There are, in addition, many people who have provided sharp thoughts, useful interventions and intellectual friendship over the last decade. It is difficult to do full justice to this list of generous folk; however, and in no particular order, I would like to acknowledge the following: Richard Twine, Anat Pick, Eva Haifa Giraud, Maan Barua, Kathrin Herrmann, Hilal Sezgin, Friederike Schmitz, André Krebber, Mieke Roscher, Jacqueline Dalziell, Nikki Savvides, Matthew Calarco, Tom Tyler, Siobhan O'Sullivan, Fiona Probyn-Rapsey, Yvette Watt, Peter Chen, Melissa Boyde, Yamini Narayanan, Guy Scotton, John Hadley, Jessica Ison, Annie Potts, Philip Armstrong, Esther Alloun, Christine Townend, Deidre Wicks, Jennifer McDonell, Robert Briggs, Angela Mitropoulos, Christiane Bailey, Frédéric Côté-Boudreau, Jacinthe Fournier, Rosemary-Claire Collard, Jesse Arseneault, Pablo Perez Castello, Jishnu Guha-Majumdar, Jack Halberstam, Zakiyyah Iman Jackson, Kiran Grewal, Meg Good, Ihab Shalbak, Danielle Celermajer, David Schlosberg, Christine Winter, Sophie Chao, Michelle St Anne, David N. Pello, Alexandra Isfahani-Hammond, Fahim Amir, Sue Donaldson, Nicola Short, Beck Pearse, Adam David Morton, Gareth Bryant, Joe Collins, Ariel Salleh, Susan Schroeder, Melinda Cooper, Nadine Ehlers, Sonja Van Wichelen, Tristan Bradshaw, Fleur Ramsay, Regrette Etcetera, Culum Brown, Cat Dorey, Victoria Braithwaite, Elisa Aaltola, Paola Cavalieri, Michael Addario, John Sanbonmatsu, Linda Alvarez, John Hutnyk, Sunaura Taylor, Nicole Shukin, Jessica Eisen, Saskia Stucki, Patricia Nonis, Vasile Stănescu, Iselin Gambert, Nekeisha Alayna Alexis and Eliza Littleton. I feel incredibly lucky to have been surrounded by deep love and support over the last decade; I would particularly like to thank Mary Wadiwel, Haresh Wadiwel, Julianne Elliott, Graham Meintjes, Jessica Robyn Cadwallader, Rhiannon Galla and Jinder Romana Elliott-Wadiwel.

Dinesh Joseph Wadiwel
Sydney, 2022

Aboriginal and Torres Strait Islander readers are respectfully cautioned that this book contains the name and words of a person who passed away during production of this text.

Value

> An hour of work may always be an equal sacrifice for the worker. But the value of commodities in no way depends on his feelings; nor does the value of his hour of work. Since A. Smith admits that one can buy this sacrifice sometimes more cheaply, sometimes more dearly, it becomes distinctly peculiar that it is supposed always to be *sold* for the same price. And he is indeed inconsistent. Later he makes *wages* the measure of value, not the amount of labour. *The slaughter of the ox is always the same sacrifice, for the ox. But this does not mean that the value of beef is constant.*
>
> Karl Marx, Grundrisse[1]

Animals involved in food production appear in at least three value forms under capitalism. Firstly, most animals are destined for transformation into consumption commodities: they will be made dead to become the food that humans eat. Secondly, animals are raw materials that circulate within economies: they are 'worked upon' within production lines in order to be transformed into products. And finally, animals labour when their placement within production necessitates that they produce value. In the case of food production, these animals work on themselves through metabolic labour to become consumption commodities, or to produce animal-based food products such as milk or eggs.

These three distinct positions within production are necessarily entangled. Some animals exist in a hybrid form embodying all three of these use values at once during their 'lifetime' (that is, alive as raw materials and labour, dead as meat). For example, the animal used for food arrives at the scene of production as a raw material, is required to work on themselves, and their life is cursorily extinguished so that they can become a consumption commodity. It is precisely the fact that animals are situated at the meeting point of these distinct forms under capitalism that suggests that these beings occupy a unique place within systems of exchange, in a fashion that is not directly comparable to most human workers. Whichever point in production animals occupy – consumption commodity, raw material, labour – it is these three intertwined 'lives' that mark out the distinct structural relation of 'food animals'[2] to capitalism, and suggest that these animals have emerged within capitalism as a distinct economic class.

Commodity

The *first position* – that is, the existence of animals, or parts of animals, as food commodities – is perhaps the most obvious to us, since most animals appear to us as consumption commodities as part of our everyday reality. The context is all around us: we are at a point in history where we use animals for food on a completely unprecedented scale. In 2020, close to 79 billion land animals were killed for human consumption; chickens alone comprised some 70 billion of these animals.[3] It is difficult to say how many fishes are killed annually, although, as I shall discuss in Chapter 6, the figure is possibly up to three trillion animals per year. It would be easy to conclude that this expansion in the use of animals has simply followed human population growth in an even manner. However, the growth rate of animals as food has exceeded the human population growth rate. In 1961, global per capita meat consumption, excluding fishes and seafood, was at 23kg per person; in 2014 this had nearly doubled to 43kg per person.[4] World per capita fish consumption has more than doubled.[5] Per capita dairy consumption has grown and is predicted to grow significantly in the Global South.[6] While there are important differences between different regions, localities and cultures in animal-based food consumption – something I shall discuss in Chapter 3 – taking a global picture, all indications suggest that animal-based foods will continue to consolidate their role as a mainstay food staple.[7]

This process of the accelerated expansion of the valorisation of animals as consumption commodities – a process Tony Weis has described as one of 'meatification'[8] – reflects what we might describe as a 'metabolic' interaction between capitalism, the industrialisation of human food supplies, and the politics of human survival. Here we cannot disconnect the relationship between the expansion of animal-based foods and the system-wide problem of the sustenance of the human workforce of capitalism. For example, Raj Patel and Jason Moore have reminded us that the industrialisation of the production of chickens for human food supplies was a central achievement of capitalism in the twentieth century.[9] For Patel and Moore, selective breeding and the industrialisation of chicken production reduced effective food prices, thus driving down the human wage cost of capitalism.[10] Part of this process involved the multiplication of animals in production to ensure large-scale human consumption.

This reality, that animals have been proliferated as consumption items and that accordingly they are relied upon for human survival, highlights the centrality of *reproduction* to these processes. In one sense, reproduction is central to the composition of the standing population of the billions of animals who are the constituents – or as I shall describe them, the 'labour force' – of the global food system. Domestication implies control over reproduction,[11] and under conditions of intensified industrial animal agriculture, the 'biopolitics' of this reproduction process must be ruthlessly managed to ensure financial viability.[12] The biological cycle of animal life is mapped onto the economic cycle of the production process;[13] for example, of the 75 million pigs in the United States, a veritable army of 6.4 million sows are continuously 'farrowed' in order to produce litters of piglets, who will be weaned, extracted and transferred to become the raw materials of food production.[14] Accordingly, feminist animal studies scholars have suggested that it is difficult to separate the politics of industrial control over animal reproduction from the human politics of gender.[15] As Kathryn Gillespie describes:

> her value is explicitly tied to her function as a reproductive machine. . . . A dollar value is placed not only on her body as a reproductive unit but also on each individual pregnancy. This is certainly a reflection of the economic interests of an industry driven by a close profit margin and the need to maximize the capital extracted from each body. Indeed, if a cow becomes infertile, or if a female calf is born sterile, her only remaining function is to be slaughtered and sold for her flesh. This industry discourse is also more generally a reflection of the way the female animal body is viewed – that because biologically she *can* reproduce, 'staying pregnant' must be the inherent function and purpose of her life.[16]

In other arenas of animal agriculture, nonhuman postnatal processes of care and nutrition are subsumed for human food commodity production: this is of course central to dairy industries, which typically use routinised, forced, industrial-scale artificial insemination to induce reproductive processes, with the aim of controlling and directing lactation towards the production of milk for human consumption.[17] As I shall describe in Chapter 4, the reproductive labour of animals – or 'gestational labour', as Sophie Lewis might describe this work[18] – is a central pillar of industrial agriculture.

But the politics of reproduction goes beyond the imperious management of the reproductive lives of animals. Animal-derived food has come to serve an essential function in the reproduction of human life. This, after all, is the implication of the massive change in diets that occurred over the last century: that is, animal life, more and more overtly, became a central necessity for the reproduction of human life. For capitalism, as an economic and social relation, this has two important implications. Firstly, human labour time has been positioned so that it requires animal life – or more particularly, as I shall describe in this book, 'animal labour time' – as a necessity for its reproduction. As Richard Twine frankly summarises: 'in a reductionist sense, animal bodies are factories for the production of protein for human consumption, for the conversion of plant material into animal commodities'.[19] The fact that animals must give up their life(times) for human survival produces a hostile logic: 'In order for me to survive you must serve me; you must die.' In many respects this logic is at the centre of what I have previously described as our 'war against animals'.[20]

Secondly, the reality that our most prominent relationship with animals involves transforming them into food for our survival has implications for how we understand 'social reproduction theory' more generally. Social reproduction theory attempts to comprehend not just what happens for workers in the scene of production, but also, as Tithi Bhattacharya describes, 'the complex network of social processes and human relations that produces the conditions of existence for that entity'.[21] This means paying attention to energy and labour outside of the formal sphere of production, including care labour regimes, forms of facilitation and the role of 'nature' in enabling formal production to occur. As we shall discover, animals pose a number of challenges to how we understand these forms of reproduction. On one hand, the positioning of animals within human food supplies means that animals are central to human social reproduction of the human worker: in other words, animals are required to reproduce human social reproduction, or alternatively, all human labour, whether formally 'productive' or not, today appears to require animals as a means of its reproduction. On the other hand, the lives of animals within intensive agriculture provide an illustration of seamless interconnection of formal production and social reproduction. Contemporary theoretical perspectives suggest that increasingly all production is indistinguishable from social production; indeed, as Michael Hardt and Antonio Negri point out, not only is formal production increasingly immaterial in nature, but 'the exploitation of living immaterial labor immerses labor in all the relational elements that define the social'.[22] In this context, it is worth emphasising that animals subsumed by capitalism, particularly food animals, have no necessary distinction between formal and social labour, no distinction between formal production and 'care', no distinction between work and home; on the contrary, the life of factory farm animals has been completely enveloped by capitalism so that it would seem that every moment of their life is potentially value-producing. The animal confined within intensive production typically has highly limited movement, ruthless management over diet, sociality, sexuality and reproduction, and controls exerted over when they live and die based on the rhythms of the economic cycle. All time for these animals is production time. There is no distinct social reproduction within the worlds of food animals under capitalism, since their whole lives, all their sociality, has become tied to the productivity of capital. Social reproduction is production for these animals. Thus, as I shall discuss in Chapter 4, what happens to animals in industrial production under capitalism conforms absolutely, and formidably, to what Marx described as a 'real subsumption'.

Raw material

The *second position* I identify relating to food animals under capitalism describes their existence as a raw material within circuits of production. This understanding of a 'raw material' reflects the appearance of objects of labour under capitalism as ready for value transformation.[23] Here, animals are deployed within production chains, and they circulate as matter worked upon as a means for the production of future value. At least according to a typical view of the labour process, production involves the application of labour to a raw material, which, through the application of energy and instruments, transforms this material into a product with a new use value. On the production side of capitalism, while it is perhaps jarring to our contemporary values to imagine that animals are prominently understood as mere raw materials, in reality this is exactly how they are treated on the balance sheets of industrial animal agriculture. They are perceived as entering production as assets to be value added, grown, arranged, located, harvested and depreciated like other raw materials within production processes.[24] But of course, animals are unlike other raw materials. Herein lies one of the many contradictions we will encounter through this book; indeed, as we shall see, and as stated by Marco Maurizi, 'animals express a living contradiction'.[25] Production processes will treat animals merely as raw materials; yet everywhere the reality of the technologies used to overwhelm, tie down, restrict and extract value from animals affirms that these beings are not mere raw 'inert' materials, and cannot be treated as such. Certainly, as I shall discuss below, the fact that animals are *not* mere raw materials is essential to their 'value proposition' under capitalism. At the level of normative value, we face other contradictions. Many animal advocates have responded to the contradiction described above – that animals are treated as mere raw materials when they are in fact sentient creatures – by arguing that we should instead value animals differently. And this has generated two prominent forms of critique: animal rights and animal welfare. Both of these forms of critique represent a response to the crisis presented by the construction of animals as mere raw materials and commodities under the historical conditions of industrial capitalism.

Animal rights theory has stressed the *intrinsic value* of animals, highlighting animal sentience, capabilities or ontologies in order to determine just or ethical treatment. Tom Regan's approach in *The Case for Animal Rights* is one example of this. Acknowledging that moral status usually rests upon awarding recognition based upon a capability for agency, Regan develops a concept of 'moral patients' as a means to include human and nonhuman others who are owed rights but lack the requisite traits to be recognised as agents in themselves.[26] In these cases, Regan argues that beings who are 'subject-of-a-life' should have their intrinsic value recognised.[27] In a similar vein, Martha Nussbaum develops the 'capabilities approach' to include recognition of the flourishing needs of all living beings, including nonhuman animals.[28] In order to arrive at animal capabilities, Nussbaum argues for reliance on 'species norms' to inform 'what the appropriate benchmark is for judging whether a given creature has decent opportunities for flourishing'.[29] In both Regan and Nussbaum, apparently 'natural' differences (between agents and patients and between humans and other species) have a bearing on the kind of moral recognition that is awarded to humans and animals in an ethical system. Intrinsic qualities determine moral worth (or value). The implications for the recognition of intrinsic value usually suggest that animals have a right to non-interference, and perhaps by extension, at least in some animal rights theory, we have duties to allow animals to flourish and be part of communities.[30] At the level of appearance, these arguments are intrinsically reasonable. However – and this is the contradiction within which animals today find themselves enclosed – demands for the abolition of human utilisation of animals are often treated as impractical, unrealistic and unthinkable. As I have elsewhere described, this is part and parcel of the epistemic violence that is an effect of the prevailing hierarchical anthropocentrism which informs most human relations with animals today.[31]

As a result, animal welfare approaches, on the other hand, appear to offer a much more 'realistic' response to the problem posed by the fabrication of animals as mere commodities. It is not that animal welfare rejects intrinsic value; rather advocates for welfare argue that considerations of intrinsic value must be weighed in relation to the realities of extrinsic use value, determined by and large, if not exclusively, by monetary prices within an economy. In this view, the intrinsic value of animals does not outweigh their value to humans as use objects; we can only value animals to the extent that they are useful to us. There is a strong impulse here to reconcile two systems of value that, at least on the face of it, are impossible to reconcile. John Webster, one of the most prominent advocates for an animal welfare approach, puts this issue plainly:

> Truth may be eternal but our perception of truth evolves. Two great pillars of truth as we view it today are, in fact, very new. The first is that Descartes was wrong. The animals we exploit for food are not mere machines but sentient creatures with the capacity to recognize quality in life, both suffering and pleasure. It follows therefore that the greater our dominion over any animal the greater our responsibility to provide it with a good life and a gentle death. The second great, but very new, truth is that the needs of mankind are better served by the free market than by the command economy; the supermarket is more comfortable than the Kremlin. Those however with a more oriental slant upon philosophy would argue that the Western pursuit of absolute values is ultimately futile since absolute values are unachievable and incompatible. Those (coming rapidly down to earth) concerned with animal production have to reconcile the ideal and incompatible goals of good welfare and economic advantage.[32]

Webster here curiously highlights a paradox within the value system of capitalism, where a growing everyday knowledge that animals feel pain, think, experience emotion and have worlds, is at odds with the flattening of animals into commodities with use values determined only by humans within monetary exchange markets. For Webster, capitalism does not answer this paradox, but offers a mechanism – through the market – to resolve a contradiction in value, albeit in a non-ideal way. We should note here that Webster places faith in the market not necessarily because it is the ideal mechanism but because it is fatalistically assumed to be relatively permanent and preferable to 'the Kremlin'. According to this view, capitalism is a reality we can't imagine living without. This creates a barrier with regard to how we treat animals, as under capitalism we cannot possibly recognise the true value of animals; their 'absolute value'. Instead we must reconcile ourselves to the reality of good welfare being driven by economic advantage.

The reconciliation Webster proposes is a reconciliation of the violence of anthropocentrism with the commodity form under capitalism. Abandoning the idealistic project of intrinsic value, Webster urges instead an engagement with the values that shape this commodity form: that is the reality of the fabrication of animals into commodities under capitalist agriculture, and the reality of their extrinsic use value as consumption items.

This interplay between the animal rights and animal welfare perspectives has, to a certain extent, been addressed by Gary Francione's important and influential critique of animals as property.[33] Francione argued that the property status of animals systematically shapes how animals are seen, so that often perceived conflicts over the utilisation of animals are in essence conflicts between those with property interests in animals.[34] To an extent Francione's critique remains fresh today and is certainly applicable to animals used within food systems, since these animals, including those captured on the seas, require their transformation into property in order for them to enter into processes of value and exchange. However, property is just the starting point for understanding the specific modality of domination that shapes the relation of animals to capitalism.[35] This is because we must tie the property status of animals with a historical understanding of their relation to the circumstances of economic production, which in turn constructs logics of value.

Animals, and particularly food animals, emerge under capitalism with a distinct form; a distinct use value. It is very clear that while animals have been property within a range of different cultural contexts and historical traditions, their use today differs from other historical utilisations. For example, uses of animals as investments (or stores of wealth) in different historical periods would shape how they were regarded as property, meaning that these animals may have lived long lives and been 'valued' by the households they were captured within. An animal that is useful to a small-scale farmer because they represent a store of wealth which can be drawn upon in a time of crisis, will be treated in a different way from an animal in a factory farm. Thus, as Erica Fudge notes, there were hybrid realities for animals owned as property within seventeenth-century smallholder production: the 'animals that people worked with and lived alongside in this period are *simultaneously* beings with individual status and nameless objects of purely economic value'.[36] This sort of use of animals differs dramatically from the contemporary rationalities of capitalist production. The subsumption of animals within capitalism marks their emergence as a raw material with a particular use value as a means for the realisation of surplus.

Here we might pause to narrow down what capitalism actually is; though in truth, our understanding of capitalism will have to be refined and augmented through this book as we go further in understanding the place of animals within it. We might define capitalism as an organism and mechanism that seeks to extract value and accumulate it in the form of capital: the latter comprising a social relation which is invested in its own continual accumulation. This conforms to the classic definition of capitalism outlined by Karl Marx in the first volume of *Capital* as essentially a circuit which circulates between money (M) and capital (C) in a movement that could be represented by M-C-M.[37] Money is used to purchase commodities, which are intended to be returned to their money form. If this process of transforming money into commodities and back again aimed only at recovering the money that was lost, then it would be pointless. However, the money-owner is incentivised to engage in this incessant process of conversion because of the promise that money invested will be returned with a surplus attached:

> the possessor of money becomes a capitalist. His person, or rather his pocket, is the point from which the money starts, and to which it returns. The objective content of the circulation we have been discussing – the valorization of value – is his subjective purpose, and it is only in so far as the appropriation of ever more wealth in the abstract is the sole driving force behind his operations that he functions as a capitalist, i.e. as capital personified and endowed with consciousness and a will. Use-values must therefore never be treated as the immediate aim of the capitalist; nor must the profit on any single transaction. His aim is rather the unceasing movement of profitmaking.[38]

Thus, capitalism does not merely accumulate wealth and profits as an object; but seeks instead to liberate a productive value that continually, incessantly, seeks its own reinvestment in order to generate more value. Importantly, as the quote above describes, capitalism operates as a drive which inhabits its actors and infiltrates relations; it is for this reason that methodologically speaking capitalism is less a description of a group of persons – capitalists – exploiting another group of people – workers – but instead might be better understood as the somewhat 'inhuman' process of life being drawn into a circuit which establishes an endless cycle of production and exchange aimed at generating surplus money (capital): what David Harvey has described as a 'bad infinity'.[39]

Food animals in industrial agriculture today are caught up in this 'bad infinity'; their proliferation a symptom of capitalist production forming a partnership with a hierarchical anthropocentrism. It is true that animals are property today as they were 500 years ago in some systems of small-scale animal agriculture. And certainly, forms of this small-scale agriculture continue today.[40] However, the rise of industrial-scale animal agriculture, and its role within capitalist food systems, suggest that the meaning of this property status of animals has shifted today. True to Marx's formulation – M-C-M – the existence of animals in their commodity form under capitalism is always only intended to be transitory. Industrial animal agriculture is driven by the quest for surplus, like any other profit-making industry under capitalism. And like any other capitalist industry, mass accumulation is a goal only because it allows for an expansion in money (or capital) as a result. Thus, animals appear in today's historical context as a peculiar source of value. However, this does not represent an inherent value; but instead animals appear as commodities with a use value for humans, and as a use value for exchange in order to gain profit. Thus, to an extent, I don't think we can contest Webster's perspective above, since animals almost certainly appear today, 'in reality', in exactly the way Webster describes: that is, as a commodity that presents as a contradiction in value; a contradiction we ask the market to resolve for us.

But the welfarist perspective only tells us one part of the story. It is certainly true that animals have a 'value' in our social, political and economic systems; a value that is produced by social relations.[41] But this value also reflects the process of fabricating animals to appear as a 'reflection' of value. The violence that animals are subject to in their commodification is a product of these rela-tions. This highlights the importance of focusing not only on the ontological or intrinsic meaning or value of animals as a means for grounding ethics; but instead exploring the systems of exchange and production that generate values in animal life (and death) and understanding the dynamic of their violence.[42]

Capitalism comes armed – both materially and symbolically – with a prevail-ing logic which arguably 'colonises' other ways of thinking about and valuing animals. This 'colonisation' might be understood as following the contours of the colonial project, as an epistemic enterprise. Here, we can be alerted to the way in which capitalism coincided with the colonial project to effect both a massive historical and continuing violence as part of European expansionism, and simultaneously, a process which established hegemonic cultures in the uti-lisation of animals. As David Nibert observes, this process tied together colonial violence and the emergence of settler colonial states with the development of large-scale animal agriculture: 'The immeasurable violence and oppression experienced by both humans and animals in the Americas and the accompa-nying terror, trauma, and deprivation created the enormous wealth necessary for the development of mercantilism and the rise of the capitalist system.'[43] In a direct sense, we cannot separate out the prevailing ways we view animals from this historical context; as Danielle Taschereau Mamers observes, 'colonial processes of extraction centrally involved animals and human–animal relations from the beginning'.[44] In settler colonial contexts, the ongoing process of 'settle-ment' included the location of grazing 'livestock' and other imported animals on stolen land; these animals helped to continue the process of altering landscapes and displacing traditional economies.[45] Further, colonialism is not merely positioned as a process at the level of material violence but also puts into action an epistemic violence and reorientation of values, knowledge and relations; it is a process that has 'marginalised "natives", animals, plants and all things of the natural world'.[46] As Kim TallBear notes, European colonisation relied on a deliberate project of displacement of a different relational system with non-human natures:

> Whether the settler state wants to farm, build a mine or a city, pump oil, or cordon off a national park, the 'resources' used to build these nation-states include the lands, waters, and other-than-human beings with whom Indigenous peoples are co-constituted. Indigenous peoples came into being as Peoples in longstanding and intricate relation with these continents and the other life forms here. Many Indigenous people have been eliminated. And for those of us who remain, our intimate relations with these lands and waters continue to be undercut and our memories relentlessly erased when the extractive nation-state continues to be dreamed. The late nineteenth-century assimilative mantra 'Kill the Indian, save the man' implies not simply an attack on our cultures but more precisely an attack on the relations – both human and other-than-human – that make us who we are.[47]

In this context we are reminded that the violence that accompanies the imposition of capital's values came hand in hand with, and perhaps was preceded and fortified by, other projects, such as that of imperialism and colonialism.[48]

This history, which has altered how many of us see animals, shapes the realities for how animals are used today, so that globally most food animals are subject to conditions of production within industrial animal agriculture that are without historical precedent. These conditions include mass accumulation, containment and slaughter on an unimaginable scale; complete control over reproductive life and the massification of forced gestational labour; and end-to-end management of the conditions of production and labour which means that every moment of these animals' lives is ruthlessly controlled, including the length of life, which is curtailed swiftly, and without hesitation, at exactly that point which proves most profitable. Arguably these conditions of production are without compare to any period of human history, and reflect how animals are valued within some dominant systems of knowledge. Again, the distinct 'use value' of animals under capitalism is important to comprehend; it is, after all, the evolving perception of how many of us humans imagine animals as useful to us that shapes the modalities of violence, control and production we apply to them. And here, a historically constituted *use value* (as commodity, as exchange value) is the important substitution for the concept of 'property interest'; the property status of animals is important, but it is only the beginning in understanding the pattern of domination which shapes the lives of the animals we see around us.

Labour

While it is relatively easy to 'see' animals as either consumption commodities or as raw materials within production processes – prevailing knowledge systems continually ensure that animals 'appear' as such – the *third position* I describe in this book – that is, animals as labour – is less apparent. To an extent, because prevailing knowledge systems make animals appear as raw materials and consumption commodities, this produces an epistemic effect which hides their active role as labourers: 'we' perceive that production processes *act upon animals* in order to produce value, rather than the reverse: *that animals act within production processes in order for value to be produced.* At base this attitude, which assumes their passivity, might be traced to a particular form of anthropocentrism which haunts how many of us, including animal advocates, look at animals and perceive them and their power. Tom Tyler neatly describes this form of anthropocentrism as *evaluative*, in so far as the human views the non-human through a gaze of supremacy, which holds that humans have particular propriety or unique characteristics, and with this 'the bald belief or supposition that the human species is, in some sense, of greater importance and value than all else . . . [it] . . . implies a hierarchy, or chain of being, from the summit of which humanity gazes down on lesser creatures'.[49] It is precisely this hierarchical anthropocentrism that haunts conceptions of animals in production, which results in framing these beings purely as raw materials, rather than as agents within production which animate productive processes through their creative labour. Certainly, managers of agribusiness imagine that animals are merely resources that are worked on in order to become 'products'. But it is disarming to recognise that many animal advocates implicitly imagine animals in this way too: as simply beings who are forced to become raw materials in order to produce food, rather than active subjects who have created, through their labour (forced or otherwise) the world that we see. It is of course true that animals are subject today to intense modalities of violence and domination which limit autonomy: they are thus victims of large-scale systems of violence. However, animals are also *agents* of production: it is their capacity to generate value that shapes their use value to capitalism; it is this use value that has been leapt on and parasitically 'sucked' by capitalist production systems.

Understanding animals as *labour* – indeed seeking to frame animals, in a primary sense, as agents of production – helps us to look at the relation of animals to capitalism in a different way. Firstly, from the perspective of power, it allows us to recognise that animals are co-producers of the world we see before us. Against the view that would suggest that we humans have one-sidedly created the world, the recognition that animals are active as labourers offers an antidote to this anthropocentrism in the form of the recognition that this same world we see before us would not be possible without the energies of animals. If animals labour, then the value that is derived from this work has helped generate the 'wealth' we see before us: buildings and roads, chemicals and technologies, money and commodities.[50] Further, in a material sense, the reality that animals exist as a mode of subsistence means that their labour produces 'us' humans: at least for those who consume animal-sourced foods, animal labour fabricates bodies and existences, which in turn allows these bodies to also labour.

Secondly, recognising animals as labour means something for how we understand the production of value under capitalism. And as I shall discuss, it is in the realm of value that recognition of animal labour is most profound, since this both disarms how we analytically examine capital as a relation, and simultaneously offers an explanation for why utilisation of animals under capitalism has endured, thrived and proliferated. Rather than imagine, as many appear to do, that the growth in human utilisation of animals has its causation in an unrelenting desire by human consumers for animal-based foods,[51] this analysis on the contrary allows us to understand that what has driven the massive change in how humans use animals is the drive for surplus value, not merely extracted from the human workers involved in animal agriculture and its associated value chains, but also, and perhaps primarily, in the distinct value that animals produce when they are deployed within these circuits of production. Capital demands that surplus is extracted from labour, human or nonhuman. And the means of consumption are arranged in order to allow this labour to be reproduced. From this perspective, it is not simply consumption that drives production; rather, we cannot understand consumption without understanding the drive for the capture of surplus within the sphere of production. The production of surplus creates an imperative which drives forward capitalist production; this means we cannot naïvely focus on the demand for consumption items as if industrial animal agriculture only exists because meat is too tasty for consumers to resist: 'capitalism is already essentially abolished once we assume that it is enjoyment that is the driving motive and not enrichment itself'.[52] Production, reified under capitalism as the source of surplus, is the engine which impels capitalism forward.

I note here that I deliberately understand value as arising through production, setting aside more recent considerations of 'financialisation', or what John Bellamy Foster describes as the 'long-run shift in the center of gravity of the capitalist economy from production to finance'.[53] While financialisation has implications for the economic functions of contemporary industrial animal agriculture,[54] a focus on animals as labourers highlights the essential continuing role of material production and the work of animals, material work, which as I outline, is irreplaceable for the production of value.[55] From this standpoint, we need to understand how animals function as value in both spheres of production and consumption; it is the movement of animals between these spheres that defines the metabolic relations of animals to humans under capitalism.

Finally, recognition that animals perform labour shapes how we view their relation to capitalism, and importantly what it means to end the capitalist relation. It allows us to resist the view that animals are mere commodities for consumption or mere raw materials. They are instead more than this; they are quite literally a labour force of capitalism, *perhaps the most significant labour force of capitalism*, and certainly one that is more numerous, as a mass of labourers, than that comprised by human workers. This has ramifications for both how we analytically view capitalism, and what we understand as the goal for the transformation of capitalism into a new economic order. My argument is that food animals were fabricated as a distinct structural class under capitalism, not only attached with a peculiar set of value relations, but simultaneously, politically positioned in relations of domination that remain unique in character. Understanding these relations is important for both animal advocates and leftists (and perhaps, animal advocates *who are* leftists): the relation of animals to capitalism is important if we are to challenge human domination of animals and the domination of life by capital. If the aim of resistance to capitalism is to free labour from its subjugation, then the revolutionary project is not faithful to its goal if it does not consider this massive animal labour force and its contribution to everything we see before us. This book seeks in no uncertain terms to imagine a pathway to democratic control over production, surplus and labour time that includes nonhuman animals as constituents: what we might describe as a 'communism'[56] which displaces a hierarchical anthropocentrism.

Reading Marx

Any critical analysis of capitalism must include an engagement with Marx, and this book is no exception.[57] Indeed, much of this text is a theoretical engagement with Marx and the implications for animals of the value theory he described, particularly, but not solely, in the first volume of *Capital*.

An immediate challenge is that it is difficult to decipher where Marx stood on animals, and whether his framework can be saved from the anthropocentrism that appears, at least in some ways, integral to it. This does not mean that animals are absent from the pages of Marx's text; far from it. One of the curious things about reading Marx is the continuing references that are made to animals and their situation within the pages of these foundational texts. Marx repeatedly refers to animals: they 'appear' as raw commodities that are worked on in agriculture, as instruments of consumption for industrial production, as food for workers, and as 'living tools' that provide traction for industries.

This of course does not mean that Marx expressed a normative interest in the plight of animals under capitalism. Instead, the appearances of animals within these texts, at least in part, represent the reality of the context within which Marx (and those who he responded to, such as Adam Smith and David Ricardo) wrote. Animals and animal products, like corn, iron and cotton, were the raw materials, traction and consumables that capitalist production worked with, and as such, animals appear everywhere; capitalism could certainly not do without them, and Marx could not help but notice them. But this does not mean that Marx took a passionate interest in animals in the same way in which he took an interest in human labour power. Animals were important factors of production within the capitalism Marx analysed, but of no political importance to his project. This is perhaps reflected in the attitude Marx displayed towards animal advocates; there is certainly evidence that Marx was highly sceptical of the animal welfare movements active during his time, perhaps epitomised by the mocking tone applied to the association between bourgeois and animal concerns: 'You may be a model citizen, perhaps a member of the RSPCA, and you may be in the odour of sanctity as well; but the thing you represent when you come face to face with me has no heart in its breast.'[58]

This dispassionate interest in animals is heightened by the ontological assumptions advanced within Marx's project, most forcefully in the early works. It is relatively well known that early Marx reserved the creative activity of productive labour for humans alone. We find stark evidence for this in the *1844 Economic and Philosophic Manuscripts*, where Marx differentiates the labour of animals from that of humans, arguing that while animals cannot distinguish themselves from their life activity,[59] humans, on the other hand, are purported to labour consciously and can produce regardless of necessity,[60] realising what Ted Benton describes as a collective human 'historical potential'[61] (that is the capacity for artifice, and with this the ability to memorialise the being of the human species within a historical context).[62]

It is not accidental that Marx drew a line between humans and animals here. We should recognise that what was at stake in Marx's division between humans and animals was the attempt to mark an ontological schism that allowed for the creation of a particular philosophical outlook. In this sense it is a function of this analysis that Marx saw a strong division between humans and animals in these early manuscripts, since this imagined division served a productive purpose in helping to craft fundamental philosophical concepts. We see this clearly in the construction of the philosophical and sociological concept of 'alienation', which relied on the division between human and animal for its legibility:

> As a result, therefore, man (the worker) no longer feels himself to be freely active in any but his animal functions – eating, drinking, procreating, or at most in his dwelling and in dressing-up, etc.; and in his human functions he no longer feels himself to be anything but an animal. What is animal becomes human and what is human becomes animal.[63]

Here animals are not neglected by Marx: instead they are central to the production of Marx's theoretical concepts, since in this example, the concept of alienation, a concept which is central both to Marx and also to the genealogy of social theory,[64] relied upon a negative or antagonistic positioning of animals as a raw material for producing the theoretical concept. Here, a conception of animals (or animality) allows Marx to normatively position the experience of alienation under capitalism within a teleology that promises it relief. As Michel Foucault observes:

> Thrust back by poverty to the very brink of death, a whole class of men experience, nakedly as it were, what need, hunger, and labour are. What others attribute to nature or to the spontaneous order of things, these men are able to recognise as the result of a history and the alienation of a finitude that does not have to have this form. For this reason they are able – they alone are able – to re-apprehend this truth of the human essence and so restore it.[65]

The formula is set: capitalism transforms humanity to the state of animality; this experience is disorienting since humans recognise they are not animals.

(Human) workers: rise up and reclaim your humanity in order to escape your alienation!

There has certainly been some disagreement from scholars over whether it is fair to level an accusation of anthropocentrism against Marx, since, true to his method, his somewhat impoverished view of animals may simply have been reflective of an attempt to provide an unflinchingly accurate portrayal of the 'dialectical' position of animals as they were historically situated within material relations.[66] In this view, 'animals play a rather passive role in Marx's critique of political economy, since we have always seen them as productive factors'.[67] In this respect, defenders of this view believe it would be unfair to criticise Marx for his anthropocentrism, as all he was doing was frankly relaying the position of animals as factors of production within capitalism, just as he describes without apparent sentimentality the deployment of human labour as a commodity with a use value for generating surplus.

As we shall see, I am less sympathetic to the cause of defending Marx from the charge of anthropocentrism: in my view, we can almost certainly find examples of this anthropocentrism, which, as I shall argue, prevented Marx from providing a complete picture of capitalism as an economic and social relation. However, while I advance this scholarly view in this book, the charge of anthropocentrism against Marx is less relevant than the substantive problem which followed it: namely the legacy of anthropocentrism within left thought following Marx, and its impact for the shape and concerns of anti-capitalist movements today. For even if we can leave aside Marx's views, the sense that pro-animal struggle is not centrally connected to the problem of overthrowing capitalism, or is perceived to have reflected a bourgeois set of concerns, haunts the history of left movements.[68] It has meant that while there have been long histories of animal advocacy that have accompanied the history of industrial capitalism, ranging from early attempts to impose basic welfare protections on industries, to contemporary animal rights and vegan movements, there seems to be little or no correspondence between these social movements and those of the organised left. Where there are obvious intersections – such as in the writings of socialist Henry Salt[69] – these appear as almost erroneous exceptions to the rule. More worrying is that when it comes to animals there seems to be almost no discernible difference between the position taken by progressive movements and their opponents, at least with respect to radical demands made by animal liberationists to end human domination of animals. Thus, John Sanbonmatsu offers the blunt diagnosis:

> the Left with few exceptions has historically viewed human violence towards other beings with indifference . . . it is one of the ironies of social thought that

the views of leftists and rightists converge on the question of animal rights. Both sides affirm the sovereign right of members of *Homo sapiens* to exploit and kill other living beings as they wish; both view animal liberation as a danger to established human society.[70]

Certainly, 'indifference' is a useful way to describe the attitude of left movements, who have by and large failed to prioritise, and in some cases completely ignored, the intensification of violence towards animals that has marked the growth of capitalist agriculture.

We should certainly not pretend here that there is a self-evident solidarity possible between pro-animal movements and anti-capitalist forces: indeed, as this book will continually remind us, there is no easy alliance, due perhaps to the structural difference of location of the human worker *vis-à-vis* the food animal. And it is instructive to note, in this context, that predominant strategies by animal advocates have not always been shaped in ways which might create solidarity with anti-capitalist movements. In part this is because much animal advocacy has, by and large, and relevant to Marx's critique of the RSPCA above, been framed by what might be understood as 'bourgeois' demands and interests.[71] The recent history of Global North animal advocacy, at least from the publication of Peter Singer's *Animal Liberation* onwards, has been largely shaped by the language of analytic philosophy and political liberalism: as Paola Cavalieri observes, 'the discourse on animals tended to be relegated to the realm of so-called practical ethics . . . analytic authors, though being extremely radical in the theoretical area, were not always politically equipped to develop a critique of established social institutions'.[72] Given these theoretical underpinnings, it is perhaps unsurprising that much work within animal ethics and animal rights theory tended to leave unattended the relationship between the domination of animals and the domination of life inherent to capitalism. And given this theoretical backdrop, it is perhaps not surprising that the predominant visible strategy of animal advocacy has focused on the politics of consumption: namely, in campaigning that seeks to convince individuals to change their consumption purchases and practices, encouraging the avoidance of animal products or purchases of animal products that are produced in less cruel conditions. Here, individual and personal choices are given primacy, and political strategies aim at securing the ability and imperative of individuals to *choose*; whether in the form of campaigns to expand available plant-based products, convince individuals to 'go vegan' or even advance legal protections for individuals who choose to identify as vegans.[73]

I should stress that in focusing on consumption, it is not that animal advocates have ignored production. Indeed, this is the paradox. Despite the predominance of individual focused action as a mainstay strategy (for example, 'go vegan'), the curious aspect of pro-animal politics is that it is not necessarily 'indentitarian' in a strict form, since it derives its energy from reflection on the brutal reality of the collective conditions for animals within capitalist production, and not necessarily the identity of the human advocate. Of course, I don't mean to imply that the emergence of fashionable vegan cultures in urban centres today is not about the politics of identity; far from it. However, the politics of animal rights has also curiously resisted individual identity politics at the same time. For example, consider the performative repertoire of contemporary animal rights groups during soundless street vigils, which emphasise the individual anonymity of human protestors (such as with the use of masks) in order to highlight to viewers the conditions of suffering of animals within industrial agriculture. Here animal protest does not appear in a straightforward way as a politics of 'recognition', as Nancy Fraser might describe it, in so far as animal advocates do not necessarily seek non-discrimination and inclusion for themselves; the demand to abolish industrial animal agriculture in this sense looks more like a demand for redistribution, aimed at structural change to the basis of production within society.[74]

Here, despite the close alliance between animal ethics and the politics of consumption with liberalism and individualism, the structural issues at stake within pro-animal movements have had, at their heart, the problem of capitalist production as the primary site of antagonism. This means that in a sense, pro-animal movements can be understood as a 'symptomatic' response to the altering structural position of animals within capitalist agriculture. Consider the emergence of radical animal rights movements in the 1970s, often associated with the publication of Singer's *Animal Liberation.* In many respects, these movements responded to the horror associated with the rationalised, industrialised production of animals: that is, the factory farm. The factory farm represents the full immersion of animals within the rhythms of the production cycles under capitalism, connected with a global project of massification of animal products as a means of sustenance for human populations. As I shall discuss in Chapter 4, what marks out the factory farm is the absence of the 'human–animal relation'; humans have largely disappeared from the scene (since one aim of intensification of animal agriculture is the reduction in necessary human labour time), setting the stage for the direct antagonism between animals and fixed capital. It is for this reason that Singer's *Animal Liberation* is not so much a treatise against anthropocentrism or 'speciesism' itself (although these concerns loom in the background of the text) but a manifesto that problematises market-oriented industrial animal production: that is, the factory farm as the precise meeting point of a violent anthropocentrism with the rationalised modalities of industrial capitalism, and the associated massive expansion in deployment of fixed capital.

In this context, the wave of pro-animal struggle against the factory farm which followed the publication of Singer's text seems inescapably connected with the problem of industrial capitalism and its relation to animals. Here, human–animal relations are problematised and become contentious when they come into view through the historically specific structural condition of animals under capitalism.[75] Pro-animal movements do not merely respond to the animal as an isolated abstract intrinsic rights holder; on the contrary, they engage with animals in a historical, material, political and economic relation, and the horror of animals in direct relation with enclosures, machines and instruments of production. That is, contemporary advocacy is motivated by the image of animals confronting fixed capital – tight enclosures, automated feeding mechanisms, conveyor belts, stunning machines, etc. – as part of the production process. Animals 'appear' to us today in this context. Perhaps, in this sense, it was only through industrial capitalism, and its vast exploitation of animals on a hitherto unimaginable scale, that animals became perceptible to many humans as political subjects, and 'liberation' became imaginable:[76] indeed, it is perhaps a curious historical combination of the consciousness of the violence animals endure under industrial capitalism, the emerging knowledge of animals' sentience and capacities, and the growing technical capacity to imagine human life without animal life as a means of subsistence, which has enabled contemporary forms of radical pro-animal politics to come into existence.[77] Certainly, as I shall argue in Chapter 3, contemporary debates about consumption and ethical veganism occur, for better or worse, upon this distinct historical terrain.

That the site of production should have such a profound effect on the development of animals as a political subjectivity to be fought for within contemporary politics makes the absence of strategy from animal advocates relating to altering capitalist production all the more puzzling. Animal advocates have by and large constrained themselves to making moral demands relating to the treatment of animals *in* production, rather than seeking to *take control or democratise production itself*. This in a sense marks the apparently fundamental schism between radical animal advocacy and labour movements: while radical pro-animal movements have demanded the end of production as a moral goal (close factory farms, stop animal testing), radical labour movements have instead produced demands for the control of production itself (reduce labour time, increase pay, socialise or democratically control the means of production). As I shall argue, if there is any strategic potential in building an alliance politics between the project of animal liberation and that of anti-capitalism, it surely depends on the ability to find a connection between these two very different attitudes towards production under capitalism. We should not pretend that reconciling these two movements will be easy: if animals appear as the means of production and as the means of subsistence, then democratic control over the means of production has peculiar, and perhaps contradictory, meanings for animals as political subjects. (As I shall discuss in Chapter 2, perhaps the unique structural position of food animals under capitalism might foreclose any such solidarity.)

An animal labour theory of value

If collaboration between pro-animal movements and leftists is possible, then there is also a lot of theoretical work to do. We certainly must deal squarely with a failing in traditional left scholarship to pay attention to animals; that is, to take account of *all* the constituents of capitalism. Addressing the anthropocentricist failure of the left theoretical project to acknowledge the distinct place of animals is no doubt a massive undertaking. But this is a familiar problem, in so far as this history of the contestations in left thought in the twentieth century and beyond has arguably been shaped by the demand to account for lives, subjectivities and structural positions that were neglected in earlier analyses. It is no secret that there were numerous failures within classical left theory to articulate a range of potentially unique formations and subject positions under capitalism. These failures have in turn generated the need for alternative readings of capitalism and its history. Amongst these alternative readings, we could include here Sylvia Federici's project to understand the domination of women as part of the primitive or original (*'ursprünglich'*) accumulation, and the role of women's resistance in the history of capital.[78] Alternatively, we could point to Cedric Robinson's work highlighting the role of race relations and slavery in racial capitalism and narrating the emergence of Black liberation movements.[79] Or we could highlight the early work of disability social model theorists, such as Michael Oliver, to locate the disabled person within the evolution of capitalism as an economic and social relation.[80] In this respect, Federici, Robinson and Oliver all offer useful correctives that allow for a reappraisal of how we understand capitalism, which simultaneously challenges the taken-for-granted assumptions of left theory.

Is such a corrective possible when it comes to animals? Incorporating animals into left theory faces a number of challenges, including, perhaps most prominently, the avowedly anthropocentric theoretical legacy we find in Marx, which I have discussed above. One view, and certainly a view which is not without its rationality, is that the anthropocentrism within modernist thinkers such as

Marx prevents this theory from being salvaged for a contemporary analysis of the nonhuman. Certainly, this attitude would follow from Dipesh Chakrabarty's important interventions, which have pointed out that the existential crisis of anthropogenic climate change forces us to reconsider, and perhaps discard, humanist perspectives on modernity and capital, at least in so far as these logics have participated in the production of the environmental crisis before us.[81] Perhaps in this vein we need new models of thinking, new ontologies, and this means rejecting humanist philosophies and narratives of the European Enlightenment (I shall examine the promise and limitations of 'new materialisms' in Chapter 2).

Alternatively, we could seek to salvage the Marxist tradition. Here we would seek a corrective that undoes the anthropocentrism of Marx and highlights the role of animals as agents of production within capitalism. However, while there are now a range of accounts within green Marxist and ecofeminist theory which take animals into account, it is not clear that these deliver this sort of corrective, or at least one adequate for the work I do in this book. Allow me to consider a few of these accounts here. One view is that Marx has been fundamentally misread, and has always accounted for nature, and with this, provided a way for thinking about animals. Perhaps one of the most prominent commentators here is John Bellamy Foster, who offered a highly influential rereading of Marx, challenging the view that Marx simply reflected a prevailing modernist antagonism towards nature.[82] Against this, Foster offers the provocation that Marx had indeed theorised nature and the looming environmental crisis generated by capitalism in the concept of the 'metabolic rift':

> It was in *Capital* that Marx's materialist conception of nature became fully integrated with his materialist conception of history. In his developed political economy, as presented in *Capital*, Marx employed the concept of 'metabolism' *(Stoffwechsel)* to define the labor process as 'a process between man and nature, a process by which man, through his own actions, mediates, regulates and controls the metabolism between himself and nature'. Yet an 'irreparable rift' had emerged in this metabolism as a result of capitalist relations of production and the antagonistic separation of town and country. Hence under the society of associated producers it would be necessary to 'govern the human metabolism with nature in a rational way', completely beyond the capabilities of bourgeois society.[83]

For Foster, this metabolic rift is culpable for the contemporary conditions faced by animals within industrialised animal agriculture: 'the metabolic rift is not limited to external nature, but also encompasses the expropriation of corporeal beings, where nonhuman animals are reduced to machines in a system predicated on constant expansion, which ignores and increases their suffering'.[84] Here, Foster offers a defence of Marx through a rereading.[85] Animals are considered part of the nature which capitalism 'super-exploits' as its material base.[86] While Foster is clearly critical of the factory farm, there is nothing in Foster's perspective that would suggest that human domination of animals is a problem *per se*; rather, in this view the industrial conditions faced by animals in production are merely a reminder of the rupture that has been created in the metabolic exchange between humans and nature.

Jason W. Moore provides an alternative viewpoint.[87] Moore does not offer the same spirited defence of Marx which we find in Foster; instead, a less anthropocentric reading of the history of capitalism is provided, one which seeks to highlight that informal unpaid labour and nonhuman energies are required to continually supply the material base for capitalism. Moore's innovation is to argue that capitalism does not represent only a material relation (or the non-relation of the 'rift' as described by Foster),[88] but instead represents a project reconfiguring capital and nature, both materially and epistemologically. In this reading, Moore utilises posthumanist approaches to problematising the society/nature split, decentring humans from the story of capitalism and instead treating capitalism as an ecology in itself; here Moore declares that the 'key to understanding the unfolding systematic crisis of the twenty-first century is a historical method – which implies a radical new praxis – in which human and extra-human natures co-produce historical change'.[89] Moore suggests that the binary between nature and society operates as an abstraction which shapes the material politics of relations within the ecology of capitalism, establishing a unique correspondence between the exploitation of formal productive labour and a cheap nature which must be appropriated to a massive degree in order for value to be produced under capitalism: 'wage-workers are exploited; everyone else, human and extra-human, is appropriated. . . . Value does not work unless most work is not valued.'[90]

Animals used for food are central to the account Moore advances, as well as in the later framework developed by Moore and Raj Patel.[91] Here we find that intensification of animal agriculture served a function in reducing the costs of the reproduction of human labour, and that the process of making animal-based food 'cheap' required these forms of intensification, including, for example, shortening the lives of broiler chickens in order to reduce the turnover time for this production.[92] Moore offers the innovation – one which is useful for this book, at least – of noticing that the logics which inform the factory farm are interconnected with those that inform human labour, and only a dualistic division between society and nature means that we treat these as separate phenomena: 'the danger is to see "factory farming" as an environmental question and "factory production" as a social question'.[93] However, like Foster, Moore has not produced an account that is critically concerned with human domination of animals. The excesses of factory farms are instead presented as an example of how nature is fabricated as 'cheap'. The distinct place of animals in this story does not appear to extend beyond this. And in this context, it is notable that Moore explicitly rejects the idea that animals labour in a 'valuable' way.[94] Alternatively, according to Moore, animals exist as part of the extra-human natures which are appropriated (rather than exploited) by capitalism in order for human labour to be perceived as producing value. Animals thus do not act as agents of value production in a way that is comparable to human labour.

Ariel Salleh's *Ecofeminism as Politics* offers a different approach to questions of capitalism's relation to nature, and a different response to Marx. Salleh calls for 'an embodied materialism, asking for thinkers and activists to recognise the historical significance of "othered labour", that unnamed class of hands-on workers who catalyse natural processes, so enabling life-on-earth to flourish'.[95] Salleh's ecofeminism aligns the domination of nature with the domination of women,[96] arguing that capitalism embodies these values simultaneously.[97] This lens guides Salleh's reading of Marx, which situates the importance of Marx (and of Friedrich Engels) for left movements while still calling into question the elements of this scholarship which are problematic, including faith in productivism and technology. Importantly, Salleh argues that women's labour and its importance appears missing for Marx: 'Symptomatically, while Marx's text cascades with imagery of the powers of Man and even technology, the powers and "labours" of women rest unspoken in his interpretation of human existence.'[98]

One of the unique features of Salleh's approach is that human domination of animals is treated as a distinct problem. Unlike Foster or Moore, who do not necessarily see an inherent issue with human domination of animals, only reading the character and intensity of this domination as symptomatic of the rise of capitalism, Salleh's ecofeminist politics offers the view that the factory farm is an outcome of 'the subjection of all Others to white middle-class masculine will'.[99] Salleh thus endorses animal liberation tactics and vegetarianism as left strategies for change.[100] Here the argument put forward is that ecofeminism represents a space that allows for a merger of a range of different emancipatory projects representing constituents who have been traditionally locked out of left movements; ecofeminism here is argued to carry 'forward four revolutions in one':

Ecofeminist politics is a feminism in as much as it offers an uncompromising critique of capitalist patriarchal culture from a womanist perspective; it is a socialism because it honours the wretched of the earth; it is an ecology because it reintegrates humanity with nature; it is a postcolonial discourse because it focuses on deconstructing eurocentric domination.[101]

Whether it is possible to unite such diverse social movements is a question, and anxiety, that will continually be interrogated in this book. However, we can note that Salleh's framework at least recognises the diverse constituencies under capitalism, their different interests, and imagines what unique strategies might be required for emancipation.

All three perspectives – Foster, Moore and Salleh – offer very different views on how we might read Marx: for Foster, we just need to read Marx more carefully; for Moore, Marx offers some key perspectives and language, but these must be amended and reinterpreted to understand how history produces a changing set of relations between nature and society; and finally, for Salleh, Marx illustrates the problem posed by masculinist systems of knowledge, which reproduce the domination of nature in the same way, and according to the same logics, as the domination of women. However, I raise these three very different perspectives on Marx not to highlight their divergence, but also to show what they share. For when it comes to animals, all three perspectives place animals within 'nature' as a resource to be used by production rather than as an active agent within production itself. For Foster, the factory farm represents a perverted relation with nature, a symptom of the metabolic rift between capital and ecology. For Moore, animals represent a fundamental interconnected aspect of what happened to human food supplies under capitalism as part of a reconfigured nature; this configuration of nature allows for the mass appropriation of animals, like other resources produced on the 'cheap'. For Salleh, what happened to animals under capitalism reflects an extension of that same logic of domination which has shaped the lives of women, Indigenous peoples and other racialised groups, and environments that have experienced the violence of capitalism. In all of these accounts, animals are placed outside of, fabricated into, or assumed to be part of 'nature', and thus do not formally belong within the sphere of productive labour; indeed, what marks animals out is that they are *other* to the process of *formal* production, they are not the engine or agent of this production. In all three accounts, animals are simply one more sign of the excesses of capital, rather than representing a distinct structural position and being important for how we understand capitalism as a relation. Further, because animals belong to a nature that is externalised from production and are thus not a 'formal' source of labour within production, they do not beckon separate analysis. Against this perspective, it is my intention in this book to place animals within 'formal production'.

Here, as I shall discuss in Chapter 4, while I am putting forward an argument that might be accused of being 'capitalocentric'[102] – in so far as I am seeking to place animals within formal labour circuits and as such, explicitly situate animals within a value theory of labour – my aim is not to suggest that informal labour is not valuable, nor to fetishise 'formal production'. On the contrary, my goal is to more accurately see animals and their relation to capital. We are dealing here with a problem of 'vantage point': that is, how does our analysis change once we take into account the unique situation of animals with respect to capital? The problem of vantage point was central to Bertell Ollman's approach in understanding Marx's philosophy of 'internal relations': namely that capitalism reflects a totality, rather than an assembly of interdependent wholes, and that where we view capitalism from allows us a different perspective on this whole.[103] It is not necessarily clear, nor will I argue, that the treatment of animals wholly represents an aspect of the 'internal relations' of capitalism; after all, as I shall discuss in Chapter 2, the appearance of animals under capitalism at least reflects *both* an interaction of capitalist relations, and a hierarchical anthropocentrism which arguably preceded the arrival of capitalist relations. However, in many ways, the problem facing the left and its relationship to animals relates to an almost complete failure to recognise the unique vantage point – that is, the unique abstraction – animals occupy with respect to capitalism. In my view, our inability to fully comprehend the relationship between animals and capital reflects an anthropocentric failure to extend in a consistent way the analytic tools available to left social movements to understand human relations to animals. And here, I refer in particular to perhaps one of the most important conceptual approaches available to the left: that is, the *value* of labour power.

One of the important achievements of Marx, and of those working in the critical tradition that followed, was to narrate the structural position of the worker. By nominating the worker as a 'persona' or political subjectivity, Marx provided a unique standpoint which is always contrasted with the structural position of the owner of capital. These two viewpoints cannot be reconciled; they are at odds, *antagonistic*:

> he who was previously the money-owner now strides out in front as a capitalist; the possessor of labour power follows as his worker. The one smirks self-importantly and is intent on business; the other is timid and holds back, like someone who has brought his own hide to market and now has nothing else to expect but – a tanning.[104]

Importantly, Marx does not describe this person through reference to their physical characteristics, personality or social status; rather this political subjectivity emerges through a relation to *labour power*; and as Marx tracks, the latter force is quantified, sought after and exploited in unprecedented ways under capitalism. Here, Marx's critical approach is to ask questions in a different way to coax a different answer; to reveal through a distinct vantage point what was previously unrevealed but essential to the story of capital. The story of Marx's *Capital* is thus to systematically dismantle this set of *appearances*: capital as a relation allows things to 'appear' to us; they are made available to our perception, though not everything is revealed in this appearance.[105]

Louis Althusser reminds us that the key to Marx's approach as a philosopher was to develop a mode of reading, where a surface reading of a text is accompanied by a second reading which offers a different perspective that reveals what was absent in the first reading:

> Such is Marx's second reading: a reading which might well be called '*symptomatic*' (*symptomale*), in so far as it divulges the undivulged event in the text it reads, and in the same movement relates it to *a different text*, present as a necessary absence in the first. Like his first reading, Marx's second reading presupposes the existence of *two texts*, and the measurement of the first against the second. But what distinguishes this new reading from the old one is the fact that in the new one the *second text* is articulated with the lapses in the first text. Here again, at least in the way peculiar to theoretical texts (the only ones whose analysis is at issue here), we find the necessity and possibility of a reading on two bearings simultaneously.[106]

For Althusser, this approach was critical for Marx in the development of the unique text that is *Capital*, volume 1. This approach allowed Marx to ask questions of classical economics which were implicit to previous approaches, but failed to be elucidated: 'That is why Marx can pose the unuttered *question*, simply by uttering the concept present in an unuttered form in the emptiness in the *answer*.'[107]

The key question Marx asks in this context relates to that abstracted quality which is seemingly attached to the worker and defines their political subjectivity: namely labour power. Thus, Althusser points out that Marx offers innovation not simply in asking, 'What is the value of labour?' but instead in asking, 'What is the value of labour power?'[108] The latter question allows Marx to treat labour power as distinct from the labourer, as something that is structurally and historically positioned, as something that is sought after as a use value, abstracted and commanded by capital. In other words, by drawing attention to how the use value of wage labour under capitalism differed in character, Marx's formulation of the question ('What is labour power?') allowed for a critical problematic that had evaded classical economics. At least for Marx's problematic, this question allowed for an interpretation of capitalism which placed the problem of value centrally in relation to the abstraction of labour power: capitalism seeks to accumulate wealth in the form of capital; however, this accumulation is not possible without a process of production which is able to 'absorb' value from abstracted labour deployed in production.

Althusser's observation on Marx's method is useful here for a number of reasons. Firstly, it is apparent that those who should have been interested – animal advocates, leftists – have failed to ask the right questions about animals. Advocates for animals, often informed by animal rights theory from analytic and liberal traditions, have been concerned about the *intrinsic value* of animals and worry about this value being squandered, destroyed and besmirched by industrial agriculture. This informs the strategies of these advocates, who wish to rescue animals from production and boycott the products that emerge from this violent production process. Leftists, on the other hand, when they have noticed animals, have regarded the treatment of animals as a symptom of a prevailing relation (or failure of relation) with nature: a nature that is imagined as perverted, appropriated, dominated.

The question that has been missing is about value. Exactly how are animals valuable to capitalism? Why have they been sought after as objects of use value? And how does this value dictate and shape their relation to capital? As I have discussed, at the level of value, we can notice at least three different lives for food animals under capitalism. It is relatively easy to see food animals as either consumption commodities or as raw materials within capitalism. The more difficult question, and one that is harder to answer, relates to labour. Who does the work of transforming animals from one state to another – raw material to consumption item; lamb to lamb chop? Clearly humans are involved in the labour of this production, notably as participants in the intense forms of domination of life – controls over movement, nutrition, sexuality, powers of life and death – that accompany animal agriculture. Pigs don't contain themselves. Nor do they slaughter themselves. Human hands wrought this transformation. And certainly, it is true that on the 'surface' of relations, it is the abstracted value of human labour that appears to make this cycle of life and death occur: it is, after all, humans (or at least some humans) who are paid a wage for this labour. But animals are not inactive in these processes. And this is where Althusser's question – 'What is the value of labour power?' – remains informative.[109] For it's apparent that we do not fully understand the specific value role of animal labour power. Asking 'What is the use value of animal labour to capital?' deliberately forces us to consider the value role of animals within the production side of capitalism; that is, the place of animals within the exchange of money for capital (and capital for money), which relies on a productive process where abstracted labour power is deployed in concert with fixed and circulating capital in order to produce value. As I argue in this book, understanding these lives of animals – as consumption items, as raw materials, as labour – reveals the highly unique structural position of food animals under capitalism. In many ways, as I shall discuss, animals exist as hybrids, as amalgamations, as contradictions. And I don't mean only the fact that animals exist as valued commodities within the circuits of capital – both alive as raw material and dead as meat – but that they are frequently positioned precisely as a hybrid of both object and subject, or at least more accurately within the terms of Marx's value theory, as *simultaneously constant and variable capital*, as both a raw material that is treated as a static object, and as labourers who are asked to work on themselves in order to produce value.

Secondly, employing this method of reading Marx reveals in a 'symptomatic' way the anthropocentrism within Marx which stood in the way of the full realisation of the promise of his method. The brilliance of Marx's approach in *Capital*, and its usefulness for thinking about animals, is precisely its 'anti-humanism': that is, a commitment to a description of relations of power without recourse to humanistic categories of analysis. This was what Althusser identified as innovative in Marx's method, since it allowed for the detachment of labour power from the labourer. For Althusser this marked the difference between the early Marx of the *1844 Manuscripts* and the 'mature Marx' of *Capital*: in the latter case, there is a rejection of an overt humanism in favour of a careful application of method without any particular nostalgia for humanistic categories.[110] We actually find this 'anti-humanist' approach to labour power expressed perfectly, even before *Capital*, in *Grundrisse*:

> For capital, the worker is not a condition of production, only work is. If it can make machines do it, or even water, air, so much the better. And it does not appropriate the worker, but his labour – not directly, but mediated through exchange.[111]

This helps us, of course, to get closer to understanding the value role of animals as labour power. It is clear that *human* labour is very much the focus of the volumes of *Capital*; indeed, as I shall discuss in Chapter 4, although Marx opens the question of animal labour in volume 2 of *Capital*, the distinct value role of animals is not a concern for his project. However, we can see that there is an opportunity to apply Marx's methods in ways which he did not. To what extent does capitalism function to extract labour power from everything in order to produce value?[112] And if this is the case, what specifically does this mean for animals? As I shall discuss, this allows us to see that animals occupy a unique position, but also allows us to examine capitalism in a new light. It further allows us different dreamings for post-capitalist societies which might enable 'multispecies' flourishings.[113]

Scope and limits

A few necessary notes on the scope and limitations of this book. This work is primarily a work of political theory. While the focus is upon concepts which overlap with political economy, the aim of the book is not to provide an empirical investigation of the economics of industry and exchange relating to animals, nor advance new economic concepts to explain acquisition, production and financing within the context of animal industries. As discussed above, the method employed in this book understands capitalism as an organism and mechanism that tirelessly organises production to suck energy from life – human and non-human – in order to produce surplus. In this context, I am less interested in questions such as: 'Who profits?' or 'Exactly who are the capitalists?' These questions would be important if we were to map the value structure of global animal agriculture for strategic purposes. However, for the theoretical analysis I present here, this sort of 'personification' of capital is less important than the task of clearly comprehending the value components of the economies we find ourselves amidst. Here, the goal of the book is to better understand the structural relation of animals to capitalism, and thus provide conceptual clarity on the patterns of power, violence and domination that shape animal lives today.

The book is *not* a work of ethics, though of course contemporary animal ethics has shaped the normative directions of the text. As such, my focus is on the development of a structural analysis of the relation between animals and capital, not to provide ethical guidance on how we should, on an individual level, relate to animals. This means while this book has a strong normative dimension in openly seeking to reduce violence against animals, dismantle forms of domination, and enable freedom and flourishing, I do not provide worked-out philosophical positions on matters that are subject to contemporary debate within animal ethics, such as subsistence hunting, companion animals or cultivated meat products. These matters are important topics for consideration; however, they are out of scope for my analysis.

The primary focus of the book is upon animals who are raw materials, consumption commodities and labour within capitalist animal agriculture and fisheries. As discussed above, I understand capitalism as an organism and mechanism that has an overarching drive to extract value and accumulate it in the form of capital. In this context, I am interested in capitalist food systems, often industrial in nature, which aim at the production of profit, and not merely subsistence. The choice of focus is deliberate, in so far as food animals within capitalist agriculture and fisheries represent the largest and perhaps most apparent site of direct entanglement between humans, machines and animals within our economies. This choice of focus does not mean that the analysis in this book cannot be applied more broadly. While 'food animals' are my focus, many of the concepts engaged within this text can be applied to other spheres of human–animal entanglement; for example, the concepts of metabolic labour in Chapter 4 can be applied to animals used in research; while the broad structure of commodities, use values and exchange values, discussed in Chapter 3, are applicable to better understanding the place of companion animals within expanding pet industries.

Certainly, it might be objected that my focus in this text on food animals is too narrow to account for the totality of relations between animals and capitalism. After all, in a very broad sense, most (and perhaps all) animals on the planet interact with capitalism as an economic system, at least in so far as this economic system and its attendant and interactive processes –industrialisation, land clearing, resource exploitation, pollution, climate warming – shape almost all life on the planet. A text on animals and capital could certainly be written to account for the total relations between capitalism and the extraordinary expanse of life on the planet, ranging from whales to microbes.[114] However, such a text would be different in shape and concern. My focus instead is upon the visible, expansive and direct interaction with animals fabricated as commodities within capitalist food systems. That capitalist animal agriculture and fisheries are prominently implicated as a core problem within that hot mess that characterises the relation of the global capitalist economy with planetary systems – indeed, capitalist food systems are directly related to land clearing, resource exploitation, pollution and climate warming[115] – highlights the significance of this focus area and its implications for a wider understanding of how life on the planet, in the broadest sense, is subject to the ripples, interventions and rhythms of capital.

Finally, the focus on the politico-economic dimension of human–animal relations under capitalism neglects other assemblies of power and domination that might be relevant for a structural analysis and for strategies of change.

32 | ANIMALS AND CAPITAL

Of primary concern here may be the need to theorise *the State*, that dominant nodal point for institutional political power within human societies. I have previously explored the relationship of sovereignty, law and private dominion to the systems of violence and domination that shape animal lives, and to an extent my analysis in this book dovetails with that prior research.[116] However, I concede that the problem of the State and its relationship to animals, while considered by a range of different authors,[117] beckons deeper analysis, perhaps in a future study. Certainly the State, as a mechanism of violence, authority, taxation and expenditure, and legitimation, is highly important for consideration of the strategic questions for animal advocates and left movements which follow from this book.

Structure

This book is organised to provide building blocks for understanding the structural position of animals under capitalism, exploring their existence as commodities, as labour, as objects of circulation, as agents of resistance. In Chapter 2 ('Material') I provide a methodological overview of the form of material analysis I will engage with in this book. I discuss recent 'new materialisms' and try to understand how these differ from the 'old materialism' of Marx. I draw attention to the ontological monism which has arisen in some accounts – such as that of Jane Bennett and Rosi Braidotti – and the effect that this has for thinking about political conflict and antagonism (the latter central to the 'old' materialism of Marx). Drawing on Frank Wilderson, I argue that charting structural antagonism is important for a materialist account that frankly engages with relations of power. Building on this, I compare Wilderson's account of political antagonism and the intersectional analysis developed by Kimberlé Crenshaw, to highlight the limits of political solidarity where antagonism structures relations. As I discuss, food animals occupy a site of political antagonism with respect to the human (at least because these beings exist as a material means of subsistence for humans), thus limiting the prospects for solidarity. Responding to this antagonism is a central task for animal advocates.

Chapter 3 ('Commodity') explores the two commodity forms food animals take which I have described above: namely, raw materials and consumption commodities. As I discuss, these conform to two spheres: the sphere of production and the sphere of consumption. I unpack the philosophical elaboration of the commodity that Marx offers in chapter 1 of *Capital*, and its implications for animals who enter production as a raw material. As I discuss, animals here are 'fabricated' in particular ways: both made to appear as having a use value for production and simultaneously established as a form of currency that highlights human supremacy. Within the sphere of consumption, animals circulate as animal products. They function as a material within the biopolitics of the reproduction of human populations, and in this sense participate, as I have described above, in the reproduction of reproduction. Animal products exist as an object of human wages and thus their availability is determined by prevailing living standards; this view allows us to appraise the relation of animal-based food consumption to the politics of freedom under capitalism and also, simultaneously, to position and problematise the politics of veganism as a strategy.

In Chapter 4 ('Labour') we move to understand the distinct role of animals as a labour force under capitalism. As I argue, there is value in moving away from describing animal labour through analogies to human labour processes (including slavery) and instead understanding the distinct value role of animal labour power within contemporary industrial animal agriculture. This allows us to see some curiosities associated with animal labour power. One of these is that, against Marx's suggestion that labour time reduces as fixed capital increases, we find instead a curious situation within animal agriculture where the expansion of fixed capital is accompanied by the multiplication of animal labour, which produces the capitalist demand to shorten animal lives in order to abbreviate the production cycle. Here, we also glimpse the distinct confrontation that exists between animals and capital: where the arrival of machines conventionally displaces humans (they lose their jobs as fixed capital increases), animals are instead confronted by fixed capital as an adversary.

Production must deal with the movements of raw materials and finished commodities with potentially slow turnover times: in other words, production must respond to the problem of circulation. In Chapter 5 ('Circulation') this book examines the case study of the globalised transfer of animals as living assets in the form of live animal transport. As I discuss, this is an example of circulation where animals are moved from one production phase to another within a value chain. Tracing the unique character of the movements of live animals, this chapter looks at the way this circulation alters with the advent of mechanisation, and in concert with attempts to make the application of human labour more efficient. However, recognition of animal labour power significantly alters how we see this circulation. Firstly, animals are required to labour if they are moved live: they must complete a metabolic labour on themselves in order to preserve the value in the raw material of their own bodies. Secondly, against a view that would see circulation as a disruption to production, the reality of animal labour makes this time 'productive'. This means, for example, that producers can rely on the fact that animals can be shipped as raw materials and arrive, miraculously, as a 'finished product' which is ready for slaughter.

Through this book, I chart the confrontation that animals experience in relation to capitalist industrial animal agriculture. As I describe, this is often a battle between fixed capital (machines, enclosures, instruments) and animals who are compelled by this machinery. It is thus resistance that is the central marker of animal agency in the face of capital. In Chapter 6 ('Resistance') I look at the case study of industrialised fisheries, exploring how resistance might be conceptualised, and the ways this resistance can be read against deployments of fixed capital. As I argue, looking at the fish hook, the purse seine net and aquaculture, the technologies of capture reveal the parasitic relation at the centre of capital's orientation to these beings, which seeks continually to subdue these animals in order to suck value. But a focus on resistance is also useful, as it reminds us that animals are co-producers of the world we see and thus point us towards the potential productivity of a reimagined world without this violence. As Hardt and Negri state: 'It is not a matter of pretending that we are powerful when we are not, but rather recognising the power we really have; the power that created the contemporary world and can create another.'[118]

In Chapter 7 I explore the implications of this book for thinking about how we move forward. I turn to Marx's notes on communism in *Critique of the Gotha Program* to ask how animals are placed with respect to the means of production, and what liberation might mean. As I outline, and in line with Wilderson's observations explored in Chapter 2, human worker control of the means of production does not necessarily entail freedom for animals in their roles as raw materials, labour or their eventual transformation into the means of subsistence – quite simply because food animals under capitalism *are* the means of production. However, as I argue, a post-anthropocentric focus on reduction in necessary labour time offers a useful trajectory for imagining a world where animals are freed of the necessity of having to labour in order to become a means of subsistence for humans. Perhaps this route provides one way to overcome the structural divisions that mark the difference between the human worker and the food animal under capitalism.

2   Material

> Perseus wore a magic cap so that the monsters he hunted down might not see
> him. We draw the magic cap down over our own eyes and ears so as to deny
> that there are any monsters.
>
> Karl Marx, Capital, vol. 1[1]

In the first chapter, I have advanced a conceptualisation of the relation of
animals to capitalism which is *materialist* in flavour. It is materialist in so far as
my analysis of the structural positioning of food animals – raw material, labour,
consumption product – begins with the 'life' of animals as factors of production;
that is, as beings who are thrown into existence and circulate as objects and relations with use values. To an extent, this reflects the methodological materialism
devised by Marx, which treats matter as the starting point for analysis, and not
the ideal or the abstraction; the latter is only possible to understand after comprehending the specific life of the object within a social relation. As Althusser
describes, 'the thingness of commodities is a social thingness, their objectivity
an objectivity of value'.[2] This approach establishes a very particular relation, at
least in traditional Marxism, between matter and knowledge. In an oft-cited
section of the Preface to *A Contribution to the Critique of Political Economy*,
Marx declares:

> it is always necessary to distinguish between the material transformation of
> the economic conditions of production, which can be determined with the
> precision of natural science, and the legal, political, religious, artistic or phil-
> osophic, in short, ideological forms in which men become conscious of this
> conflict and fight it out. Just as one does not judge an individual by what he

thinks about himself, so one cannot judge such an epoch of transformation by its consciousness, but, on the contrary, this consciousness must be explained from the contradictions of material life, from the conflict existing between the social forces of production and the relations of production. No social order ever perishes before all the productive forces for which it is broadly sufficient have been developed, and new superior relations of production never replace older ones before the material conditions for their existence have matured within the womb of the old society.[3]

In this view – which sets out the foundation of the traditional Marxist approach to ideology – the analysis of matter, and the social relations that emerge from these material relations, tells us everything we need to know about relations of power. The field of ideas is deceptive in so far as there is a gap between knowledge of these relations and the 'true' understanding of the material forces behind perception. Note as well the teleology assumed by Marx which suggests a narrative of progress structuring history; 'new superior relations of production never replace older ones', while the ideas which provide an understanding of this evolution will necessarily follow in a delayed manner, 'with the change in the economic foundation the whole immense superstructure is more slowly or rapidly transformed'.[4]

There is of course much we can say about this approach to the material and its problems. Antonio Gramsci would add increased sophistication to the problem of the relation between ideas, history and materialism through the theory of hegemony, aiming to 'get people into the habit of a more cautious and precise calculation of the forces acting in society';[5] while a range of scholars, such as Stuart Hall, would build on Gramsci's critique to emphasise the importance of ideas and culture in social change.[6] Foucault drew attention to the problematic distinction between the 'truth' of material relations and our potential ideology, and also reacted to the assumed notions of progress behind this traditional Marxist conception of truth.[7] More relevant to this chapter, recent scholarship within emerging animal studies and posthumanities has provided a different critique in the form of *new materialism*, a tendency that, inherent in its name, either displaces, or perhaps continues, the project of the 'old' materialism, while also providing some necessary correctives.

In this chapter I think in a methodological fashion on how I will approach my 'materialist' analysis in this book. As I have indicated, my goal is to understand the place of food animals in production, explore what this means at the level of value, and derive from this an understanding of the relations of power that shape the existence of animals within capitalism. While this approach is clearly influenced by Marx, there are a number of differences between Marx's materialism and my own analysis. Overtly, as indicated in Chapter 1, I understand animals as both raw materials *and* as labour; I thus assume, against Marx, that nonhuman entities enter production as agents. This reflects a 'posthumanist' orientation to capitalism, in so far as the human is 'decentred' within the analysis. As such, I am interested in how recent new materialist approaches are useful in helping to construct an analysis, since, as I shall discuss, new materialists are seeking to provide a materialist account that is not anthropocentric. However, there are different layers to understanding what is 'new' within new materialism, something that will become apparent below. The first part of this chapter explores new materialisms and tries to situate their usefulness politically. As I shall discuss, my main concern with these new materialist approaches for my analysis is that they avoid structural *antagonism*, and thus displace oppositional politics in their analysis of relations of power. In the second half of this chapter, I look specifically at antagonism as a central part of a structural analysis. Here, I compare the views of Kimberlé Crenshaw and Frank Wilderson, to highlight the problem posed for solidarity between diverse groups where antagonism structures material relations. As I argue through this book, an analysis of the material relations of food animals under capitalism creates vexed questions for human social movements, including in the structural antagonism I uncover between human labourers and animal labourers. Resolving this antagonism – if at all possible – is key to addressing the mass-scale violence experienced by animals within capitalism.

New materialism and political monism

Pinning down exactly what makes up new materialism is not straightforward; as Vicky Kirby describes, 'its identity is often contradictory and its crossdisciplinary rationalisations and commitments quite muddled'.[8] Perhaps one definition provided by Christopher Gamble, Joshua Hanan and Thomas Nail gives us a possible direction: 'new materialism embraces a non-anthropocentric realism grounded in a shift from epistemology to ontology and the recognition of matter's intrinsic activity'.[9] Different definitions emphasise a more active sense in which new materialism engages with the 'natural' or 'physical' sciences, and that it explicitly moves towards a reformed view of ontology. For example, Simon Choat provides the following characterisation: 'There are three central features of new materialism: a reappraisal of science, an emphasis on the agency of all things and, underpinning all this, a "flat" ontology.'[10]

Some of these elements are certainly present in Diana Coole and Samantha Frost's commonly cited introduction to new materialisms.[11] Coole and Frost highlight the demise of textual-based analyses and radical social construction-ism.[12] Further, they declare a revised method that includes stronger engagement with the natural sciences.[13] With this, there is a commitment to challenge the limits of the humanities and social sciences, in part by 'taking heed of developments in the natural sciences as well as attending to transformations in the ways we currently produce, reproduce, and consume our material environment'.[14] Recent transformations in scientific enquiry are seen as prompting a need for the humanities and social sciences to similarly reform: to continually reinterpret their ground for action, and indeed question the separation of the 'human' sciences from the natural sciences. Coole and Frost state that a reason:

> for turning to materialism is the emergence of pressing ethical and political concerns that accompany the scientific and technological advances predicated on new scientific models of matter and, in particular, of living matter. As critically engaged theorists, we find ourselves compelled to explore the significance of complex issues such as climate change or global capital and population flows, the biotechnological engineering of genetically modified organisms, or the saturation of our intimate and physical lives by digital, wireless, and virtual technologies.[15]

Here, in a sense, the appeal for a return to materiality is a reflection on a lost connection between the human and natural sciences. The arrival of radical new technologies, plus complex problems such as anthropogenic climate change, which require diverse but joined-up disciplinary approaches, suggests the possibility of reunification.

However, this declaration of the end of the 'humanities' as we know it, and the call to re-embrace materialism, is not intended as an uncritical return to the 'old' materialism of Marx.[16] Coole and Frost argue that the quest for a 'new materialism' is also driven by a need to reinvent this materialism:

> this legacy does remain important, not least because traditionally Marxism has been the critique of capitalism par excellence. A critical understanding of global capitalism and its multifarious effects remains crucial for contemporary critical materialists, for some of whom a Marxist label has helped to signify their opposition to dominant neoliberal trends. But coming after poststructuralism and its criticisms, no workable version of Marxism can advance a historical metanarrative, aspire to the identification of determining economic laws, valorize an originary, pristine nature, or envisage communism as history's idealized material destiny.[17]

Certainly, we could sympathise with some of these sentiments. Perhaps the 'old' materialism of Marx might be associated with a universalist approach which denied difference, and with an anthropocentric view of the relation of humans to nature (our alienation, our capacity for dominance, etc.), a view I have already discussed in Chapter 1 (and will return to in Chapter 4) on Marx's writing on animals in the early manuscripts. Coole and Frost also correctly challenge a functionalist view of history which came with a teleological attachment to seeing contradiction and change (such as the 'falling rate of profit') as prophetic signs of the predestination of capitalist societies towards communism. As discussed above, we certainly see elements of this deterministic teleology in the way in which Marx rendered his materialist analysis, and its relation to knowledge and 'truth'.

While I respect the above adjustments for how we read Marx, we also need critical caution in how we understand Marx's materialism; at least to more carefully consider if it is unilaterally and definitively true that 'no workable version of Marxism can advance a historical metanarrative, aspire to the identification of determining economic laws, valorize an originary, pristine nature, or envisage communism as history's idealized material destiny'. For example, I would certainly agree that a 'historical metanarrative' which assumes that past, present and future are predetermined is problematic. However, I would argue that we should be wary of jettisoning an analysis of materiality which is historically situated. Arguably, it is through understanding the place of matter within a historical situation that we can make sense of it.[18] Today, as I have outlined in Chapter 1, animals 'appear' in context with machines, enclosures and factory processes; the factory farm as a sociotechnical apparatus makes animal bodies appear as mass consumption products in a way that is perhaps historically without precedent. While previous historical periods may have similarly made animals available to us as food, we must also acknowledge that an unprecedented assembly of fixed capital, techniques, labour and bodies allows for the mass appearance of animals today as a means of subsistence which cannot compare to any period of human history. This observation is an example of a 'historical materialism': rather than simply understand the animal as a biological entity abstracted from a sociotechnical environment, I have instead insisted on understanding the animal as a commodity within a contemporary system of production. The importance of history also has implications for how we understand macropolitical change. Clearly, we have no reason to believe that we are in the midst of a predetermined set of historical circumstances which will allow us to predict the future. However, Marx's historical approach allows us to understand the way in which economic structure prepares the ground for the political potentialities which may emerge from it (such as a post-capitalist future). As Hanna Meißner observes:

> Marx's analysis of capitalism offers important social explanations that account for the fact that many of our relations to (human) others (and their differences) are formed as relations of competition, that many relations to ourselves and to others are formed as relations of subjects/owners/users to resources, objects of utility, commodities. This perspective makes available options of addressing the conditions set by the capitalist mode of production as globalized structural impediments to ethically adequate relations – conditions that are socially transformable.[19]

Here, history is important in making sense of how matter relationally appears to us today, and providing avenues to address inequalities and violence. Thus at least one problem noted by critics in relation to new materialisms is a tendency 'towards ahistorical analyses that ignore, or at least downplay, relations of power and ownership'.[20]

Perhaps related to this question of history, another concern with Coole and Frost's perspective described above is their view on 'determining economic laws'. It seems somewhat fraught to provide any critical analysis of capitalism without exploring the ways in which economic values and imperatives drive forward the assembly of commodities, production and labour that comprise capitalism. Capitalism is a system of value relations which is governed by a distinct determining rationality. It seems difficult to understand the usefulness of Marx without engaging with the 'determining economic law' which informs the rationality of capitalism as a social relation: that is, 'the law of value'.[21] *Value*, and hence 'capital', is by definition an abstraction; it operates at the level of the symbolic and is given sense within social relations. Yet this does not mean it is not material. This value relation is embodied in material relations within the historical period of the capitalist relation. The point for Marx is that the analysis of material relations gestures towards the operation of a unique abstraction within capitalism, and not the other way around; 'the thingness of commodities is a social thingness', as Althusser put it. And this abstraction of value continually materialises and dematerialises within concrete relations. This is of course plain when we think about animals as commodities: an animal in animal agriculture has a use value as a raw material, appearing as a materialised value which continually transforms through the production process. This value will determine how the animal is treated; as we know, the fact that animals are only treated in ways which reflect their 'value' underpins the horrific material reality these beings face. We can make sense of this through an analysis of the reality of this material appearance of animals within production, the peculiar constellation of violence they experience within a specific historical period, and the implications this has for their 'fabrication' by production processes. From this standpoint, and despite Coole and Frost's objection to identifying 'determining economic laws', I don't believe Marx's theory of value need be at odds with a 'new materialist' approach.

I make the above observations not with the aim of returning to the 'old' materialism, but instead attempting to sharpen focus on what exactly is 'new' in the materialist approach being proclaimed today. Certainly, I am not the first to ask this question. Kim TallBear, for example, has argued that many Indigenous peoples already maintained knowledge systems that did not inculcate strong binaries between nature and culture, and thus stresses that 'we should remember that not everyone needs to summon a new analytical framework'.[22] This highlights that we are not necessarily talking about a 'new' materialism, but an approach to materialism that reflects on the exclusions which have been highlighted by a range of movements and critical scholars. From my standpoint, rather than proclaim a 'new' materialism, the pertinent questions are: how does a 'materialist' approach function today, in light of the valid critiques, including decades of poststructural theory? How does this approach or method allow us to reveal economic relations through an analysis of the material, without a recourse to anthropocentrism, colonial logics, or an attachment to a deterministic narrative of historical progress? There is certainly no reason to imagine that the materialism that emerges today, after poststructuralism, after posthumanism, is incapable of a critique of capital. Jason Edwards suggests that what 'remains at the heart of historical materialism [after new materialism] . . . is an ongoing analysis of the current social and political conditions of contemporary capitalist societies in light of their historical development, their embedded institutions and practices, and the contingent circumstances that serve to reproduce them – or that threaten their reproduction – over time'.[23] Note this rendering certainly does not mean the end for 'historical materialism'; on the contrary, there is an urgent need for this sort of historical materialist analysis to guide future political projects.

However, even if we could resuscitate Marxism in light of these critiques, new materialisms offer a deeper and perhaps more contentious challenge which relates to their 'ontological' mission, and the presumed implications this has for politics today. Informing this approach is a rejection of dualistic oppositions (subject/object, society/nature) as structuring forces of interpretation, in favour of understanding relational entanglements in multi-dimensional and complex systems; the latter focus promises to 'radically' rewrite 'the dualisms of modernity'.[24] In seeking to move beyond binaries there is often a commitment to a 'monist philosophy', which Rosi Braidotti describes as that 'which rejects dualism, especially the opposition "nature–culture", and stresses instead the self-organizing (or auto-poietic) force of living matter'.[25] Part of the rationale for this is commendable, and highly relevant to this book: namely in the desire to unseat a hierarchical anthropocentrism which places the human as the authoring agential subject, in contrast to nature, which is the object of 'man's' work. In response, new materialisms (and many posthumanisms and animal studies approaches) have expressed the need to recognise nonhumans (animals but also other nonhuman natures) as agents or actants. As I have suggested above, following from TallBear's observation on the ontologies and knowledge systems of some Indigenous peoples, we have no reason to believe that this is a novel proposal. However, it is true that such a corrective is vital for contemporary materialist analysis of capital that does not rehearse an old anthropocentrism. Thus, from the standpoint of ontology, once we declare that nonhumans also shape, constitute, evade and resist, then we must account for a range of entities within networks of relations, but also put in question the whole operation of fundamental categories of being – not only 'subjects' and 'objects', but also identities, forms of communication and the ways in which they materialise: as Kirby states, 'if the spatio/temporal order of things is truly muddled and any one thing (e.g. photon, person, concept) is inseparable from another, then what we mean by mediation and identity require review'.[26]

While the implications of an ontology that does not centre the human are becoming more clear at the level of analysis of being, institution and subject, what this means for 'politics' and how we conceive of the 'political' appears as an unresolved question within new materialisms.[27] For thinkers such as Jane Bennett, the flattening of ontologies found in new materialisms and actor network theories[28] have implications for how we delegate responsibilities within a political field, since we can no longer attribute causality to a single actor:

> it is a safe bet to begin with the presumption that the locus of political responsibility is a human-nonhuman assemblage. On close-enough inspection, the productive power that has engendered an effect will turn out to be a confederacy, and the human actants within it will themselves turn out to be confederations of tools, microbes, minerals, sounds, and other 'foreign' materialities. Human intentionality can emerge as agentic only by way of such a distribution. The agency of assemblages is not the strong, autonomous kind of agency to which Augustine and Kant (or an omnipotent God) aspired; this is because the

relationship between tendencies and outcomes or between trajectories and effects is imagined as more porous, tenuous, and thus indirect.[29]

Note the explicit use by Bennett of the political terms 'confederacy' and 'confederations', indicating alliance or union between different entities for common purpose. This is indicative of a general move away from a singular view of agency in the analysis of relations of power. For Bennett, the inability to attribute sole authoring political responsibility for effects of power, and the sense that outcomes can never be determined by strict lines of causality, encourages a degree of care and modesty; indeed, this approach is regarded as an example of a 'presumptive virtue'.[30] Here, the flattening of ontologies moves towards a flattening of the *antagonisms* within politics. Doing politics well becomes a process of 'cultivated discernment':

> Outrage will not and should not disappear, but a politics devoted too exclusively to moral condemnation and not enough to a cultivated discernment of the web of agentic capacities can do little good. A moralized politics of good and evil, of singular agents who must be made to pay for their sins (be they bin Laden, Saddam Hussein, or Bush) becomes unethical to the degree that it legitimates vengeance and elevates violence to the tool of first resort. An understanding of agency as distributive and confederate thus reinvokes the need to detach ethics from moralism and to produce guides to action appropriate to a world of vital, crosscutting forces.[31]

In this rendering, flatter ontologies produce a retreat from antagonism as structuring political contestation; in a sense, ontological monism is perceived to demand *political monism*.[32] In this regard, Bennett opposes strong political binaries and antagonisms in favour of a world of shared responsibilities and agencies stretching across networks comprising human and nonhuman actants. Braidotti similarly puts forward a vision of 'political monism' or 'monistic politics' which resists 'dialectical oppositions':

> Because power is not a steady location operated by a single masterful owner, monistic politics identifies differential mechanisms of distribution of power effects at the core of subjectivity. Multiple mechanisms of capture also engender multiple forms of resistance. Power-formations are time-bound and consequently temporary and contingent upon social action and interaction. Movement and speed, lines of sedimentation and lines of flight are the main factors that affect the formation of non-unitary, neo-materialist subjects. They

express political agency not in the critical and negative sense of dialectical oppositions, but rather rely instead on affirmation and the pursuit of counter-actualisations of the virtual.[33]

On one hand, this call for care and sophistication in how we approach political problems appears reasonable, since empirically, of course, it is not contestable that political transformation cannot be attributed to one single causal agent. For the political monist, the fact that deep conflict is not present at an ontological level leads to a political retreat from a 'negative' of dialectics,[34] and a move towards 'confederacy' and 'affirmation'. However, political contestation is not a reflection of empirical realities: if it were, we could simply employ an automaton to realise just ends which would prove politically satisfactory for everyone. But such an automaton does not exist, and all political decisions exist in spaces of deep contestability.[35] As such, 'dialectical opposition' happens in the space of 'ideology', perspective, viewpoint and framing, and not in a political neutral zone of 'ontology'.[36] In this regard, there is something insipid in imagining a political engagement that is not heated, appears to deny deep conflict, anger and disillusionment, and treats strong opposition as potentially 'unethical'. Violence, inequality, oppression, exclusion, alienation, colonialism, disappropriation and exploitation are all political relations which will invite immediate, oppositional and sometimes impolite responses, particularly from those who experience the harm of these relations.

Perhaps more significantly for my analysis, this political monism is at odds with the conception of the political which sees *antagonism* as defining. Certainly, this does not appear compatible with a reading of Marx, which by necessity highlights antagonism, contradiction and violence as structuring the reality which we perceive. As Mario Tronti observes, 'a class relation is a struggle between antagonistic classes. This is why the production process – as a process that produces capital – is inseparable from the moments of class struggle, which is to say, is not independent of the movements of working-class struggle.'[37] However, there is a wider importance for a form of political analysis that incorporates the possibility of structural antagonism. The rationale for understanding political relations in terms of antagonism is that it unveils the irreconcilability of particular political positions; this irreconcilability suggests a structural incompatibility that cannot be resolved without system change. We see this reflected in the way in which Wilderson understands the structural position of the Black subject within contemporary racial economies. In *Red, White & Black*, Wilderson advances a precise understanding of the concept 'structural antagonism' which is differentiated from 'conflict'.[38] Situations of conflict between parties carry the possibility of resolution if both parties have grounds for agreement, or if the excluded party is capable of being recognised and empowered without threatening the lives of those who are included. On the other hand, antagonism between two parties cannot be resolved without destruction of a world, since the excluded party exists as a negation of those who are included; that is, the terms of inclusion depend upon the absolute exclusion of this other.[39] For Wilderson, understanding this antagonism is essential for describing the ontology of the Black subject, who is not able to be saved by liberal humanism, since this subject exists in antagonistic relationality with whiteness. This is why Wilderson argues that liberal humanism essentially cements an antagonistic relation between the Black subject/slave and other racialised groups, since Blackness continues to be structured as a negation even as liberalism reforms itself and attempts to include other rationalised subjectivities: 'the moment in Western history in which Humanism becomes hegemonic (and detrimental to the Indian's way of life) is not a moment in which the Slave achieves relationality (even as a subaltern) except in that his or her negativity stands now in relation not only to the Settler/Master, but to the "Savage" as well, and so becomes all the more nonrecuperable and all the more isolated'.[40] As we shall discover later in this chapter, Wilderson also suggests animals are located in a position of structural antagonism with respect to the human; and this is indeed a continuing feature of relations between humans and food animals that we will encounter in this book.

Relevant to new materialisms, a key problem here is how we interpret the movement from ontology to politics; and how pronouncements of a 'new' ontology, or a new ethics which might flow from this ontology, connects with the politics of exclusion and political projects of transformation. This is certainly a pressing challenge given the global problems we now encounter, including mass-scale racial injustice, economic inequality and climate change. As Michiel van Ingen observes, 'whatever political strategy we may wish to adopt in order to counter the various challenges that are inherent to the anthropocene all presuppose much more than a flat ontology is able to provide us with'.[41] Here, standpoint[42] remains fundamental to political action, and by necessity, in so far as political actors are located within distinct historical fields of contestation, violence and inequality in resources, then these standpoints produce unique effects which are particular to the positioning of these actors within a political field. At least one aspect of this is that we can dispense with the fantasy that ontologies can be represented in a politically 'neutral' way; as Zakiyyah Iman Jackson observes, 'the resounding silence in the posthumanist, object-oriented, and new materialist literatures with respect to race is remarkable, persisting even despite the reach of antiblackness into the nonhuman – *as blackness conditions and*

46 | ANIMALS AND CAPITAL

constitutes the very nonhuman disruption and/or displacement they invite.[43] Adopting a political starting point which is located within a concrete terrain thus allows for different ontological projects, including, for example, resisting colonial constructions of humanity.[44]

This certainly tallies with work by Eva Haifa Giraud, who has provided a timely reminder of the need to move beyond simply acknowledging the fact of human–animal entanglement, arguing that a focus on exclusion which is inherently political in orientation 'holds potential for opening . . . to future contestation and the possibility of alternatives'.[45] For Giraud, understanding how relational entanglements are connected with exclusion moves consideration to the space of political responsibility: 'exclusion is not just something that happens, an inevitable component of the ever-evolving, entangled composition of the world, but is often bound up with particular sociotechnical infrastructures and political decisions'.[46] Giraud argues thus that a political conceptualisation of exclusion is required which goes 'beyond an ethics oriented around proximal relations and encounters, to instead force attention to longer histories and intersectional inequalities that inform these relations'.[47] In other words, we need a structural analysis of material relations that is alive to entrenched and constitutive divisions and contestations. Here I would argue that antagonism is an important concept, as it allows for politics to take place in a way that historicises relations, reflects on power, and resists dominant narratives and ruling political ontologies.

If we don't recognise structural antagonism, we are left with a view of politics that simply hides the deep schisms which mark structural relations behind a fantasy of a benign and aseptic ethics.[48] This model of politics hides life-and-death forms of antagonism, and replaces them with tacit agreement and the assumption that behind disagreement lies entangled solidarity.[49] In the context of a discussion of Friedrich Nietzsche's concepts of *ressentiment* and 'slave morality', and commenting on the slave's quest for freedom and triumph, Jared Sexton points out the necessity of the oppositional viewpoint in articulating the life-affirming will of the oppressed subjectivity:

> In the absence, or repression, of the political antagonism between slavery and freedom, politics as such (including its extension as war) withers away and moralism fills the ethical vacuum. Once inside the universe of morality, however, further de-politicization feels like a deeper, more authentic form of politics because it is guided by reference to traditional (moral) values and buttressed by the felt need to survive. Meanwhile the prospect of repoliticization, which requires cultivating an antagonistic sensibility driven by an uncompro-

mising ethic of freedom, feels like an insult to cherished (moral) values and, moreover, a threat to survival, individual and collective. In fact, it is such a threat. But, on this account, a threat to survival is not life threatening here, but rather life-affirming.[50]

Sexton's comments appear useful for articulating the problems with a 'new' materialism which, by embracing an entangled flattened ontology, rejects antagonistic dichotomous political relations. Sexton here problematises a focus on ethics, as if this was the same as antagonistic politics. The latter demands action; it is driven by a real, historically situated quest for freedom. It demands a revolt against systems, institutions and structures. Here political interests are shaped by deep forms of exclusion and violence which threaten freedom, security and life; and those who experience this violence and exclusion respond in uncompromising ways. We certainly see this starkly in the politics of colonialism; as Frantz Fanon observed: 'in the colonial context the settler only ends his work of breaking in the native when the latter admits loudly and intelligibly the supremacy of the white man's values. In the period of decolonization, the colonized masses mock at these very values, insult them, and vomit them up.'[51] In this view, by necessity, politics is *partial*; it does not make a claim of impartiality and when it does, it does so fraudulently. Instead, politics uses partiality to express a unique standpoint, shaped by structuring forms of violence, exploitation, theft and exclusion – antagonism – to illuminate demands within a concrete, material, political terrain.

The aim of all of this is to stress that while much of this book is in relative harmony with many of the demands of new materialisms – including, notably, displacement of the human as the centre of analysis, and the need to develop or *recognise* more complex relational ontologies – this work is nevertheless suspicious of a *political monism*, which would eject antagonism and conflict from the political project. In order to contest capitalism, we need to frankly understand antagonism and how this shapes interests. Antagonism also informs the structural position of animals and their own 'interests'. The reality is, taking food animals into account, that a life-and-death antagonism informs their structural position under capitalism, and this is enforced by an all-encompassing and unrelenting violence which aims at complete domination. Taking this structural position seriously produces a political demand which animals arguably make of us: that is, to end this violence. It is an uncomfortable and uncompromising demand because it asks us to fundamentally rearrange the world as we know it in order that animals do not need to suffer and die for us. As such this demand operates as a 'life-affirming' threat to our way of life. It is antagonistic.

Antagonism and 'intersectionality'

Recognising the unique and antagonistic structural position of animals does not rule out forms of analysis that highlight the way in which different struggles 'intersect' and coalesce; for example, between animals and systems of racialisation, or gender and anthropocentrism. In Chapter 1, I have highlighted the way in which a hierarchical anthropocentrism combines with capitalism historically to produce the present reality experienced by animals. To an extent, we might, at least at face value, suggest this is an 'intersectional' analysis since it examines the overlap between two different forms of oppression. And we might extend this hybrid, or perhaps 'intersectional', approach to look at how different modalities of violence and oppression have shaped what we see today. There are some notable forms of scholarship which have provided this analysis. Claire Jean Kim, for example, has carefully described the way in which anthropocentric orderings of life conform with racialised logics, meaning it is difficult to disentangle contemporary violence against animals from colonialism, racialisation and anti-Blackness.[52] Similarly, feminist and ecofeminist theory has consistently drawn connections between the industrial farming of animals and gender relations;[53] for example, as I have discussed above, Gillespie tracks the ways in which industrial animal agriculture rehearses and reproduces gendered power structures.[54] Sunaura Taylor has done pioneering work exploring the relation of disability to animal liberation, arguing that:

> inattention to disability and animality (and how they intersect) is a mistake, because both concepts are so deeply implicated in other categories of difference and in the many social justice issues that oppressed populations face – from poverty, incarceration, and war to environmental injustice – that they cannot simply be relegated to the margins.[55]

However, although 'intersectional' analysis is essential as a method for understanding the terrain we work from, I also express some hesitation at the limits of an *intersectional politics*, particularly one which too easily assumes that diverse political subjectivities can be reconciled towards shared goals. Here, I draw the distinction between intersectionality as a way to bring together different frames in order to understand the unique political position of a subject, and intersectionality as a call for or claim to political alliance and coalition with multiple social movements – women, people of colour, people with disabilities, workers and queers – where an 'intersectional approach' is declared as a method of working with others. While the latter use of 'intersectional' is now pervasive across social movements, it is the former usage of intersectionality – as a method of analysis of a terrain of power – which I think is most useful for my discussion here.[56]

Kimberlé Crenshaw sought in establishing the concept of intersectionality to respond to a particular set of problems: in part, the failure of mainstay structural analyses of power – that is, feminism and antiracism – to account for the unique location of women of colour as targets of violence; and secondly, the inadequacy of identity politics in providing an adequate pathway forward.[57] 'Intersectionality' was thus proposed as a methodological approach to designate 'the location of women of color both within overlapping systems of subordination and at the margins of feminism and antiracism'.[58] For Crenshaw a failure to take an 'intersectional' approach between race and gender produced a schism that negated political recognition of women of colour: for example, as Crenshaw discusses, a failure to acknowledge intersectional positions creates a feminism that only problematises sexual violence when it impacts white women; or an antiracism that explains away the sexual violence experienced by women of colour as simply a product of racism.[59]

In a sense here, Crenshaw argues that intersectionality is methodological in nature. It is a method of analysis that allows us to recognise the unique structural position of different agents; a unique position that cannot be understood by solely using one structural explanation.[60] Crenshaw's method of analysis allows for a starting point for coalition-building, as it creates the basis for a politics that does not rely on the subordination of women of colour in order to produce political resolution,[61] but instead offers an understanding of race itself as necessarily a point of alliance; in Crenshaw's words: 'intersectionality provides a basis for reconceptualising race as a coalition between men and women of color'.[62]

However, while an intersectional approach is the starting point for coalition-building, there is no reason why such a coalition is inevitable. Crenshaw makes clear that what is described as 'structural intersectionality' would position women of colour very differently from other subjects.[63] Indeed, Crenshaw points out repeatedly the potential non-commensurability of the position of women of colour with any other political subject positions; in Crenshaw's words, 'women of colour are differently situated in the economic, social and political worlds'.[64] This resonates with other feminist theory which has articulated a unique subject position for women of colour, ranging from Gayatri Spivak's identification of the 'subaltern' as unrepresentable within knowledge systems[65] to Hortense J. Spillers's observation that the historical reality of racial slavery casts doubt over how Black women might be assimilated to the same concept of gender as that

50 | ANIMALS AND CAPITAL

articulated by white feminism.[66] The point here is to emphasise that intersectionality provides a method of analysis, and perhaps a starting point for building coalitions, but we cannot assume that we can easily overcome the structural divisions that might prevent alliance-building, particularly where political interests are not in alignment. Here, the problem of structural antagonism comes once again into view.

It is at this point that I would like to return to Wilderson. Here I focus on a 2003 essay: 'Gramsci's Black Marx'. This remarkable text does not merely explore the problem of how to imagine political change in the face of structural antagonism; it goes further, in that it explicitly allows us to assess the prospects for human political projects to challenge the structural position of animals under capitalism.[67] Wilderson's essay is thus a central theoretical text that informs this book.[68] As I have already described, Wilderson has a distinct view of antagonism, advanced in the later text, *Red, White & Black*. 'Gramsci's Black Marx' aims to situate the unique political ontology of the Black subject, but in doing so Wilderson articulates the nature of the antagonism which circulates both Blackness *and* animality, putting these positions at odds structurally with the subject of emancipation within the Marxist left project.[69] As such, the earlier essay is of a high degree of relevance not only for theoretical consideration of race, but also for animal studies. Wilderson's claim is that the continual violation of the Black subject forms the taken-for-granted basis of social relations, and thus progressive political change is unlikely to change the status of the Black subject, who will remain the subject of violence: 'Why is American civil life, whether regressive or expansive, predicated on black death? Why are black folk the indispensable sacrificial lamb vital to its sustenance?'[70] Wilderson here distinguishes between the worker and the slave as two different structural positions:

The worker calls into question the legitimacy of productive practices, the slave calls into question the legitimacy of productivity itself. From the positionality of the worker the question, 'What does it mean to be free?' is raised. But the question hides the process by which the discourse assumes a hidden grammar which has already posed and answered the question, 'What does it mean to suffer?' And that grammar is organised around the categories of exploitation (unfair labour relations or wage slavery). Thus, exploitation (wage slavery) is the only category of oppression which concerns Gramsci: society, Western society, thrives on the exploitation of the Gramscian subject. Full stop. Again, this is inadequate, because it would call white supremacy 'racism' and articulate it as a derivative phenomenon of the capitalist matrix, rather than incorporating white supremacy as a matrix constituent to the base, if not the base itself.[71]

The aim for Wilderson is to articulate the unique structure of antagonism which animates race and is not addressed by the Marxist project; that is, not represented within the material 'base' of productive forces within the left project. Indeed, in emphasising the worker alone as the priority subject of capitalism's exploitation, and side-stepping the constitutive and ongoing place of racial slavery within social and economic relations, the left stands accused of simply rearticulating and intensifying racial hierarchisation: 'what many political theorists have either missed or ignored is that a crisis of authority that might take place by way of a Left expansion of civil society, further instantiates, rather than dismantles, the authority of whiteness. Black death is the modern bourgeois-state's recreational pastime.'[72]

In order to illustrate the incommensurability of the position of the worker versus the Black subject, Wilderson proposes a thought experiment. In this experiment, Wilderson asks the reader to imagine the situation of human workers in a slaughterhouse that has been liberated after a socialist revolution. Perhaps the revolution will bring about democracy in the workplace, and workers will finally be freed from the unnecessary labour of producing surplus for capitalism. But liberation has only come for the humans. As Wilderson asks, what about the cows?

> First, how would the cows fare under a dictatorship of the proletariat? Would cows experience freedom at the mere knowledge that they're no longer being slaughtered in an economy of exchange predicated on exploitation? In other words, would it feel more like freedom to be slaughtered by a workers' collective where there was no exploitation, where the working day was not a minute longer than the time it took to reproduce workers' needs and pleasures, as opposed to being slaughtered in the exploitative context of that dreary old nine to five? Secondly, in the river of common sense does the flotsam of good sense have a message in a bottle that reads 'Workers of the World Become Vegetarians!'? Finally, is it enough to just stop eating meat? In other words, can the Gramscian worker simply *give* the cows their freedom, grant them emancipation, and have it be meaningful to the cows? The cows need some answers before they raise a hoof for the 'flowering of the superstructure'.[73]

For Wilderson, the cows function as an analogy for the Black subject. Through the example of the cows, Wilderson points out that the Black subject has a unique structural position, one that cannot be assimilated to any other structural position, such as that of the worker. Where the worker under capitalism experienced the wage relation as the site of antagonism, the slave, on the other hand, only experienced forced labour and with it, a terrifying regime of violence which shackles the slave to a different political ontology. Further, the alteration of the material base of society does not necessarily imply any shift in the Gramscian 'common sense',[74] which reproduces ideologically the assumed natural position of the slave as a commodity to be set to work and used within a racial hierarchy. This embeds a constellation of relations: 'The chief difference today, compared to several hundred years ago, is that today our bodies are desired, accumulated, and warehoused – like the cows.'[75]

Whether or not the cows can actually be compared to the unique political position of the Black subject – as Wilderson does – is a deeper question; as I shall argue in Chapter 4, although there are strong resonances between racial slavery and industrial animal agriculture, there are also important structural differences which show that these positions cannot be too easily aligned. However, Wilderson's perspective is also an important reminder of the role of antagonism within material relations, and the difficulty this poses for imagining solidarity. Wilderson highlights the unique structural position of the Black subject, a position that cannot be liberated by the social movements of the left, or at least Marxist anti-capitalist movements, since they focus on a different site of exploitation and hostility from that which gave force to racial slavery; the latter required the 'absolute isolation of the slave'.[76]

Although an 'intersectional' analysis might allow us to see this unique positionality, it certainly doesn't guarantee alliance: indeed Wilderson is at pains to stress that alliance with non-Black social movements is difficult to imagine, since whiteness is always invested in anti-Black violence in all its political projects, even those of the left. The fact that Wilderson draws an analogy between the political ontology of Blackness and the animal in the slaughterhouse is instructive: while socialism might liberate the factory, it would take a very different sort of politics – a different revolution – to free the cows as objects of the production of the factory (since in a Marxist sense, animals exist, almost foundationally, as the means of production and the means of subsistence and enjoyment for humans).

Here, I don't at all mean to suggest that we don't need an intersectional analysis, or approach. An intersectional analysis allows us to understand where subjects are positioned within a terrain of power and perhaps develop strategies with relevant social movements that build alliances acknowledging this terrain. This is an important political and strategic condition for animal advocacy; that is, advocacy by humans on behalf of animals. Indeed, some of the most interesting forms of animal advocacy – such as the work of Palestinian animal liberation activists,[77] or Black vegan movements[78] – are fascinating because their politics reflects a specific location with a terrain of power producing new alliances and visions (that is, they are 'intersectional' in the sense Crenshaw suggested).

But do the cows themselves demand something much more radical? Does that mean animal advocates must continually make demands that go beyond those of other left movements, since animal advocates must also deal with a structural antagonism that informs human–animal relations? Indeed, as Wilderson suggests, perhaps the victories of anti-capitalist movements are always premised on a victory over animals; they rely on the continued promise of animals as the 'spoils of victory'.[79] Here, the material conditions which form the base of our analysis – their location, their history, their constituents – are primary considerations for our analysis. Certainly, as I discuss in Chapter 7 of this book, the fact that animals are both the means of production and the means of consumption poses a challenge for what worker control over the means of production means for animals. A revolution that gave human workers control of the means of production would not be a revolution for animals if they remained the means of production and the means of subsistence. In this context, alliance between workers in a slaughterhouse and the cows they will slaughter is highly fraught. It also means that alliance between *animal advocates* and animals is similarly fraught, since it would be arrogant to imagine that the interests of human animal advocates and animals perfectly align. Indeed, a more difficult question is to what extent animal advocates can authentically represent the political demands of animals. Do advocates themselves reproduce the logics of the violent anthropocentrism which stands in the way of 'liberation' for animals? And here we have another layer of complexity: if animal advocates feel isolated from the movements of the left, then this is nothing compared to the profound isolation of animals themselves, whose continual resistance is silenced, nullified and sequestered from sight as part of the business as usual of animal agriculture. The fact that animals need animal advocates only reminds us of the completely unchecked volume of violence experienced by animals, and the profound and absolute isolation of their structural position. Does the loneliness that all animal activists seem to feel – the sense that all those around, including members of other left social movements, are largely oblivious to the horrors of what we do to animals – only reveal the unique material position of animals themselves as largely unsaveable by existing social movements, as beyond redemption by anti-capitalism? Throughout this book, we will keep returning to this problem. The promise of solidarity and shared goals are the optimistic hope that guides my political approach here; however, this must always be tempered by a realistic appraisal of the political terrain before us, as sobering as the latter analysis turns out to be.

The werewolf

There are at least two supernatural creatures lurking amongst the pages of the first volume of Karl Marx's *Capital*. One of these is the vampire: 'Capital is dead labour which, vampire-like, lives only by sucking living labour, and lives the more, the more labour it sucks.'[80] The werewolf is the other beast that wanders through the pages of the text, a supernatural creature that is referred to repeatedly by Marx. For example, in Marx's attempt to powerfully illustrate the almost limitless capacity of capital to demand ever longer working hours from the labourer, we are offered the following characterisation of capitalism:

> in its blind and measureless drive, a werewolf's voracious hunger for surplus labour, capital oversteps not only the moral, but even the merely physical maximum bounds of the working-day.[81]

Here, Marx refers to capitalism as a being that is hyperbolic in its desires; indeed, this is a being identified not by any inherent calm rationality and calculation, but an uncontrolled, unconstrained 'drive'. This is a being with a voracious appetite – a *heisshunger* – that 'sucks' or 'vacuums' (*saugt*) all life in its path.[82] Marx thus depicts capitalism as an apparatus of complete domination, an organism that exerts a political control over life; a supernatural being that we must all succumb to; a terrifying *'animated monster'*[83] which sucks or extracts life, labour, time from everything it turns its attention to.

Marx's life-sucking werewolves and vampires appear as both *material* and *immaterial*; they present themselves as real and unreal, as being beyond the 'social' and 'natural'. The appearance of these supernatural creatures is odd in some respects, given Marx's continuing commitment to a 'materialist' form of analysis, focused on the 'real' relations of productive forces, and not ideals, nor fantasies. As I have described above, Marx emphasises in his materialism that 'it is always necessary to distinguish between the material transformation of the economic conditions of production, which can be determined with the precision of natural science, and the legal, political, religious, artistic or philosophic, in short, ideological forms in which men become conscious of this conflict and fight it out'. Here the world of ideas is divided from the material reality of its economic base; the latter only determined with the 'precision of natural science'.

How can we make sense of the non-material, supernatural force within Marx's text, which is used to describe capitalism?

To an extent Gilles Deleuze and Félix Guattari, in their profound reading of Marx in *Anti-Oedipus*,[84] provide a different way to understand Marx's supernatural creatures. Here, Deleuze and Guattari note that psychoanalysis had traditionally placed desire at odds with the real; the latter functions as the material world which desires affix through lack:

> On the very lowest level of interpretation, this means that the real object that desire lacks is related to an extrinsic natural or social production, whereas desire intrinsically produces an imaginary object that functions as a double of reality, as though there were a 'dreamed-of object behind every real object', or a mental production behind all real productions.[85]

Against this, Deleuze and Guattari argue for a conception of desire as a force of production that is unattached to the product itself, yet sits behind every production in such a way that the real becomes an outcome of desire: 'if desire produces, its product is real. If desire is productive, it can be productive only in the real world and can only produce reality.'[86] For Deleuze and Guattari this understanding of desire shapes their analysis of capitalism as a material social relation.[87] Previous social formations were bound by archaic traditional rules – or 'codes' – which shaped, limited and corralled desire towards fixed or pre-established patterns, confining production within the authority structures of the State or the religious ordering of everyday life.[88] For Deleuze and Guattari capitalism is marked, on the other hand, by a drive to liberate flows from the constraint of these codes. Indeed, what defines capital as a relation is precisely its apparent freedom: the fact that it can be expressed in either constant or variable form, and the fact that it is both everywhere, but seemingly nowhere concrete. This drive of capitalism towards liberating flows – money, labour, commodities – comes constantly into contact with the limits imposed by social orders and the State. Thus, capitalism appears, to everyone it seems,[89] as a vast liberating force whose limits are constantly surfacing at the edges of, and in contest with, prevailing social norms. As Aidan Tynan observes: 'capitalist society is distinct from every other because its limits are constantly being brought into reality as something lived, and, indeed, this occupation of the social limit is precisely how capitalist society can dispense with codes'.[90]

I draw attention to Deleuze and Guattari's reading of capitalism for a few reasons. Firstly, we can note that this reading of the relation between the realm of collective ideas (and fantasies) and that of materiality is not far from at least some new materialist conceptions, such as that of Karen Barad, which disrupt the separation between matter and knowledge by entwining them:

> Material conditions matter, not because they 'support' or 'sustain' or 'mediate' particular discourses that are the actual generative factors in the formation of subjects, but because both discourses and matter come to matter through processes of materialization and the iterative enfolding of phenomena into apparatuses of bodily production.[91]

Secondly, it is a reminder of the strongly energetic anti-capitalist project within the work of Deleuze and Guattari. This is of course quite overtly the goal of two of the famous volumes they author together, which both contain the subtitle 'Capitalism and Schizophrenia'. This is the Deleuze who remarked of himself and his coauthor: 'I think Félix Guattari and I have remained Marxists, in our two different ways, perhaps, but both of us. You see, we think any political philosophy must turn on the analysis of capitalism and the ways it has developed.'[92] This is also the Deleuze who, in the same interview, remarked of 'liberal capitalism' that 'there's no democratic state that's not compromised to the very core by its part in generating human misery'.[93] This is the Guattari who contributes in the 1960s to the *Voie Communiste* and coauthors in the 1980s, with Negri no less, the text *Communists Like Us*.[94] Throughout this intellectual history, we see that there is ongoing commitment to update the materialism of Marxism, and refine our perspective on what exactly capitalism is. But it is also a reminder of the perhaps selective reading of Deleuze and Guattari's thought by contemporary theorists: despite the strong and apparent affection for concepts such as 'becoming' and 'assemblage' within new materialism, this same energy to theorise capitalism as a material relation appears missing, or at least less apparent.

The understanding provided by Deleuze and Guattari of capitalism as an insatiable drive that transforms all material relations helps us to understand the way in which it interacts with and transforms, in a dynamic fashion, pre-existing relationships of knowledge and structure. In these cases, capitalism may act as the engine to enhance and liberate, in an intoxicated and frenzied way, the desires embedded in social relations which prefigure the capitalist economy. This point is made clearly by Cedric Robinson in *Black Marxism*, who suggests that the structural relations of racism were in place prior to the emergence of capitalism, so that 'the effects of racialism were bound to appear in the social expression of every strata of every European society no matter the structures upon which they were formed'.[95] This racism gives shape to capitalist social and economic relations: 'racialism . . . ran deep in the bowels of Western culture, negating its varying social relations of production and distorting their inherent contradictions'.[96] Thus the arrival of capitalism offers the opportunity to simply extend and expand existing modalities of social structure:

> The social, cultural, political, and ideological complexes of European feudal-isms contributed more to capitalism than the social 'fetters' that precipitated the bourgeoisie into social and political revolutions. No class was its own creation. Indeed, capitalism was less a catastrophic revolution (negation) of feudalist social orders than the extension of these social relations into the larger tapestry of the modern world's political and economic relations.[97]

These social relations are no doubt transformed through their encounter with capitalism: they are offered new consolidations, energies, modulations, they become more intense, more apparent, more horrific. They build on an earlier set of ideas and practices, allowing a pre-existing racism to be transformed and liberated by the flows of capitalism in order to realise unprecedented and constitutive forms of violence, exploitation, theft and genocide which form the material base of contemporary global economies.

This conceptualisation of the interaction between racism and capitalism pro-vides a useful analytic schema to understand the way in which a prevailing hierarchical anthropocentrism, which as Kim reminds us also overlaps with an anti-Black racial knowledge order,[98] was modified and put into effect by capitalism, reflecting a materialisation of desiring production. Following this logic through, the factory farm represents the outcome of this process of mate-rialisation. It arises within a distinct set of concrete historical conditions: a prevailing and intensifying form of hierarchical anthropocentrism; a scientific and rational application of knowledge to create technologies and techniques; an economic system bound only to expanding capital; and a State apparatus that can deploy force, command, facilitate and authorise. Importantly, as I shall discuss in Chapter 6, this materialisation had to also confront the resistance of animals themselves, producing the perverse formulations we find today which seek to quell all dissent and produce nightmarish mechanisms which we shall encounter in this book: skinning and 'harvesting' machines, trawl nets and fish pumps. The desire of this form of anthropocentrism collaborates with the free-ing movement of capitalism to materialise a non-stop reality of fast-paced birth and death which both delivers a seemingly unending supply of pleasure, satisfac-tion and sustenance, and simultaneously provides a mechanism for the capture of the value of labour time through the production of death. The living hell of industrial animal agriculture, with its primary productivity entailing the mass 'fabrication' of death,[99] represents simultaneously a process for the capture of 'dead labour'; not just human labour but, as I argue in this book, the labour of animals too.

Seeing capitalism as a werewolf requires a particular form of materialism. In line with the new materialisms, we have to dispense with the anthropocentrism of the old materialisms so that we can *both* recognise the historical interaction between anthropocentrism and prevailing systems of production and exchange *and* simultaneously notice the full extent to which nonhuman labour and energies are central to the economy of relations and the construction of 'value'. In conformity with the old materialism, though, we need to see the way in which material conditions place actors at odds with each other in systems of violence and domination;[100] that is, depend upon continuing structural antagonism. Finally, although we must certainly reject a predestined plan written into current material relations which suggests a narrative of perpetual progress and 'civilisation', we must nevertheless at the same time be alive to the reality that the historical moment of current material conditions, their contradictions and antagonisms, produces unprecedented opportunities for different futures. Certainly, as this book contends, while the twin forces of anthropocentrism and capitalism have co-produced a living nightmare for animals, the contradiction is that we have simultaneously produced the means for an alternative without this violence. This material future beckons realisation.

3   Commodity

> Production creates the material, as external object, for consumption; consumption creates the need, as internal object, as aim, for production. Without production no consumption; without consumption no production.
>
> Karl Marx, *Grundrisse*[1]

Nothing on the surface of the commodity betrays the violence of its production.[2] Instead the commodity appears mysteriously to us, its immediate use value in the foreground, other values – the conditions of its supply, its history – obscured from sight. This is without doubt the global condition for food animals associated with industrial animal agriculture under the capitalist system. Food animals appear to 'us' (capital, human consumers) – whether as raw materials (inputs) or as consumption commodities (products) – 'pre-fabricated' and ready for use.

In describing the difference between a commodity which is a 'raw material' and that which is a 'consumption commodity', I delineate two different 'appearances' for animals within a circuit of production. I should stress that this distinction is artificial, since in both cases, animals are consumed as commodities: animal lives are *consumed* in the process of creating products within production; while the consumption products that emerge as a result of this process are intended to become the raw materials for the reproduction of humans (that is, a means for the production and reproduction of human labour), also to be consumed. In both cases, animals are simultaneously a raw material and a consumption commodity. However, although we can form a general abstraction of animals as commodities by drawing an equivalence between raw materials as consumables for capitalist production and, secondly, animals as consumer commodities which are raw materials for human reproduction, there is value in separating these two instances of the commodification of animals. One reason is that there is at least one qualitative difference between these two commodity forms: the first, by and large, represents the space where animals are living and therefore endure production processes as lives lived; the second, the space where these animals are dead, and fabricated into a commodity suitable for consumption. Additionally, there is a difference for capitalism itself. The space of capitalist production is the space where value is sought through the transformation of use values. Because production directly produces value, this is a site of interest for capitalism (we cannot comprehend this fully until we examine labour in Chapter 4). This does not mean that capitalism is agnostic with regard to consumption. Reproduction of human life and labour is functionally important for the productivity of capitalism; and the consumption of animal-sourced foods as a means of subsistence forms part of the circulation that occurs outside of production, which aligns human living standards with the expenditure of wages (the movement of money) upon the products that capitalist production proliferates. As such, we must treat the circuit of production as interconnected with the circuit of consumption: 'without production no consumption; without consumption, no production'.

This chapter follows the 'appearances' of food animals as commodities within capitalism. I will firstly outline Marx's approach to understanding the commodity as something which is identified as an entity with a use value and interrogate what this may mean for animals as commodities at a symbolic and material level. I will then follow the movement of animals from raw material to consumption commodity, noting the transformation of use values in production, particularly marked by the event of production from which (for animals, like other raw materials) no return is possible: that is, the value-creating moment of death, which moves the animal body wholeheartedly from the space of a material fabrication into a consumption commodity. Here, the animal is literally de-faced: their materiality is altered and homogenised in such a way as to assume the undifferentiated banality of the product. Finally, I will explore the circulation of animals as consumption commodities. Here we enter the space where animal products become the means of subsistence for human populations, and thus essential for the reproduction of another labour force of capitalism: namely, the human workforce. As I shall describe, there are contradictions here – some perhaps structurally irresolvable, and others perhaps indicating the curious potentialities for shared alliances against capitalism.

Raw material

In the first chapter of the first volume of *Capital*, Marx describes the process by which an entity attains value within a system of exchange and thus transforms into a commodity. There is nothing intrinsic about an entity that establishes it as a target for commodification. Rather, as Marx observes, this process is necessarily relational: commodity exchange requires establishing a form of equivalent value between one entity and another, where one qualitatively different entity is exchanged for another in a transaction. Importantly, the two objects of exchange must be substantively different in order for a concept of value to arise. Here, as Marx notes, we find the perplexing process whereby in order for an object to attain value, another object must stand in for it as an equivalent:[3] 'the equivalent form of a commodity, accordingly, is the form in which it is directly exchangeable with other commodities'.[4] Marx summarises:

> Since a commodity cannot be related to itself as an equivalent, and therefore cannot make its own physical shape into the expression of its own value, it must be related to another commodity as equivalent, and therefore must make the physical shape of another commodity into its own value form.[5]

The process of recognising value – a process of imposing equivalence upon contextually differentiated entities in order to generate value – is, by definition, a process of 'abstraction'. It relies upon substitution to generate a value that is not inherent in the entity which is valued.[6]

There is violence – symbolic, but as we shall see, also material – attached to this process, since valuation requires erasure of the inherent qualities of one entity in order to create a generalised equivalence and identification with another. One entity is made to look like the other: 'by means of the value relation, therefore, the natural form of the commodity becomes the value-form of commodity A, in other words the physical body of commodity B becomes a mirror for the value of commodity A'.[7]

Here, initially, we can note a number of characteristics related to the way Marx sees value. Firstly, while this process of substitution necessitates a violent erasure, it is important to note that in Marx's philosophy this same process for the recognition of value is necessary for any valuation to occur. Value does not beam out of an object or relation in a way that is inherent or self-evident. There is nothing in the object or relation that arises as value in an 'intrinsic' way; instead, value emerges within the context of a relation between a community of comparable objects of value. It is for this reason that the idea of 'intrinsic value'

– as emphasised by animal rights theory (and as I discussed in Chapter 1) – is meaningless from Marx's perspective. Secondly, it is also not clear that Marx is only speaking of 'economic' value here; at least if we imagine the sphere of the 'economic' as relating to the exchange of goods, services and currency.[8] Indeed, Marx's discussion is revealing of how value might accrue within social relations more generally, including human–animal relations. I refer here explicitly to a curious footnote in the first chapter of *Capital*, volume 1:

> In a certain sense, a man is in the same situation as a commodity. As he neither enters into the world in possession of a mirror, nor as a Fichtean philosopher who can say 'I am I,' a man first sees and recognizes himself in another man. Peter only relates to himself as a man through his relation to another man, Paul, in who he recognizes his likeness. With this, however, Paul also becomes from head to toe, in his physical form as Paul, the form of appearance of the species man for Peter.[9]

The footnote is remarkable on a number of levels. Here, Marx transposes the process of commodification onto the problem of relations 'between men'. Marx speculates that self-realisation – realisation of the value in oneself – relies upon recognition of another like-self, to stand in for one's own self. Peter can only recognise himself when Paul is understood as equivalent to him. This violence, the replacement of one for another, enables value through a sociality that provides equivalence between two otherwise distinct entities.

Beyond the novelty of Marx's transposition of the process of commodification onto social relations, there are other aspects of the footnote which remain remarkable. The reference to Paul as the mirror which allows Peter to see his own value bears a remarkable resonance with Jacques Lacan's description of the 'mirror stage', as the experience of the schism between the material experience of the self and the specular image of oneself:

> the total form of his body, by which the subject anticipates the maturation of his power in a mirage, is given to him only as a gestalt, that is, in an exteriority in which, to be sure, this form is more constitutive than constituted, but in which, above all, it appears to him as the contour of his stature that freezes it and in a symmetry that reverses it, in opposition to the turbulent movements with which the subject feels he animates it.[10]

As Lacan highlights, the 'assumption' of the image of identification by the subject is a rupturing experience, since the self must become what it is not in order to be part of an order of signification (Peter becomes, or stands in for, Paul). Another layer here is the clearly gendered terms of value recognition in 'man'; Peter recognises himself, his similarity, his value over other entities by understanding his equivalence to Paul. One might speculate whether in this valuation, Peter might see value in himself when confronted by Mary; could one replace another in a commodity exchange? As I shall discuss below with reference to Luce Irigaray, the equivalence that Peter sees in Paul embeds phallocentric social relations.[11] Finally, the remarkable phrase 'the form of appearance of the species man' ('*als Erscheinungsform des Genus Mensch*') reminds us that the distinction between humans and animals, the species-specific 'dignity' of the human claimed by Peter and recognised in Paul, secures and grounds the value that arises in this economy. As I shall discuss, animals appear as commodities with both a direct and immediate use value for humans as a raw material, or as food, and simultaneously with a broader use value to secure a hierarchical human value over other animals.

We might render this picture more fully by considering the role of money in this commodity exchange. While Marx discusses money and its circulation within the pages of the first volume of *Capital*, it is in his earlier *Grundrisse* that we find a more detailed and lengthy exposition of the emergence of money, and the way in which currency under capitalism comes to dominate exchange relationships. Money complicates the story of our commodity exchange between Paul and Peter, because in Marx's model, money comes to stand in between the exchange of commodities, and becomes the universalised way in which a commodity can have its value 'reflected'. As Marx observes in *Grundrisse*, the value or price applied to a commodity refers the commodity outside of its immediate point of exchange into a sphere of abstracted value. This is an abstracted value that bears no necessary connection to the immediate use value of the commodity.[12] Money thus becomes a way to agree upon the relationship between Peter and Paul, so that Paul is not expressed through his respective value to Peter (for example, one Peter is worth one Paul), but through a third commodity – money – which represents a value with respect to which both Paul and Peter can attain relative value (for example, Peter is worth $100, and Paul $80). This has the effect of shifting exchange to the sphere of money and its circulation, and applying a price to commodities in a way that is not necessarily connected to other commodities, only money itself. In a money economy, Peter and Paul's value can only be understood by reference to money, and this money value, the abstract value, becomes a reflected aspect of the commodity itself. Thus, Marx observes:

as *price*, the commodity relates to money on one side as something existing outside of itself, and secondly, it is *ideally* posited as money itself, since money has a reality that is different from it. The price is a property of the commodity, a quality in which it is *presented* as money. It is no longer an immediate but a reflected quality of it.[13]

Once again, the process of allowing a commodity to reflect value through the image of relational commodities or money depends upon a certain erasure in the entity that is commodified, an effacement of the surface that allows it to become reflective of value. Marx notes this in *Capital*, suggesting that this is a process of stripping the skin:

> Hence, for one commodity-owner to meet with another, in the form of a money owner, it is necessary either that the product of the latter should possess by its nature the form of money, i.e. it should be gold, the material of which money consists, or that his product should have already changed its skin and stripped off its original form of a useful object.[14]

I will return below to the question of the 'skinning' that is inherent to commodification. However, we might note here that all commodities rely upon a kind of homogenisation where particular characteristics are erased in order for equivalence to be established. We saw this above in the simple exchange where we allow, for example, an apple to be equivalent to an orange, thus forgetting what is distinctive about both in order to establish an equal value. This does not change when money is involved, since money is simply the medium for this value to be established. Further, and as we shall discuss, money is itself a commodity which has been effaced of all characteristics so that it can function perfectly to 'reflect' a price.

How might the above considerations relate to animals within economies? We might be able to assemble some provisional observations. Firstly, we are aware that animals have been exchanged and traded for a long time. These exchanges, at their most elementary, such as in a barter system, required a process by which an animal was made equivalent to another entity – a foodstuff, another animal, a service, etc. – in order for exchange to occur. This represents the violence of commodification, since, under the terms laid out above, a use value is established by creating an equivalent in a relational system. But this differs greatly from animals who are traded as raw materials today within industrial agriculture, since these exchanges are mediated through exchanges of money. Money establishes a way for one animal to be valued in relation to another without a direct comparison with different commodities (thus, instead of a hundred chickens being worth one cow, we are presented with a world where chickens might be worth \$3 and cows might be worth \$2,000).[15] In either case, a barter system or a money economy, the price of the commodity is a reflection of the apparent use value to the commodity-owner or the money-owner who wishes to buy.

But there is more to say on money and what it symbolically may mean in relation to human–animal relations. In a remarkable essay, Irigaray offers a powerful reading of chapter 1 of Marx's *Capital*, volume 1.[16] Here, Irigaray describes how it is that an animate body – that of a woman – should be drawn into the process of becoming both a commodity and a commodity that circulates as a means to reflect exchange value (that is, money). Importantly, Irigaray describes the experience for woman to be rendered as both a material object and as a symbolic exchange value. In this sense, Irigaray describes a moving intersection between two forms of patriarchy: women dominated as an immediate objectified use value for the purposes of male pleasure (a material oppression), and a continual pressure for women to uphold their symbolic value as maintaining and reproducing the generalised value of the phallus (a symbolic oppression).

Irigaray draws a number of conclusions that are acutely relevant to my discussion here. Firstly, Irigaray describes the movement from use value to exchange value inherent to commodification, and its materiality for women's bodies: 'just as, in commodities, natural utility is overridden by the exchange function, so the properties of a woman's body have to be suppressed and subordinated to the exigencies of its transformation into an object of circulation among men'.[17] According to Irigaray, exchange shifts the use value of a woman's body – including her intrinsic or 'natural' use value[18] to herself – into a system of commodification and exchange.[19] Secondly, in line with Irigaray's interest in the mirror,[20] Irigaray points to the specific function of women as mirrors in exchange: 'just as a commodity has no mirror it can use to reflect itself, so woman serves as a reflection, as image of and for man, but lacks specific qualities of her own'.[21] Thirdly, Irigaray observes that this specific commodification is premised, becomes urgent, due to the fragility of masculinity itself and its need for securitisation through continual circulation:

> just as commodities, despite their resistance, become more or less autonomous repositories for the value of human work, as mirrors of and for man, women more or less unwittingly come to represent the danger of a disappropriation of masculine power: the phallic mirage.[22]

Thus, Irigaray describes the intersecting symbolic experience of objectification and commodification, with an attentiveness to the materiality of this commodification.[23] This describes a political subjectivity within the exchange system of patriarchy, which enacts a simultaneous material and epistemic violence.[24]

My interest in Irigaray's account is in whether this same process might usefully describe the materiality of animal subjugation; a materiality that is caught precisely between being both a commodity with a raw use value (for example, meat or leather) and being an exchange value that circulates as a means to reflect value in other commodities. Within animal rights theory, Carol J. Adams has pointed out that patriarchy and speciesism collide to create 'the cycle of objectification, fragmentation, and consumption, which links butchering and sexual violence in our culture'.[25] For Adams, this occurs through what she describes as the 'absent referent': a set of transformations between subject and object where the original entity that might have been owed moral recognition is substituted by an object.[26] In a sense, Irigaray's reading of Marx allows for a supplementation of Adams's approach, in so far as Irigaray describes the materiality of this transformation as not merely being about the objectification of women for a masculine use value, but the valuation of masculinity itself through women as a 'reflective' commodity (money) within an economy of gender relations.

Irigaray raises a set of conceptual concerns related to the optics of the commodity (its appearance, reflections), its capacity to operate within different economies of value, and the dynamics of its fabrication. These are certainly relevant to understanding animal commodification under capitalism; but we could take other examples. Perhaps the other pressing example relates to slavery and the economy of race. Orlando Patterson certainly makes clear that trade in slaves was an essential aspect of slavery as an institution, but also observes that slaves functioned as currency.[27] Importantly, as I shall discuss in Chapter 4, the violence of slavery, and the universalised dishonour it generated, served a function in establishing and reproducing an economy of race. Perhaps of relevance, this racialised economy connects with trade in animals. Patterson points to the interrelations between human slaves and animals as commodities with money values: for example, 'in sixteenth-century Burma, 40 Indian slaves was the going price for a horse'.[28] Here, as in Irigaray's discussion, we are reminded that the commodity exists in numerous guises – raw material, labour (which I discuss in Chapter 4), currency – and operates on multiple levels; not only in a money economy, but in a symbolic, material and 'libidinal'[29] space that stratifies status and establishes political ontologies. This is why Wilderson points out the larger racial effects of slavery on forming the world as we know it:

through chattel slavery the world gave birth and coherence to both its joys of domesticity and to its struggles of political discontent; and with these joys and struggles the Human was born, but not before it murdered the Black, forging a symbiosis between the political ontology of Humanity and the social death of Blacks.[30]

This is not simply an 'economic' relation in so far as it is determined by the exchanges of money and commodities; it instead sits at the centre of symbolic relations which define the human.

We might similarly understand animals as both a raw material (one that enters production, or one that is consumed) *and* as a form of currency that reifies and cements human value in itself. Indeed, the footnote from the first volume of *Capital* that I refer to above is interesting for me because it is explicitly related to the production of human value in itself: 'With this, however, Paul also becomes from head to toe, in his physical form as Paul, the form of appearance of the species man for Peter.' The encounter with Paul enables Peter not merely to understand himself as equivalent to the specific object of exchange – Paul – but to generalise the characteristics that he finds in common with Paul as definitive of the species being of the human; and thus, the human emerges as a biological entity (*'genus Mensch'*). Peter's encounter with Paul, the man who might stand in for him as an equivalent, already also comes to mark the experience of the human as a species differentiated from other living beings and placed above other species. While the encounter and commodification relies upon a violence – an erasure of those points of difference between Peter and Paul that might prevent us ascribing equivalence – it is Paul's likeness that is productive of an immunising sociality, a sociality which generates a biological affiliation between Peter and Paul as a species. Why is it, we may ask, that 'man' becomes privileged to signify his own meaning, his own value, through reference to himself? Why is it that an understanding of oneself relies upon this biological classification?[31]

Derrida's 1971 essay 'White Mythology: Metaphor in the Text of Philosophy' perhaps provides some clues to this problem.[32] I am drawn to this essay in particular because of the transparent link Derrida makes between the commodification of the object and its circulation, the process of abstraction in generating meaning within a language system, and the way in which metaphor circulates within this system. Taking a leaf from a discussion in Anatole France's *The Garden of Epicurus*,[33] Derrida observes that language works through a substitution of the word, the concept, or the metaphor for the material phenomena of world: word stands in for object in order to generate a system of language. Each

68 | ANIMALS AND CAPITAL

time the metaphor is deployed and put into exchange, it is 'worn down', as it were; it distances itself further from the original point of equivalence so that its originary meaning, the originary signifier, is lost.[34]

As such, and this is the story retold by Derrida from France's text, the metaphor is like a coin whose surfaces are so worn through exchange that the 'value and the head' – the signification of the originary exchange and the authority underpinning exchange – are lost. For Derrida, philosophy is involved in at least two tasks. The first is employing the metaphor, putting it into circulation, and becoming an accomplice in the obliteration of the original meaning through exchange. Secondly, Derrida observes that in this process philosophy seeks, repetitively, to uncover the secret meaning behind the metaphor; the meaning that has been worn down through time. And philosophers pick the most worn-down metaphors – for example, 'being', 'truth', 'the good' – as an economical decision that aims to 'save' the labour of rubbing.[35] By the close of the essay, Derrida associates the metaphor with both the 'provisional loss of meaning' but one that orients itself towards a return to meaning: 'a history with its sights set on, and within the horizon of, the circular reappropriation of literal, proper meaning'.[36]

The section that particularly interests me here, which is relevant to animal commodification, is Derrida's discussion of metaphor in Aristotle, where Derrida examines both *Poetics* and *Rhetoric*. Here Derrida alerts us to the specific classification system that lies behind Aristotle's understanding of the process of metaphorisation as giving a 'thing a name that belongs to something else'.[37] While the basis of analogy may open the grounds for equivalence between any two entities that we might find analogous, it is curious to find here the apparent overdetermination of the relationship between metaphor and the structured comparison between species and genus, and species and species.[38] These are categorisations which in Aristotle are at once logical, and comply with a structured lexical ordering of the world, but are simultaneously biological, in a structured ordering of life. (Perhaps it is no accident that, along similar lines, Aristotle remarks in *Logic* that 'Not every animal is a man; but every man is an animal.')[39] The repetition of language here rests upon assumed similarity, on the ability of the metaphor-maker to replicate and imitate the original in order to produce meaning.

Derrida observes that according to the Aristotelian system, only humans have the ability to metaphoricise, since only humans, for Aristotle, possess language. Here, both humans and animals are able to utter sounds, but only human sounds may be signified: 'This is the difference between animals and man: according to Aristotle both can emit indivisible sounds, but only man can make of them a letter.'[40] The reason, Derrida suggests, is that for Aristotle humans posses a unique capability for mimesis, for representation through imitation and mimicry. As such, Derrida characterises the difference Aristotle draws between humans and animals in relation to language as founded upon a 'teleological'[41] judgement on the nature of 'man' (rather than through any evidence about animal communication). Derrida observes:

> What is proper to nouns is to signify something, an independent being identical to itself, conceived as such. It is at this point that the theory of the name, such as it is implied by the concept of metaphor, is articulated with ontology. Aside from the classical and dogmatically affirmed limit between the animal without *logos* and the man as the *zōon logon ekhon*, what appears here is a certain systematic indissociability of the value of metaphor and the metaphysical chain holding together the values of discourse, voice, noun, signification, meaning, imitative representation, resemblance . . . *Mimēsis* is never without the *theoretical* perception of resemblance or similarity, that is, of that which always will be posited as the condition for metaphor.[42]

In this reading, 'man's' difference from other animals rests upon a human ability to craft, to 'fabricate', the metaphor, to excoriate the differences between entities in order to 'see the double'; this name is 'articulated with ontology'.[43] Derrida suggests that it is this capacity that Aristotle refers to, that defines the human relationship with nature, as a form of reason which finds the double, the resemblance, within the natural world, including itself: '*Mimēsis* is proper to man. . . . The power of truth, as the unveiling of nature (*physis*) by *mimēsis*, congenitally belongs to the physics of man, to anthropophysics.'[44] But this is a 'theoretical' rather than empirically verified mimesis. It occurs by abstraction and *fabrication*. The metaphor can only arise through an interlinked string of signifiers, themselves fabrications, which is why Derrida wants to emphasise that we are dealing here not merely with the metaphor, but with a theory of the metaphor. The theory of the metaphor accompanies the metaphor; in order to see the double, the resemblance, we need to partake in the theory that accompanies it – that is, a human system of language that authorises itself and its own internally constituted resemblances. This theory accompanies a particular philosophical and historical tradition of thought – Western metaphysics – that sees animals in particular ways, authorising a systematic categorisation that allows for both a hierarchical order and one that enables comparison, analogy, similarity and difference.

To return to our Peter and Paul, we can understand that the species being that both Peter and Paul represent, at least in the Aristotelian schema, emerges from not merely a simple capacity to recognise a likeness, but an apparently distinct human capacity to use logic to theorise a pattern of repetition in nature and apply generality – species, genus, etc. – across otherwise distinct entities. A human capacity that simultaneously, first in theorising and then in seeing repetition, violently erases difference at the point at which a common value is sought.[45]

We also recognise that Peter does not directly commodify Paul in order to recognise human value. On the contrary, the animal stands in as the means for this social relationship to occur. Peter fabricates the animal as a way to reflect his value, as a mirror to his own humanity, a common value he shares with Paul. And the only way for this value to be reproduced is for animality to continually circulate as a currency that reflects human value (superiority, dignity, etc.); just as, in capitalism, the continual circulation of money underpins financial value. We might further observe that capitalism thrives upon the continual expansion of value; the expansion of capital, its promise of an increase in value, is dependent upon an exponential increase in the circulation of money. As Marx is at pains to note, capitalism as an economic system thrives not on the production of commodities as a goal, but on the production of capital, which appears in money form amongst other guises, and promises future production of capital as an end in itself: 'exchanging money for money makes no sense, unless, that is, a quantitative difference arises, less money is exchanged for more'.[46] Perhaps, therefore, one way to read the explosive acceleration of large-scale containment, breeding and slaughter associated with animal-sourced food systems[47] is that it represents a process by which animals have been produced as both use values (for example, as meat for human consumption and nourishment) and as exchange values expressed in a kind of currency which reflects human value – human superiority, dignity, prerogative – which is reaffirmed with each act of killing or animal utilisation. The former commodity is deployed to enable the subsistence of human populations. The latter 'money' value, which occurs within the 'economy' of hierarchical anthropocentrism, is always precarious and perched upon maintaining an absolute value in human superiority, even where evidence might suggest that this has no factual basis.[48] As I have previously argued, human sovereignty over animals, maintained and regulated through systemic institutions of violence, underpins systems of value.[49] This value production is not merely about animals as food – that is, the price of steak – but is simultaneously the reproduction through an authorising violence of the rationality that accompanies a human sovereign prerogative: to paraphrase Irigaray, the violence upholds 'the mirage' of human sovereignty.

We are here at the point where we can offer a summary of how animals are commodified as raw materials. Firstly, in order to be transformed into a commodity, animals, like any other entity to be commodified, must be made equivalent to other commodities within an economy. The 'price' of this commodity – whether this is expressed within a system of barter, or in money exchange – 'reflects' a use value. The 'appearance' of this use value is a fabrication within a relational system of meaning, since the commodity must have its distinct characteristics effaced in order for it to appear as a use value. Finally, the animal commodity is not merely a raw material, or later, a means of subsistence with an immediate use value, but simultaneously acts as a symbolic currency that stands between humans to reflect and confirm human superiority through their circulation. Within this logic of value, the fact that animals appear as commodities reinforces, in an everyday way, that humans appear superior to them: the exponential and frenzied circulation of animal-sourced foods for human satisfaction and pleasure establishes a continuing mirror that allows humans to see themselves – sovereign, victorious – in the corpses which are fabricated.[50]

Skinning machine

As I have discussed, Derrida reminds us that money is 'worn down' by exchange. The surface of the coin is gradually effaced so that even the signified value inscribed on the surface is worn away. Marx devotes much space in *Grundrisse* to considering the emergence of so-called 'metallics' as the preferred physical form of money, the pure reflection of value.[51] Prior to the prominence of metal currencies, economies relied on the trade of a range of non-metallic commodities: as Marx observes, 'salt, hides, cattle and slaves' all served the function of money.[52] However, metals emerge as the chosen format for money because of their material qualities: they can be divided and remain equal in quantity,[53] they can be transported without risk of damaged stock, and, importantly, 'precious metals last, they do not alter'.[54] This is related to the 'perishability' of other commodities in comparison to precious metals, the reason why hoarding metallic forms of money, the universal commodity, is preferred to hoarding other goods: 'It maintains itself as wealth at all times. Its specific durability. It is the treasure which neither rust nor moths eat up.'[55] As such, metallic money requires no particular skill or equipment to be deployed in order to maintain its value.[56]

Marx's observations remind us that the process of creating money, and the process of exchange itself, is both symbolic and material. A symbolic erasure occurs to allow a commodity to act as money; its unique qualities are forgotten, and in its place a veneer of durability and pure value is fabricated. The surface of money must not betray any qualities that would allow it to be differentiated from the currency it must be identical to. Money must be able to perfectly reflect

72 | ANIMALS AND CAPITAL

back value, even if this value is fleeting and changeable; its materiality is required to be present but qualitatively absent in order to enable exchange:

> It *is* the price; it is a given quantity of gold or silver; but in so far as this reality of the price is here only fleeting, a reality destined constantly to disappear, to be suspended, not to count as a definitive realization, but always as an intermediate, mediating realization; in so far as the point here is not the realization of the price at all, but rather the realization of the exchange value of one particular commodity in the material of another commodity, to that extent its own material is irrelevant; it is ephemeral as a realization of the price, since this itself disappears; it exists, therefore, in so far as it remains in this constant movement, only as a representative of exchange value, which becomes real only if the real exchange value constantly steps into the place of its representative, constantly changes place with it, constantly exchanges itself for it. Hence, in this process, its reality is not that it is the price, but that it *represents* it, is is its representative – the materially present representative of the price, thus of itself, and, as such, of the exchange value of commodities.[57]

If it is true, as I am asserting here, that animals circulate as a means to underpin the human and its value, then the materiality of the transformation of animals is one which allows for the animal to be fabricated as not differentiated; as equivalent to other animals; as being able to be present, yet never betraying a qualitative difference; as seamlessly allowing exchange between humans. One lamb looks like another; one lamb chop like another lamb chop; and each is understood within social and political relations as self-same.[58]

Animals in food production must undergo a material transformation in order to be fabricated into meat. They are born through biotechnologies into a life of containment, then nurtured carefully by sophisticated techniques which participate in the crafting of bodies for market, often held upon the line between life and death in order to maximise profitability and use value to capital. This relies on a specific fabrication of the body, an effacement to create uniformity, homogeneity, predictability in the commodity, so that one lamb should come to represent another, one chicken should be replaceable by another; thus almost perfectly exchangeable, and durable in material character.[59] And of course, death marks a material point of transition in this process. As Jan Dutkiewicz has noted, the death of animals within industrialised food production is a value-producing moment: the moment where a number of converging processes which fabricate the animal as a universal and uniform commodity mature into the value form:

The product (the pig) must be preconceived as having certain biological characteristics (growth rate, ability to efficiently convert feed of a certain kind into mass, high fertility for females, and a specific yield of meat desired by consumers, among others); the pig must then be raised in such a way as to maximize its biological capacity for meat creation while controlling for the risk posed by its animality (preventing disease, certain behaviors, escape); the pig must then be killed and its carcass efficiently mined for saleable goods, which in turn need to be sold to consumers.[60]

It is at this moment, when the animal is converted from living to dead, that the value of the animal can be realised in the market; where the raw material emerges from the production process to become the consumption commodity. As Marx notes, all exchange requires that which is being exchanged to undergo a transition from one state to another as part of the production process: from 'nature' to commodity, use value to exchange value, commodity to money. In the case of animals in food production, the materiality of this transformation point is from living being to dead meat. It is perhaps telling that Marx in *Grundrisse* points to the analogy between the 'arbitrary and senseless abstraction' that characterises the circulation of money and commodities, and the circular process of life and death.[61] For animals the circulation of money and commodities is materially interrelated with the cycle of industrialised birth, death and rebirth in order to both satisfy a commodity use value for humans and to underline and cement, through an incessant, growing and hyperbolic circulation, 'the form of appearance of the species man'.

The event of transforming living being to dead meat involves a material, physical transformation, and not just one where the life of the living being is pried away in order for the animal to be transformed into the consumption commodity. Not only is the living soul extinguished, but there is also a material effacement of the body: these animals are both symbolically and materially 'skinned'.

Above, I noted that for Marx the process of commodification is described as akin to being 'excoriated'. Here we can explore the meaning of this. In chapter 6 of *Capital*, volume 1, Marx observes that human workers under capitalism are exposed to a dubious freedom: a freedom that operates in a double sense, since workers are *both* free to commodify their own labour power and free of the means of realising the value of their own labour. Both these 'freedoms' are framed by necessity, since the worker is only free to commodify their own labour because they have nothing else to sell in order to survive.[62] Marx then closes the chapter by calling upon the reader to leave the simple sphere of exchange and turn to the heart of production:

When we leave this sphere of simple circulation or the exchange of commodities, which provides the 'free-trader vulgaris' with his views, his concepts and the standard by which he judges the society of capital and wage-labour, a certain change takes place, or so it appears, in the physiognomy of our *dramatis personae*. He who was previously the money-owner now strides in front as a capitalist; the possessor of labour-power follows as his worker. The one smirks self-importantly and is intent on business; the other is timid and holds back, like someone who has brought his own hide to market and now has nothing else to expect but – a tanning.[63]

This is not the first time in *Capital* that Marx makes reference to the removal of the skin, or the hide, as a metaphor for labour commodification.[64] The hide, tanning and skinning are repeated through the text, and become a way for Marx to describe a moment of transition – from subject to commodity; from commodity to money – a way to describe the process of becoming something that one is not through effacement of one's appearance.[65] This effacement allows for the fabrication of a new value, a new 'appearance'.

Certainly, the process is as material as it is symbolic: 'With this, however, Paul also becomes from head to toe, in his physical form as Paul, the form of appearance of the species man for Peter [*Damit gilt ihm aber auch der Paul mit Haut und Haaren, in seiner paulinischen Leiblichkeit, als Erscheinungsform des Genus Mensch*]'. The phrase '*mit Haut und Haaren*' translates as 'with skin and hair'. The etymology of '*mit Haut und Haaren*' traces to ancient German punishments – *Strafen an Haut und Haar* – which took the skin and hair as their object: punishments involving cutting or pulling hair out of the victim, and punishments such as flogging which took the skin as their object.[66] One devotes oneself to an activity 'with skin and hair' (at least in the contemporary rendering of the phrase) because one is consumed wholeheartedly, materially invested, by that activity. Irigaray notes that the materiality of this effacement is important to understand:

> One commodity cannot be mirrored in another, as man is mirrored in his fellow man. For when we are dealing with commodities the self-same, mirrored, is not 'its' own likeness, contains nothing of its properties, its qualities, its 'skin and hair'. The likeness here is only a measure expressing the *fabricated* character of the commodity, its trans-formation by man's (social, symbolic) 'labor'.[67]

In industrialised slaughter, the act of stripping animals of their hide marks the material threshold where the once-was-alive animal becomes meat and the body of the animal is commodified in such a way as for an exchange value to be realisable on the open market. The process of commodification here rests upon an imposed equivalent value, of the exchange of living lamb for dead chop, upon the forced exchange of one for the other as a way to generate value. This process of commodification simultaneously demands the erasure of those qualities that might mark a qualitative difference between the living and the dead, including those signs of animal resistance to the process of commodification – the body kicking and struggling – all of which is subject to a material erasure in order to sustain the commodity exchange value pursued.[68] Removing the skin of the animal[69] is an important aspect in the generation of value, as it enables the homogenisation of what was previously uniquely differentiated.

Timothy Pachirat, in his ethnographic work *Every Twelve Seconds*, carefully documents the segmentation within the modern slaughterhouse which materially separates between life and death. Pachirat observes that the slaughterhouse is partitioned not only to offer a multi-staged separation between each labour process involved in disassembling the living animal to become dead meat; the partitions also function to shield from view different phases in the production process, particularly between the clean, aseptic space where dead animal bodies are processed into various cuts of meat, and the hot and dirty space where animals are stunned and killed. The presence of the hide becomes a marker of these two different zones of value: 'Sometimes the clean side and the dirty side are also referred to as the hide-off and hide-on areas.'[70] At least in the case of industrialised bovine slaughter, the removal of the skin ('three large hydraulic machines rip the hides from the flesh')[71] is a potentially fraught process, not only (from a food safety perspective) because of the potential for contamination of the meat, but also because this is perhaps the most visceral moment at which a living animal becomes unrecognisable as such for those processing the animal:

> If the presence of an animal's hide is a proxy for clean and dirty from the standpoint of the food-safety planner, it also operates as a proxy for animal and carcass from the standpoint of what the workers see. To watch the movement of a cow from the chute to the down puller is to witness the transformation of a creature from fully animal to carcass. In the chutes, each of the cattle has its own unique characteristics: breed, sex, height, width, hide pattern, level of curiosity, eyes, horns, sound of bellow. From a phenomenological standpoint, after the cattle are stunned, shackled, and suspended upside down in the air, the entire process seems geared to stripping them of these unique identifiers in order to begin the process of turning living animals into homogenous raw material.[72]

The hide thus represents a border between two different worlds that in theory cannot communicate with each other: the 'arbitrary and senseless abstraction' between life and death; the transfer from qualitatively different value to another; the movement from endless differentiation to monotonous homogeneity. The stun gun and the skinning machine stand between these two worlds.

Human workers and animals are both commodified by capitalism; however, the substance of their 'tanning' is different. For the waged human worker under capitalism, the alienation of their labour typically requires a false freedom where the worker submits themselves to a process of effacement – the alienation of one's own labour – a skinning that is largely symbolic, even if 'free' labour is always material in its effects. The specificity of this material alienation, where the worker puts their own self wholeheartedly, 'with skin and hair', into production, is described by Marx, at least in his early work, as essentially animalising: 'what is animal becomes human and what is human becomes animal'. Labour commodification will thus be experienced for the human worker as investing oneself in a process that one is detached from, and where one's own self will become detached for the purpose of commodification, in a way which seems to resemble animals disassembled as part of production into an unrecognisable form: like bringing one's own hide to market. As we shall discuss in Chapter 4, it is of course true that in reality not all waged labour can be said to be 'disembodied' in this way; however, for our purposes here, the 'skinning' Marx refers to is intended as metaphor.

This situation is of course different for animals. The dubious freedoms enjoyed by human workers – the freedom from ownership of the means of production, and the freedom to commodify one's labour – are conspicuously absent from the lives of animals used by humans. This is why Wilderson's perspective on the cows in the slaughterhouse, described in Chapter 2, remains useful for interpreting the different structural position of animals, particularly with respect to their unique demand for liberation, which is not directly reconcilable with that of the human proletariat. Animals are not free of the means of production – the means to realise the value of their labour – since food animals *are* the means of production. Nor is there an in-principle freedom to sell one's own labour, since animals do not own their labour to sell. Compulsion cloaked under the guise of freedom (as implied by the human labour contract under capitalism) is replaced by outright compulsion. There is no constrained freedom here to alienate one's own labour; rather there is a directly forced extraction of the creative 'labour' of animals that produces capital in the body of the dead 'labourer' themselves: 'Capital is dead labour which, vampire-like, lives only by sucking living labour, and lives the more, the more labour it sucks.'[73]

Further, the materiality of the process of commodification differs. Animal hides are literally removed as part of their subsumption to capital; in this sense, while animals circulate as symbolic value, they simultaneously submit to a material excoriation. While it is true that the classically understood proletarian must endure the degradation and deterioration of their own bodies as part of their own labour commodification ('the premature exhaustion and death of this labour-power itself'),[74] the material body of the proletarian, at least as Marx conceived it, is not structurally situated as both a means and object of production.[75] In order to be fabricated into a commodity – a commodity that is both a use value as meat, but also made uniform to be exchanged like money – the skin and hair of animals, the outward features of their appearance, must be removed, and their bodies must be disassembled prior to exchange. One lamb is made to look like another; a pig becomes pork. The end of this process of fabrication is a product whose value rests in a complete extinguishment of previous markers of identity, without trace or ceremony. In this sense, the tanning that beckons for the animal has to be both metaphorical and material: both processes are required here, and each feeds into the other.

Consumption

The animal – sans living soul – leaves production as the product; now dead rather than alive. Thus begins a 'new life' as a consumption commodity. The use value of this commodity has altered. Where the animal in production was seized upon as a raw material towards the creation of value, the dismembered body which departs as the product enters a different world, this time assuming the appearance of a commodity that exists to sustain human life.

In describing this different world where the consumption commodity takes on a new 'life', I am pointing to the existence of at least two economies or zones of circulation occurring at once within capitalism. On one hand, there is an economy of production which aims at producing more capital. In this story, the owners of production processes buy labour power, which in combination with raw materials and machines produces value. In the second zone, consumption commodities proliferate as a means of subsistence which allow humans to reproduce their lives and themselves.

I am here deliberately alluding to the 'two departments' described by Marx in the second volume of *Capital*. Here, Marx attempted to deal with the problem of how money, commodities and labour moved through circuits of production, and the challenges associated with alignments of these flows to allow for the reproduction of these circuits. In order to develop a schema for the 'simple reproduction' of capital, Marx proposed conceptually dividing 'society's total product' into 'two great departments': the first representing the 'means of production', which described commodities with the capacity to, or engaged in, productive consumption (that is, productive of value); the second department engaged with the 'means of consumption', namely 'commodities that possess a form in which they enter the individual consumption of the capitalist and the working classes'.[76] This simple model of reproduction aims to describe a self-reproducing but growthless economy.[77] However, in Marx's analysis this model paved the way for the development of an 'enlarged' model of reproduction, one which could account for an overproduction of commodities as a method of accumulating capital.[78]

For our purposes, we don't need to enter into Marx's theory of accumulation or the difficult problem of how, or whether, these circulations of value translate to 'prices'.[79] More relevant for us here is the separation of the sphere of consumption from production. It is not that the circuit of consumption is disconnected from production in a fundamental way (indeed, the point for Marx is to show the interconnections between these two spheres) – rather that the enlargement of production has a central place in shaping the flows of consumption that follow, even if the circulations of consumption operate within a somewhat discrete world.

For food animals, as we have seen, the connection between these worlds is one of life and death: animals enter production alive; they are transformed systematically by production; and then as part of their metamorphoses into a product, they must be made to die. In the sphere of production, animals are consumers: they consume raw materials (feed, water, pharmaceuticals) which are combined with them through a metabolic process, allowing for their transformation into a consumption product when they leave the sphere of production (we shall discuss the labour of animals in this sphere of production in Chapter 4). For humans, the two spheres are experienced differently: in the first sphere, humans labour for a wage; in the second sphere, humans expend their wages on the means of subsistence which allows them to reproduce their labour. The connection between these worlds for humans is thus mediated by the *monetary wage*: it is through the wage – earned in one sphere or spent in the other – that those human workers continually participate in two different zones of circulation.

Here we should note that the wage is a particular *technology* of capitalism which is available to some humans. The wage is paid in monetary form to humans in exchange for labour power expended over a given period of time. The wage under capitalism is by definition exploitative: the wage represents only a portion of the value the worker produces through the labour process. But also, the wage is the goal of labour effort for the worker, since it allows the worker to survive. In Marx's analysis, the function of the wage is to allow the worker to purchase their subsistence and reproduce their own labour power: that is, buy food, clothing and other 'essentials' in order to continue to live and go back to work. The wage also serves the function of supporting those humans who do not receive wages. It thus contributes to the costs of the social reproduction of capitalism, through this contribution; for example, in meeting the costs of unpaid labour in the home (they are a 'disguised form').[80] That the wage paid to the human worker is in the same form (that is, money) as the profit gained by the capitalist does not mean that the two circulations I have outlined above are the same: 'the fact that the same money serves one purpose in the hands of the seller and another in the hands of the buyer is simply a phenomenon inherent in all purchases and sales of commodities'.[81] Here, a 'class relation' segments worker from capitalist:

> The class relation between capitalist and wage-labourer is thus already present, already presupposed, the moment the two confront each other in the act M-L (L-M from the side of the worker). This is sale and purchase, a money relation, but a sale and purchase in which it is presupposed that the buyer is a capitalist and the seller a wage-labourer; and this relation does in fact exist, because the conditions for the realization of labour-power, i.e. means of subsistence and means of production, are separated, as the property of another, from the possessor of labour-power.[82]

At least in Marx's view, the whole point of the wage was that the money paid for labour time was not paid at a level to actually allow workers to purchase the means of production, only their own subsistence; as Ernest Mandel summarises, 'under capitalism workers are not supposed to spend their money on any commodities other than consumer goods'.[83] The two economies (the circulation of production, and the circulation of wages and consumption) are ruthlessly kept apart. For Marx at least, this is why most people in the world are wage-earners and not capital-owners, a situation that cannot be altered without major structural change.[84]

But despite these structural limitations, the technology of the wage represents a kind of 'freedom' for humans, and it is this freedom that is potentially troubling for the appearance of animals as consumption commodities. As indicated above, the wage relies on the workers owning themselves as persons: the worker is free to enter the labour relation, and accepts the wage in exchange for their labour time. However, the nature of this relationship is that the worker has no other way to survive except by selling their labour for whatever wage is on offer.[85] The wage thus has a specific role in mediating human freedom under capitalism. Firstly, it is a material symbol of the relative freedom of the worker; the fact that the worker is paid a wage operates as a marker of their free consent to being exploited. Secondly, it allows the person who has earned the wage to purchase their own means of subsistence, a freedom that is not available, for example, to animals within production. With the technology of the wage the worker has the autonomy to expend their wage on the things they need to survive, and, where available, exercise choice in relation to consumer goods. This 'autonomy' is constrained by the structural limits described above: namely, that the worker is only meant to purchase the means of subsistence and not capital. It is also constrained in the sense that any choice is limited by the quantum of money, and more particularly, the buying power of that money is determined by the present availability of consumer commodities for purchase. Prevailing standards of living would dictate what consumer choices look like: for example, in rural India or other low-income regions, a larger proportion of money might be spent on food[86] in comparison to areas with relatively high living standards and expanded worker capacity to expend wages on property, mobile phones, televisions and holidays as a means of living. But whether culture and tradition determine that workers spend their wages on what in other contexts might be deemed 'luxuries'[87] is separate from the function of the wage and its relationship to consumption: the structural role of the wage is as a medium by which to 'produce' the worker, that is, to enable the reproduction of labour power and social reproduction generally.

My aim in positioning the wage as *a technology for the reproduction of human labour power* is to avoid fetishising the monetary payment which *some* human workers – and certainly not *all* or even *most* – receive in exchange for labour time. Certainly, the monetary wage takes centre stage for Marx in the calculation of surplus value. For Marx, the difference between the exchange value of labour (that is, the monetary wage) and the actual value produced by this labour is of central importance for the calculation of surplus. However, from the perspective of value, we need not assume that the monetary payment marks out the proletarian as the priority site for capitalist exploitation.[88] While Marx places the monetary wage at the centre of his analysis of capitalism, we can certainly find somewhat heretical examples relevant to this book where Marx deviates from this obsessive focus. For example, consider the following sentences from *Capital*, volume 1:

> The fact that the worker performs acts of individual consumption in his own interest, and not to please the capitalist, is something entirely irrelevant to the

matter. The consumption of food by a beast of burden does not become any less a necessary aspect of the production process because the beast enjoys what it eats.[89]

These two sentences allow us to critically reappraise the monetary wage and its function. And we can perform this critical appraisal without any nostalgia for the humans who are the target of these wages. This is because Marx points directly to the value role of the means of subsistence within the capitalist production process, seemingly unconcerned about whether this means of subsistence arrives in the form of a pay cheque or a feedbag. Here Marx compels us to avoid being distracted by the form of the means of subsistence, or the pleasure it generates for the worker who consumes it, or indeed whether the worker is a human or an animal; instead, in all cases, the value of the means of subsistence remains the same for the capitalist. In Chapter 1, I pointed to the opportunities to read Marx in a way that highlights an 'anti-humanist' perspective; one that allows for us to understand capitalism as relatively agnostic in relation to which species is privileged as a site for the absorption of labour power. Here we have an opportunity to deploy Marx's anti-humanist method. It is true that species difference produces variations in capital's relations: as we have seen, humans in theory have the capacity to exchange their labour for a wage, animals do not.[90] But this is merely a difference in the character of exploitation and not object. The point is that capitalism has a variety of strategies for the extraction of value; but in all cases, the extraction of value remains the goal. The above fragment from Marx is revealing in multiple ways, as it shows that from the perspective of capital, *only the reproduction costs of labour matter* (since this is essential for the extraction of surplus): other considerations, such as whether or not a wage is paid, how this wage is spent, and whether this expenditure is a source of enjoyment, are not necessarily of direct interest to capitalism. Note that these observations are not merely relevant to the unwaged labour of animals, but all unwaged labour performed under capitalism. The latter does not need to be paid for by monetary wages in order for it to be considered exploitative; instead, as long as there is a positive difference between the value produced by labour versus the reproductive costs of this labour, then we can understand this work, in a broad sense at least, as performed under conditions of exploitation. As we shall see in Chapter 4, this anti-humanist understanding of the 'wage' will be important for making sense of the value produced by animal labour in capitalist animal agriculture.

We should also note, as I have discussed in Chapter 1, the 'biopolitics' of human reproduction which accompany the above circulations. The economy that accounts for the movement of wages in relation to consumption commodities is an exchange devoted to enabling the reproduction of humans: humans in a general sense; but also more specifically, the reproduction of human labour power and the reproduction of human social reproduction. 'Biopolitics' refers here to Foucault's identification of a shift in the organisation of modern power away from episodic, spectacular violence as a mechanism of control towards a focus on biological life and population.[91] Foucault argues for a shift in logic, where power today is less associated with the older logic of 'the ancient right to take life or let live' but is instead identified with a 'power to foster life or disallow it to the point of death'.[92] Modern power is instead seen through instruments that seek to continuously regulate the biological life of populations, in some cases securitising one 'flock' in the name of the other.[93] One aspect of the development of 'biopower' was the coincidence between the emergence of this rationality and the emergence of capitalism. As Foucault makes clear, a rationality of power focused on population was essential for the distinct productivity of capitalism:

> This bio-power was without question an indispensable element in the development of capitalism; the latter would not have been possible without the controlled insertion of bodies into the machinery of production and the adjustment of the phenomena of population to economic processes. . . . The adjustment of the accumulation of men to that of capital, the joining of the growth of human groups to the expansion of productive forces and the differential allocation of profit, were made possible in part by the exercise of bio-power in its many forms and modes of application. The investment of the body, its valorization, and the distributive management of its forces were at the time indispensable.[94]

Here Foucault is explicit about the meaning of biopower for the alignment of 'human groups' with capitalism: at least one implication is that human biological reproduction, and the governance of those with a reproductive capacity, became a target for power.[95] But Foucault was largely uninterested in what this view of the modern rationality of power meant for animals.[96] This is an unfortunate omission, as animals belong firmly to the story of modern biopolitics. In part this is because industrial agriculture relies upon a ruthless application of the biopolitical management of population: every aspect of the life of animals will need to be controlled, including when the animal is born and when the animal dies.[97] In addition, and as I have discussed in the Introduction, the reproductive processes of animals must also be ruthlessly controlled in order to allow for the accumulation of animals as raw materials and as consumption commodities. Again, nothing about the commodity reveals the violence of its production: in the case of animals who are raw materials, or animals who become dead meat, one of the forms of violence that prefigures the appearance of these commodities is forced reproduction which allows for new life to be born (I shall explore this further in the context of animal labour in Chapter 4). Finally, the production of animals as a means of subsistence draws these beings into the reproductive cycle of humanity: animals exist as the raw material that allows humans to reproduce themselves. Under capitalism, animal-sourced foods have taken a priority place as the meat and milk of human sustenance: they are positioned to allow the worker to reproduce their labour in the scene of production; and simultaneously, they allow all humans, including those who provide 'non-productive' labour, to reproduce themselves. In other words, animal products *are positioned to allow for the reproduction of reproduction.*

It is for this reason that we can extend Patel and Moore's suggestion that the 'cheapening' of food, including animal-based products, is aimed at driving down the cost of human labour under capitalism.[98] 'Cheap food' is certainly one dimension of capitalist animal agriculture. But there is more to say: the proliferation of animal-sourced food as commodities under capitalism also served a manifold biopolitical function. Intensive biopolitical processes were utilised to allow for the production of animals *en masse*, which in turn allowed the securitisation of human populations in their ability to reproduce productive and unproductive labour, and reproduce themselves.[99] Thus, capitalist animal agriculture brought together, and intertwined, human and animal populations in an unprecedented metabolic relation: human populations, more than ever before, have become reliant upon the multiplication of animals within animal agriculture as a means of survival. Rising global per capita consumption of animal-sourced foods highlights that this process has not as yet been exhausted: the biopolitical 'entanglement' of human and animal populations continues apace.

What does all this mean for how we think about animals and their relationship to the circulations of production and consumption? Firstly, as I have noted above, the two spheres of circulation – production and consumption – give animals complex and sometimes contradictory roles. This is because animals appear on the side of production as a use value for capitalism, *and* on the side of consumption as a use value for consumers. One implication of this, and one that has been tracked by numerous animal studies scholars, is that animals as commodities have a number of different lives within capitalism, leading to almost absurd paradoxes or perhaps, as I shall discuss below, 'contradictions'. For example, as many scholars have already asked, why is it that dogs might appear as experimental animals or as working dogs or as racing greyhounds or as food or as companions, and be offered vastly different treatment, welfare and protection in these different zones of life?[100] The view I have provided here gives us one perspective; namely that the different and contradictory ways dogs are treated reflect their roles in different circulatory processes under capitalism. For example, the experimental animal is an animal whose sole function is as a reactive test model for pharmaceuticals and chemicals, many of which are tested for commercial purposes. This animal is both a raw material and a productive labourer within economic processes. The companion animal, on the other hand, exists within the wages/consumption cycle of capitalism: companion animals are positioned as consumption products for humans to expend their wages on, with the aim of pleasure and companionship, and this fundamentally shapes the value placed on these animals in a way that is completely incomparable to the treatment of animals in sites of production, which have a very different function within this site of circulation. Research animals (and 'livestock') are mere material assets to production, they allow for the absorption of value through production; companion animals, on the other hand, are the site of human freedom in so far as they are the objects of wages.

Secondly, and related to the above, we can get a sense of the unique problem faced by animal advocacy in attempting to make change, particularly in relation to animals used as food, since advocates must respond to these two realities.[101] On the production side, animals appear as useful for the creation of value: that is, for the expansion of capital. On the consumption side, animals appear as sustenance that is purchased as a product using wages, which allows for the biopolitics of human reproduction (the reproduction of reproduction). The former sphere is interconnected with the survival of human economies; the latter with the survival of humans themselves. For animal advocates, this means fighting a battle on two fronts, and dealing with competing and contradictory value systems depending on whether advocates are focused on the horrors of the circulations of production, or alternatively, on an apparent failure of interpersonal ethics from those who make purchasing decisions within the circulations of consumption.

But it is the 'affective' dimension of this struggle that is most perplexing. As discussed above, expenditure on consumption items is positioned as a site of freedom for those humans who receive wages; that is, the sphere where the worker exercises choice and liberates pleasures:

> The worker, then, finds himself only in the relation of simple circulation, of simple exchange, and obtains only *coin* for his use value; subsistence; but mediated. This form of mediation is, as we saw, essential to and characteristic

of the relation. That it can proceed to the transformation of the coin into money – savings – proves precisely only that his relation is that of simple circulation; he can save more or less; but beyond that he cannot get; he can realize what he has saved only by momentarily expanding the sphere of his pleasures. It is of importance – and penetrates into the character of the relation itself – that, because money is the product of his exchange, general wealth drives him forward as an illusion; makes him industrious.[102]

Given this context, it perhaps is no surprise that animal advocates face some of the most fierce resistance to change over consumption decisions, since meat, milk and leather are not a mere arbitrary choice of subsistence material, but rather are saturated by the promise of freedom and its necessity, so that it would seem that giving up animal-sourced products becomes akin to a loss of world or death itself.[103] We only need to look at the spectacles that circulate debates about food to see the intensity by which the apparent 'freedom' to eat meat becomes configured as the same as 'political freedom', 'rights' and the possibility of living itself. Perhaps, in a historical sense, this makes sense. For most of human history, for most humans, food choices were dictated by available resources, climate and social organisation.[104] Today, particularly for consumers in the Global North, capitalism has provided a world where at least some individuals can source seemingly any food from anywhere in the world, in any location, at any time. This means that food – as a core component of recognised living standards – becomes a site intensely associated with the everyday experience of freedom and choice. Higher living standards come hand in hand with an expanded consumption of food, so that the increasing political freedom to spend wages becomes also the freedom to purchase more and more food, of which animal products comprise an increasing proportion. As mentioned above, this perspective on the political economy of food aligns with the argument made by Patel and Moore on the expansion of 'cheap food' as a strategy of capitalism;[105] but also with a tangential observation made by Elspeth Probyn, reflecting on Foucault's *History of Sexuality*, that suggests food, alongside sexuality, might be another site for the investment of pleasure and ethics.[106] Thus, there is not only a drive for cheap food, but also a market for 'ethical' food. Like Foucault's analysis of the ethics of Greek male citizens, deliberation over the ethics of our pleasures and consumptions only becomes possible where freedom allows for such deliberation: the wage and the living standard it buys – whether through the magnitude of money at the disposal of the consumer or the availability of goods and services – mediates the possibility of freedom and ethics in relation to the means of subsistence.

There is in all of this a curious question about the politics of veganism. Contemporary consumer veganism has grown on this terrain, where vegans have similarly treated waged consumer consumption decisions as a site of intensified ethics and freedom and campaigned for others to change their consumption decisions in the hope that this will impact the horrors of production. But in doing so, these campaigners for ethical veganism have similarly been caught in the same conceptual frame, where the expenditure of wages on consumption items is imagined as an important – if not primary – site for political agency, political identity, and freedom. This form of politics has not necessarily challenged the accelerating expansion of food as a consumption item; as discussed in the Introduction to this book, global per capita consumption of animal-based food products continues to expand; indeed, all per capita food consumption continues to climb.[107] In line with the view that the drive of capitalism is precisely to proliferate commodities as a mechanism for the production of value, food is one more site for overproduction (albeit not accompanied by fair distribution), whether this involves the overproduction of animal-based foods or the overproduction of foods derived from plants.[108] This has meant some vegans have simply made use of (and perhaps helped exacerbate) the proliferation of food choices offered, as an outcome of campaigns for people to spend their wages in alternative ways. In what sense is this politics simply a pitched battle between vegans and non-vegans on how wages should be spent, or what options should become available for those with wages to spend? What are the limits of this politics which aims at stimulating the expansion of consumption choices? In what ways are the politics of veganism a symptom of a reality that under capitalism, this is the only site where many humans can exercise freedom in their day-to-day lives? In other words, how has the failure of the collective political project to intervene meaningfully in the cycle of capitalist production (that is, how have the dismantling of trade unions, the decimation of public institutions by neoliberal restructuring, and the end of organised movements against capitalism) intensified the emphasis on consumption as our only site of freedom – a freedom that, we should note, is proportionately most available to those who have access to higher wages (that is, those who enjoy the highest living standards)?[109]

Asking these critical questions of veganism as a strategy, something I will return to at the close of the book, is not at all intended to sideline or minimise the paradoxes that relate to the mass emergence of animals as consumption commodities under capitalism, or to belittle the symptomatic response of veganism to this reality. Indeed it is the space of contradiction that we find ourselves within: the contradiction of sentient beings rendered as mere commodities; the contradiction of animals living two lives, two use values within two spheres of production; and the problem that even if we agree that animals should not be mere commodities for human use, we are confronted by the reality that animal products exist as a means for the reproduction of human reproduction, and that simultaneously animal-based foods have been positioned today as a site of freedom and ethics. Growing per capita global meat consumption, and the rapid development of an industrialised globalised production and trade system to facilitate this growth, seems only to attest to the fact that any ethical contradiction here does not in itself have the necessary force to counter the trend towards continuing utilisation.

Of course, contradiction plays an important conceptual role in Marxist-oriented analysis of capitalism.[110] Marx infamously predicted a tendency of the profit rate to fall, describing the crises that capitalism would generate through overproduction.[111] Rosa Luxemburg acknowledged this contradiction, but resolved it by showing that imperialism was the outcome for capitalism as it approached the limits of its own internal markets.[112] James O'Connor proposed a second contradiction[113] where overproduction created an internal contradiction within capitalism; the environment was established as one site of an external contradiction with capitalism, the latter of which potentially participates in creating 'its own barriers or limits by destroying its own production conditions'.[114] Moore builds on O'Connor and bends Marx's law of profit to declare instead a 'tendency of the ecological surplus to fall'.[115] In many of these accounts of inherent contradiction within capitalism there is a 'teleological' prediction of limit, crisis and change, where according to the dialectical resonances in Marx, the crisis contains the potential for resolution within itself.[116] As such, at least for many Marxists, contradiction is a process that is both violent and productive. It is violent because of the material damage it imposes on those who bear the force of the contradiction: in the case of workers under capitalism, for example, this means poverty and deprivation, meaningless drudgery and alienation. The flipside of this process, though, is that the contradiction provides the basis for resistance against power, and the generation of previously unimagined modes of organisation and collectivity.

I am not about to announce here a new 'law' of capitalist development that relates to animals. However, I do want to flag the political potential of a 'positive teleology' relating to the contradictions that circulate animal-sourced foods as consumption commodities. In particular, I point here to the contradiction, or at least paradox, that while, on the one hand, capitalism has exposed animals to exploitation, suffering and death that cannot really be compared to any previous time in human history, it has, on the other hand, simultaneously provided the mechanisms by which we might imagine ending or at least minimising this mass-scale industrialised violence towards animals. Capitalism is thus both the problem and, potentially, the cure.

Let us consider this 'positive teleology'. It begins with the question of the 'intrinsic' use value of animals for human food supplies today. The question of whether we 'need' animals for food is of course a contentious one. And in some ways, at least for animal advocates, this question is infuriating. Those who dare suggest that there is no 'intrinsic' need to eat animals are barraged with a variety of perspectives, ranging from the view that humans are evolutionarily or biologically predisposed to eat meat;[117] to the view that meat-eating is a fundamental aspect of cultural and linguistic heritage (and therefore represents a cultural right);[118] to the view that humans do a favour to domesticated animals by using them for food, since this is a better life than the animals would face in the wild (in terms of exposure to starvation, disease and predation);[119] to the view that a world shift towards plant-based diets is not as environmentally beneficial as imagined;[120] and, perhaps most recently, the view that eating a plant-based diet contributes to more animal deaths (for example, in the extermination of rodents) than a meat-based diet.[121] But these diverse, and sometimes frankly strange, viewpoints fail to notice the extraordinary scale of plant-based food availability today. The very same processes of industrialisation and intensification that have increased the use of animals have also increased the production of vegetables and grains worldwide: per capita consumption of vegetable-based proteins has continued to climb.[122] Despite much press which would appear to indicate otherwise, animal-based proteins do not make up the majority of the world's food intake. Certainly, we know that the per capita intake of animal proteins in the Global North is relatively high. However, plant-based foods make up the majority of the protein intake for Global South countries:

> Consumers in low-income countries will continue to obtain roughly 70% of total calories and protein from staple foods, while only 20% of protein will come from animal sources. People in higher income countries will still consume around 40% of calories as staple foods and obtain over half of their protein from animal sources.[123]

We see these different consumption patterns very clearly reflected when we examine the astonishing variance between countries in relation to per capita (land animal) meat consumption. Typically, the highest (land animal) meat per capita consuming nations are the United States and Australia, consuming well over 100kg per person per year; meanwhile, India typically has the lowest per capita meat consumption, at around 4kg per person per year.[124] In other words, most of the world relies on plant-based proteins for survival. Despite stark divisions between different countries and their consumption patterns, and despite a growing per capita consumption of meat, vegetable proteins remain the main way almost all of the world, particularly the Global South, gets its protein.

Just because the world produces a lot of plant-based food does not, of course, mean that this food can be made available to all. There are vast inequalities which relate to food, its distribution and availability. We know that people don't starve because there is a lack of food in the world.[125] There are acknowledged problems in how to distribute available food efficiently: capitalism proves inefficient in responding to hunger and poverty through fair distribution, and as the wastage statistics demonstrate, similarly inefficient in using food resources effectively.[126] Paradoxically, globalisation and developments in transportation and refrigeration systems have enabled vast international distribution networks that might effectively respond if there were market incentives: today there is a global export market for fruits such as strawberries from California, or bananas from Central America; frozen vegetables on the shelves of supermarkets might come from China, Chile or Belgium. This globalised system of food transport is far from sustainable,[127] though it illustrates that the technical capacity is there to distribute food despite regional and local differences in availability.

The point of the above is not to argue for the continuing industrialisation and globalisation of food supplies, nor the overproduction of plant-based food. Rather, it is to illustrate the way in which the evolution of capitalist agricultural processes have undermined the 'intrinsic' necessity of animal-sourced foods through the simultaneous expansion of plant-based food production and distribution. Here the paradox, or perhaps contradiction, we face in relation to animals as food is that at the same time as animals have been made to proliferate as consumption commodities, and have been sewn into a new and seemingly intractable metabolic relation with human populations, these same forces have created the productive and distributive possibility of imagining living without animals as food. The developments I have described that are part and parcel of capitalism, industrialisation and globalisation have reduced the 'intrinsic' necessity of animals as a means of subsistence to most humans (at least for food) to an absolute low point. Human economies have developed the capacity to grow plant protein on a massive scale and distribute it to respond to human needs; indeed, and despite the acceleration in the use of animals for food globally, plant-based materials remain the main way most of the world's human population is fed.[128] Certainly, as indicated by the Intergovernmental Panel on Climate Change, arresting the expansion of animal agriculture through a shift towards 'diets that feature plant-based foods' would be an important mitigation strategy in relation to anthropogenic climate warming.[129]

And thus the paradox confronts us. We will continue to see exponential growth in the use of animals for food despite this food not being strictly 'necessary' for human survival, and despite this exponential growth in animal agriculture taking a wrecking ball to planetary systems. Yet, at the same time, the technical means have been developed for the large-scale replacement of animal-based food as consumption commodities, though their promise has not been realised. This paradox in some ways highlights the contradictions which circulate around all use values and their limited connection to 'intrinsic' concepts of need, since what humans, and the planet, actually need is not an outcome or aspiration of our global economy. Here lies precisely the tactical problem facing animal advocates today. Certainly, there is the challenge of overcoming the fetishism associated with animal-sourced foods.[130] Campaigns to 'go vegan' or technical developments to produce meat substitutes may conceivably mitigate the acceleration of animal agriculture. But there is also the deeper problem of understanding fully why animals are useful to capitalism, not merely as a means of subsistence, but also as agents of production. And this is why we cannot place too much faith in the alteration of the consumption sphere of capitalism alone. This misses the driving force for the overproduction in the first place, which is derived from the value that can be attained from the 'controlled insertion of bodies into the machinery of production'. Why did capitalism leap upon animals, overproduce them, fabricate them as commodities, and then place them in a seemingly indispensable relation to human population survival? As I shall discuss in the next chapter, the driving force of production – in this context, the enduring attachment of capitalist production to animal agriculture – gains new meaning once we understand the labour value of animals themselves.

4 Labour

When Marx writes that it is a sad fate to be a productive worker, he is not issuing a moral protest but recognising this fact. To be productive means to produce capital, thus also to continually produce the dominion of capital over the worker.

Mario Tronti, *Workers and Capital*[1]

No equal capital puts into motion a greater quantity of productive labour than that of the farmer. Not only his labouring servants, but his labouring cattle, are productive labourers. In agriculture too nature labours along with man; and though her labour costs no expense, its produce has its value, as well as that of the most expensive workmen. . . . The labourers and labouring cattle, therefore, employed in agriculture, not only occasion, like the workmen in manufactures, the reproduction of a value, equal to their own consumption, or to the capital which employs them, together with its owner's profits; but of a much greater value. Over and above the capital of the farmer and all its profits, they regularly occasion the reproduction of the rent of the landlord. This rent may be considered as the produce of those powers of nature, the use of which the landlord lends to the farmer. It is greater or smaller according to the supposed extent of those powers, or in other words, according to the supposed natural or improved fertility of the land. It is the work of nature which remains after deducting or compensating everything which can be regarded as the work of man.

Adam Smith, *The Wealth of Nations*[2]

In Chapter 3 I described the fabrication of food animals as objects of value: their arrival at the scene of production as a raw material, their transformation into a commodity with a use value for food, and their double existence, at least symbolically, as a currency to reflect human value. I have so far treated these animals as 'passive objects': that is, as a circulating material that is worked upon in order to congeal value within the production process. But animals are not merely 'passive' material that is worked on by humans. Indeed, at least one contradiction we face today is that almost everyone, including the most shrewd managers of industrial animal agriculture, would agree that animals are not *mere objects*; however, the reality is that they are treated as such on the balance sheets of global economies. While we might be able to understand the value of animals as a raw material or a consumption item, we are less clear on the value of animals as useful for generating capital within a production process. It is the later value role for animals that a focus on labour can help unveil.

In this chapter I seek to provide a description of animals as labouring subjects under capitalism. While, as I shall discuss, there are numerous examples provided by a range of scholars of how we might conceptualise this labour, I am centrally interested in establishing an understanding of the use value of the labour of food animals to capitalism within the production process: in other words, in the context of industrial food production. How is animal labour power useful for producing surplus value? As we shall discover, this focus not only helps us to re-describe and understand intensification within animal agriculture, but also, simultaneously, to define the characteristics of human and animal labour within production, and the role of mechanisation within these processes.

Animals as labourers?

As I have discussed in the Introduction, Marx appears antagonistic towards the idea of animal labour. The early Marx differentiates the labour of animals from that of humans, arguing that while animals cannot distinguish themselves from their life activity, humans on the other hand labour consciously and can produce regardless of necessity.[3] This is, as I have discussed, the philosophical worldview the early Marx puts forward which generates a schism between humans and animals at the level of ontology, which does 'work' in establishing the essentially alienated character of human labour under capitalism (that is, capitalism is seen as alienating humans by transforming their labour into something animalistic). Whether this antagonism extends beyond the early writing of Marx is perhaps contentious. For example, John Bellamy Foster has rejected a view that Marx attributed value solely to human labour, arguing that for Marx, 'nature, which contributed to the production of use values, was just as much a source of wealth as labor'.[4] Further, against critics who have raised concerns about the 'speciesism' of Marx, Foster and Brett Clark have argued that 'it is important to recognize that Marx's discussions of animals were primarily historical, materialist, and natural-scientific in orientation. Marx and Engels's examinations of the position of animals in society were therefore not directed at issues of moral philosophy, as is the case for most of their critics.'[5]

Certainly, and in favour of the perspective put forward by Foster and Clark, Marx says many things about animals. This can make it difficult to determine Marx's own perspective. Importantly, as Foster and Clark emphasise, Marx's project was not aimed at offering a humanistic moral philosophy but instead at understanding, in the terms of political economy, the elements and dynamics of capitalist production, and the structural positions of various actors within this story. Indeed, as we shall discover, Marx was certainly aware of the tendencies within capitalist production towards the intensification of animal agriculture, and perhaps with this, the dramatic pressure this would place on social traditions on how animals should be treated.[6]

However, even if we accept that Marx was contradictory and may indeed have expressed concern for animals, there remain many instances, including in late Marx, where he makes his commitment to a hierarchical anthropocentrism clear. At least one example of this is the responses that Marx poses to Adam Smith in the second volume of *Capital*. In a remarkable section of Smith's *The Wealth of Nations*, the economist puts forward the view that both animals and nature as a whole work in the production of value:

> But it must be considered that the price of any instrument of husbandry, such as a labouring horse, is itself made up of the same three parts; the rent of the land upon which he is reared, the labour of tending and rearing him, and the profits of the farmer who advances both the rent of this land, and the wages of this labour. Though the price of the corn, therefore, may pay the price as well as the maintenance of the horse, the whole price still resolves itself either immediately or ultimately into the same three parts of rent, labour, and profit.[7]

Marx's response in *Capital*, volume 2, is characteristically scathing:

> We leave completely aside here the fact that our Adam was particularly unfortunate in his choice of example. The value of corn can be resolved into wages, profit and rent only by depicting the feed consumed by the draught cattle as their wages, and the draught cattle as wage labourers – hence depicting the wage labourer in his turn as a draught animal.[8]

For Marx's schema, the draught animal has to appear as an instrument of production, as fixed capital, rather than as labour. This is because value appears for Marx through the application of human hands to production.[9] The draught animal sets production in motion, but only has this capacity because this animal has been crafted by human hands and embodies human labour. As such, in Marx's story, only human labour has the capacity to create value.

My point in raising this commentary by Marx on Smith is not to put forward the perspective that Smith was correct in his analysis. Rather, the example highlights the way in which Marx was intent on centring value creation solely upon labour by humans within production.[10] As I have pointed out in the Introduction, Althusser reminds us that Marx invents a powerful 'anti-humanist' mode of analysis in *Capital*. The above commentary by Marx on Smith is one example where Marx's unflinching anti-humanism slips, and we are instead offered an analysis where there is avid attachment to humanistic categories; indeed, Marx seems almost offended that a draught animal should be compared to a human worker. As I shall discuss below, 'depicting the feed consumed by the draught cattle as their wages' is actually an important innovation, as it allows us to remove the dazzling glitter applied to the wage, and recognise it for what it is: namely, as described in Chapter 3, a technology that allows for the cost of the reproduction of labour to shape the value which can be extracted from that labour. From this perspective, whether the wage is paid in feed or in money is immaterial from the standpoint of capital; the main importance is that there is a difference between the reproduction costs of labour power, and the value produced by that same labour power.

In other words, we need to approach the labour of animals in value terms. Here I note that there have been a number of scholars who have gone some way towards addressing Marx's anthropocentric response to animal labour: for example, putting forward views that animals labour in ways that resemble the creative labour of humans;[11] or that animals are 'alienated' in specific ways when they labour under capitalism;[12] or that animals might be said to be 'part of the working class';[13] or that animals are owed rights as labourers.[14] While all this scholarship has laid useful foundations for thinking about the place of animals under capitalism, it does not approach the problem of animal labour power from the perspective of value. Many of these approaches share a tendency to associate by comparison, or analogy, the structural condition of animals in production processes with those of humans, rather than seek to understand what is distinctive about animal labour power. This inevitably leads to difficulties in analysis, particularly when we move the analytic frame to animals used for food, since the labour of food animals looks very different from the labour of a draft animal who is forced to work a mine or the labour of a police dog. The challenge with this view, which treats labour as visibly working on an external world using tools of production, is that it cannot account for the kind of labour performed by a food animal, where the body of the animal is itself the object of production. Thus, Kendra Coulter observes:

> When an animal's sole 'task' is to eat and fatten in order to physically become meat or fur, I am uncertain about whether to argue that they do work, other than perhaps some very constrained and limited subsistence labor to sustain themselves and their offspring.[15]

Coulter goes on to explore 'body work',[16] which resonates with what I shall describe, drawing from other scholars, as 'metabolic labour'; a term that perhaps provides a route to explain work that has the *character* of an activity tied closely to the individual metabolism of the body. Yet, to an extent, the character of the labour animals – whether it is physical, metabolic, affective – is distinct from its value form; focusing on the latter, as I shall discuss below, relieves us of the necessity of only recognising as labour an activity that appears to us to look like 'work'. The process of animals consuming feed, growing and transforming into a new product, counts as productive labour because it is positioned within production to be productive of value.

Before we move to thinking of an approach to labour that centres on the problem of value, I want to address here a different issue that relates to the characteristics of animal labour: namely its possible relationship to (human) forms of forced or coerced work.[17] We might be tempted to suggest that what differentiates wage labour and the contemporary labour of animals is the 'forced' nature of the latter: in this sense, the labour of animals represents a form of slavery, perhaps comparable to other examples of forced labour as it applies to humans. In a direct sense this is true: animals are not paid a wage, and overt force is utilised to ensure compliance with production. Thus, it seems to make sense *prima facie* to compare forced animal labour to forced human labour.

However, there also intricate histories to disentangle in relation to how we draw these analogies or assumed similarities between the labour of animals that are owned as property and forms of forced human labour, including chattel slavery. For example, the comparison of the conditions of animal labour to racial slavery, made within some pro-animal scholarship,[18] fails to disentangle abstract concepts of coerced labour from the specific dynamics of racial slavery. At least one difference is that the latter aimed at production of a racialised subject, or as I have discussed in Wilderson's rendering, generated an 'ontological' political status which continues to inform present-day anti-Black violence and racism.[19] Indeed, the tendency to imagine animal labour as equivalent to human slavery produces an analysis that potentially obscures crucial characteristics and histories of violence experienced by human subjects; as Zakiyyah Iman Jackson has urged, we must consider 'New World slavery as an ever-present mode of violent ontologizing that includes but exceeds the animalization of the slave, as blackness was always subject to something more.'[20]

Once again, the point here is to recognise the distinct structural position of animals, or at least animals used for food; a structural position that should not be confused, or too hastily adjoined with, other political subjectivities, even if the dynamics of violence and domination appear similar, or even share entwined histories. Here value relations assist us to elucidate this distinct structural position, since the existence of animals as a raw material, as a consumption commodity and as labour shapes the unique position of these subjects. Perhaps one way to make sense of this is to look at one specific example – meat grading and 'quality' – which shapes the value relations surrounding animals, but simultaneously marks out the distance between the modality of domination experienced by animals and that of the human slave. Here we need to pay attention to the fact that animals leave production as a consumption product. Because food animals will become *the* product – that is, their bodies will assume a new use value as a consumption commodity – the qualities of the final product play a determining function for the conditions that animals in production face. For example, producers will seek to ensure that meat is of a quality that is 'desirable' (has use value) for consumers as a subsistence item, avoiding meat that is 'pale, soft exudative' or 'dry firm dark'.[21] As I shall discuss in Chapter 5, avoidance of stress, particularly prior to slaughter, is essential for avoiding these 'undesirable' outcomes in the final product, and thus a degree of attention to the 'welfare' of these animals becomes an aspect of the production process. This may extend, for example, to avoidance of particular forms of injury – such as skin lesions[22] – where these can be demonstrated to impact the final product and therefore the possibilities for value extraction. Violence is still present here, but managed so as to protect value. The imperative will be to treat the body of the animal with particular forms of care in order to safeguard the integrity and saleability of the final product; that is, the consumption commodity.

Such consideration was clearly not extended to those who were dominated under racial slavery in the antebellum era. As Orlando Patterson outlined, the distinct character of racial slavery was defined by natal alienation ('the loss of ties at birth in both ascending and descending generations'),[23] generalised dishonour and excessive, unlimited violence.[24] Fundamental natal alienation is a resonant modality of violence directed against animals, since domestication implies a ruthless control over biological reproduction. However, the economies of dishonour and ultra-violence operate differently. The social death of slavery has the psychological aim to mark out its target and instil inferior status as an indelible mark: 'the slave could have no honor because of the origin of his status, the indignity and all-pervasiveness of his indebtedness, his absence of any independent social existence, but most of all because he was without power except through another'.[25] There is no question that animals are almost universally dishonoured by prevailing hierarchical anthropocentrism.[26] But the dishonour that permeated racial slavery and its aftermath had, and has, a distinct function within the racial politics of intra-human relations, and produces distinct 'sociopsychologies' and worldviews that operate in material relations between humans.[27] Since animals do not participate in the same way in human cultural and linguistic communities, racialised logics cannot be said to shape power relations between humans and animals *in the same way* as inter-human relations, even if there are strong interconnections between racial logics and contemporary hierarchical modalities of anthropocentrism.[28] But it is the differential character of *violence* that most sharply distinguishes between the operation of human slavery and animal agriculture, and highlights the unique structural position of the human slave *vis-à-vis* the food animal. The brutal, excessive use of violence within the context of racial slavery had no particular limits beyond those prescribed by the economics of labour production and the racial economics of the reproduction of Blackness. Prevention of skin lesions was certainly not a goal of racial slavery; quite the reverse. The theatre of violence that was characteristic of racial slavery – the routine use of whipping;[29] the use of tortures such as cutting ears, branding and castration which truncated and marked the body; the frequent examples of violent deaths where the body of the slave was quite literally torn apart[30] – all highlight that 'welfare' was not part of the economy of racial slavery, since protection of the body was not an object. Importantly, as Saidiya V. Hartman carefully demonstrates, white pleasure is gained at the spectacle of violence visited upon the Black body, and this carefully choreographed violence 'confirmed the slaveholder's dominion and made the captive body the vehicle of the master's power and truth'.[31]

This is not to imply that routine violence is not part of animal agriculture; on the contrary, the factory farm is a concentrated site of hostility. However, we are dealing with a different economy, and structure of value. The conditions of production, dictated by its unique value structure, mean that the body of the animal is safeguarded in such a way as to protect its transformation into a consumption commodity. Daily torments exist – branding, tail docking, mulesing, pain and injury from long periods of standing in confined cages, injury from other animals, even the use of shared technologies, such as the bull whip – and these tortures produce intensities of pain that animals must endure throughout the production process. However, this violence has a different functional operation, and pain does not as prominently serve an instructive function in disciplining the body as was the case in racial slavery; pain here is not an object or incentive within production; instead it is merely a 'necessary' side effect of, and accessory to, the inevitability of production.[32] The logic of animal agriculture dictates that the system will prevent violence which threatens the integrity of the product, since this will impact the value structure of the industry and bleed profitability from operations. Hence the extraordinary proliferation of research aimed at ensuring the improved taste and texture of meat through better animal welfare: the fact that animals will become the product means that the body of the animal must be safeguarded, within particular bounds, to ensure the financial viability of the corpse as it is fabricated. Importantly, violence does not operate within intensive animal agriculture as spectacle. Visibility is obscured and production carefully sequestered to hide from external scrutiny the violence within animal agriculture.[33] Thus violence is everyday, it is routine, everywhere, but there is little 'theatre': indeed, as Pachirat demonstrates, this violence is carefully partitioned in such a way that not only do animals not see what is to come, but the vision of human workers themselves is controlled to manage what is seen and not seen.[34]

The above analysis highlights the potential of focusing on value for understanding the distinct place of different subjectivities within broadly 'economic' relations. As I have stated in Chapter 1, we are asking the wrong question when we ask: 'Do animals labour?' Instead, the question we must ask is something like: 'What is the use value of animal labour power to capital?' As I have indicated above, asking this question allows us to usefully differentiate animal labour in food systems from forms of human labour, including chattel slavery. From this standpoint, focusing on value is productive.

There are certainly some useful recent analyses we could draw on to understand how animal labour operates in a value context. For example, Donna Haraway has argued for the modification of Marx's value theory, inserting a concept of 'encounter value' alongside the concepts of 'use value' and 'exchange value'.[35] Haraway elucidates the idea of 'encounter value' to deal with the effect of cross-species interaction with animate beings (or 'lively capital') that are not passive or static in relation: 'Trans-species encounter value is about relationships among a motley array of lively beings, in which commerce and consciousness, evolution and bioengineering, and ethics and utilities are all in play.'[36]

While Haraway opens the door to a new conceptualisation in describing 'lively capital', the fine detail of how encounter value connects with Marx's value theory is left unattended; and Haraway certainly does not provide a detailed description of the relationship between animal labour and lively capital.[37] However, there have been attempts to extend Haraway's concepts in ways that might inform an augmentation of Marx's value theory so that it might concretely account for animals. Maan Barua, for example, has provided a significant extension of Haraway's concept of 'encounter value', suggesting that it 'is a process of value-generation where lively potentials and nonhuman labours of an organism constitute and make a difference to those very historical and material relations that render or transact it as a commodity'.[38] In this understanding of encounter value, Barua illustrates that generation of use values in production requires a grappling between human and nonhuman (including nonhuman labour) which helps to produce the animal as a commodity: 'encounter value can be thought of as that *process* of value generation where bodies, ethologies and liveliness of an animal *makes a difference to*, and *is constitutive* of, those very relations that render or mobilize it as a commodity'.[39] Here, within a production process, the encounter generates a relation that potentially shapes both the commodity and the commodity-making process; while this encounter also participates in generating the allure of the animal whom buyers may want to engage with as a consumption item. Barua, for example, describes the movement of lions from hunting trophies to conservation icons in India as an example of a process where animals are not merely 'passively' commodified, but through their evolving encounters and agency participate in engaged ways to produce different modalities of commodification.[40] Encounters between human and nonhuman natures make the value process fraught or potentially valuable. These uncertain, and resistant, encounters disturb the process of extracting value: production will have to deal with a being who is slippery, who develops co-shaping relations with others in the production process, and who actively resists complete subordination by production. We might read this sort of engagement, or encounter, in a relatively benign way as 'mutually productive'. However, as I shall argue below, such 'encounters' are sites of antagonism or conflict; they represent a messy grappling with potentially non-compliant natures which will have to be 'tamed' or subordinated, including through coercive means, into the rhythms of production in order to generate value. As such, animal labour is tied to the process of resistance to that labour.

A different refraction of Haraway's approach is provided by Rosemary-Claire Collard and Jessica Dempsey, who focus on a notion of 'lively commodities' which they argue 'produce capitalist value as long as *they remain alive and/or promise future life'.*[41] Here a biopolitical process of making life/keeping alive is central to value production: this is a commodity who must remain 'alive for the duration of its commodity life and whose life is central to its value, like Tillikum/ Shamu (Sea World's "killer" orca whale), a trafficked human, a rodeo bull, or an exotic pet'.[42] The need to stay alive is also a biopolitical reality for human labour power utilised in production processes. However, this requirement characteristic for animal labour seems to be highly relevant to understanding what is distinctive about the food animal, where it is only the 'mere' or 'bare' fact of living in the biopolitical sense[43] – that is, being housed, constrained and fed in an intensive environment during a predetermined production cycle – that is required for the generation of value.

Collard and Dempsey's approach strongly resonates with the work of Melinda Cooper, who explores the self-generative processes of the body as sources for surplus; for example, examining biotechnology, Cooper points out:

> When patent law apprehends the value of the stem cell line, it is not in the first instance as an exchangeable equivalent (Marx's definition of the commodity) but as a self-regenerative surplus value, a biological promise whose future self-valorizations cannot be predetermined or calculated in advance. In this way it redefines the value of life as self-accumulative, both on a material level (cell line technology as a deliberate cultivation of the self-regenerative potentialities of living tissue) and a commercial level (the intellectual value of the cell line is not pregiven in the cell line in its unicity but accumulates and multiplies as the cell line is subdivided, expanded, and circulated among researchers).[44]

This idea of self-generative or metabolic processes as value-creating bends how we might understand labour, offering useful ways to think about the labour of animals used for food, whose bodily processes are transformed into value. Les Beldo offers a similar view of life as a vital self-generating force that produces value through 'metabolic labour'.[45] Examining chicken production, Beldo notes that chicken labour does not need to be voluntary or conscious, and draws a productive distinction between the 'macrobiological' processes of the organism and those 'microbiological' processes that are internal to the organism itself, arguing that both processes occur together, producing a unique hybrid:

> Pasture chickens, for instance, labor at both the macrobiological and microbiological levels – by eating, rooting, and laying eggs, on one hand, and by metabolizing feed into eggs or animal flesh protein on the other; but they have the additional burden of enduring their own metabolic labor, of constantly

feeling the effects of the cellular processes within them that generate eggs at the rate demanded by capital.[46]

Perhaps all labour (human and nonhuman) is a combination of both macrobiological and microbiological processes; however, what is distinctive about intensified animal production is that systems of domination concentrate in such a way that all labour time for food animals comes to depend on the control of these microbiological processes to produce value. As such, the battery chicken appears to barely move within their constrained environment as the labour process aligns with the metabolic duration of life itself: these animals eat, they defecate and, when the time comes to realise value, they are slaughtered.

For Beldo, 'labour' offers an opportunity for an affirmative and active rendering of animals within production that is a counterpoint to the accounts which offer a 'negative' reading of systems of domination over animals; against these negative readings, Beldo suggests that the ever-present vitality of animal life, that which produces value, confirms an affirmative force that animals possess that is relied upon by systems of production.[47] This means that Beldo's analysis appears to deliberately distance itself from a theory of resistance,[48] even though, as Beldo acknowledges, the sort of labour performed by animals in production systems makes the category of 'labour' (at least in the sense of labour as a consensual process) fraught.[49] As I shall argue below, there is no reason to imagine that animal labour and resistance are not interconnected: indeed, animal resistance to systems is intrinsic to the character of this labour, and the adaptation of human and machinic labour processes to this resistance is precisely what produces value.

Before I move to my own proposal for understanding the labour of animals from a value perspective, I want to pause here to think about 'reproductive' labour and its relation to the work of animals in industrial animal agriculture. My analysis in the section below will be directed at food animals who will themselves become consumption commodities: that is, the billions of animals who exist within intensive industrial systems, entering production as a raw material and leaving as a consumption commodity. As I have outlined in Chapter 1, the reproductive functions of animals are subsumed by capitalism in a number of distinct ways: not only are animals with the capacity to reproduce pulled into labour in order to create products such as dairy foods or eggs; but ruthless controls over reproduction are required to allow these processes to conform to the rhythms of production, so that 'gestational labour' becomes essential to not only dairy and egg products, but also the continual supply of new animals to meat production.

This work of gestation, accompanied by forced insemination prior and removal of progeny after, is routine and necessary to production, despite its horror. And this horror betrays no apparent trace in the finished item on a supermarket shelf: again, as stated in Chapter 3, nothing in the commodity reveals the violence of its production. Gillespie, drawing on a case study of a dairy cow, describes the repeated violence that is central to their life:

> When she reached 15 months of age, she would be impregnated through artificial insemination for the first time. Artificial insemination is the most common method of reproducing cows in the dairy industry. To artificially inseminate a cow, the farmer inserts his/her left hand into the cow's rectum in order to manipulate the reproductive tract. . . . Meanwhile, the right hand is inserted into the cow's vagina and an insemination gun is used to reach the cervix. . . . Three weeks before giving birth, she would be moved into a 'maternity pen' with other cows nearing their due dates. When the time came, she would be isolated and monitored while she gives birth to her calf. Several hours after the calf is born, it would be taken away from the cow and she would be moved into the milking string. . . . About 60–90 days after the cow gives birth, she would be artificially inseminated again and continuously milked through her pregnancy until 60 days before giving birth (the 'drying off' period). This cycle of artificial insemination, birth, and milking would be repeated for several years until lameness, mastitis, infertility, and/or declining milk production set in. These conditions are common in cows used for dairy because of the immense physical strain and nutrient depletion (hence their frequent emaciated appearance) caused by the excessive milking and forced impregnation inherent in the industry. At this point, the farmer would make a careful calculation of her profitability as a milk producer weighed against the cost of maintaining her. When she is deemed 'spent', she would end up at auction, or she might be sent directly to the slaughterhouse.[50]

The dairy cow performs a 'metabolic labour' here, but one that uses the bodily processes of the cow to produce a continuous flow of milk. While these animals may eventually become food (though perhaps not for humans), and these animals produce other beings as part of their dairy work (that is, new dairy calves, and disposed-of 'bobby calves' – calves that are separated and either reared for products such as veal, or immediately slaughtered),[51] Gillespie's description highlights the way in which milk, as the object of production, informs the value structure of this labour. The animal is treated as a machine that is progressively worn down by production. And since the primary object of production is not the body of the animal itself, a value structure emerges in which all activity aims towards the stimulation of lactation as the product, even at the cost of the destruction of the animal themselves.

This sort of labour process – where the body is utilised as a machine for the repeated production of a product which is created by the metabolic processes of this body – differs from the animal whose primary 'purpose' is to become food (I will examine the latter in the next section). Because of the unique logics of violence, it is very difficult to find human comparisons to the labour performed by animals under capitalism who will become food; quite simply, because we don't eat humans. The labour processes which enmesh these food animals are geared towards the horizon of their death, since their distinct commodification depends upon a metamorphosis beyond the limits of life. However, the reproductive or gestational work of animals, such as the dairy cow described by Gillespie, does have some resonance with existent forms of human labour, where metabolic processes are drawn on to produce a product which can be alienated from the body of the producer, allowing for repeated production cycles to be completed by this same body. I pause here to consider the distinct character of this modality of metabolic labour, before we press on to look at the labour of animals who will themselves become food.

Here we can draw on work within feminist labour studies which has situated the body itself as a means of production, particularly in relation to commercial surrogacy,[52] emotional labour,[53] care labour, sex work and other 'body work'.[54] Critical interrogation of commercial surrogacy from a labour perspective is particularly relevant, since this provides one example of a human labour process where the body is utilised as a means of production to enable a particular 'product' to be realised and alienated from the body of the producer, at least from the standpoint of the production process.[55] Amrita Pande's analysis of commercial surrogacy in India is of particular relevance to my analysis here. Pande observes that commercial surrogacy occupies a unique position as an embodied form of labour:

> there are profound differences in expectations about embodied dispositions of workers in service industries and the kind of worker embodiment required in surrogacy. Surrogacy is an extreme example of the manifestation of worker embodiment, where body is the ultimate site of labor, where the resources, the skills, and the ultimate product are derived primarily from the body of the laborer. The worker's embodiment is essentially living in the commodity produced – literally in the form of the worker's bodily fluids, her blood and sweat.[56]

104 | ANIMALS AND CAPITAL

Pande suggests that surrogacy provides a different way by which to understand 'embodied labour', defined as 'a rental of the use of one's body by somebody else, in which the body of the worker is the fundamental and ultimate site, resource, requirement, and (arguably) product'.[57] While perhaps all labour necessitates the 'rent of the body' (or the purchase of labour power for a market-determined price), perhaps what marks commercial surrogacy is the unique way in which the body's metabolism is subsumed by capitalism so that the outcome of this metabolism, one intimately connected with the body of the labourer, becomes the product. In this production process, the body becomes the means of production; and the product itself must be materially alienated from this body.

Pande stresses, for the work of commercial surrogacy, that this aligns production with the gendered politics of reproduction:

> A fundamentally paradoxical characteristic of commercial surrogacy resonates with other gendered forms of labor like domestic work and sex work. On the one hand, commercial surrogacy becomes a powerful challenge to the age-old dichotomy constructed between production and reproduction. Women's reproductive capacities are valued and monetized outside of the so-called private sphere. As surrogates, women use their bodies, wombs and sometimes breasts, as instruments of labor. But just as commercial surrogacy subverts these gendered dichotomies, it simultaneously reifies them. When reproducing bodies of women become the only source, requirement, and product of a labor market, and fertility becomes the only asset women can use to earn wages, women essentially get reduced to their reproductive capacity, ultimately reifying their historically constructed role in the gender division of labor.[58]

The subsumption of gestational labour into the rhythms of capitalism thus offers a bittersweet opportunity to name and value labour that has previously been privatised; but this comes, at least for Pande, at the cost of its inscription within a normative gender system.

Sophie Lewis, in a recent analysis of commercial surrogacy, provides a different perspective: commercial surrogacy is undoubtably a sign of the continuing expansion of the logic of capital and produces exploitation; but for Lewis it also presents an opportunity to situate all gestational labour, and not just commercial surrogacy, as 'work'.[59] Lewis provides a useful intervention in challenging normative assumptions on who does gestational work – Lewis points out that gestating work is performed by bodies who do not necessarily identify as 'women'. Further, there is little that is pleasurable about gestational labour, nor should it be accepted as *fait accompli* because it is purported to be 'natural';[60] it is instead work that is often forced upon those who do this labour by norms or law. This labour connects to a system of property which valorises a biological connection between parent and child, and treats as natural the connection between the child and the gestational labour of their parent. For Lewis, commercial surrogacy thus creates the opportunity to challenge and re-understand reproductive work under capitalism:

> Narrating capital's evolving history then becomes a matter of revealing a web of surrogacy relations at the heart of empire, reaching into every intimate abode. Social reproduction theory becomes a matter populated by a whole raft of 'surrogates': provisioners, test subjects, helps, and tech supports. 'Surrogate', more than 'reproductive' or 'feminized', might be a word that proves useful for that field in bringing together the millions of precarious and/ or migrant workers laboring today as cleaners, nannies, butlers, assistants, cooks, and sexual assistants in First World homes, whose service is figured as dirtied by commerce, in contrast to the supposedly 'free' or 'natural' love-acts of an angelic white bourgeois femininity it in fact makes possible. Surrogacy, in its current connotation, is the lie and the truth of their situation. It speaks of the millions of living bodies secretly crouching inside the automatons, and behind the customer-service machine interfaces, of what Kalindi Vora has called 'surrogate humanity'.[61]

For Lewis, commercial surrogacy thus provides the impetus to rupture social relations surrounding human reproduction, challenging gender and sexuality norms and dismantling the family as a revolutionary project. 'Full surrogacy' then becomes a demand for a collectivised reimagining of how this labour might be organised and distributed:

> For if babies were universally thought of as anybody and everybody's responsibility, 'belonging' to nobody, surrogacy would generate no profits. Would it even be 'surrogacy' at this point? Wouldn't the question then simply be: how can babymaking best be distributed and made to realize collective needs and desires? Formal gestational workers' self-interest, like that of their unpaid counterparts, is an anti-work matter, and anti-work in the domain of care production is admittedly sometimes bloody. Their tacit threat to reproductive capitalism, whose knowledges and machinery they embody, takes the world a few steps toward queer polymaternalism. Terrifyingly and thrillingly it whispers the promise of the reproductive commune.[62]

Lewis's analysis is potentially productive for thinking about animals. However, Lewis leaves unattended the gestational labour of animals.[63] This means that the ruthless incorporation of animal reproductive processes within capitalism – where a significant proportion of the world's food supply relies on the forced gestational labour of billions of animals – is not explored as a facet of analysis. This feels like a missed opportunity, as industrial animal agriculture raises some curious questions for how we might see the work of surrogacy.[64] Firstly, in unhinging gestational labour from gender, Lewis offers the opportunity to consider how this labour operates within different regimes, including as a central pillar of the domestication of animals. Forced gestational labour is after all the story of human domestication of animals; this labour intensifies and assumes industrial proportions under capitalism. Inclusion of animals in how we understand the interaction of capitalism and gestational labour is useful, as it allows us to see the different ways in which regimes of biopolitical control and property rights play out around gestation – not only noting, as Lewis does, that the politics of gestational labour shifts when we look outside of the boundaries of the white heterosexual family, ranging from histories of racialised slavery and dislocation of Black families, the theft of children from Indigenous families, and the politics of trans parenting – but also noticing the way in which a technically mediated, industrial-scale, forced gestational labour becomes the norm where we move outside of the bounds of the human. Secondly, under capitalism 'full surrogacy now', dominated by the social relation of capital, is already a reality for animals globally, since there are no propertied connections that bind an animal who performs gestational labour to their progeny; indeed, central to the reality of the lives of these animals is the continual loss of this connection.[65] Animal agriculture thus provides a compelling account of gestational labour as a key pillar of capital's domination of life; total control over the reproductive lives of animals is a central structuring force in human–animal relations. Finally, thinking through the end of this violence – for both humans and animals – has profound effects for the societies we are imagining. I don't at all mean to imply that Lewis's proposals for the abolition of the family and collectivised responsibility for reproductive work are a problem: on the contrary their implications if they were applied to animals under capitalism would be significant. (Again, as I have emphasised in this book, noticing the place of animals in production allows us to both look at capitalism in a new way, and imagine very different futures.) Quite simply: if animals had the right to refuse gestational labour, then this would be the end of animal agriculture. From this standpoint, this forced gestational labour is crucial for the whole capitalist system of industrial agriculture, and thus, as I shall discuss in Chapter 7, tactically useful for advocates to pay attention to. Further, if we recognise animals who exist as a mass of gestational labour, the project of transformation of capitalism takes on a new form. If animals and humans were together collectively responsible for reproductive futures, then this would be a very different form of production; a different form of 'communism'.

Food animals as a hybrid of constant and variable capital

We have so far examined a range of theoretical tools which are useful for understanding the value structure of the labour of food animals: in particular, we have noticed the way in which 'lively', intimate, metabolic processes might be subsumed as part of the production of capital (that is, how metabolism might become 'productive labour'). In these forms of production, biological processes of the body themselves are relied upon to generate the product. But describing the character of this labour does not take us closer to understanding its distinct value relation. To make sense of this, I will now focus in particular on the food animal, defined as the animal who is required to deploy their own metabolic processes to convert themselves into the consumption commodity. As I have described above, this metabolic labour differs in its object from other work that animals do in the context of intensive agriculture (such as that of dairy cows), in so far as the primary aim of production is to transform the body of this animal into a product.

It is here that I would like to return to Marx to consider the structural position of this unique form of labour. In a section of *Capital*, volume 1, Marx provides an account of the microdynamics of labour's role in creating value:

> While productive labour is changing the means of production into constituent elements of a new product, their value undergoes a metempsychosis ['*Seelenwanderung*']. It deserts the consumed body to occupy the new created one. But this transmigration ['*Seelenwanderung*'] takes place, as it were, behind the back of the actual labour in progress. The worker is unable to add new labour, to create new value, without at the same time preserving old values, because the labour he adds must be of a specific useful kind, and he cannot do work of a useful kind without employing products as the means of production of a new product, and thereby transferring their value to the new product. The property therefore which labour-power in action, living labour, possesses of preserving value, at the same time that it adds it, is a gift of nature which costs the worker nothing, but is very advantageous to the capitalist since it preserves the existing value of his capital.[66]

Here, Marx describes a remarkable 'process' by which an object is transformed through the application of labour power, while the 'soul' of this same object – its value – is nurtured. In the idealised terms Marx lays out here, the worker applies their labour power (*Arbeitskraft*) on an object of production that is distinct from one's own body, and this process, while 'consuming' a use value, simultaneously produces a new use value which contains the old use value within it: 'what is produced is a new use-value in which the old exchange-value re-appears'.[67] The worker, for example, sands a table, but must in the process of sanding the table maintain the old value in the table (that is, not destroy the table) while simultaneously adding value through the sanding work. Here the money-owner 'trusts' the worker with the object of production; the worker faithfully does not damage the value of the object of production while at the same time transforming it into something new. The 'soul' of the object of production moves ('*Seelenwanderung*') seamlessly as it were to a new object with a new use value, even if this 'object' itself appears as one and the same.

The above process appears at first glance limited in its applicability to the metabolic labour I described in the last section. Because the above section from Marx deals with a conception of a labour process where the worker applies energy to an object external to them, it is highly disembodied in its narrative: it fails to account for labour where the object of production is the body of the labourer themselves. This means it is not immediately useful for thinking about the labour of food animals, since for food animals it is their own bodies that are created as the product of processes through production.

However, we might apply some flexibility to the categories that Marx imposes on the labour value process by approaching this in a creative way. For Marx, capital enters the production process as either constant capital – that is, 'raw material, the auxiliary material and the instruments of labour'[68] – or as variable capital – that is, labour power which 'both reproduces the equivalent of its own value and produces an excess, a surplus value'.[69] This separation between constant and variable capital is somewhat 'fetishised' in Marx, in so far as it aims to establish two different appearances for capital in production, as either that of materials, equipment and machines or that of labour.[70] However, as discussed above, this separation between constant and variable capital makes little sense when we discuss various modalities of metabolic labour: for example, the gestational labour of a commercial surrogate or a dairy cow effectively treat the biological body as a machine for the generation of a product which can only be crafted by the metabolic processes of that body. Here, constant and variable capital collide. Thus, against Marx's presumption of a separation between constant and variable capital, we can suggest that food animals enter the production process *as a hybrid of both constant and variable capital.*

This collision of constant and variable capital is, as we shall see, productive for understanding the distinct role of this sort of labour. Food animals are deployed as *both* a raw material that will be 'finished' as a product by the production process, *and simultaneously* as labour that must work on itself through a 'metabolic' self-generative work. The primary alienation from the means of production which Marx describes as part of the process of value transmigration for the human wage labourer (behind the worker's back) is actually located in close proximity to the labouring animal: in this case, the animal works on their own body, consuming old use values and producing new use values seamlessly in their body's own materiality. For the economics of food production, it is vital that these animals reproduce their own value in themselves (as a raw material) and simultaneously labour, without injuring the original raw material, so as to ensure their transformation into a new use value. This is the specific use value of food animals for capitalism: this animal enters production as a special raw material that produces a new use value in their own bodies, the latter of which is destined itself to become a product of the production process.

We are now in a position to more specifically understand animal-based food production in value terms. For Marx, for any product (that is, a useful object) to come into being, there is a requirement for raw materials and instruments of production to be brought together with expended labour power. Labour power, expended for a definite period of time, or variable capital, is deployed in combination with constant capital – that is, raw materials (or circulating capital) and instruments of production (or fixed capital) – in order to generate the product. One way to express this is that fixed capital (FC), circulating capital (CC) and labour time (LT) come together to make the new use value/product (P); or in value terms:

$$P = FC + CC + LT$$

Relevant to my analysis, Marx is very clear that labour time, the definite period for the expenditure of labour power, relates solely to *human* labour. Animals here only appear on the side of constant capital: in Marx's analysis animals will be treated in a traditional value sense as circulating capital – raw materials to be worked towards a product with a new use value, or in some guises, as in draught animals, as instruments of production or fixed capital; that is, as a capital item that embodies a previous expenditure of human labour, which is gradually 'used up' in the production process.

110 | ANIMALS AND CAPITAL

However, inserting animals into production as workers rather than as mere circulating capital – that is, recognising metabolic processes as potentially value-producing – complicates the picture above. This is because we must allow for the unique position of animals as both capital assets that are worked on, and simultaneously labouring subjects who, at least in the case of food animals, work on themselves over a definite period of time. We cannot simply treat animals as a passive raw material, nor a machine that reflects previously expended human labour time. Instead, animals arrive as a hybrid of both capital and labour, and this has an effect on values in a given production process.

Here, it is not my contention to argue that the general characteristic of Marx's formula must change.[71] Rather, I am curious how acknowledging that animals labour 'productively' (that is, animals have labour power that is deployed for a definite time with the aim of generating surplus above the relevant time-specific costs of the reproduction of that labour) alters how we look at the components of value in production. If we were to imagine the incorporation of animal labour, the fundamentals remain the same: the product (P) requires a combination of capital (C) and labour time (LT). However, the fine detail alters. We must allow for the inclusion of animal value as a raw material that enters the production process to be worked on (that is, animal capital or CCA), differentiated from other circulating capital (CC) items (such as animal feed) and differentiated from fixed capital (or FC) (such as machines used in production, or instruments of production in animal agriculture such as barns, fences and other containment facilities). But we must also allow for animal labour: that is a definite expenditure of animal labour time (LTA) to be part of the production process, which must be differentiated from human labour time (LT) for the purposes of analysis. This leaves us with the following:

$$P = FC + (CC + CCA) + (LT + LTA)$$

Note again that the above formula does not deviate from the essence of Marx's formulation, which rests on the assumption that the product is merely the combination of capital and labour time. What I have done here, though, is to recognise animals in a discrete fashion as both a circulating raw material and as providing labour time. While there is nothing revolutionary about the form of the formula, what does differ is that by insisting on identifying specifically the role of animals as both a raw material and a source of labour simultaneously, we are now in a position to observe a number of curiosities associated with how we might understand a production process that deploys the metabolic labour of animals.

At least one thing the formula allows us to see is that the social relationship between factors of production (human and nonhuman) shifts remarkably depending on how far animal agriculture processes are intensified and mechanised. On one hand, we can glimpse the conditions for animal agriculture before the arrival of the factory farm. Under non-industrialised conditions of production, where there is a low involvement of machinery and tools (fixed capital) in the production of animals, then the business of creating the animal as a product is of a low 'inert' capital intensity. Circulating capital is required to ensure the flock is nourished; however, these raw materials can be attained by cycling animals through different pastures to maintain subsistence.[72] But in these production systems there will potentially be a high degree of human labour time involved. The lack of automated processes means that humans must be present to facilitate production processes.[73] There will also be a high degree of animal labour here too, in the form of the 'metabolic' labour involved by animals in producing themselves (staying nourished, growing, moving, developing muscle, cultivating desirable flesh, etc.) that will enable a desirable product (a product with a new use value). We can represent this low-intensity animal agriculture scenario with the following:

$$P = (CC + CCA) + (LT + LTA)$$

Here, fixed capital is minimised. There are relatively few capital items (housing, machines, fences) that mediate the relationship between humans and animals; instead, there is a direct relationship between human labour time (LT), animals as circulating capital or raw materials (CCA), and the manipulation of the conditions by which animals can expend labour power (LTA). In some such systems, animals may graze on commonly owned property so that it appears that there are no other capital items present – merely animals confronting humans in direct relation with each other. As a result, in the above representation I have removed other capital items (FC) completely. This is of course fictitious and for illustration only, since the implements used by humans in this system, such as the shepherd's branding iron or staff, would appear here as capital items; and if rent or a tithe were payable for pasture, this would also appear. The point, however, is to illustrate that in a low capital intensity agriculture scenario, fixed capital would tend towards zero, placing the spotlight on the other factors of production. In a sense, this low capital intensity labour environment of animal agriculture will look mostly like an everyday intimate entanglement between humans and animals (perhaps what is often romanticised as the traditional pre-industrialised 'pastoral' shepherd/flock relation).

This relation establishes specific roles for humans and animals. Humans and animals both labour in this production process; however, the circumstances and orientation of this labour differ. In this sense, while Haraway is correct that animals and humans might be considered coworkers in some contexts,[74] this is only the beginning of the story: the labour of animals and humans in these processes differs due to their different structural position. Human labour in animal agriculture aims to generate, enforce and extract animal labour. The function of human labour in these industries is to compel animals to labour within the strict bounds of the productive processes. Domination is the overall characteristic of this relationship; humans dominate animals to compel them to labour on themselves in order to achieve a desirable product. This imperative shapes human labour tasks, which are designed to compel this specific form of animal labour into being; these human labour tasks can include husbandry and reproductive controls, feeding and nutrition regimes, herding animals under fear of the whip or a dog's bite, forced body modifications including sterilisation, removal of body parts (such as tails or horns) or bodily identification regimes (for example, branding). In other words, human labour here aims to generate the animal as a self-labouring subject: animals are compelled by this human labour (that is, domination) to obey the metabolic regime imposed upon them in order to realise themselves as a product to be sold.

I note here that animal resistance is an implied aspect of this labour process, since humans only labour to compel animal labour because animals do not surrender this labour of their own volition. The fact that animals resist this labour means they must be compelled. In so far as human labour time is expended to compel animals to labour, then human labour time is generally equivalent to animal resistance time. We shall return to the role of resistance in this labour process below, and examine this more closely in Chapter 6.

I have so far described low capital intensity animal agriculture, where machines and built infrastructure are minimised. As discussed above, this produces a direct and antagonistic relationship between humans and animals: in this agricultural system, humans work to make animals do what they would prefer not to do. But what happens when animal agriculture intensifies? That is, what happens when the factory farm materialises? An important part of the intensification of animal agriculture is the deployment of enclosures and machines to conglomerate, automate and accelerate production. Today we are seeing dramatic progress towards fully automated systems of animal agriculture, such as the implementation of robotic dairy farms[75] or the use of automation in aquaculture – for instance, the development of processes to sort fishes by size so that they are suitable for other automated processes within the value chain.[76] In Marx's view, such developments would highlight a changing 'technical composition of capital' – that is, the increasing mass of constant capital (machines, raw materials, fixed assets), in contrast to a reduced variable 'mass of labour-power' – where human labour increasingly appears to be supplanted by machines and raw commodities.[77] Thus the intensification of production is accompanied by the expansion of fixed capital (FC) in animal agriculture – intensive enclosures, industrial-scale feeding systems, systems for getting rid of waste, industrialised forms of breeding, forms of automation applied everywhere, including in slaughter – as well as an expansion of circulating capital (CC), such as feed, water and pharmaceuticals essential to the production of animals. This intensive animal agriculture scenario also signals the massive expansion in animals as raw materials (CCA): more and more animals enter the system to be produced as an increasing supply of consumption commodities. To an extent, these elements so far describe the explosion of intensive animal agriculture over the last hundred years.[78]

But what about animal labour? While it is true that under the factory farm scenario animals have expanded as raw materials, my analysis is also signalling their expansion as workers: that is, there is an expansion in animal labour time (ALT) required to produce ever more product. Indeed, the only thing that relatively decreases in this scenario of capital intensification is human labour time (HLT), as human labour productivity increases create efficiencies that 'save' on the mass of human labour (that is, an increase in the 'technical composition of capital'). As we know, producers are globally working towards fully automated processes in animal agriculture which effectively remove all human labour from the equation. Under a system of imagined full automation of animal agriculture, this scenario looks something like this:

$$P = FC + (CC + CCA) + LTA$$

It is here that we start to glimpse what is unique about a value approach that takes account of animal labour time. It is also here that I hope we gain a sense of how Marx's anthropocentrism leads to a distorted view of how value is generated within the productive processes of animal agriculture. In Marx's story, a rising technical composition of capital puts humans out of work by reducing labour time and increasing the presence of machines and raw materials in productive processes; that is, rising labour productivity (a reduction in abstract labour time) is driven by technological developments and a rising investment in machinery. Thus, we are told, full automation will effectively dispense with the need for direct inputs of labour time. However, we can no longer maintain Marx's strict division between constant and variable capital, since in the case of contemporary industrialised agriculture, animals arrive as both. It is here, if we take a non-anthropocentric perspective on labour, that Marx's view that relative capital intensity would rise – that 'a smaller quantity of labour will suffice to set in motion a larger quantity of machinery and raw material'[79] – becomes unstable within the context of live animal-based industries. This is because, just when human labour appears to vacate animal agriculture (as a result of capital intensification), animals increasingly arrive as *both* a mass of raw materials and a mass of labourers (in the hybrid form I have described above). Thus, if we include animal labour time into the story, we cannot assume in a straightforward way 'that a smaller quantity of labour will suffice to set in motion a larger quantity of machinery and raw material'. It is true that the intensification of animal agriculture has led to an explosion in the capital contribution to production: in the form of fixed capital and circulating raw materials, including massive flows of living animals into production as raw materials and voluminous flows of feed that animals will metabolise. However, animal labour time also expands in this scenario; indeed, as total human labour time diminishes within the production process (relative to total output of product), total animal labour time would seem to expand almost proportionately with the expansion in the total production of animals as products.[80] In other words, it is not quite correct to say that intensification of animal agriculture has resulted in a relative reduction in labour time. The truth of the factory farm is more complex; human labour time has progressively declined and even been eliminated, while the mass of animal labour has expanded substantially as part of this model of surplus creation.

While the focus of the above analysis has been animals who work on their own bodies to be transformed into a consumption commodity, the dynamics of the above scenarios are useful for interrogating other situations of metabolic labour such as the lactation work of dairy cows, discussed earlier. In the case of the latter, the same tendency will apply. Intensification of production in dairy industries will reduce human labour time, but animal labour time cannot be replaced, since this metabolic labour by animals is directly essential for the creation of the product. It is possible to use strategies to make animal labour time more efficient[81] (we shall explore these below) but, since animals are required to be deployed to make the product utilising their own bodies, they cannot easily be replaced. This same logic accompanies reproductive work, such as the production of eggs for human consumption. Industrialisation and massification has apparently removed humans from the scene of production; however, animal labour cannot be replaced, since this metabolism is directly required for the products that are the object of production. Within animal agriculture, the mass of human labour can conceivably be removed through automated processes, but since the metabolic labour of animals is essential to 'the product' then animal labour time cannot directly be replaced.

In saying that food animals cannot be replaced, I must stress here that I am assuming that animals are used in this way by production because they have the capacity to produce surplus. Naturally they can be 'replaced' if capital finds other sources of labour or other materials that might be useful to work on in production:

> If we look at the creation and the alteration of value for themselves, i.e. in their pure form, then the means of production, this physical shape taken on by constant capital, provides only the material in which fluid, value-creating labour-power has to be incorporated. Nether the nature nor the value of this material is of any importance. All that is needed is a sufficient supply of material to absorb the labour expended in the process of production. That supply once given, the material may rise or fall in value, or even be without any value in itself, like the land and the sea; but this will have no influence on the creation of value or on the variation in the quantity of value.[82]

Capital is agnostic about where it extracts value from, 'whether cotton or iron'.[83] Animals are seized upon by capitalist production because a hierarchical anthropocentrism makes them available, almost without limit, and because they are *not just* a mere raw material for humans to labour on, but have the capacity to labour on themselves; that is, they are good at producing value. Yet a condition of this production, assuming that animal products are the outcome, is that this labour force cannot be dispensed with, since these animals appear as both a raw material, as labour and, finally, as the product. And this means that while human labour can be replaced by machines, the same cannot easily happen for the metabolic labour of animals, since their three lives under capitalism – raw material, labour, consumption commodity – must occupy a continuous, but continually transforming, materiality throughout the production process.

We thus face a paradox here if we include animals as labourers. Where intensification would ordinarily imply a reduction in the mass of labour deployed, the intensification of animal agriculture appears, counterintuitively, to lead to an expansion in the mass of animal labour, despite a reduction in human labour time. But note that I have used the phrase 'mass of animal labour' rather than 'animal labour time'. This has been deliberate, because we are here thinking about animals as a mass of labourers rather than as a quantity of labour power deployed over a definite period of time. From a value perspective, it is labour time that is of interest: capitalism is an antagonistic relation with *labour time*, and the drive to reduce the given quantity of labour time required to produce the commodity, or more particularly to expand the surplus extracted from the production process over this time, will remain.

Before I turn to think about what the above analysis means for animal labour time, I would like to address an issue that I raised in Chapter 1 over the placement of animal labour within the formal circuits of value production; namely the concern over whether such a move risks creating an overly 'capitalocentric' analysis of animal agriculture.[84] In this context, J. K. Gibson-Graham has advanced an important critique of contemporary left thought; they have expressed concerns about narratives which position capitalism as a central, dominating and 'phallic' economic relation:

> When we say that most economic discourse is 'capitalocentric', we mean that other forms of economy (not to mention noneconomic aspects of social life) are often understood primarily with reference to capitalism: as being fundamentally the same as (or modeled upon) capitalism, or as being deficient or substandard imitations; as being opposite to capitalism; as being the complement of capitalism; as existing in capitalism's space or orbit.[85]

For Gibson-Graham, the problem with this framing is that it totalises our conception of social and economic life and fails to take note of different economic relations which provide alternatives to capitalism; this understanding of capitalism produces 'economic monism as an implication or effect' and 'the subordination of noncapitalism'.[86] This perspective has informed other thinkers who have highlighted the value of alternate economies and different forms of informal labour, such as Lynne Pettinger's analysis of the many forms of unpaid work and productivity: 'non-economic relations are everywhere, if only we would look'.[87]

I raise these perspectives from Gibson-Graham and Pettinger to highlight that I am unapologetically moving in the contrary direction by insisting that the work food animals do in intensive animal agriculture occurs in absolute conformity with the rationalities of formal capitalist production. I insist on this orientation for the work of food animals for three reasons. Firstly, while there are many forms of production involving animals, such as subsistence farming, which move outside of formal circuits of capitalist production, industrial animal agriculture, and its distinct contribution to the transformation of the means of human subsistence, represents an unquestionable example of capitalist economic transformation. Capitalist animal agriculture has not only transformed human relations with animals; it has transformed humans as well. Secondly, as discussed in Chapter 1, while animals within animal agriculture have previously not been regarded as workers, this presumption has been shaped by a prevailing hierarchical anthropocentrism that has prevented an accurate understanding of formal production under capitalism. My analysis above highlights the potential for a comprehensive analysis of the dynamics of capitalist animal agriculture if animal labour time is considered. Finally, it is certainly not clear that the labour that animals do is 'unpaid' or is informal. Certainly, animals do not receive a monetary wage. However, intensive animal agriculture must meet the costs of the means of subsistence for animals, and this is an input cost to production, just like a wage. As I shall argue in the following section, this input cost – its volume, its timing – is one of the sites of contestation for animal agriculture in its drive to extract the difference between the value produced by labour and it reproduction costs. For these reasons, contemporary intensive animal agriculture is certainly front and centre within capitalist economies; the animals within are usefully understood as a formal labour force.

The battle over animal labour time

During that long, spiralling, but central chapter on 'The Working Day' in *Capital* volume 1, contestation takes centre stage. The chapter reveals the way in which capitalism struggles to increase the productivity of the working day: that is, struggles against social norms and worker resistance to expand working time, and then struggles to use other means to compel labour to be more productive within the social limits placed on the working day.[88] These two trajectories of attack – lengthening the working day and intensifying labour productivity – are described by Marx with the concepts 'absolute' and 'relative' surplus value:

> I call that surplus-value which is produced by the lengthening of the working day, *absolute surplus-value*. In contrast to this, I call that surplus-value which arises from the curtailment of the necessary labour time, and from the corresponding alteration in the respective lengths of the two components of the working day, *relative surplus-value*.[89]

As we shall see, these two drives have implications for thinking about the lives of food animals. Importantly they produce a unique pattern of domination, one that aims to literally steal life. Marx makes the stakes of this clear:

> 'What is a working-day? What is the length of time during which capital may consume the labour-power whose daily value it has paid for? How far may the working day be extended beyond the amount of labour-time necessary

for the reproduction of labour-power itself?' We have seen that capital's reply to these questions is this: the working day contains the full 24 hours, with the deduction of the few hours of rest without which labour-power is absolutely incapable of renewing its services. Hence it is self-evident that the worker is nothing other than labour-power for the duration of his whole life, and that therefore all his disposable time is by nature and by right labour-time, to be devoted to the self-valorization of capital. Time for education, for intellectual development, for the fulfilment of social functions, for social intercourse, for the free play of the vital forces of his body and his mind, even the rest time of Sunday (and that in a country of Sabbatarians!) – what foolishness! But in its blind and measureless drive, its insatiable appetite for surplus labour, capital oversteps not only the moral but even the merely physical limits of the working day. It usurps the time for growth, development and healthy maintenance of the body. It steals the time required for the consumption of fresh air and sun-light. It haggles over the meal-times, where possible incorporating them into the production process itself, so that food is added to the worker as to a mere means of production, as coal is supplied to the boiler, and grease and oil to the machinery. It reduces the sound sleep needed for the restoration, renewal and refreshment of the vital forces to the exact amount of torpor essential to the revival of an absolutely exhausted organism. It is not the normal mainte-nance of labour-power which determines the limits of the working day here, but rather the greatest possible daily expenditure of labour-power, no matter how diseased, compulsory and painful it may be, which determines the limits of the workers' period of rest. Capital asks no questions about the length of life of labour-power. What interests it is purely and simply the maximum of labour-power that can be set in motion in a working day. It attains this objec-tive by shortening the life of labour-power, in the same way as a greedy farmer snatches more produce from the soil by robbing it of its fertility.[90]

I have included this extended quotation from *Capital* because it is highly useful for our analysis. Firstly, although the context here is the length of the working day, the 'working day' is itself an arbitrary duration shaped by human social relations: the key question here relates to the limits, if any, that might be placed upon extending labour time for a given entity, human or otherwise, within production. Secondly, Marx outlines a relation of power that is explic-itly biopolitical. The antagonism between the living entity and capital is one determined by a political contest where capitalism seeks to make available the duration of life for productivity, and has no hesitation in extending, shortening and depleting this life towards the goal of expanding surplus value. Here we should note that conflict over labour time is explicitly biopolitical because it deals with the limits of biological life. Time matters to living animals as it is time endured; it can be extended or diminished and it can, in a qualitative sense, be assessed as time that is enjoyed, tolerated or suffered, depending on how this time is deployed. As Marx vividly describes, time stolen by capitalism is life lost that could be more meaningfully spent. On the other hand, time of life matters to capitalism where it represents a potential towards the production of surplus value. As such, and if it were possible, capitalism would be happy to take all time. As we shall see, this is a characteristic of the life of the food animal. Finally, Marx's flourish in the final sentence of the passage above (capitalism 'attains this objective by shortening the life of labour-power, in the same way as a greedy farmer snatches more produce from the soil by robbing it of its fertility') points us to a non-anthropocentric reading of the biopolitics of capitalist production. It is not merely human life that is stolen in this arrangement, but all life – human and nonhuman – is sapped.

There are two trajectories of antagonism related to animal labour time: the first relates to the shortening of animal lives as a means of reduction of labour time; the second to the emergence of the human–animal relation as a mediated relation with fixed capital and machines.

The first trajectory relates to the concrete reality that capitalism will continuously seek to shorten animal lives in order to expand relative surplus value. As Collard and Dempsey have suggested, the role of animals as a 'lively commodity' is one where being alive is central to the production process.[91] However, we can expand on this to note the overt sense in which life and death mark the production process in a fundamental way. Within the value chains of animal food production, death is configured as a value-producing moment;[92] it is when death arrives that the living commodity ceases to exist as a raw material and attains a use value. As discussed in Chapter 3, where capital is often represented as 'dead labour', the movement of animals from alive to dead materially illustrates this relation:[93] 'On one side of the sticker are the living; on the other side, the slaughtered. Each animal hangs head downwards at the same regular interval, except that, from the creatures to his right, blood is spurting out of the neck-wound in the tempo of the heartbeat.'[94] All workers look out at a world which includes artifice embodying dead labour; animals in production confront a world where they are continually becoming this artifice through their own self-labour. When biological life ends, the life of dead labour begins.

This highlights that in essence, for animals, the production process is equivalent to life: for food animals the whole of life is subsumed within production so that all labour time is equivalent to the fact of living, and will only reach its completion at slaughter. Thus, for food animals, labour time is *not* regulated by the normative limits imposed by the 'working day'.[95] On the contrary, a prevailing hierarchical anthropocentrism places almost no meaningful limits on what we can do to animals, and thus there is no working day for these creatures. Instead, labour time equals life. That is, the production system incorporates the whole of the animal life as it is lived – converts life into life lived as metabolic labour – within the production cycle. For example, in intensive systems, chicken labour time equals the time the chicken is alive: this is exactly how much labour time is required from the chicken to produce 'the chicken' as a product.

The reality that lifetime represents labour time shapes the nature of attempts to wrest more value from this labour. The tendency of productive processes towards increasing 'relative surplus value' is to reduce labour time for the production of the same use value. This has a peculiar meaning for animals in animal agriculture. Long before the factory farm, Marx recognised this as a tendency within capitalist animal agriculture, and its meaning for animal life:

> It is impossible, of course, to deliver a five-year-old animal before the end of five years. But what is possible within certain limits is to prepare animals for their fate more quickly by new modes of treatment. This was precisely what Bakewell managed to do. Previously, British sheep, just like French sheep as late as 1855, were not ready for slaughter before the fourth or fifth year. In Bakewell's system, one-year-old sheep can already be fattened, and in any case they are full grown before the second year has elapsed. By careful selective breeding, Bakewell . . . reduced the bone structure of his sheep to the minimum necessary for their existence.[96]

While the above passage reveals that Marx was aware of the tendency within capitalist animal agriculture to shorten lives, he did not see this in the terms I have framed; that is, as a mechanism to increase relative surplus value. This is of course because Marx did not see animals as providing labour; they are instead only capital that is worked upon. However, if we set aside this anthropocentric conception of labour, we can see that within capitalist animal agriculture the driving rationality for the evolution of production systems would be the promotion of both human *and* animal labour efficiencies. For humans, this means that the average labour time to produce consumption items such as food, televisions and automobiles has progressively been reduced through the introduction of machines, technologies and techniques. The 'working day' required to produce these goods has been effectively shortened; or more accurately, human labour has been freed to be elsewhere deployed to produce additional surplus. For food animals, on the other hand, since labour time equals life, there is no possibility of shortening the working day. Instead, increasing relative surplus value has relied on the shortening of life: for example, over the last fifty years broiler chickens have been genetically selected to effectively halve 'growing' time.[97] This has led to the perverse situation where animals are bred to grow faster in order to die quicker, reducing the production phase: therefore, literally, through the shortening of life it is possible to shorten animal labour time.[98] Thus the factory farm can more or less be described as a combination of the arrival of fixed capital and rationalised production techniques to animal agriculture; the withdrawal of human labour as automated processes 'took command';[99] and the ruthless control of animal metabolic labour to increase production turnover by reducing animal life.

While shortened animal lives reduce the production cycle, expansions in 'yield' also effectively improve relative surplus value. Here we are reminded that the producer controls the raw materials consumed by animals in order to reproduce their labour. This is precisely controlled to manage the metabolism that follows.[100] As Richard Twine describes:

> If we think about the biopower of animal science broadly (not just genetics), we see an approach to the bodies of pigs, cattle, chicken and sheep that is about the precise and economically efficient control of inputs in order to try and control a particular qualitatively standardized meat, milk or fibre product. The sequencing of the genomes of these animals is an attempt to widen the toolkit and to heighten the degree of control in breeding. Just as important as genetics is research into feed, feed efficiency and animal health (which have a genetic component).[101]

One focus here is to generate as much growth in as limited a time as possible, and maximise 'yield' or 'feed conversion rates'; that is, to make most efficient the ratio between the amount of feed provided to the animal and the final weight attained.[102] Feed is a fundamental driver of the economics of animal agriculture because it contributes a significant portion of inputs to production; for example, in the context of intensive hog production, feed 'accounts by approximately 65–75% of pig production cost'.[103] Intensification has driven industry to develop accurate calculations in relation to 'a mathematical construct, based on the component variables body weight, weight gain, feed intake, and possibly some measure of body fatness, that is meant to convey the ability of an individual to convert nutrients obtained from available feed into useful product'.[104] Thus precise and imperious control over feed and the conditions for their conversion

122 | ANIMALS AND CAPITAL

into weight (that is, the conditions for animal labour on their own bodies to metabolise this feed) will determine profitability. This profitability of the production process will be directly interrelated between feed conversion ratios; the costs of feed, which produce an 'economic conversion ratio'; and the final number, weight and price of animal-sourced foods produced.[105]

Here, feed conversion rates effectively pin down the costs for capital for the animal's reproduction of their own labour: that is, in almost exactly the way Smith outlined, feed represents a component of the 'wage' for animals. Indeed, the parameters of this 'wage' – that is, the cost of the reproduction of labour seen from the vantage of capital – are naturally fixed by the demand to produce surplus over and above these reproduction costs, or the difference between 'necessary labour time' and 'surplus labour time'.[106] As Marx points out, the 'value of labour-power' – that is, its cost to production – 'can be resolved into the value of a definite quantity of the means of subsistence';[107] in the case of animals, this is resolvable into the costs required to allow the animal to pursue metabolic labour, reproducing their own life for capital. Marx's formula for the daily cost of human labour production ('365A+52B+4C+ ... /365') averages out human means of subsistence (fuel, food, shelter, clothing, etc.) over a twenty-four-hour period.[108] The 'Feed Conversion Ratio', on the other hand, offers a different form of brute accounting, one that measures in a direct sense the efficiency of the costs of reproduction in generating a final product. And everything matters for this conversion efficiency, including the temperatures of the feed lot, the number of animals in each pen, segregation and control to minimise inter-animal aggression, and constrained opportunities for movement in order to conserve energy expenditure.[109] In other words, through controls over the environment metabolic labour efficiencies can be attained, increasing relative surplus value derived from this process. Thus, every element of the animal's life must be controlled to maximise this conversion efficiency; that is, pin down the animal 'wage'.

This complete immersion of the lives of animals into production is a 'subsumption' in the technical sense described by Marx. In this understanding, Marx drew attention to the means by which an existing labour process is drawn into productive labour (that is, 'formal subsumption'), differentiated from a 'real subsumption', which involved the transformation of labour through technologies, machinery, collective processes and the metamorphosis of production techniques such that labour is no longer separable from the production process around it:

> The *social* productive powers of labour, or the productive powers of directly *social, socialised* (common) labour, are developed through cooperation,

through the division of labour within the workshop, the employment of *machinery*, and in general through the transformation of the production process into a conscious *application* of the natural sciences, mechanics, chemistry, etc., for particular purposes, *technology*, etc., as well as by working on a *large scale*, which corresponds to all these advances, etc. [This socialised labour alone is capable of applying the *general* products of human development, such as mathematics, etc., to the *direct* production process, just as, conversely, the development of the sciences presupposes that the material production process has attained a certain level.] This development of the productive power of *socialised labour*, as opposed to the more or less isolated labour of the individual, etc., and, alongside it, the *application of science*, that *general* product of social development, to the *direct production process,* has the appearance of a *productive power of capital*, not of labour, or it only appears as a productive power of labour in so far as the latter is identical with capital, and in any case it does not appear as the productive power either of the individual worker or of the workers combined together in the production process. The mystification which lies in the capital-relation in general is now much more developed than it was, or could be, in the case of the merely formal subsumption of labour under capital. On the other hand, the historical significance of capitalist production first emerges here in striking fashion (and specifically), precisely through the transformation of the direct production process itself, and the development of the social productive powers of labour.[110]

This perspective allows us to read the history of domestication in a novel way. Domestication of previously 'wild' animals, aimed at co-opting the metabolic labour processes of animals for human purposes, represents an example of 'formal subsumption'. Arguably, the history of animal agriculture moves this formal subsumption towards a 'real subsumption', in so far as animals become inseparable from the productive processes within which humans place them, such that the morphology and livelihoods of animals become intertwined and interdependent on human utilisation. Intensive animal agriculture under capitalism marks a very clear example of a real subsumption, where the productive rhythms of capital are placed in direct alignment with the metabolic labour of animals; thus, as animals live, they produce; every moment of their life is geared towards the moment of their death, when they will transform into a new commodity with a new use value.

This understanding of subsumption allows us to makes sense of the particular violence animals experience within intensive animal agriculture. Here, I want to stress that the violence experienced by animals in this production process is shaped by this mix of imperatives to make life endure in such a way as to maximally congeal value, *and simultaneously* shorten life in order to reduce animal labour time (and the production cycle itself). Human control in animal agriculture aims at both of these things through a close alignment between productive processes and biological life. On one hand, production innovation relies on the use of beneficent techniques of welfare and regulation to make life endure towards the production of a final product. Thus, the production and reproduction of animals within animal agriculture conforms to a biopolitical form of violence, in so far as it involves the scrupulous and infinite management of life, with deep controls over nutrition, movement and reproduction.[111] On the other hand, production processes deploy practices and technological innovations to hasten life to its death: whether in the use of devices and techniques to expedite the transfer of living assets between phases of production (using cattle prods and other means of coercion) or in the use of genetic selection or hormones to progressively increase growth rates and therefore reduce the animal labour time between birth and death. There is here the economic reality of disposability that accompanies this production, which means that unplanned early death is part and parcel of the life cycle; whether in the form of attrition rates within the production system,[112] or mortality in transport.[113] In so far as these techniques of violence tend towards fostering death, they conform to Achille Mbembe's understanding of necropolitics as the 'subjugation of life to the power of death'.[114] The food animal is caught in the terrain between these two forces of life and death, as if the dream of these production processes is to bring animals to life *en masse*, only to 'depopulate' them in the shortest possible time. Within this intoxicating intersection of hostile force, resistance for the food animal becomes equivalent to the will to persevere despite the aversive environment around. Because these animals can at least be said to prefer to live – against production systems that aim to make them die ever more quickly – life will be experienced as essentially resistant, against an apparatus that looms with the continued and actualised threat of life extinguishment in the name of value.

The second trajectory of antagonism is the emergence of the human–animal relation as a mediated relation with fixed capital and machine. Here, and relevant to the intensification that has accompanied mechanised industrial animal agriculture, the character of resistive encounters with animals shifts away from engagements between humans and animals towards encounters instead between animals and the instruments of mechanised production. Automation in animal agriculture is as much a story about the replacement of human labour with machines, as it is simultaneously the story of the expansion of the mass of animal labour, which now confronts fixed capital directly as their object of domination. This is after all the peculiar horror associated with intensified animal agriculture: that is, not only the increasing massification of production, but the progressive displacement of human labour from the production process itself, which disrupts all nostalgic imaginings of a 'pastoral' relation between humans and animals. From this standpoint, we might wonder why we talk of 'human–animal relations' rather than capital–animal relations, since the bulk of interactions in animal agriculture and fisheries comprises a confrontation between animals and fixed capital.

It is here in this context – the confrontation between animals and fixed capital – that we find a story of resistance that is central to animal labour within intensive mechanised (and increasingly automated) agriculture. For Marx, the fundamental antagonisms that developed in early capitalism between human workers and machines arose as a result of the sense that machines were replacing the labour and livelihoods of workers:

> Since machinery is continually seizing on new fields of production, its 'temporary' effect is really permanent. Hence the character of independence from and estrangement towards the worker, which the capitalist mode of production gives to the conditions of labour and the product of labour, develops into a complete and total antagonism with the advent of machinery. It is therefore when machinery arrives on the scene that the worker for the first time revolts savagely against the instruments of labour.[115]

The machine, for Marx, was the product of past human labour: the machine absorbs labour in a 'coarsely sensuous form'[116] and immediately in its deployment supplants the labour of the worker.[117] As such, the antagonism between the human worker and the machine is one of 'competition', where the machine threatens to replace human labour power: 'the worker appears as superfluous to the extent that his action is not determined by [capital's] requirements'.[118] For animals, however, the antagonism takes on a completely different character. Food animal labour cannot be replaced by inorganic machines, since these animals are not only labour power, but they are also raw material and finished product. Instead, the arrival of machines is merely the replacement of the antagonistic relationality between humans and animals in this production process with a new hostility: that between animals and machines.

One example of this is the introduction of automated processes to 'catch' or 'harvest' chickens.[119] As described in Chapter 1, humans killed approximately 70 billion chickens in 2020 for meat. Such large-scale slaughter requires mechanised forms of production. However, even in capital-intensive forms of killing, the business of making chickens available for slaughter typically involves the mass deployment of human labour at crucial points in the value chain. For example, chicken-catching prior to transport or slaughter is usually performed by human hands. This process is intensely frictional and involves a tussle between human workers and the chickens, who would prefer not to be caught. Chicken-catching in the context of industrialised animal agriculture is usually dangerous for both animals and humans.[120] Routinely, chicken-catching is performed by human hands; many chickens will sustain injuries in the process,[121] and many will be 'dead on arrival' when they finally reach the slaughterhouse.[122] Human workers too will sustain injuries as a result of the repetitive work of engaging with struggling chickens.[123] Partly due to the intensity of human labour involved in chicken-catching, there has been a steady introduction of automated 'chicken-harvesting' machines into production processes. These technologies are quite directly an example of the deployment of techniques that seek to increase 'relative' surplus value by reducing human labour time. But beyond simply making chicken-catching labour performed by humans more productive, the automation of the chicken-harvesting machine also holds the promise of almost completely displacing the need for human labour itself. As such, chickens increasingly no longer confront humans in production processes, but instead almost always encounter machines instead. The harvesting machine takes different forms: some look like wide-mouthed vacuum cleaners, larger than a motor vehicle, while another variation uses 'foam paddles to place birds on inclined conveyor belts that carry the birds into crates'.[124] This device is usually rolled over a darkened compound containing thousands of chickens, who desperately climb over each other to escape. The speed of capture is dizzying. As the chickens succumb to the machine, they are sucked into its internality, whisked away almost seamlessly, and thrust into crates. In this process of capture, the chickens do not directly experience interaction with humans.

Where animal resistance might previously have been directed against human workers whose labour power aimed at making animals productive (that is, making animals labour), intensified production instead shifts this relation to the technologies of control: it is the machine that now confronts the animal as a force of domination aimed at compelling labour, right up until that point where value can be realised through death. The increasing intensification of animal agriculture, including progress towards full automation, means that animal labour now increasingly faces an environment where capital everywhere dominates: patterns of birth are completely overcome by mechanised processes; every aspect of the environment becomes enclosed within a weaponised aversive living space determined by economic necessity; and animals are moved between phases in the value chain, including to death, through automated processes which chase them down, shackle them and drive them towards the death of value realisation.

It might be objected that the arrival of technologies in animal agriculture should not be understood purely through the lens of conflict, antagonism and resistance; and that animals 'actively assent' to the technologies that have arrived within animal agriculture.[125] A complicating factor here is that the technologies used within animal agriculture aim to nullify resistance and thus create an epistemic effect of absence of friction and peaceability, constructing the recipients of violence as willing participants (this is something we will examine further in Chapter 6).[126] An example of this is the arrival of 'fully automated' or robotic milking machines. These machines replace the twice-daily milking of the dairy herd with a system of restrictions and incentives which 'allow' cows to move themselves to the milking machine more or less frequently.[127] A very clear driver of these changes relates to the removal of human labour time from milking activities,[128] and promotion of increased 'yield'.[129] The industry gloss has presented the robotic dairy farm as a site of freedom which allows cows newfound autonomy:

> Can you imagine a robot milking a cow? It's a reality in Australia, thanks to the development of automatic milking systems that make the entire milking procedure free of human assistance! The cow voluntarily enters the milking shed for milking and is recognised by an electronic transponder. The suction cups are attached to the cow's udder by a robotic arm and are removed after milking has finished.[130]

The reality is more complicated. As Holloway and Bear describe, while cows have increased autonomy in choosing when to approach the milking machine, this is dependent upon forms of individualising training, discipline and deeper modalities of control: 'an ability to manage and discipline what Foucault refers to as "counter-conduct" more closely in new, technologically mediated ways'.[131] Holloway and Bear further stress that cows and their subjectivities are moulded in relation to the machinic technologies in production.[132] Thus, cows are selected to conform to the machines, and are incentivised – with feed, electric fences, etc. – to align their own rhythms with the routines of the robots (that is, the demands of production).[133] Intensive computerised monitoring of individual cows ensures continued productivity.[134] In this sense, new technologies respond to and mitigate animal non-compliance, bending subjectivities in line with the demands and rhythms of production; that is, as human labour time diminishes, the mass of animal labour is not replaced, but rather animal labour time is intensified, made more productive. Finally, while automation generates new routines which appear to offer 'freedom' and lack of coercion, the signs of antagonism and violence remain, including routine interventions such as teat and horn removal, and continued use of forced insemination (and calf removal) which is central to milk production. Violence is still present, though it is often materially and epistemically cloaked.[135]

Within posthumanist theory, Haraway has deployed the concept of the 'contact zone' to account for material co-shaping encounters between humans and nonhumans.[136] Haraway draws this term from Mary Louise Pratt, but redeploys it to account for human–animal relations.[137] In Pratt's view, contact zones represented 'social spaces where cultures meet, clash, and grapple with each other, often in contexts of highly asymmetrical relations of power, such as colonialism, slavery, or their aftermaths as they are lived out in many parts of the world today'.[138] Pratt's interest was in trying to describe complex interactions between agents, where exchanges (such as linguistic adaptation) were co-shaped despite entrenched inequalities in power.[139] As such the 'contact zone' for Pratt is something of a methodological tool in enabling an analysis of fine-grained, mutually evolving interactions in the midst of deeply structured violence:

> The term 'contact' foregrounds the interactive, improvisational dimensions of imperial encounters so easily ignored or suppressed by accounts of conquest and domination told from the invaders perspective. A 'contact' perspective emphasizes how subjects get constituted in and by their relations to each other. It treats the relations among colonized, or travelers and 'travelees', not in terms of separateness, but in terms of co-presence, interaction, interlocking understandings and practices, and often within radically asymmetrical relations of power.[140]

Haraway redeploys this concept of 'contact' in potentially productive ways to examine the interaction between dogs and humans in agility training, highlighting that this training enables a 'chance for joint, cross-species invention that is simultaneously work and play'.[141] However, whether this method of analysis – where a sole focus on overarching modalities of structural domination is suspended to enable a more fine-grained examination of co-shaping relations – is useful for understanding the 'contacts' between humans and animals (or machines and animals) in the context of industrial animal agriculture remains an unsettling question.[142] The 'contact zone' risks forgetting this overarching reality; and risks also forgetting the structural differences between humans, animals and machines within productive processes, in particular, glossing over fundamental antagonism. Certainly, within animal agriculture, food animals have a unique position: unique because the constellation of violence that is directed towards them, and the forms of resistance they deploy, are structurally positioned in a way that is potentially quite different from other agents. Would it be better to talk about 'conflict zones' rather than 'contact zones'? After all, a conflict zone is also a space where agents interact and co-shape each other; but the idea of a 'conflict zone' highlights the ever-presence of violence in shaping relations, and stresses the structural antagonism between combatants. In the conflict zone of intensified animal agriculture, violence is everywhere, and it blends with the rationalities of capitalist production to produce patterned deployments of capital and (human and nonhuman) labour power. In this conflict zone, humans labour to coerce animals to work to produce themselves as commodities. As production intensifies, technological innovation and the deployment of fixed capital displaces human labour power and confronts animal labour power in an antagonistic relation: the aim of these deployments is to overcome the resistance of animals, bending wills towards human prerogatives. This is indeed 'contact' between material bodies which press and shape each other; but its character is all-out conflict, antagonism, asymmetry, living resistance only interrupted by slaughter. In so far as the lives of animals are almost completely subordinated by these processes, this resistance is equivalent to a will to live in the face of an aversive environment where all time is labour time, and the final product of labour is the animal's own body itself. We shall turn to look in more detail at this resistance in Chapter 6. However, before we move to exploring the relation of animal resistance to the form of capitalism, we must address the problem of circulation – where, as we shall discover, both human and animal labour time provide the distinct shape of the movement of animals as living commodities.

5 Circulation

Nothing is more common than to bring transport etc., to the extent that they are connected with trade, into the pure circulation costs. In so far as trade brings a product to market, it gives it new form. True, all it does is change the location. But the mode of the transformation does not concern us. It gives the product a new use value (and this holds right down to and including the retail grocer, who weighs, measures, wraps the product and thus gives it a form for consumption) and this new use value costs labour time, is therefore at the same time exchange value. Bringing to market is part of the production process itself. The product is a commodity, is in circulation only when it is on the market.

Karl Marx, *Grundrisse*[1]

In the preceding chapters I have offered the building blocks for how we might perceive the three lives of food animals under capitalism: as raw material, as consumption commodity and as labour. These categories allow us to look at animals and their relation to capital from a value perspective; that is, as embodying different use values depending upon their positionality with respect to production and consumption. However, although production depends upon swiftly, and without ceremony, switching animals and animal bodies between these use values, we don't encounter seamless material movements between these different moments of positionality. In reality, despite appearances, the movements between production and consumption – and between the conversion of money to the commodity, and to money back again – are abrupt and often violent. As we saw in Chapter 3, the conversion of the living animal who is a raw material into a consumption commodity as meat is far from frictionless;

instead, in the intermediary zone between life and death, animals face violence and struggle as they confront mechanised fixed capital in the forms of corrals and chutes, live hang and conveyor belts, captive-bolt stun guns and skinning machines. Here, smooth movement from one stage of production to another is central to the process of value creation. But for animals, these transitions are fricative.

Animal agriculture requires frequent movement. There are often continual movements of animals, alive or dead, between stages of production. Broadly, capitalism requires the continual circulation and movement of raw materials and finished commodities to enable the simultaneous movement of money. Efficiencies require these endless movements to occur smoothly, quickly and with precision, always 'just in time' to enable the next scene of productivity or consumption to occur. These efficiencies are required because circulation effectively adds to turnover time; as Marx makes clear, circulation time is a component in the movement of capital: 'the turnover time of capital is the sum of production time and its circulation or rotation time. It is self-evident, therefore, that circulation times of varying length make for different times of turnover and thus different turnover periods.'[2] This has implications for animal agriculture, where the movement of living animals is part and parcel of the production process. As discussed in Chapter 4, the turnover time of animal agriculture is interconnected with the biological life of the living animal. It is for this reason, as we shall see, that the movement of living animals imposes particular challenges and opportunities for production processes; differentiated from non-living commodities, the capacity of animals for metabolic labour shapes the decision whether to move these commodities alive or dead.

This chapter seeks to look at the problem of circulation through an examination of the transport of live animals. I will explore the meaning of live animal transport within the context of supply chains as a process for transferring and realising value. I will offer some characterisations of different meat industry value chains and the potential role transport plays within them. As we shall see, mechanisation and globalisation have had a hand to play in the expansion of live animal transport.

My focus on live animal transport is aimed at highlighting the importance of animal labour from a value perspective. In Chapter 4, I highlighted the way in which recognising animal labour in value terms provides insight into the development of intensive animal agriculture and a different way to account for the peculiar form it has taken. Similarly, as we shall see in this chapter, recognising animal labour alters how we see the problem of circulation. As I shall argue, animal labour is essential to the live animal transport trade: if animals did not maintain their own value through their own metabolic labour, then the economics of the live animal trade would not 'add up'.

Live animal transport and value transfer

Live animal transport refers to the transport of living animals by road, sea or air in order to physically locate animals (as raw materials and labour) within a specific phase in a value chain. The function of transport is fundamentally to realise a use value; it is the process of transference between one phase of a value chain and another that allows for the realisation of this new value. Thus, for example, a sheep may leave a breeding facility as a product, to be moved to a feedlot to be 'finished': in this latter phase of production, the sheep arrives as a raw material with a use value to be worked upon in order to produce a new use value. From the standpoint of the productive process, transport thus serves a purpose in transferring and realising value.

At a basic level, the historic capacity for animals to function as a mobile store of wealth (the 'walking larder')[3] is dictated by the intrinsic bio-capacity of live animals to move and be moved, maintaining their own value and thus ensuring their own convertibility to money (thus, as we shall discuss below, the essential role of metabolic labour in the apparent 'durability' of animals for transport). Live animal transportation is a key feature of the long historical development of agricultural technologies aimed at refining production efficiencies within animal-related industries.[4] For example, the ability of an agricultural producer to move animals from pasture to market, either by foot or by mechanised transportation system, enables farmers to access a market and thus (potentially) realise a use value from the animal.

The segmentation of production chains – between, for example, breeders and 'growers' – itself creates demand for the live transport of animals to transfer raw materials and commodities (and therefore value) between successive stages within a production process. Developments in slaughter technologies and geographic/spatial location also play a part in generating live animal transport need. The centralisation of slaughterhouses, away from smallholder backyard slaughter towards coordinated and centralised slaughter facilities,[5] generated the need to transport animals between a smallholder farmer and the slaughterhouse. This means that today, most animals produced globally as part of meat industries are transported at some point in their lives.[6]

While there are important differences between value chains within the global meat industry, for the purpose of this analysis of live animal transport, we might note three different models. A simple model is described in Figure 5.1.

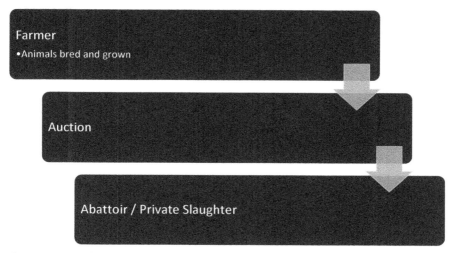

Figure 5.1 Example Simple Model Value Chain – Meat Production

Here, the animal is born and raised by the same operator, transferred to market for sale (or alternatively to a cooperative or association),[7] and then transferred to a centralised slaughterhouse. I have excluded the stages of production post-slaughter, as they are not immediately relevant for my discussion of live animal transport.

This sort of value chain exists where smallholder farmers take control of raising animals, with little segmentation of production phases prior to the sale of the animal.[8] Here the structure of production, even in this simple formation, generates the need to transport live animals; at minimum, from smallholder to a market or cooperative, and then, assuming there is no co-location between this phase and the slaughterhouse, transport will be required to the abattoir. We know that a significant change in the structure of meat industries in the twentieth century, at least in the Global North, was the vertical integration of production; that is, the exertion of control by meat packing/processing firms, particularly in relation to pork and chicken meat supply, over the whole value chain of animal production to final sale ('from squeal to meal').[9] The capacity for one firm to exert control on the supply chain – either through ownership or through contracting arrangements – need not generate the need for transport; on the contrary, this can reduce the need for transportation within some aspects of the supply chain. This was certainly the case for early vertically integrated meat businesses, where the kill floor was located directly (vertically) above the processing phase, allowing body parts to be gravity fed to the floors below in 'large multistoried packing plants'.[10]

However, even within vertically integrated models, the staging of production in order to maximise value will potentially generate the need for transport, and not just between the farm and the slaughterhouse. An example is the structuring of production between operators who breed and nurture young animals (for example, using farrowing stalls, such as in pork production) and operators who intensively feed these animals, preparing them for their eventual realisation of value as consumption commodity at slaughter. Here, a feedlot operator can place an order for a large number of calves which form the basis of the next phase of valorisation.[11] But calves do not arrive from nowhere. They of course must be born, through the forms of forced gestational labour described in Chapter 4. And further, even before calves are ready to be sold, there are many preliminary stages required in the value chain, including, for example, preparing animals ('preconditioning') through processes such as dehorning, castrating, and acculturating animals into self-feeding regimes, to fabricate them for suitability within the next production phase. Producers may also segment later stages of production. One area of specialisation, for example, is the development of specialised 'finishing' production phases prior to slaughter (or 'feeder to finish' operations), which aim to intensively feed animals in order to attain the desired weight before they are sent to the abattoir.[12] This means, at least in the case of pork production, that there may be very different segmentations within value chains introducing complexity, even within vertically integrated businesses ('Farrow to wean', 'Wean to feeder', 'Farrow to feeder', 'Feeder to finish', 'Farrow to finish').[13]

Live animal transport is potentially demanded between every phase of this segmented value chain. And each of these phases demands additional transport roles, including in providing 'inputs' to production such as grain (note that the location of food may determine the need to transport animals, such as in the case of the foundation of the Iowa pork industry, where it was discovered that it was 'cheaper to transport the livestock product than to transport its grain equivalent').[14] Figure 5.2 provides a simple example of a meat industry value chain within a vertically integrated model. This model is indicative and not representative of every type of vertically integrated meat production; the intent here is to demonstrate the way in which a value chain creates the need for transport in order to transfer commodities for value realisation between different phases of production. Again, I have excluded the stages of production post-slaughter, as they are not immediately relevant to my discussion of live animal transport.

While vertical integration is common within industrialised animal agriculture, it is far from ubiquitous within the global meat industry. On the contrary, global value chains differ greatly, and there appear to be as many examples of

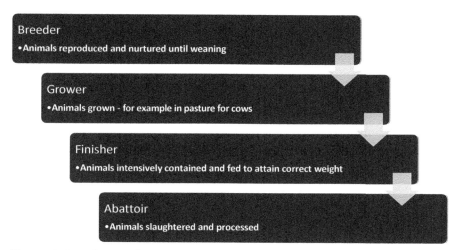

Figure 5.2 Example Vertically Integrated Value Chain – Meat Production

disintegrated models of animal-based production as there are vertically integrated models. There are a number of reasons to emphasise this heterogeneous model of meat production. The first is that vertical integration has been applied in earnest to intensive farming practices for some species (such as chicken or pork production), while within other industries (such as beef production) there has been far less integration.[15] The second reason is the capacity of disintegrated models to provide boutique 'high value' types of meat ('lean meat', 'organic', 'grain fed' and 'free range', for example) through unique specialisations in the value chain. In some cases, this means producers within specific phases of the value chain assert themselves within a market by directly marketing to consumers (this is the case in relation to the emergence of 'locavorism').[16] One industry-oriented fact sheet advises:

> Sharing with your customer how you raise your animals, the breed of the animals and about your farm adds value to your product. Consider creating clear statements about the type of production, your animals' access to fresh air, clean water and shelter which will help you address any animal welfare concerns or questions that might arise. Use of antibiotics and artificial hormones; whether you are using these in your operation or not. Having an understanding [of the] public's concerns and addressing them with your product or farm description will ultimately add value to your livestock products.[17]

Naturally, vertically integrated models of production are capable of controlling diverse 'value added' product lines, for example through contracts with suppliers

136 | ANIMALS AND CAPITAL

to market an 'organic' line of meat. However, given the growing global interest in various 'happy meats' as an alternative to factory farm-sourced meat,[18] there is probably an argument to suggest that we may see more specialisation and disintegration within particular supply chains.

The third reason why it is useful to understand disintegrated models of meat production is that outside of the Global North and its tendency towards large, integrated animal-sourced food businesses, we find alternative forms of production. For example, today China is the world's largest producer of pork; however, some 80 per cent of this pork production is derived from 'backyard feeding' operations.[19] The situation appears similar for beef production: China is the third largest beef producer, with some 16 million low-income households across China involved in this production.[20] This has led to a confusing situation where in the beef industry, for example, smallholder production aimed at producing 'low'/'generic' and 'medium value' meat remains dominant, despite Chinese government incentives to facilitate the emergence of industrialised slaughter and feeding facilities in order to enable 'high value' meat production.[21] This does not mean that vertical integration does not exist in China; on the contrary, there are vertical models. But in some cases, they do not look like those elsewhere. For example, in the case of chicken production, Wen's Food Group has developed an innovative model, effectively outsourcing the growth of the animal to private households while retaining breeding, slaughtering and processing functions:

> The Wen Family Food Conglomerate Company, founded in 1986, provides chicks (at five yuan per chick), feed, drugs, and handbooks to participating households on fixed dates at fixed locations for breeding through a well-organized network with a computerized database. The company follows up with provisions of information and services against disease, repurchases the grown chickens on a fixed schedule, and pays for those following delivery of matured chickens. It then processes the chickens at its plants for sale.[22]

These heterogeneous examples of value chains within meat industries suggest a different example model for disintegrated systems of production, as outlined below in Figure 5.3. Once again, in this figure I have excluded the stages of production post-slaughter.

Note that the lack of vertical integration in this disintegrated model creates additional opportunities for the segmentation of the value chain between different sites of production, and thus for an increased need for transport to arise between each segment. Here, intermediaries may be required within the value chain to link one phase of production to another: for example, a specialised

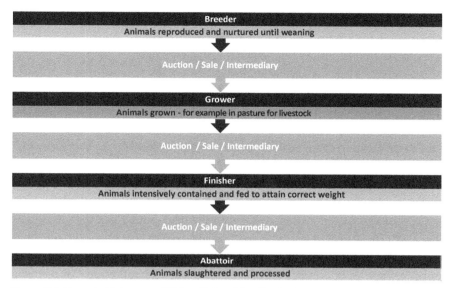

Figure 5.3 Example Disintegrated Value Chain – Meat Production

breeder may use a market or trader to link with 'growers'. Transport will be the key to making these connections real, even if this is simply about a breeder taking an animal to market.

In a sense, much of this transition in the development of animal agriculture industries resonates with the development of manufacture generally, where in small-scale production, efficiencies come from bringing together stages of assembly; while in larger-scale mass production, there is specialisation, isolation and mechanisms generated for commodities to move between localities. For Marx this was an inherent product of the division of labour power under capitalism, where production is staged to maximise the productive force of workers engaged in repetitive specialised actions which discretely produce value: 'The establishment and maintenance of a connection between the isolated functions requires that the article be transported incessantly from one hand to another and from one process to another.'[23]

Incessant transportation might describe the evolving nature of the global meat industry, which has seen the development of segmentations in the production processes, with live animals transported by road over long distances within countries (such as across the United States or Australia) and across nation-state borders (such as in inter-European Union trade). Production segmentation has also seen animals transported long distances by sea, often between different continents. In the case of 'high-value' animals (such as animals used for breeding purposes), transport can occur by air. While air transport makes up a minority of global transfers of live animals, there is no reason to assume that air transport won't grow in importance: the 'world's first luxury animal terminal' has recently been constructed at John F. Kennedy Airport, New York.[24]

Although my focus here is live animals, naturally the transfer of dead animals and/or the parts of dead animals is part of the larger context. A broader analysis might pay attention to this in the global transfers of animal bodies and animal body parts that are part of international trade. For example, China today is one of the largest exporters of seafood products, and specialises in 're-processing' fish products. Thus, fishes may be caught in the waters off Southeast Asia, processed in China and then exported for sale in the United States.[25] The vast logistical and technological expenditure required (for example, industrial-scale refrigeration) to facilitate this global transfer of commodities tells us something about the potential for value creation involved in staging production, and in utilising transport networks to access different production specialisations. Transport here is a necessary stage for enhanced valorisation. Just as a smallholder farmer may only realise the exchange value of their cow if the animal is walked to market, we might equally observe that today's segmentation of global meat industries generates a transport task in transferring commodities in order that the exchange value of these commodities can be realised.

The mechanisation and globalisation of live animal transport

Mechanisation and globalisation form part of the back story to this process. Firstly, mechanised transport by land (road or rail),[26] sea and air have facilitated large-scale movement of live animals over great distances.[27] Today, some of the world's largest sea-based livestock carriers, such as MV *Ocean Drover*[28] (formerly MV *Becrux*)[29] and MV *NADA*,[30] have a fearsome capability to transport tens of thousands of animals (MV *NADA* has a stated capacity to transport 110,000 sheep).[31] Developments in land-based transport also facilitate the movement of large numbers of animals. In Europe there are now livestock vehicles fitted with onboard watering systems and tracking systems;[32] in Australia, large triple-decked trailers take advantage of reduced rural and remote-area road regulation requirements to transport large numbers of animals over potentially vast distances.[33] In some cases, there is an integral link between land transport systems and sea transport of animals. This is because the logistics involved in making large numbers of animals available to be loaded onto a transport ship means coordination between multiple factors including land transport, shipping docks, and the deployment of human labour. In 2011, the operator of MV *Ocean Drover* 'celebrated' a world record for the largest shipment of live cattle (25,817 animals).[34] This sort of record is only achievable through large-scale coordination: every component in each phase of production must play its part.[35]

Secondly, the long history of the centralisation and mechanisation of aspects of meat production, particularly intensive feedlots (that is, 'Concentrated Animal Feeding Operations' or CAFOs) and industrialised slaughter facilities, have voraciously demanded live animal transport in order to supply the 'raw materials' for these phases of production. Centralisation has reduced the number of slaughter facilities; however, mechanisation has increased their capacity to 'process' animals. This has increased demand for live animal transport.[36] This sort of locational substitution in the structure of animal food production generates transport demand not only for the transfer of live animals, but also for inputs such as human labour and grain.[37] In these cases the transport task becomes massive, and coordination between production phases becomes more important. These shifts no doubt suggest that transport efficiencies will contribute to the profitability of animal industries; the tendency will be towards improved logistics to avoid costly delays, such as long queues at slaughterhouses.[38]

However, this is not merely a question of transport and logistics keeping up with expanding industrial 'processing' capacity, but this capacity itself keeping up with supply systems which threaten to overwhelm and destroy the viability of production chains. For example, within the context of fish meal production, processing plants must be able to cope with potentially high volumes of fishes delivered during peak catch seasons, where dead animals must be neither too old nor too 'fresh':

> If raw material is too old there is an increase of losses and a decrease in fish-meal quality. If fish is too fresh (e.g., in *rigor mortis*) there are working problems to grind and transport the raw material and the quality of the resulting fishmeal may not be acceptable for the customer.[39]

There is an 'organic' interdependence here between the development of transport systems and production systems within a value chain: evolution in production techniques and capacities pulls upon transport systems and their own capacities, while improvements in transportation efficiencies make possible changes in production systems, which suddenly are provided with the incentive to produce more live animals more quickly than ever before.

A range of geopolitical factors will drive these shifts. For example, in April 2014, during a period of international tension over the annexation of Crimea, Russia announced a ban on chilled and frozen beef from Australia, claiming concerns over growth hormones.[40] Perversely, within a matter of weeks and despite

140 | ANIMALS AND CAPITAL

lots of continued hand-wringing from beef suppliers, Australian exporters filled an order for Russia, which was claimed to be 'the largest single contract for live cattle ever from southern Australia'.[41] Frozen meat was exchanged for live flesh. However, this shift in the nature of the supply chain was not accidental. Here the productive capacities of Russian industry are important, as are the existence of supply-chain capacities such as live animal transport machinery. It is because of a capacity to slaughter live animals (and to profitably absorb the costs of this slaughter and necessary live transport within a value chain) that it is possible to substitute a chilled and frozen meat supply with a live animal supply. If Russia did not possess slaughter capacity, then, quite simply, this large-scale live animal transport would not be possible. Similarly, if the transport capacity did not exist – in this case, one of the world's largest live animal transport carriers, the MV *NADA*, was pressed into service – then there would be little potential to so seamlessly shift supply from chilled and frozen meat to live animals. Certainly, this suggests that the task for animal advocates is to seek to elucidate the value chain in its entirety – its capacities, its phases, its systems of transfer – in order to identify where to disrupt or interrupt value flows. Given the massive changes afoot in the global restructuring of the meat and dairy industries, including in the locational dynamics of production, this sort of strategic and coordinated overview will be vital.[42]

'Globalisation' is also an important factor in understanding the contemporary processes of live animal transfer. Of course, globalisation has been much debated within social and economic theory over the last three decades, understood variously as a restructuring of world economic markets[43] and its impact for the movements of commodities, including labour;[44] as an ongoing narrative within a converging global human history of 'world systems';[45] as a political force towards the internationalisation of sovereign power with attendant effects for law, rights and democracy;[46] as a system of cultural and linguistic exchange through mediated technological networks;[47] as a mechanism for expanding capitalist markets and exploiting differential wages;[48] and as an example of the spread of hegemonic powers.[49] For my purposes here, I will treat globalisation as the progressively enhanced capacity for transfers of commodities (products and services with a use value) and money to occur seamlessly between international exchange markets. It is beyond my scope here to advance a new theory of globalisation to accommodate animals (nor is there a clear need to) but it is worth observing that, at least in relation to live animal transport, the globalisation of capital has had some concrete impacts for animal agriculture.

One factor is that the value chains for animal production now more than ever do not need to be constrained by national borders; global trade liberalisation has allowed for different phases of the animal production process to occur in different international localities. In the case of live animal transport, for example, this means that animals can be bred and 'grown' within one nation state, and then transported across a border to take advantage of productive slaughter efficiencies (or reduced regulatory costs)[50] in another nation state: this occurs through intensive systems of transfer by road (such as inter-European trade) or by sea voyage (such as Australian or New Zealand live animal export). International transaction systems exist to allow for money to be transferred seamlessly in exchange for these movements.[51] Here we find an enlargement of the same processes of transfer that occurs within domestic markets, where animals are moved from one phase of production to another in order to transfer and realise value. The only difference is that a nation-state border has been traversed. In this case, the globalisation of markets, and with it the erasure of barriers to international trade, facilitates this structural change. We need not constrain our understanding of these processes to transfers for the purpose of slaughter. For example, within the global racehorse industry there is an active trade in 'studs' for breeding purposes, which interconnects a range of global markets centred on gambling, racing and breeding.[52] Nor need we only focus on live animal transport to understand the full extent of the impact of globalising forces on animal-related capital. As I have discussed above, the emergence of some national markets as specialists in, for example, fish product reprocessing, means that dead (rather than live) animals or animal parts may be transferred over very long distances before they find their end point with the consumer. Similarly, regional and national differences in consumer preferences for animal products can create differentiated demand, and generate surplus commodities for export: thus, for example, 'China imports chicken feet and wings and exports the higher value processed cuts.'[53]

Another related factor is the spread of technologies relevant to animal production processes, which innovate in how to maximally extract profit from each stage of a value chain. In a broad sense, the history of animal domestication is a history of techniques designed to increase the efficient 'yield' of animals used by humans;[54] that is, in the terms laid out in Chapter 4, increase the relative efficiency of animal labour. This has, in essence, become a global story, as the twentieth century oversaw a convergence of animal industries and sharing of 'stock' and technology.[55] For example, there has been an active development of a global semen industry for the artificial insemination of dairy cows, often relying on a small pool of 'donors'.[56] Here again, the globalisation of markets enables both the transfer of commodities and capital (including animal parts), but also the transfer of technologies and knowledge as new techniques and machinery come into 'general use' within a globalised economy.[57] Industrialised slaughter and intensive farming technologies have also transferred under conditions of globalisation so that in general, how animals are bred, raised and slaughtered in one part of the world doesn't necessarily differ from how this happens in another part of the world. While there are always exceptions, such as the predominant use of grass-fed systems for some animals in Australia, Africa and Southeast Asia, intensive farming remains the main way most chickens and pigs are produced globally; continued growth in intensive farming systems is a worldwide norm,[58] and new forms of intensification, such as aquaculture (which we shall explore in Chapter 6), are emerging.

It is worth noting that some of these transfers of technology can also relate to innovations that both improve efficiencies in the utilisation of animals and promise improved 'welfare'. For example, the development of 'best practice' stunning techniques potentially reduces suffering but also makes killing more seamless and efficient.[59] In these cases, at least as far as technologies aim at innovation in relation to the efficiencies and thus expansions in animals produced, then we can surmise that this technological change likely leads to increased transport demand, either as living commodities or as dead meat, to be processed within the next phase of production.[60] These changes have implications for human labour: as discussed in Chapter 4, human labour becomes more 'productive' as technologies are introduced, with implications for the value of labour and the necessary labour time required to 'produce animals as commodities'. In this way, the dynamics of labour within the global meat production industry, whether in relation to deskilling or through increased use of temporary, low-paid labour, does not substantially differ from the structural changes that have occurred elsewhere as a result of globalisation and which have opened migration flows.

The effects of these interconnected processes – mechanisation of transport, centralisation and mechanisation of production phases and slaughter, globalisation of animal trade and cross-border location of different production phases in value chains – has led to a continued increase in global live animal transportation. United Nations-derived trade data allows us to get a sense of the extent of this expansion. In 2001, approximately one billion (932,653,6560) land animals were exported globally; by 2011 this figure had grown to more than 1.5 billion animals (1,606,675,998).[61] These figures only tell part of the story in relation to the global transfer of animals as value commodities. Hiding behind this increase in the number of animals transported is a growing industry dependent upon the use value of live animals which are transferred from one production process to another. The World Trade Organization/International Trade Centre data on the value of live animal trade provides a unique picture in this regard, with a growth in the annual value of international live animal exports increasing from close to USD $9 billion in 2001 to over USD $23 billion in 2021.[62]

According to this data, in 2021 the most significant national interests in live animal exports are, in order of trade value, France, Netherlands, Canada, Germany, the United States of America, Denmark and Australia.[63] However, there has been a steady emergence of countries such as Brazil, Ethiopia, Jordan, Saudi Arabia and Somalia as exporters of live animals.[64] In some respects, the growth of the latter trade is reflective of the entry of these nations into globalised animal agriculture markets, taking advantage of the financial possibilities attached to moving live animals across borders. Live animal exports from Ethiopia are a good example of this, since Ethiopia has reported dramatic expansions of the value of its live animal export trade since 2001.[65] Part of this recorded growth is the increasing recognition in national accounting statistics of informal cross-border trade as part of the live animal export industry.[66] But the other side of this story is the capture – or quite accurately, 'subsumption' – of existing animals within a global circuit of production. Ethiopia has 'the tenth largest livestock inventory in the world'[67] in part because of widespread household-level private ownership of animals. This offers opportunities to expose these animals to wider markets through trade and to develop technologies and labour within Ethiopia to maximise value extracted from this 'stock'.[68] Here, agencies such as USAID are active in promoting the expansion of trade and the development of intensive systems to 'exploit' value:

> the promise and potential of the Ethiopian livestock value chain is to become a thriving industry that can produce packaged meats destined for Middle Eastern, European and East African markets, or fashion gloves and shoes that sell in volume on the high streets and boutiques of Europe.[69]

And the promise, according to these international development agencies, is the potential to use livestock industries to address structural inequalities in Ethopia (including in relation to gender inequalities where, we are told, 'livestock . . . has a huge potential to reduce gender asset disparities commonly found in households in most developing countries such as Ethiopia').[70]

It is beyond my scope here to demonstrate causal links between globalising processes in the world economy and the expansion of live animal transport. However, it seems reasonable to suggest that powerful economic forces are incentivising the expansion in live animal transport; and further, that this is sometimes occurring in ways that appear *prima facie* non-intuitive. The contradiction isn't merely that there has been an expansion in live animal transport at the same time as normative welfare concerns for animals who are transported have been escalating; although this is a contradiction worth contemplating. It is also that some of the economic drivers – such as increased transport costs or increased regulatory compliance costs – which might very well have stymied live animal transport, have failed to reduce the practice. We might find evidence for this in the experience within the European Union (EU) after the implementation of regional regulation of live animal transport systems.[71] In so far as the 2005 EU regulation imposed requirements for road transporters to install water systems in motorised transport and utilise tracking devices for transport carriers, significant additional costs were imposed on the industry. When the impact of the regulation was evaluated in 2011, evaluators expressed the expectation that the costs of implementation would increase the costs of transport.[72] Presumably these cost drivers would reduce the number of live animals transported within the EU as part of interstate trade. However, on the contrary, live animal trade increased over the period: 'there was no break in the upward trend in the volume of international trade in live animals after the implementation of the Regulation in 2007'.[73] Indeed, although the regulation imposed significant costs on providers (of an average of €13,000 per vehicle),[74] providers found means to absorb these costs. By all accounts, transport is a high-cost item within the supply chain; however, its capacity to facilitate the process of realisation of use value remains indispensable to an industry that is actively restructuring itself across borders.[75] It is for this reason that we need to perceive the underlying economic forces which make transport – transport of a living commodity – essential for the realisation of value within a world market. As such labour (both human and nonhuman) is one of the components in understanding this problem.

Mobile violence

The above sections have provided an overview of the context of live animal transport internationally. As we have seen, this transport is central to the production processes of animal agriculture, and increasingly a component of the circulations inherent to globalised capitalist agriculture. The mechanisation of transport has allowed for a significant expansion in the transfer of live animal bodies by road, rail, sea and air. This transfer aligns with the globalisation of production, the acceleration of the availability of animal-sourced foods, and the evolving profitability of animal agriculture industries.

However, the picture so far provided deals largely with the broad-brush features of global circulation, and does not attend to the fine detail of what is involved for human and animal labour within the process of transportation. As we shall see, this circulation – that is, the transport of animals to different points within the production process – is a sphere of intense friction and antagonism between human labour and animal life; indeed this antagonism is inescapably part of the transfer. Amidst the tricky and delicate business of transferring value embodied in live animals from one production locale to another, the labour conditions of human workers, the potential violence animals are exposed to, and therefore the labour conditions of animal workers, will be constantly evolving 'variables' of the process. For example, a driver employed by a logistics company or a processing company will likely be expected to be available to work weekdays and weekends, public holidays and overnight; they will need to handle heavy loads in order to load and unload animals; they will have to balance hectic schedules against welfare prerogatives (such as routinely checking for 'downer animals'); they will have to work with respect to prevailing regulations, and are likely to feel pressure to take a flexible approach to rules to get the job done faster. In these circumstances, the material practices relating to the transfer of value, facilitated by labour (human and nonhuman), are fraught with potential violence delivered as part of the business of maintaining the optimal level of value for each transport operation. Thus, human labour conditions have a role in determining animal welfare conditions; and as we shall see, also determine the conditions of animal metabolic labour.

In noting this inherent antagonism, we should not imagine that there is a direct economic benefit in 'protecting' animals from harm. The aim of live animal transport is not directly about protecting each living member of the cargo. On the contrary, the aim of transport logistics is to efficiently preserve the net value of the cargo (while accepting some loss) and potentially make this cargo available for the realisation of value. Thus, the aims of the transport enterprise are only tangentially or indirectly connected with ensuring safe passage. The economics of this process means that loss of animal life, or severe injury delivered to some animals as part of this process, is not a problem for the value chain unless it threatens the ability of the cargo to realise value within the next phase of production.[76]

This will produce all sorts of differentiated logics; for example, it will mean that relatively 'low-value' animals – such as livestock or chickens – will be subject to more violent treatment with risk of severe suffering, injury and death than 'high value' animals – such as stud horses – where valorisation depends on ruthlessly maintaining the integrity of the stock in order to realise value. It is also worth emphasising that the value of the stock depends upon its readiness for valorisation at the next phase of production. This means suffering imposed on animals that does not generate injury, or creates injury that is immaterial to valorisation at the next stage of production, can be 'afforded' as part and parcel of the transport process. For example, Clive Phillips estimates that five to ten per cent of animals transported by sea have conjunctivitis, a painful eye irritation which is caused by dust stirred from animal feed.[77] A solution to this would be to supply higher-quality feed that does not disintegrate as easily.[78] However, there is no financial incentive for this: conjunctivitis does not compromise the final value of the stock, and therefore the suffering of animals in this case is immaterial to the value chain. This is of course why the persistent claims made by the animal industry that it has a vested interest in the welfare of animals are nonsensical. Producers only care about the welfare of animals where this welfare has a material impact on the value chain. Where preventing suffering, injury or death have no impact on systems of value (for example, where the economics of live animal shipping tolerates large numbers of animals dying on the voyage without unduly compromising profit), producers and transporters will have no interest in welfare. Similarly, if animals are injured on the journey, but not in a way that compromises the value of stock at destination, then these injuries are immaterial as part of the value chain process and there will be no direct incentive to prevent them.[79]

Given this context, it is perhaps no surprise that the transport of live animals, as it is currently practised, exerts extraordinary violence against the animals who are transported. Perhaps the headline indicator which measures the impact of transportation on animals is the 'mortality rate' over the length of a given journey. 'Conscience-shocking' incidents, usually in the context of sea-based transport,[80] such as the loss of 50 per cent of the animals on the MV *Becrux* in 2002,[81] or the death of 5,500 sheep on the MV *Cormo Express* in 2003, or the extinguishment of 2,400 sheep on the *Awassi Express* in 2017,[82] are useful reminders of the capacity of live animal transport to routinely inflict mass injury and death for large numbers of animals. However, the everyday, mundane and apparently 'humane' mortality rates experienced within transport operations are also telling reminders of the relationship between the economic imperatives of the industry and the impact on the welfare of animals. For example, up until recent changes, the Australian Government's 2011 Australian Standards for the Export of Livestock created a regime of compulsory reporting for mortality rates above an agreed threshold, with threshold mortality rates of up to 2 per cent for some animals such as sheep and goats, and 1 per cent for cattle for journeys over ten days.[83] The reality of these threshold rates is that for a large shipment of animals – such as MV *Ocean Drover*'s record shipment of 25,817 cattle in 2011 (see above) – only a mortality of above 258 cattle would be reportable; presumably, anything below would constitute an acceptable norm. Acceptable animal death becomes more extreme with 'lower value' animals: the 2 per cent reportable figure for sheep and goats would suggest that if MV *NADA* actually filled its 110,000 sheep-carrying capacity, then even a 2,000-sheep mortality over a long voyage would be considered non-reportable (that is, 'humane').[84]

The example of sheep transport on a large animal carrier demonstrates that observed mortality rates need to be understood in the context of the number of animals transported, which will impact the raw number of lives lost as part of the transport process. For example, one British study indicates an average mortality rate of 0.27 per cent for chickens in a 2009 survey.[85] On the face of it, this would seem to be a 'low' observable average mortality rate. However, the study included 13.3 million chickens, suggesting that the number of animals killed as part of the transport process equated to approximately 36,000 animals over the survey period; hardly an insignificant number.[86] It is also useful to note that mortality rates are 'dead on arrival' figures, so they do not include non-lethal injury rates.[87]

The fine detail of commonplace practices within the context of live animal transport provides a more complete perspective on the potential violence experienced by animals as part of the circulation. One important detail is that the mortality of animals during transport is in part affected by their treatment prior to transport. Sick or injured animals are more likely to not survive the journey.[88] For example, one study of broiler chicken mortality during transport found that dead on arrival rates were 'dependent not only on the pre-slaughter steps but on the rearing conditions as a whole, which also led to losses before loading'.[89] Note that in the case of chickens, as discussed in Chapter 4, catching and crating methods, whether by human operators or machines, have a direct capacity to inflict lethal harm prior to transport. The stress animals experience during transport will also be related to their experiences interacting with humans prior to transport: 'if pigs are handled gently on 2–3 days during development, they are easier to handle and their welfare is better during transport'.[90] It is also worth noting that animals are often denied food prior to transport, sometimes as a method to 'keep the trucks clean'.[91] This highlights that the outcomes for animals in relation to welfare – stress, injury, death – are potentially cumulative within a supply chain, and not isolated to a specific phase of production.

As the above indicates, along the whole pathway of transferring animals from one location to another, we encounter sites of friction and antagonism. For example, the processes involved in loading and unloading animals onto transport are a hotspot for injury to animals (and, as I shall discuss below, a potential site of friction between human labour and animal labour). This is in part because production processes have to work directly against the resistance of animals to being transported: 'when being loaded on to a vehicle, animals have to be moved into an unfamiliar, restricted and darkened area, an experience which may be aversive'.[92] Animals have to further encounter narrow chutes and difficult terrain, including steep inclines such as ramps. This space of stress produces resistance, which is countered by open coercion:

> The animals may refuse and even turn their sides towards the ramp. . . . In addition, because pigs balk on these steep ramps, handlers may become frustrated by the hesitation leading to harsher handling and increased use of the electric prod. . . . Pigs that are difficult to handle tend to receive 'harsher' treatment during loading than pigs that are easy to handle.[93]

The electric cattle prod, or similar 'moving devices'[94] such as paddles, induce pain and stress as a means to coerce animals to undertake transport.[95] The use of fear-inducing techniques, such as trained dogs, achieves a similar effect. Forms of coercion that visibly scar and damage animals, such as beating them or dragging them into the transport vehicle, will reduce the value of the animal at the destination and risk mortality during transport; thus technologies such as paddles, whips[96] and cattle prods have been a useful innovation in creating methods to incentivise motion while applying a 'clean' violence which leaves little trace and thus does not injure value.[97] As I will discuss in Chapter 6, the development of techniques which incentivise animals to move towards a new phase of production, such as the use of curved cattle races, are an example of the way production systems continually seek to respond to, capture and redeploy animal resistance towards improving the productivity of the system itself.[98] But in many cases brute force replaces gentler techniques; for example, 'downer' animals – that is, animals who have been severely injured during transportation – may simply be dragged off the carrier with ropes or chains.[99]

The transport journey itself is a site of stress, injury and death for animals: this is of course one of the main reasons why transport has been such a focus of sustained animal advocacy.[100] It is tempting to imagine that journey length alone determines the welfare of animals. However, the issue of journey time is complex because a range of adjacent factors will determine the level of potential harm experienced by animals.[101] These different factors, including the environmental conditions (such as temperature[102] or the availability of water and food)[103] of the transporter, the driving style and route of the transport operator,[104] and the loading density of the transport[105] will impact the 'welfare' of animals. Journey length intensifies all of these factors: a road-based cattle truck without a watering system may result in minimal mortality or injury over a short distance, while the same truck carrying many animals over sixteen hours in above 30° Celsius temperatures is more likely to impose severe suffering and death. Journey length thus can multiply risks for animals:

> as journeys continue, the duration of the journey becomes more and more important in its effects on welfare. Animals travelling to slaughter are not given the space and comfort that a racehorse or showjumper are given. They are much more active, using much more energy, than an animal that is not transported. As a result, they become more fatigued, more in need of water, more in need of food, more affected by any adverse conditions, more immunosuppressed, more susceptible to disease and sometimes more exposed to pathogens on a long journey than on a short journey.[106]

As I have observed above, there are a number of structural factors within the global meat industry that suggest long-range transport is a reality for many animals. This means that the geographic expansion of the production process has probably increased average journey times for live animals used as food. In some markets, extraordinarily long-range transport is a structural condition of the business; thus, for example in Australia, over 50 per cent of livestock journeys occur in the hot regions of the north, with most journeys exceeding 500km and some reaching 3,000km.[107] This situation is more extreme for animals transported by sea, where, in the case of Australian live export ships, the length of transport extends to between seven and twenty-three days, as animals are shipped over many thousands of kilometres.[108]

The minute detail of this transport reveals its particular cruelty. Transport in itself need not impose suffering; however, the economies of scale that are required to make mass transport of live animals financially viable are essentially antagonistic to creating an environment which does not exert stress, discomfort and pain, and for at least some animals, mortality. In the case of sheep who are transported by ship, approximately 100 animals will be placed in a pen 8 x 4 m; they will spend the whole journey in this space, pens will not be cleaned: 'in the sheep pens the excreta builds up over the duration of the voyage, and providing it is not too hot or humid, a relatively soft and crumbly material develops, which is suitable for the sheep to lie on'. In humid climates, this underfoot material will turn to a slurry which sheep will need to navigate and lie in.[109] In addition, animals over long journeys will need to endure heat stress, ammonia exposure from animal excreta, high levels of noise and motion sickness.[110]

In a sense here we strike at least one of the many contradictions between achievement of 'welfare' goals (however they may be defined, in whose interests, and how they might be regulated) and the reality of the economic structure of meat production, which pulls in the other direction.[111] Almost everywhere we find that 'welfare' must be balanced against profitability; and thus the level of violence applied to animals becomes a measure of the surplus that it is possible to extract.

One area where animal welfare is in clear competition with the economic viability of animal transport is in relation to the stocking densities within transport carriers. High stocking densities compromise the welfare outcomes of animals transported.[112] But stocking density is a key factor in the economic viability of transport: the impulse for transporters would be simply to transport as much stock as possible to reduce the unit cost of transport. It is true that high stocking densities can damage 'stock' and therefore impact financial viability, particularly if animals arrive dead or so severely injured that this in turn injures their economic value. Considerations of stocking densities will be paramount for 'high-value' animals that are transported, such as breeding animals. However, the economics are arguably very different for 'low-value' animals transported for food, where stock losses will be weighed against total profits gained by maximising density. Here a cruel balance is struck; production gambles between the potential loss of animals, affecting profitability, and the potential gain of maximising the value of each shipment through expanding the available stock for sale. Meaningful adherence to 'welfare' principles in this picture becomes extraordinarily abstract and will quickly be compromised to meet the economic imperatives of industry.

Thrift is everything within the context of an efficient competitive global supply chain. This is where steering towards questions of value rather than 'welfare' is starkly clarifying if we want to understand the particularities of the relation between animals, capital and circulation. In particular, this helps us get closer to understanding why live animal transport – that is, the movement of animals as raw materials – rather than transport of refrigerated meat – that is, the movement of the dead, 'finished' consumption commodity – is preferred. Why is the transport of live animals 'cheaper and easier than the refrigerated transport necessary for the long-distance carcass trade'?[113] At least one answer is this: the industrial-scale refrigeration systems required for the transport of dead animals, adequate to sustain the integrity of the commodity within a value chain, are expensive. The value of being able to consistently chill meat for transport is dependent on a market being available at a destination that can effectively realise the value of chilled meat. Thus, in destinations without effective refrigeration capacity, or markets where the domestic transport infrastructure is not able to support transfers of refrigerated products, then live animals become more economically viable (marketable).

But this perspective is treating the value chain as simply being driven by available technologies. If we focus on labour instead then we can complete the picture, as labour, both human and, as we shall see below, animal, generates opportunities for value creation which, as a result, come to dictate the structure of value chains. In a simple sense, the use value of human labour is an important determinant of the structure of value chains in the meat industry (as it is for any industry). Transport of live animals would not be possible if there was not a labour force available to perform the difficult task of transferring live animals from one part of the value chain to another. If the labour involved in transporting live animals was comparatively high value, then this would impact the viability of live animal transport, perhaps making refrigerated meat a more viable option for a supply chain (and perhaps influencing investment decisions, such as refrigeration capacity at destinations). Similarly, and this is a vital observation, the capacity of destination countries to efficiently slaughter animals will determine the viability of a live animal transport business; slaughter and processing labour costs will be one of the chief cost drivers that will determine the comparable ability of a destination to receive live animals. If slaughterhouse labour costs in a destination market are high, then this will fundamentally impact the economics of the demand for live animals.

In a material sense, then, human labour is one variable component within the live animal trade; this labour can be twisted, shaped and redeployed in ways that can extract or suck ever more value from existing processes. It is perhaps for this reason that, as I described above, European Union legislation mandating improved welfare regulation for the transport of live animals did not lead to reduced live animal transport despite the significant cost imposed on transporters.[114] Indeed, the audit report indicated that the continuing increase in live animals transported was a result of a failure by some unscrupulous, 'unfair' competitors to enforce the mandated welfare regulations or pay respect to regulations on driving times.[115] In other words, some supply-chain operators were happy to find productive efficiencies in lowering both animal welfare and labour rights standards. This is perhaps indicative of a general interplay between human labour and animal welfare within transportation processes in the global meat industry, sometimes generating points of friction between the interests of humans and those of animals in the supply chain. One example I have already given above relates to the use of coercive measures, such as whips or cattle prods, to coax animals onto transport. The frequency of the use of such measures is arguably related to a number of factors, including the design of loading facilities.[116] But it is also influenced by the pressure on human labour to meet the demands placed upon it by the timing of production processes. Where human workers are pressed to meet deadlines imposed by the supply chain, then animals will also be pressed to conform to these same deadlines. Human workers will utilise available means, including outright modes of physical coercion, in order to meet production deadlines.[117] It is perhaps for this reason that loading and unloading animals into and from transport carriers is a potential site of stress and injury for both animals and humans.[118] The economics of transport means there is no time to gently convince animals to board a transport. On the contrary, there will be every pressure to force animals to take the journey, and human workers almost invariably will be compelled by material circumstances to take on this dangerous physical labour of coaxing animals onto transport.[119] In a sense, transport is merely one locality of struggle within a broader global meat industry that is restructuring itself, and with it, restructuring the value of labour: 'they have stepped up the pace of mechanisation and intensified the labour process, increasing the risk of workplace injury'.[120]

It is for this reason that the transport journey is potentially a space for not only violence towards animals, but towards human workers as well. Naturally the tendency of transport operations will be to keep labour costs to a minimum, either through the use of low-wage labour, or through the use of thin staffing levels, or some combination of both. Staffing levels, including the availability of veterinarians during the journey, will impact the capacity of workers to minimise violence towards animals: certainly, this is the case where there are large shipments of animals which do not make individual checks of animals feasible.[121] As in other parts of the meat industry, some labour within transport can be dangerous to human workers.[122] Road transport journeys can be long and drivers will bear a personal risk for industry practices which rely upon elongated transport journeys utilising few human operators.[123] Jennifer Woods and Temple Grandin's study of commercial livestock accidents in the United States suggests that long and irregular hours, and solo journeys, were a contributor to fatigue-related crashes; they note that 'some of the yearling and weaner calf loads are transported by solo drivers who may have trips over 20h'.[124] Naturally, road accidents resulting from fatigue not only risk injury and death for the driver, but also for the animals being transported: 'road accidents undo all other actions for the welfare of animals'.[125] But time is everything for the production processes, and the compulsion for transporters will be to ensure that the cargo is delivered 'just in time'. This means that other considerations – whether animal welfare or labour rights related – will become variable as the rhythms dictated by the global flow commodities within production processes take ultimate precedence. Thus a simple decision, such as a decision taken by a ship captain to avoid disembarking animals in the midst of high temperatures, will work against the rhythms set by the supply chains themselves: 'when the animals are at risk of heat stress the ship's master could delay entry to port until adequate crosswinds are assured, although they operate to a tight, co-coordinated schedule that would be a deterrent to such action'.[126]

Here, as elsewhere, we find human labour conditions in conflict with the conditions experienced by animals. In Chapter 4 I noted that within animal agriculture, human labour time is devoted towards the deployment of force relations to compel animal labour time. This relation is essentially antagonistic. Within the above study of circulation, we have found the same antagonistic relation between humans and animals. And this antagonism is not merely between humans and animals, but, also as discussed in Chapter 4, represents a contest between animals and fixed capital. Machines and enclosures (or more accurately, if we think of transport vessels, machines which are enclosures) dominate the social world of animals in circulation, so that the experience of transport is directly an antagonistic relation with this fixed capital. In this sense, circulation of live animals 'mobilises' the violence found in animal agriculture; it makes portable that antagonistic relation. Today, the circulation of animals that is part of capitalist animal agriculture has established a mobile hell for the animals who are compelled to endure it. But, in describing the purgatory that sits between stages of production, I have neglected an important 'factor': namely, I have not so far addressed the role of animal labour within the process of circulation. Animals do not enter circulation as passive commodities. These beings are alive; moreover, as we shall discover, they continue to perform metabolic labour along the long, arduous transport route. It is the latter activity which establishes all possibility for the maintenance of value during circulation. If animals did not perform this metabolic labour, then live animal transport would not be possible.

Animal labour within circulation

In this chapter, I have so far treated animals as simply another raw non-variable commodity that is worked on for the purposes of valorisation within a value chain. This framing assumes, as per mainstay approaches, that animals are passive materials that are moved, laboured upon and transformed. However, animals are not mere raw materials. In this sense the question of animal labour is also fundamental. As discussed in Chapter 4, productive processes which derive value from animals depend upon a capacity for animals to both reproduce their own value and produce surplus. Allow me to repeat the formulation that Marx provides in *Capital*:

> While productive labour is changing the means of production into constituent elements of a new product, their value undergoes a metempsychosis ['*Seelen wandrung*'/'transmigration']. . . . The worker is unable to add new labour, to create new value, without at the same time preserving old values, because the labour he adds must be of a specific useful kind, and he cannot do work of a useful kind without employing products as the means of production of a new product, and thereby transferring their value to the new product.[127]

For much human labour (though, as discussed in Chapter 4, certainly not all) this means that this labour works on an object of production which is understood as distinct from one's own body, and this process 'consumes' a use value and, simultaneously, produces a new use value which contains the old use value within it ('what is produced is a new use-value in which the old exchange-value re-appears').[128] As we have seen, this narrative must be amended for food animals, at least with respect to the fact that the primary alienation from the means of production which Marx describes as part of the process of value transmigration (behind the worker's back) is actually located in close proximity to the labouring animal: in this case, the animal works on their own body, consuming old use values and producing new use values seamlessly in their own body's materiality. Food animals are both constant and variable capital, simultaneously.

Relevant to the circulation of capital, what is vital here is that animals must reproduce their own value in themselves (as a means of production) and simultaneously, through their labour, make themselves available for additional value to be realised at a different stage of production. Live animal transport relies absolutely on this labour; if it were not for this labour then live animal transport would not exist. Above I posed Phillips's question: Why is the transport of live animals 'cheaper and easier than the refrigerated transport necessary for the long-distance carcass trade'? One solution, as I discussed, is that the capital costs involved in exporting meat (that is, the costs of refrigerated transport and/ or slaughter costs before export) are high, relative to the costs of exporting live animals. Another solution, and one that is implied by the previous alternative, is that the human labour costs at destination to slaughter and process animals, and the human labour costs involved in transporting animals, provide an incentive for live animal transport. Presumably, if the capital costs of transport were too high, or the labour costs of transport or labour costs at destination were relatively high, then live animal transport would not occur.

However, both of these perspectives rely on treating animals as mere raw material, since human labour and available technologies and infrastructure are foregrounded as a priority for the value exchange. But a different view is this: *it is cheaper to transport live animals because of the low relative cost of the labour of animals*. This amounts to the same thing as saying that the value animals produce, including while they are being transported (that is, surplus value in addition to the costs of reproducing the capital value of animals themselves) is relatively high; this value is high enough to eclipse the value that might be gained through converting live animals to dead meat at an earlier stage in the value chain. Here, we treat the metabolic labour of animals upon themselves as essential to the process of live animal transport. Quite simply, if these animals did not labour upon themselves to reproduce their own life during the period of circulation time, then it would not be possible to realise value through transport.

We can see this animal labour time in effect when we look at different examples of circulation. In its most basic form, we see this reality in the decision of a smallhold farmer to walk animals to a marketplace or a place of slaughter in order to realise an exchange value for them. Assuming this farmer has no access to mechanised transport, or no capacity to slaughter and refrigerate animals, then the argument for walking animals to a locality where they can be 'processed' remains strong: it is more cost-efficient to rely on slaughter efficiencies that exist elsewhere in the value chain (for example, a local town abattoir where there are economies of scale and available technologies and human labour), and take advantage of a local market where meat can be exchanged for money. So, in this case, animals are made to walk themselves to their own deaths. Animal labour is deployed profitably in the value chain. This labour of animals is potentially fraught; some may not survive the journey. Yet if enough animals survive, then this labour makes absolute sense to exploit, since the farmer can trust the animals to both maintain their own value in themselves (reproduce their own capital value, 'maintain old values') while also, in the process of transferring themselves from one site in the production process to another, enabling a new value to be realised (that is, for the animals to become meat). If animals could not move themselves, then they could not transfer their value or realise a new value. More importantly, if animals could not survive the journey to market – that is, reproduce their own value in themselves by continuing to live – then value could not be transferred. Here, the character of the labour of these animals includes a metabolic labour on themselves (to maintain their value) and simultaneously a power of movement (or 'automobility')[129] which allows for value realisation.

Perhaps it might be argued that the mass transport of animals by machines removes the necessity of animal labour, since it is through the investment of producers and businesses in technologies and infrastructure in mechanised transport that animals are 'saved' the labour of having to transport themselves over long distances. However, once again, this sort of perspective defers back to a view that animals can simply be regarded as raw commodities that are carted passively across large distances, like 'cotton or iron'.[130] A different view, one which foregrounds the labour of animals, cannot avoid the reality that once again, at a primary level, the reason that a decision can be taken to transport living animals over long distances, rather than just their dead bodies as meat, *most fundamentally* depends on the living capacity of animals to reproduce their own value – that is, to keep in place, preserve and faithfully transcribe the value of their old selves – in order to make themselves available to acquire a new value upon disembarkation. If the animals transported lacked this capacity, if they all refused to eat (as a significant number do through systemic inappetence)[131] or attained diseases or injury that damaged final exchange values, then live animal transport would not exist. It is because animals can provide this labour – a self-labour that maintains the value of the initial capital, and simultaneously is able to arrive at destination in a form upon which a new use value can be attained – that the live animal trade exists. Here, metabolic labour is essential: no metabolic labour, no live transport.

Further, recognising animal labour alters how we view circulation within capitalist economies, particularly where this relates to living beings. Under Marx's schema, circulation time necessarily ruptures production time, expanding the turnover time of capital, without necessarily expanding the time during which value is added in production:

> The general law is that *all circulation costs that arise simply from a change in form of the commodity cannot add any value to it.* They are simply costs involved in realizing the value or transforming it from one form to another. The capital expended in these costs (including the labour it commands) belongs to the *faux frais* of capitalist production. The replacement of these costs must come from the surplus product, and from the standpoint of the capitalist class as a whole it forms a deduction of surplus-value or surplus-product, in just the same way as the time the worker needs to buy his means of subsistence is lost time for him.[132]

This treatment of circulation time as the *'faux frais'* (or 'overhead costs')[133] means that transport does not necessarily alter the finished product, but merely makes possible the realisation of the use value in the product. To what extent does Marx's general rule on circulation costs apply to live animal transport? Transport certainly exerts a physical toll on animals, so that weight loss or 'shrinkage' is a standard feature.[134] From this perspective, we might take the view that these animals when transported are like a perishable raw material, similar to fruit or vegetables, that deteriorates during circulation. Certainly this appears to be the way animals are treated, and it would be in line with the general rule above, which treats circulation time as distinct from production time. In this understanding, transport moves a finished product, and thus the productivity of transport relates to efficiencies gained by and through circulation, and not in relation to a change in the qualities of the finished product:[135]

> The quantity of products is not increased by their transport. The change in their natural properties that may be effected by transport is also, certain exceptions apart, not an intended useful effect, but rather an unavoidable evil. But the use-value of things is realized only in their consumption, and their consumption may make a change of location necessary, and thus also the additional production process of the transport industry. The productive capital invested in this industry thus adds value to the products transported, partly through the value carried over from the means of transport, partly through the value added by the work of transport. This latter addition of value can be divided, as with all capitalist production, into replacement of wages and surplus-value.[136]

Transport moves a finished product to a site where its use value can be realised. Thus, productivity gains in efficiencies in transport (whether through technologies or human labour practices) produce a more effective realisation of value, but do not necessarily change the product that is transported.

However, perhaps animal transport is an exception to the above 'general law'. This is because a finished product is not necessarily transported in live animal transport, but one which is in the process of being finished. This is certainly the case for long-distance transport of animals, where transport time must be taken into account during the production phase to ensure that the animal is ready at arrival for the next phase of production. For example, in the case of Australian producers, live animal export is one avenue utilised to move animals where there is an incapacity to 'finish' them within a domestic region. One report notes that there were:

> advantages in the added marketing flexibility live exports provided. In particular, this included the ability to market unfinished livestock in situations where adverse seasonal conditions precluded those stock being finished to slaughter

weights, and the related ability to time the disposal of those stock to fit in with seasonal pasture growth or labour requirements.[137]

Here, live export serves a function in dealing with the problems of overproduction, including the incapacity of animal agriculture to provide ongoing security to animals during periods of seasonal variation and drought.[138] Regardless of whether this live export is useful as a way to 'dispose' of stock when it is not viable any longer for animal agriculture producers to meet the future costs of sustaining these lives, or whether the existence of mechanised transport allows for the structuring of production to stage the release of animals when market conditions are ripe,[139] in all cases, the metabolic labour of animals on themselves is foundational in order for these opportunities for value realisation to present themselves. And in this sense, for animals themselves, the production phase continues while they are being transported: viability will depend upon these animals continuing to feed, to stay alive, to maintain value in themselves. These animals are not 'finished': they continue to be in production on the ship, since the metabolic labour of these animals is ongoing.

This production remains a site of political antagonism. The microdynamics of this labour, the everyday toil and struggle of animals that is transformed into a value-producing activity, is here of immense importance in understanding the role that animals play within a value chain. I described above the precarious economic balancing act involved in stocking densities: a large number of animals must be placed in a small space in order to make transport viable, but there is a simultaneous reality that very high stocking densities will lead to large numbers of animals being injured or killed, compromising profitability. Animals who sit at the crux of this accounting dilemma face a 'struggle to the death';[140] their labour is simply about surviving a journey that will threaten their existence. Friction marks this whole process.

Here, labour is not merely confined to metabolic labour on oneself, but the active process of staying alive and avoiding injury. One example of animal labour in the context of transport is the maintenance of standing positions by animals being transported. It is not only transporters who have a vested interest in preventing injury or death for animals who are transported. Animals themselves too, of course, actively avoid possible injury or death during the transport process (avoidance of pain and the fear of death here are motivating).[141] For example, many cattle who are transported over road journeys are reluctant to sit. This means the road journey is a prolonged example of 'forced standing' in which anxious animals exert their strength for a long period, attempting to keep their balance while experiencing increasing fatigue in an unstable environment comprising many other potentially agitated animals. The costs for some animals – such as bovine – if they fail to maintain their balance will potentially be torturous injury (for example, a fracture) to themselves or other animals:

> Cattle do not readily lie down while being transported and this forced standing causes them to become physically tired during transport in a way that is not seen in pigs and sheep. Due to this behaviour, transport is stressful for cattle and makes them fatigue. The continuous increase in creatine kinase activity with an increase in transport time noted in this study indicates increasing muscular fatigue, which could be attributed to swaying, restlessness and loss of balance behaviours of animals during transport.[142]

Similar compensatory movement occurs within long-distance live-animal sea transport.[143] Stocking densities thus are not merely aimed at achieving human labour efficiencies, but animal labour efficiencies. Increased stocking density does improve human labour efficiencies: it means more animals are transported for each hour of paid human labour. But higher stocking density will also make the most of animal labour time, since it more efficiently deploys a mass of animal labour towards a productive end. The intensity of this labour will be pushed to the border between life and death; the labour of these animals will be characterised by a contest to survive the environmental factors that assault them, and would otherwise seek to diminish them.

Here the labour of animals to maintain the value in themselves – that is, allow for an original value to emerge undamaged and encapsulated in a new value at the end of the journey – is impossible to distinguish from a generalised struggle to survive in the face of the antagonistic environment of transport. This will be a moment-by-moment struggle, so that even a decision by a driver to approach a corner at speed, or divert a route over a rocky terrain in order to meet a deadline,[144] will have to be countered by animal labour to head off the potential threat of death or injury that may result:

> loss of balance is a major determinant in injuries in transported cattle. The author found that one-third of events where cattle were floored during transport were caused by loss of balance during cornering. These behaviours are not common in the farms and the animals showed the behaviours in an attempt to cope with the challenging environment.[145]

Animals here must work; they must sway and push themselves to stay upright in an environment that threatens to overwhelm them. In this sense, animal labour time is again equivalent to resistance: a struggle to survive against conditions that would otherwise diminish life; a struggle that is then valorised within a labour chain as a proceed from conflict. It is because animals survive that value becomes possible upon disembarkation. Animals here maintain value in themselves, and in so doing, make themselves available as a new use value. This means they labour productively. They have to, or the business model collapses.

Incorporating animal labour into the value process of the circulation of commodities allows us thus to look at live animal transport in a different way; or at least to see this circulation as more than just the movement of raw materials and 'finished' commodities. As we have seen, technological changes in transport have facilitated the globalisation of animal agriculture, allowing production to take advantage of 'specialisation' in different localities, including across borders. Here human labour is undoubtably an important factor; the relative price of labour prior to transport and at destination shapes the demand for circulation, and the price of labour during transport, where operators will seek to maximise labour efficiencies, will also shape the efficacy of transport. But the metabolic labour of animals cannot be ignored; it is essential to enable 'live' animal transport. And this labour continues the production of these animals upon themselves as raw materials into the circulation phase, almost as if production did not stop.

For animals, production always continues; its drone is ever-present in their ears. It continues throughout their lives, since for food animals, their lifetime is experienced as production time. Once again, there is no working day for animals. This means that even when these animals are transported from one site of production to another, labour does not stop; the interruption to board a ship is, in more ways than one, no vacation. They must continue to labour on themselves if they want to survive. If animals were not able to provide this labour, they could not be transported alive. Further, the more brutal the conditions of this transport – the more it reflects an unflinching and naked calculation of relative mortality rates, pre and post liveweight calculations, and seasonal prices attained at disembarkation – the more this labour of animals appears as a purely distilled resistant will to survive; that is, a struggle to survive against an aversive environment that would otherwise injure and kill. But despite the life-and-death stakes of this resistance, it is nonetheless captured by capital as a value-producing moment, a moment where new use values are miraculously brought into being. Here, as I shall discuss in the next chapter, resistance itself is subsumed by capitalist processes and turned into a parasitic productivity.

6   Resistance

Commodities cannot themselves go to market and perform exchanges in their own right. We must, therefore, have recourse to their guardians, who are possessors of commodities. Commodities are things, and therefore lack the power to resist man. If they are unwilling, he can use force; in other words, he can take possession of them.

Karl Marx, *Capital*, vol. 1[1]

Hedges and fences were erected to hinder escapes. Wooden triangular-shaped yokes would be fitted around necks to hinder movement. Wooden clogs would be fastened around back legs to hinder jumping or running. Some farmers would actually cut the leg tendons of their workers. Others clipped the wings of chickens, turkeys, and geese to prevent flight, and still others would blind animals by using a 'red hot knitting needle.' If these measures failed, there were additional implementations. Local pounds were built for the captured. Ear-marks and brands were increasingly used as a means of identification, and nose-ringing prevented the maroons, especially pigs, from digging into the local fields.

Jason Hribal, 'Animals Are Part of the Working Class'[2]

In Chapters 4 and 5, I have argued that the intensive model of animal production under capitalism continually adapts to and subsumes the resistance of animals in order to enable enhanced productivity. In some cases, as discussed in Chapter 4, this involves playing off human labour time against animal labour time: thus a human labour-saving device, such as the chicken-harvesting machine, is introduced in order to reduce human labour time, dominating animals more effectively in order to speed up exchange and turnover associated with animal labour time. Alternatively, as discussed in Chapter 5, fixed capital interacts with animal resistance in a combative fashion as part of the valorisation process; for example, in the hull of a live transport ship, or in a road-based livestock carrier, the ability of animals to survive the ordeal – that is, resist the play of forces which would otherwise send them to an early death – enables the realisation of value. In all of these cases, animal resistance is fundamental. In some cases, capitalist animal agriculture adapts to and reworks the resistance of animals to bend it towards productivity; in other cases, resistance is nullified in order to smooth and speed up processes.

This chapter turns to think more carefully about resistance itself, how it might be conceptualised in relation to animals, and the way in which we find, again and again, a contest between fixed capital and animal labour as a central antagonism of industrial capitalism. The chapter takes one main example of the role of animal resistance within food production: that is, the case study of global industrialised fisheries. In part, the choice of fishes is informed by the near complete absence of fisheries as a site of contemporary interest for animal advocates. This contrasts, perhaps paradoxically, with the extraordinary extent of global fisheries. Today fishes are reported to be the most traded global food commodity.[3] This means that trillions of fishes, alive and dead, whole or in parts, are hunted down, contained, slaughtered and made to constantly circulate across waters, territories, the globe, in order to realise value. But the other reason fishes are a focus is that, as we shall see, resistance and the development of technologies to overcome this resistance appear as central to the material interactions in production, and are arguably definitive of industrial-scale fisheries under capitalism. During this period when capitalist economies subsumed fisheries, we have seen extraordinary developments in human relations with sea creatures: not just the industrialisation of the hunting of fishes but, in the latter half of the twentieth century and beyond, the development of mechanised farming techniques – aquaculture – as a response to the problem of fish resistance. As I shall argue, fish resistance demonstrates something about the essential conflict or antagonism that circulates the utilisation of animals within industrial capitalism, a friction that is co-productive of the world we see before us.

Fisheries in context

In 2016, Daniel Pauly and Dirk Zeller provided a new global overview of the extent of industrial, subsistence and recreational fishing.[4] The study attempted to provide a more comprehensive global perspective on fisheries, including unreported catches and subsistence fishing. Perhaps the most pressing policy driver for this sort of data is the growing global crisis in relation to the sustainability of wild fish capture. The UN Food and Agriculture Organization claims that in 2011, some '28.8 percent of fish stocks were estimated as fished at a biologically unsustainable level'. To an extent this pillage is 'epochal' in character, representing a planetary shift. It is little wonder that Nobel Prize winner Paul Crutzen, in proposing the geological time period of the Anthropocene, singled out mechanised fishing as one example of a significant site of planetary-scale human impact.[5] The crisis ahead is that the depletion of fish populations may have reached an irreversible stage. In other words, we may have reached the point where there is a fundamental asymmetry between the mass self-reproduction of fishes (their gestational labour) and the insatiable drive of industrial fisheries to suck the oceans dry.[6]

It is no secret that it was the industrialisation of wild fish capture that helped generate the crisis taking place within the oceans. Indeed, Pauly and Zeller make this clear; their construction of data shows that from 1950 onwards, industrial fish capture comes to dominate all global fish capture, as local small-scale fishing continues to account for a proportionately smaller and smaller part of the global picture.[7] Note that there is a strong geopolitical aspect that shapes how we should see this data: we know that over the last half-century, increasingly large multinational interests have hunted for fishes in the waters of developing countries, competing with local subsistence fishers. Today these large-scale international businesses capture creatures who will become commodities; most of these fishes will be processed and sold elsewhere, often ending up on the plates of consumers in the Global North.

We are presented here with the image of fishes being subsumed by capital: industrialised fishing aims to capture the labour and energies of fishes as a surplus-generating activity. In so far as industrial wild capture fisheries hunt down fishes in 'nature', this conforms to a process of 'formal subsumption' as described in Chapter 4. As discussed, a process of formal subsumption involves immersion of an activity which was previously outside of the formal productive circuits of capitalism into a surplus-creating activity. Wild fish capture conforms to this model of formal subsumption. Fishes perform the labour of life in the oceans: gestational labour bringing new life into the world; metabolic labour growing, developing; networks of care labour that allow this social reproduction. Industrial fisheries hunt down and drag these products of labour from the seas, effectively subsuming a labour process that was previously 'unproductive' (at least from the standpoint of capital, not for the fishes) and reorienting this work as 'productive' of surplus. All capitalist extraction is essentially parasitic, at least in so far as it sucks value (and value measured in life; that is, time) in a way that is, by definition, exploitative. Wild capture industrial fisheries are an extreme vision of this parasitism.

And this parasitism is hardly efficient. At least one disturbing aspect of this global business is the large number of fishes that are 'discarded' as part of the fishing industry. Discards mean by-catch and other species that are not marketable, who are thrown back into the ocean after they have been hunted down and killed – often because they are too small for market, belong to a non-marketable species, or because a more profitable species is subsequently caught by the fishing vessel, forcing a financial decision to jettison the less profitable haul. As Pauly and Zeller highlight, 'discards' account for a large proportion of animals caught: noticeably more than global subsistence fishing, and approaching the numbers globally caught by small-scale commercial (or artisanal) fisheries.[8] These industrial-scale discards represent an extraordinary example of the way in which capitalist overproduction interacts with waste, and not just at the consumption end. From the perspective of capitalist value, 'wastage' is not value production – hence the tragedies of production we see everywhere under capitalism, which routinely disposes of lives and resources without any need for ceremony. This conforms to what Collard and Dempsey have described with their concept of 'outcast surplus'; that is, objects and relations that might be considered 'superfluous as far as capital accumulation is concerned'.[9] Gillespie, for example, discusses male calves disposed of by the dairy industry:

> these calves are sometimes killed at or shortly after birth as 'waste' or 'discards' from the dairy industry and may be composted on the farm or sent for rendering. Their value is low and teeters on the edge of a failed cost–benefit calculation regarding cost of feed versus potential capital that might be generated from their slaughter.[10]

Gillespie extends this analysis to pay attention to dairy cows who are disposed of as soon-to-be-slaughtered commodities at cull auctions;[11] animals who have outlived their primary 'purpose' in production and become, at best, opportunities for low-value commodification as a method of recuperating input costs. These animals have been sucked dry by capitalist animal agriculture; the cull auction becomes an opportunity for an additional line of income. However, the example of 'discards' I am describing here in the fishing industry differs from the 'death worlds' of cull auctions that Gillespie narrates. Within industrial fisheries, the fishes who are discarded go through a quick transition from unproductive to productive to unproductive again. At first, these animals find themselves hauled on decks, their lifetime of labour subsumed formally within the value structure of capitalist exchange. And then, seemingly moments after their lives are extinguished, they are returned dead to the oceans, exchanged for more promising 'stock'. During their ordeal their lifework was treated momentarily as 'productive'. It glimmered in the oceans with the promise of value, and was seized upon. The commodity was born. Yet this labour can become unproductive in a moment, and the organic body, destroyed in this process of fossicking for value, discarded. The commodity is no more again, replaced by another. For fisheries, this process of sorting through the oceans to find value is part of the business of turning a profit. Each new day offers opportunities for value to be seized; some days, we presume, are profitable, some days less so. For fishes, on the other hand, the movement from unproductive to productive to unproductive is not an ordeal they can recover from.

Before we move to the problem of fish resistance, it is worth understanding the totality of human interaction with fishes within capitalist fisheries. Today, human wild fish capture certainly accounts for a large proportion of all fishes caught globally; however, industrialised fishing is shifting from the use of mechanised predation towards intensive fish farming in the context of aquaculture. Following an explosion in the use of aquaculture since the 1990s (at a growth rate of around 9.5 per cent per year),[12] farmed fishes now account for more than half of the fish consumed by humans.[13] Today fish farming has overtaken beef farming globally as a source of animal protein.[14] Aquaculture – factory farms for fishes – looks to be positioned as an essential element within global food supply. Fish farms are of course interesting from the perspective of value, as they represent a 'real subsumption' of fish labour; I shall return to this below.

Data has been available from national and international organisations on commercial fishing quantities; but most of these measures, such as those maintained by the UN Food and Agriculture Organization,[15] refer to sea animals produced for food by weight rather than number, and thus veil from public perception the actual number of sea animals used by humans. In 2010 a UK-based organisation, Fishcount.org.uk, released a pioneering report which attempted to estimate the number of wild sea animals killed each year as part of commercial fishing. Based on their own research, Fishcount.org.uk and the report's lead author, Alison Mood, proposed a sobering statistic: namely, that between 0.97 and 2.7 trillion wild fishes are slaughtered every year through commercial fishing.[16] Fishcount.org.uk suggests that in 2017, between 51 and 161 billion fishes were slaughtered in aquaculture.[17] As discussed in Chapter 1, and to put these figures in perspective, the UN Food and Agriculture Organization data indicates that around 79 billion land animals were slaughtered in 2020.

166 | ANIMALS AND CAPITAL

As I have suggested in Chapter 3, perhaps all processes of commodification, including that of human labour commodification, 'efface' the material body in some way. But the massive volume of suffering for fishes associated with this significant industry is particularly nightmarish and worth highlighting.[18] Despite the huge scale of the industry, there is little evidence of significant 'welfare' precautions taken in the context of fishing practices to reduce the suffering experienced by fishes as part of their utilisation by humans. There are a number of publicly documented welfare concerns surrounding recreational and industrial fishing practices, including around line fishing, net fishing and the trauma associated with the capture and transport of live fishes.[19]

However, arguably, the mode of slaughter used to kill fishes in most fishing industry practices offers us the most telling insight into the poverty of current basic welfare protections available to fishes that are used by humans. By far, the most prevalent means of slaughter utilised by the fishing industry is death by asphyxiation, where fishes are left in the open air to die slowly as their bodies are deprived of oxygen. Fishes usually take a long time to die this way, and studies have shown that the period until stunning – that is, the period fish suffer for before they are unconscious – is considerable. Rainbow trout take some 15 minutes before they are stunned; sea bream 25 minutes and sea bass, 60 minutes.[20] The prevalent practice of placing live fishes on an ice slurry is no better; indeed, it is likely to further prolong the period before fish are effectively stunned. Studies have shown that trout take between 28 and 198 minutes to be stunned using this method; salmon 60 minutes, sea bream 20 to 40 minutes.[21] Many fishes are subject to live gutting as part of the slaughter process. Some fishes continue to live during and after being gutted; one study indicates that stunning times vary between 25 and 60 minutes for gutted fish.[22] The use of carbon dioxide to stun fish may speed up stunning periods; however, it may also lead to a 'quick and violent reaction, such as repeated swimming around, attempts to escape from the tub and abnormal activity before stunning'.[23] In some cases, sea animals may take a relatively long time to be stunned using carbon dioxide; for example, 109 minutes for eels.[24] Many fishes are *indirectly* killed or injured by nets, hooks or other fishes before they land on board a ship (something I will discuss below). However, many forms of suffering are *directly*, intentionally, imposed on fishes as part of the killing process, often as a means to produce a desired marketable commodity at the end of the process (that is, fish meat). One example of this sort of metabolic labour is the practice of cutting fishes across the gills and returning them alive to water. This uses the beating hearts of fishes while they are still alive to flush blood from their bodies, supposedly to produce a desirable effect on fish meat in terms of taste and appearance. In the case of eels, a common practice is to place them in a salt-water bath to 'deslime them' – a process that eels are aversive towards – before they are eviscerated alive. The whole ordeal takes some 20 minutes.[25]

Despite these visceral horrors that are part and parcel of fishing and fishing industries, the advocacy challenge for pro-animal activists, scholars and workers remains daunting. While there are legal protections offered to many land animals that are routinely used for food, the same protections are not available for fishes.[26] In part, this situation is the result of a lack of agreement that fishes are capable of suffering, or at least that this suffering matters. There is some recognition that land animals used for food, experiments and recreation can suffer at human hands, and this shapes welfare laws and regulation aimed at minimising that suffering.[27] This in turn shapes the arguments made by animal advocates on behalf of land animals – which, in an environment where sentience is used as a measure of protection, usually involve balancing animal suffering against human utility.[28] In the case of fishes, there is no universal acceptance that fishes suffer, which in turn shapes the advocacy task. Advocates are forced to argue first that fish do indeed suffer (since this is contentious) and then, subsequently, to argue for minimal (often very minimal) welfare measures to be adopted to mitigate the intense volume of this suffering.[29]

This situation – in which advocates must argue that fishes feel pain, since this knowledge is not taken for granted – is at least in part a result of the uncertain science on fish suffering. There are indeed many scientific studies which have shown that some fishes do feel pain, and that this has significant welfare implications. Lynne Sneddon and her colleagues, for example, in 2003 performed experiments on rainbow trout, observing aversive behaviours in relation to potentially painful experiences, and they also observed that administering morphine to the fish significantly reduced the pain-related behaviours.[30] These studies, and the problems they raise, were further expanded upon by one of Sneddon's co-researchers, Victoria Braithwaite, in her 2010 book *Do Fish Feel Pain?*[31] Against this view, other scientists have consistently argued, perhaps as an echo of the view attributed to Descartes that animals are mere automata (the *bête-machine* doctrine),[32] that fishes do not experience suffering, only reaction to stimuli.[33] The uncertainty within the scientific community over whether fishes feel pain, combined with a public attachment to the maintenance of existing fishing practices, produces a somewhat perverse silence in relation to fish welfare, let alone deeper questions on the relations of fishes to capitalism, and what fish flourishing might look like as a political goal. The lack of consistent agreement on the question of fish suffering leads to inaction. For animal advocates, I would argue that there is now a tactical quandary over how we might respond to the massive human violence that is directed against fishes.

Do fish resist?

The above section highlights the magnitude of industrial fisheries under contemporary capitalist production, and the inadequacies of contemporary political frameworks – in particular, sentience-based welfare approaches – in effecting large-scale institutional change. It is with this in mind that in this chapter I will abandon the question of fish suffering – at least directly – and focus instead on understanding the potential of the question 'Do fish resist?' There are a number of reasons to adopt this approach. Resistance offers a different model for considering political agency. If we award moral recognition to animals on the basis of their sentience, then we argue that moral worth depends upon some innate capacity related to sentience (for example, the ability to feel pain or to experience emotion). For instance, Singer's foundational text *Animal Liberation* uses a utilitarian approach to suffering as a basis to weigh the moral claims of animals,[34] and as discussed in Chapter 1, Tom Regan's *The Case for Animal Rights* instead argues that animals, in so far as they are 'subjects of a life', have an intrinsic moral worth;[35] while Nussbaum applies the capabilities approach to animals to argue that animals have their own needs for flourishing that we must recognise.[36] Against these approaches, my interest in resistance is that it describes a form of political agency that need not be grounded in an innate capability or worth. If we think about resistance – for example, human political mobilisation against a totalitarian dictator – we are not initially concerned with recognising the moral worth of those who resist; we are instead interested in how those who resist are involved in relationships of power. This understanding of resistance draws explicitly from the tradition established by Foucault in understanding resistance as always in relation to power; in this reading, power describes the existence of contestation.[37] For Foucault, power involves:

> mobile and transitory points of resistance, producing cleavages in a society that shift about, fracturing unities and effecting regroupings, furrowing across individuals themselves, cutting them up and remoulding them, marking off irreducible regions in them, in their bodies and minds.[38]

Foucault's view of power as a frictional tussle of forces[39] allows resistive elements within relations of power to be understood as engaging 'agentially' within those relations, without having to demonstrate that those who resist possess capabilities worthy of moral recognition (language, reason, capacity for suffering, etc.). In some respects, keeping the dynamics of power in the frame, it is enough simply to understand that if there is power, there must be resistance.

This, as I shall discuss below, is essential for understanding the character of the labour and energies that are captured by fisheries. As I have argued so far in this book, capitalism might be understood as an antagonistic relationality with life; we see this prominently in the resistance of fishes to this mass-scale subsumption.

In order to understand fish resistance, it seems worth attending to the question of 'epistemology' and then to the concept of 'epistemic violence'.[40] In some respects the question 'Do fish resist?' can only be answered by attending to the question of epistemologies; of what we 'know' and how what we 'know' frames what is possible. I will treat 'epistemology' here as a system of knowledge or truth: it is within the confines of a system of truth that we may verify whether statements may be true or false, and a system of truth renders the way in which we see and understand the world. One example of an epistemology is the system of knowledge that has been built around the scientific method, which has relied upon making systematic and repeated observations of the world and phenomena. Based upon these observations, logical inferences are made about truth.

A related consideration for epistemology is the way in which we frame a particular issue, how this frame simultaneously situates actors, and how this frame enables what is possible and impossible within any given context. This understanding of epistemology, which gives preference to understanding the contours, dynamics and effects of what we know as true, rather than seeking to verify what is in itself 'true', is shaped by an explicitly Foucaultian outlook, which comprehends epistemology as constituted by contesting social and political processes.[41] Foucault's method provides a way to understand and reframe the 'scientific' method of progressively completing the documentation of what is true through empirical observation (for example, through experimentation to conclusively determine if fishes feel pain), by allowing us to instead understand knowledge as determining what is possible, including what it is possible to think:

> I am not concerned . . . to describe the progress of knowledge towards an objectivity in which today's science can finally be recognized; what I am trying to bring to light is the epistemological field, the *episteme* in which knowledge, envisaged apart from all criteria having reference to its rational value or to its objective forms, grounds its positivity and thereby manifests a history which is not that of its growing perfection, but rather that of its conditions of possibility.[42]

Here the focus of Foucault's approach is not to evaluate knowledge, or the history of knowledge, by understanding its potential 'proximity' to an objective truth. On the contrary, of more interest to Foucault is understanding how a regime of truth conditions possibility, and in turn how this inflects relations of power.

This approach is incredibly useful for unpacking human relations of power with fishes. As I have discussed above, one of the tensions when considering whether fishes that are utilised by humans are owed welfare is the current scientific debate over whether fishes suffer. The epistemological framing here is important to take into consideration. The fact that fish suffering is in question, the fact that we need scientists to answer this question before we – humans – decide to take action, demonstrates a problem of framing, where it is impossible to imagine offering welfare to fishes – or indeed stopping fishing – until verification arrives that fishes do indeed suffer.[43]

Perhaps of more concern is that this framing creates apparently rational positions which are, in some respects – at least when examined using a different perspective on 'truth' – easily rendered as irrational, and certainly unjustifiable. At present humans kill trillions of fishes; many of these fishes are hunted and slaughtered (or bred, intensively contained and slaughtered) with minimal (or no) welfare precautions taken. Humans apparently feel able to continue their practices because there has been no science which has consistently verified whether fish suffer. There is insufficient evidence to support change; and change is costly.[44] However, against this apparently rational worldview, we could, on the other hand, equally argue that we should *not* use fishes until we are clear on the science of fish suffering. Given the gravity of the volume of potential suffering that we may impose on trillions of fishes through our use of them, the 'rational position' could easily be that we should not harm fishes, or alternatively offer maximal welfare to fishes, until such a time comes when we have confirmed evidence, one way or other, on the question of whether fish suffer. Certainly some of the minimal welfare provisions based on the 'precautionary principle' that have been adopted with respect to fish have occurred through this kind of cautious 'benefit of the doubt' approach; but these same precautions have been strongly criticised,[45] precisely because, as I have said, the framing of the problem of fish suffering assumes that we can continue using fishes the way we do until somebody proves that we should not.

I raise all of this not to call into question the scientific method and its capacity to answer the pressing question: 'Do fish feel pain?' Rather, I merely want to stress that the epistemology of fish suffering is shaped by a vast human investment – monetary, infrastructural, dietary, institutional – in making fishes suffer. It is in this sense that it is no surprise that the 'ethical' problem of fishes should arrive at this point, where industrialised fisheries are wreaking havoc on the oceans. Fishes have been made to appear on a mass scale as objects of production, as labour and as a means of subsistence for human populations, and this has in turn shaped the high stakes of how we see fish and the meaning of the question 'Do fish feel pain?' The fact that we utilise fishes on a monstrous scale and in such a way that they are likely to suffer, if they have a capacity to suffer – and that we do so without reliable science to confirm that they do not suffer at our hands – tells us something about the relationship of our system of truth to power, the way this frames problems and determines subject positions. Instead of asking 'Do fish feel pain?', a different order of question might be, 'How can we use fishes the way we do, on the scale we do, when we are still not certain that they do not suffer?'[46]

In this context, fisheries remind us that violence itself is shaped by our systems of knowledge, and as such many of these questions are essentially epistemic in nature. Violence, its rendering within the public space and by the politics of suffering,[47] can only be made visible within the context of available knowledge systems. It is only possible to see violence towards animals when we conceptualise this as possible.[48] The relative silence around fishing practices, the large global and industrial scale of this endeavour, the easy availability of these animals as a source of surplus value and as a means of subsistence, the reliance on the scientific project to verify fish suffering – all perhaps indicate that we fundamentally lack the knowledge systems to imagine fishes as subjects of violence, or to understand fishing as a system of concentrated violence against sea animals.

In a well-known essay, Gayatri Chakravorty Spivak describes what she calls 'epistemic violence' as a way to understand the capacity of systems of truth to silence particular subjects, and render visible and invisible particular forms of truth and possibility.[49] Spivak offers the case study of ritual widow burning in India, *sati*, a practice that was subject to legal regulation by the British as part of their colonising mission in India, and then subject to a response from Indian traditionalists claiming the practice as a 'custom'.[50] Spivak draws attention to the way in which a system of truth shaped the narratives of these two voices of the coloniser and the colonised, in such a way as to silence the voices of Indian women:

The Hindu widow ascends the pyre of the dead husband and immolates herself upon it. This is widow sacrifice. (The conventional transcription of the Sanskrit word for the widow would be *sati*. The early colonial British transcribed it *suttee*.) The rite was not practiced universally and was not caste- or class-fixed. The abolition of this rite by the British has been generally understood as a

case of 'White men saving brown women from brown men'. White women –
from the nineteenth-century British Missionary Registers to Mary Daly – have
not produced an alternative understanding. Against this is the Indian nativist
argument, a parody of nostalgia for lost origins: 'The women actually wanted
to die.'[51]

The citation from Spivak is, I believe, of very strong relevance to animal studies generally, the challenge of understanding hierarchical anthropocentrism,
and the problem of how violence renders its subject. Spivak's perspective partly
serves as a reminder that our current framing of the ethical problem of animal
suffering has its limits and creates a logical structure that is difficult to escape.
The politics of suffering – the insistence on determining whether fish feel pain,
and shaping social and political responses only to the answer to this question –
generates its own politics and its own subjectivities, which become irrefusable.
If pro-animal advocates explain that they want to save animals from suffering
or reduce the suffering of animals through welfare practices – if this is the
only frame we have at our disposal – then these advocates run the risk of being
trapped within this truth, and more importantly, of the animals they are trying to
'save' being trapped by this truth. This does not mean that advocates should not
respond to violence, or that existing responses have no value; on the contrary,
work by scholars and activists to highlight this suffering has been immensely
successful in shaping public perceptions. However, even valuable responses participate in systems of truth that generate their own violence. Speaking of the
value of the discourse of rights for women, Wendy Brown acknowledges the
bittersweet attachment we can have to some emancipatory discourses, which
both create relief from suffering and also, simultaneously, create the terms for
continuing domination:

> if violence is upon you, almost any means of reducing it is of value. The prob-
> lem surfaces in the question of when and whether rights for women are formu-
> lated in such a way as to enable the escape of the subordinated from the site of
> that violation, and when and whether they build a fence around us at that site,
> regulating rather than challenging the conditions within.[52]

Arguably, animal advocates face this same dilemma with respect to improved
welfare protections for animals aimed at reducing suffering. On one hand,
at least with respect to land animals used for food, there have been tangible
improvements in the conditions of containment and slaughter. However, a
number of critics have pointed out that a reduction in suffering has *not* been

accompanied by a reduction in use; on the contrary, there has been an exponential global increase in the scale and intensity of animal utilisation for food.[53] Recent 'thought experiments' on the possibility of bioengineering livestock to not feel pain[54] only seem to further highlight the problem related to political and ethical claims which are solely based on the reduction of animal suffering as a goal. Just as Spivak might suggest that there is an epistemic violence in imagining that the solution – the only solution – that Indian women wanted to the ritual practice of *sati* was to be saved by British colonisers, we might similarly ask if the only solution available to the problem of large-scale human utilisation of animals is to reduce or avoid suffering (to 'save' animals who suffer by saving them only from suffering, rather than from their large-scale subsumption).

But it is the final sentence of that short quote from Spivak above that most intrigues me, and is relevant to both the epistemological problem of how we imagine what animals might want, and the significant challenge in imagining that animals may not want to be used for human benefit. Spivak describes the conservative Indian response defending ritual widow sacrifice with the short, ironic phrase: 'The women actually wanted to die.' In observing that an 'Indian nativist' defence of *sati* effectively participated in reproducing the absurd logic that women wanted to die, Spivak mocks a patriarchal institutional practice that silences women in such a way that the only explanation for why women would consent to take part in the custom is the preference of death over life.

The phrase 'the women actually wanted to die' is perfectly usable as a tool to understand the material and epistemic violence humans exert against animals, precisely because our epistemic framing of animals, and the monstrous systems of violence towards animals that exist all around us, appear to rely on a logic that 'the animals actually want to die' for our benefit and pleasure. Defenders of animal use explicitly endorse this messaging when they argue, for example, that animals used by humans enjoy a better life than they would if they were not used by humans.[55] We find this logic powerfully present in at least some fishing practices, where fishes are, as the official nomenclature used by the UN Food and Agriculture Organization states, simply 'harvested' for human use from oceans, seas and rivers.[56] In these cases we are presented with the idea of fishes giving themselves passively to us to be used, with no particular preference as to whether they continue living or meet the end of life at our hands: 'the fish actually wanted to die'. Epistemic violence renders fishes as uninterested in their own lives. The flipside of this, however, is that we can see that the statement 'the fish actually wanted to die' is absurd, precisely because it implies that fishes lack any resistance to being used for our benefit and, like the fishing fantasy of fishes throwing themselves onto the decks of boats, would prefer to die at our hands (or at least, have no preference whether they die or not at our hands). As I shall discuss later, it is precisely because of the possibility of offering a different framing, indeed the need to continually explore new framings, that it is important to conceptualise the possibility that animals, including sea animals, resist human utilisation and that they prefer not to be used, indeed they prefer not to die.[57]

It is for this reason that the question 'Do fish feel pain?' is perhaps less politically interesting than the alternative I have posed here: 'Do fish resist?' Once again, as I have discussed in Chapter 1, Althusser's symptomatic approach to reading is useful for us in pushing us to ask the question that reveals what was not answered in the initial enquiry: 'what distinguishes this new reading from the old one is the fact that in the new one the second text is articulated with the lapses in the first text'.[58] Asking about resistance discloses animals who not only suffer as a result of the violence they are exposed to, but also reveals the way that animals as political agents antagonistically contest the political relations imposed upon them. Importantly, asking the second question – 'Do animals resist?' – immediately uncovers the epistemic logic that sits behind these relations of violence, which assume that, even if all welfare precautions are taken, 'the animals want to die', since it is assumed that these beings have no particular interest in their own lives.

Conceptualising animal resistance

There has been a range of scholarly work within animal studies dealing with the question of animal resistance. Perhaps most prominent is the work of Jason Hribal, which documents, through historical case studies, examples of animals breaking free from human control – breaking down fences, escaping abattoirs, tussling with human controllers, maiming those who stand in their way.[59] Hribal's method is to use historical information to construct narratives of animal resistance.[60] For example, and relevant to my focus here on sea animals, Hribal narrates the successive acts of resistance by one of the orcas at Sea World, Tilikum[61] (resistance that has since featured in the documentary *Blackfish*).[62] In these cases, animal resistance is conceptualised as comprising intentional acts of insubordination against human domination. In some respects, we have the resources to understand this sort of resistance by 'big fish' that is part of the Western cultural imaginary. Herman Melville's *Moby-Dick*, for example, is a similar story of the tussle between Captain Ahab and a white whale, a story effectively of domination and resistance.[63] Similarly, Ernest Hemingway's *The Old Man and the Sea* enacts a narrative which resonates with a view of animal resistance as reflecting an intentional tussle against human domination.[64] In both cases, it is clear that the animal would prefer not to die. I note that to an extent, recreational fishing practices – that is, fishing for 'sport', where the intention is to catch fishes for pleasure rather than food – rely on a conceptualisation of animal resistance to fuel human pleasure.[65] It is precisely because fishes resist in these cases that recreational fishing becomes a 'sport'; since the supposed pleasure and art of these fishing practices relies upon the capture of an animal who eludes the recreational fisher,[66] and will struggle against the line when hooked (more on the hook itself below). The practice of 'playing' the fish once they are hooked, which can be practised as part of recreational fishing – that is, prolonging the period of time that the fish is on the hook so that they swim themselves to exhaustion in order to get away – illustrates the extent to which fish resistance, or at least one understanding of fish resistance (resistance as comprising acts of insubordination against human domination), is conceptually an important component of fishing practice.[67]

Against the above conceptualisation of fish resistance, some may argue that fishes cannot reasonably be said to 'resist' human domination in an intentional or 'agential' way. Indeed, there are at least two arguments that could be made here against the above conceptualisation of resistance. One view might be that there is no 'scientific evidence' to suggest that fishes, as intentional agents, work against human domination; in this view, fishes lack the reasoning (or other agential) capacity to choose to resist or defy human domination, and any visible evidence of what might look like resistance (such as fish struggling at the end of a fishing line) reflects 'instinctive' rather than 'rational' behaviour (this is, as I discussed above, a version of Descartes's animals-as-automatons view). It is certainly beyond the scope of this chapter to advance an empirically grounded argument for fish agency in relation to resistance based upon observational or similar studies, and, as discussed above, the epistemological problem of framing and conceptualising fish resistance might prevent the possibility of actually 'proving' (through observational studies or otherwise) that fishes 'resist' in this way. If mainstay scientific empirical approaches cannot confirm the possibility of fish agency and cognition, then it becomes impossible to mount an empirically sound case that fishes act in intentional ways to resist human domination, and we are condemned, therefore, just as we are with the question of fish suffering, to wait for science to prove one way or another that fishes, or at least most fishes, might be able to resist. One solution for this is to rethink how we frame agency and its alignment with intentionality: this is Agnieszka Kowalczyk's suggestion that 'acts of resisting exploitation performed by non-human bodies do not necessarily have to be thoughtful . . . to be recognized as significant'.[68] However, as I will discuss below, we do not need to prove that fishes exercise what we normatively might construct as 'agency' in order to understand that they resist human domination; this depends on the conceptual model of resistance we use.

There is a second and, I would suggest, more sophisticated version of the argument that animals, and hence fishes, cannot be said to resist human domination. This argument suggests that given we have such intense systems of violence directed towards animals, it is literally not possible for animals to resist in the sense of engaging in meaningful power relations. This view argues that these forms of domination seem overwhelmingly one-sided and thus nullify any possibility of escape or interaction. This is the view put forward by Clare Palmer in an early discussion of animal resistance.[69] Resistance, in this view, is only possible where entities that are subject to violence have some means of response or reaction in order to engage with relations of power. Where there is no freedom to move by the victim of violence, then there is no possibility of power.

Against the view put forward by Palmer, I would suggest that resistance is possible to imagine if we focus on the instrumentation of violence used to dominate animals, and the way in which these apparatuses effectively work against the active resistance of animals even if, from the outside, these relations appear to involve no contest or to be unilaterally one-sided in character. Here I expand on an argument I have previously advanced,[70] but do so with the purpose of aligning animal resistance with the contemporary context of industrial animal agriculture under capitalism, where technologies are deployed precisely to counter, subdue, cathect and capture resistance in order to generate surplus.

This view of resistance as generated by, and working intimately against, systems of production correlates with what I would describe as an 'autonomous' or *operaist* model of resistance. In understanding this model of resistance, I have been influenced by both the Italian Marxist operaist tendency[71] and by the more recent work of Fahim Amir, who explores operaism as a way of explaining animal subordination in systems of production.[72] In this view, systems of production and exchange, such as capitalism, feed upon the productive capacities and creativity of the bodies that labour within these systems. This is essentially a parasitic relation, where resistance is captured and redeployed through systems of subordination.[73] Here, even extreme forms of domination that appear to lack any movement or resistance are in fact the product of active forms of creative resistance by those who are subordinated, a resistance that is subsequently co-opted in the process of domination. Thus, the means used to restrain and intensively dominate animals are themselves a product of the active forms of resistance employed by animals themselves against human instrumentalisation. This autonomous or operaist model of resistance dynamically re-understands the way production occurs so that systems of domination must keep pace with new forms of resistance in order to extract productivity (this is part of the process of 'subsumption' inherent to production). For example, as Michael Hardt and Antonio Negri have argued, the flexibilities that characterise post-Fordist workplaces (flexible work hours, work from home arrangements, teleworking, etc.) are the result of capitalism adapting to the resistance of workers to Fordist modes of disciplined production: it is because workers actively dropped out of labour through absenteeism, through cultural experimentation, through everyday resistances and sabotage, that capitalism needed to adapt and re-mould work itself in order to maintain productivity.[74] Here resistance is always present, but only becomes apparent where there is organised confrontation; without this there is an apparently seamless view of production, in which those who are subject to intense forms of domination and discipline appear to be working cohesively with the production apparatus. As Mario Tronti observes:

> Workers' struggles determine the course of capitalist development; but capitalist development will use those struggles for its own ends if no organized revolutionary process opens up, capable of changing that balance of forces. It is easy to see this in the case of social struggles in which the entire systemic apparatus of domination repositions itself, reforms, democratizes and stabilizes itself anew.[75]

We might apply this operaist view of resistance to understanding the relationship between emerging technological and production processes and confrontation in the context of animal containment, breeding and slaughter. One example of this is the curved corrals that are made use of in slaughterhouses.[76] The traditional chute led animals straight into the arms of the stun gun; perhaps unsurprisingly, animals would halter and stop in response to the sight and sounds ahead. The introduction of curves into the chutes or races leading cattle towards death minimised the possibility of the animals balking at the prospect of proceeding along the pathway to slaughter.[77] In so far as the curves work to coax animal compliance in the face of insubordination, these curved corrals are directly a means of responding to animal resistance.

I should be clear here that this co-opting of resistance need not lead to outcomes that increase the suffering of animals; quite the reverse. Working to counter resistance in this sense can work to promote enhanced welfare outcomes; the curved corrals arguably reduce the suffering of animals prior to death (suffering at least with respect to stress, and the cognition and anticipation of the death to come). However, the curves also function to manage resistance and enable a smooth process of slaughter, maximising the efficacy of human utilisation. In other words – and emphasising again why the question 'Do animals resist?' provides a useful way to interrogate violence – the curved corrals serve a function in enabling a more effective extraction of value from animals. And they do this through the familiar route of reducing both human and animal labour time: the time-intensive and fricative human labour involved in forcing animals up the slaughter chute is dispensed with, while the productive inefficiency of animals resisting the act of walking themselves to their deaths is removed, thus optimising turnover time and making animal labour time more 'productive'. Bodies shape productive processes, while production shapes bodies; in this sense the 'agency' of animals (at least as resistive agents) is generated as a political subjectivity. As Hardt and Negri state: 'The great industrial and financial powers thus produce not only commodities but also subjectivities . . . they produce producers.'[78]

In some respects, thinking about resistance in this sense is a different way to conceptualise a 'relational approach' for thinking about how we engage with animals.[79] At least some of these approaches aim quite explicitly to question 'dualistic' accounts of human–animal relations – such as animal rights accounts which emphasise one-sided domination of animals by humans – by focusing upon forms of shared relationality and working, where animals and humans 'co-shape' each other and might derive mutual benefit from their relationships. The view I advance here differs from these approaches. As I have argued in Chapter 2, in so far as antagonistic conflict is the starting point for thinking about relationality, we are in relation with animals, but this is a relation of hostility.

Three technologies: hook, purse seine, aquaculture

Above, I have outlined a method of interpreting animal resistance. But how might this apply to understanding animals in interaction with human production systems? Building on the above conceptualisation of resistance, I would like to offer three examples – the hook, the purse seine and aquaculture – of how we might conceptualise fish resistance, through a focus on the technologies used to capture, utilise and slaughter fishes. This identification of technologies conforms to the autonomous or operaist view of resistance described above. All of these examples are framed by the understanding that these technologies aim precisely to counter and put down resistance; as such, the technology itself tells us something about the active politics of restraint and resistance involved in fishing practices, without having to demonstrate that fishes display normatively defined intentionality and agency. Importantly, in so far as I focus on technologies, we are dealing with a confrontation between animals and fixed capital. As I discussed in Chapter 4, an altered technical composition of capitalism sees machines and fixed capital replace human labour; however, in this deployment of fixed capital, animal labour is not substituted – rather, a direct confrontation between humans and animals is replaced by an antagonistic relation between fixed capital and animals.

Hook

The hook is possibly one of the oldest human technological innovations for the capture of animal life.[80] This technological development allowed sea animals, who otherwise evade capture, to be hunted along with land-based animals. However, fish resist in a different way to buffalo;[81] they are elusive and thus have additional resources to escape capture. It is only when fishing gear is developed that it becomes feasible to counter this resistance.[82] The hook would not be necessary if fishes allowed themselves to be passively 'harvested'. On the contrary, it is precisely because fishes elude human capture that the hook was devised. In this sense the hook is one of the technological innovations that shifted the nature of human hunting practice and opened the sea as a 'commons'[83] for the human pursuit of animal-based food; in 2006, *Forbes* magazine listed the hook as one of the twenty most important tools ever invented.[84]

The fish hook is an ingenious capture and kill device.[85] It is a sharp point with a bend in it which can be affixed to a line, allowing its operator to work at a distance. The bend is crucial, in so far as the hook aims not merely to impale its recipient but to snag the body of the fish to the hook, allowing them to be drawn in by a line. The hook frequently works with a lure or bait. In these cases, the hook is a stealth device; it aims to deceive an animal who would evade capture by other means. The hook was thus fundamentally conceived to work against fish resistance to capture. Elaine Scarry in her classic study of torture, *The Body in Pain*, points out that the most ingenious torture devices use the body of the victim against itself.[86] The fish hook is no different. When it finds sinuous flesh to impale and bind itself to, the body of the fish is effectively turned against the self; the fish will struggle against their own mouth (or elsewhere – the gut,[87] the eye) which has been caught by the hook, sometimes deepening the hold of the hook on the flesh. The technical innovation of the barb in the hook – a counter-facing point near the point – heightened the capacity of the hook as a technology to refuse resistance. The barb makes it more difficult for fish to free themselves once impaled; freedom from the hook is only possible through further laceration.

180 | ANIMALS AND CAPITAL

The discussions that are presently occurring within the recreational – 'catch and release' – fishing community on whether barbless hooks should be used on ethical (and sustainability) grounds are interesting in this regard.[88] Recreational fishing derives its supposed pleasure from the resistance of fish to capture. Recreational fishing is not interested in merely impaling fishes, but the whole process of drawing in a struggling fish and then, if the animal survives, setting it free.[89] The barb in the hook offers an additional safeguard that the fish will not slip away once impaled; however, it risks further injury and death to the fish, particularly if the fish is impaled in the gut, working against the stated aim of recreational fishing to merely catch and return fish as sport. In some respects, it should be no surprise that hook development can work to maximise resistance in order to enhance the 'sport' of fishing. For example, 'circle hooks' incorporate a wider curve to more efficiently facilitate sport fishing; this:

> unique hook shape causes the hook to slide toward the point of resistance and embed itself in the jaw or in the corner of the fish's mouth. The actual curved shape of the hook keeps the hook from catching in the gut cavity or throat.[90]

The Florida Sea Grant research circular I quote from here goes on to explain that 'fish hooked in the corner of the mouth or jaw tend to fight better than fish that are hooked in the gut'.[91] Here resistance itself – maximising the intensity of resistance, making it persist – is the objective of productive activity, its *raison d'être*. On one hand, recreational fishing tells us a lot about the sorry state of fish welfare and the limited impact welfare considerations, or the possibility of fish suffering, have upon some fishing practices. On the other hand, though, it tells us something about the investment recreational fishing has in fish resistance, since this practice is only deemed productively pleasurable (for the fisherperson) if the fish remains bound to the line until the fisherperson releases the fish, even if this process of struggle and resistance leads to the unplanned death of the fish itself.

While the hook is a familiar and everyday device deployed within recreational and subsistence fishing practices, it remains a highly useful tool within the context of industrialised fisheries, particularly in pole and line tuna fishing[92] and longline fishing. In the latter case, the capacity for suffering to be exerted on sea animals is amplified due to the expansive reach of the hooks deployed and the length of time fishes might be left to struggle:

> By this method, vessels trail a monofilament fishing line, often more than 60 miles long. Every 100 ft or so, a secondary line (called a 'gangion' or a 'snood')

branches off carrying additional baited, barbed hooks as it dangles. These lines themselves can be up to 1200-ft long. Often, there are as many as 2000 of these secondary branches over the 60 miles that the line stretches. Hooks are typically baited with squid, mackerel, or sometimes shark and a single longline may carry up to 10,000 hooks. The longline is buoyed by Styrofoam or plastic floats. Most of the longline boats have freezer capacity, a small working crew, and can stay at sea for months covering vast ranges of ocean. They know the fish they seek and use sophisticated fish-finding equipment such as sonar and computer-guided imaging to find schools of fish. Every 16–24 hours, they haul in the lines they trail, retrieve their catch, mechanically rebait the hooks, and reset the lines.[93]

Approximately 12 per cent of tuna caught globally are captured through longline fishing,[94] and it is estimated that in 2012 some 10 billion longline hooks were deployed in seas.[95] Here, the same characteristics that make the hook a useful weapon – its capacity to facilitate deception and to maintain distance from the operator, and its ability to use the physiology of the target body against itself – are put to maximum use, aiming as it were to exhaust the oceans of target species, subsuming the productivity of these animals towards the generation of value. In a sense we are dealing here with an altering technical composition of capital; industrialisation has taken this simple device – the hook – and through a massification of fixed capital, an abundance of production becomes possible. But note again the curious dynamics of this in relation to labour. An expansion in this form of fixed capital almost certainly reduces effective human labour time, since it would be much more time-consuming for humans to individually capture all fishes that are ensnared by longlines. However, from the standpoint of animal labour, the aim here is to efficiently subsume a mass of fish labour time, converting the product of a previously 'unproductive' metabolic labour to one that now becomes productive and 'valuable'. This capture of value can only happen in context with fish resistance. The fishes do not want to give themselves up; the mass deployment of hooks works against this resistance to guarantee minimal capacity for escape.

Purse seine

The net is another innovation in fish capture and, like the hook, has a long history of human utilisation.[96] The net, at least in some respects, is a discriminating capture device: the use of rope or twine in a mesh pattern allows water and small creatures to move through the device, while ensnaring larger target fishes.

In relation to mechanised fishing, there has been a great degree of focus on the environmental impacts of net-based fishing, particularly trawling (where a net is pulled through the water at speed) and the *lack of* discrimination in net fishing with respect to particular 'high-value megafauna' who are caught as 'by-catch' (for example, dolphins).[97] Like the hook, the net is a technological innovation designed to capture animals that would otherwise evade capture. As I have stated, net fishing is an old technique of human hunting; today, industrialisation has mechanised this practice of predation in order to massively increase its efficiency. Trawl netting, for example, frequently uses motorised speed and net breadth and depth to run down groups of fishes in the water; fishes will swim themselves to exhaustion before they finally surrender to the net.[98]

An example of a net that is commonly used within industrialised wild fish capture, and a technology that works to counter the resistance of fish, is the purse seine.[99] The purse seine is like a huge drawstring bag. A large net – which can be up to a kilometre long and 200 metres deep – is threaded over an area, and then pulled inwards to trap the animals within. This method is very different from trawl fishing. Rather than using sheer speed to capture fishes, the purse seine uses stealth to encircle them. Decoys can be part and parcel of the fishing operations: for example, floating objects, or 'Fish Aggregating Devices' (FADs), which attract fishes, can be used to congregate fishes prior to the deployment of the purse seine.[100] The net technology can work to selectively discriminate with respect to target species: 'the geometry of the net during the set is also significant for understanding the vertical dimension of the operation, and the volume enclosed, which may determine which schools and individuals are captured'.[101]

This sort of industrial-scale net fishing exerts extraordinary violence against its object. When the net is drawn in, many fishes will die, being crushed by other fishes on top of them. Here, fish resistance can be used directly as a means to facilitate human utilisation. As the net is drawn in, the fishes will thrash and struggle. The closing encircling space means that fishes will come into violent contact with one another, and many will injure or kill themselves in this process.[102] One practice in industrial purse seine fishing is to progressively close the net and allow fish to struggle and injure each other as the compression by the net increases (this is why blood will surface on the water as the net constricts).[103] A pump or a 'brailer' (a smaller scooping net) is then used to extract fishes nearer the surface, many of whom may be injured or already dead. Once these fishes are pumped or brailed onto the ship, the net is tightened further and the process begins again. Fish resistance, against the prospect of their own death, is here subsumed and utilised as a means to facilitate human productivity in wild fish capture.

Purse seine fishing is another example of how we might conceptualise fish resistance in relation to technological innovation. The purse seine itself, like the hook, is an ancient technology. However, when utilised with contemporary technologies, and obeying the logics of industrial capitalist production, this form of capture takes on diabolical proportions: helicopters are used to search out fish schools; mechanised sea transport, including speedboats, is utilised to chase down fishes and to string the encircled area; the development of the Puretic Power Block,[104] which is capable of hauling large nets into the boat, enables the mass capture of sea animals; and pumps are used which can smoothly extract fishes from the water directly to ice slurries below deck. These technologies are accompanied by techniques which are refined year after year to more efficiently capture fishes; for example, the use of floating devices, or the use of the compression and pump technique I have described. All of these techniques and technologies aim at countering resistance; their promise of improved efficiency relates to their ability to capture entities that evade and resist capture.

Aquaculture

Commercial wild fishing is a modality of hunting[105] operating today as a peculiar industrial form of mechanised predation. In this respect, commercial fishing is unlike any other large-scale form of animal utilisation for food by humans. In so far as, at least at present, fish numbers in the wild are abundant enough to sustain this sort of hunting industry, and simultaneously the evolved techniques and technologies for wild fishing are effective enough – that is, effective in countering fish resistance to them – this sort of predation on a large scale remains economically viable.

However, as I have stated above, there has been an extraordinary explosion in the development of aquaculture, at least over the last forty years, which has substantially shifted the nature of large-scale fishing industries, positioning 'farmed fish' as the majority route by which human populations attain fish-based food. In some respects, the development of aquaculture is itself a technological response to fish resistance. We know that since the 1980s, the number of wild fishes caught on a global level has more or less stayed the same.[106] Yet per capita fish consumption has increased. It is aquaculture that has filled the gap in terms of supplying the other fishes that have been used for human consumption. On one hand, there is an environmental explanation for this: as experts have repeatedly warned, wild fishing is at capacity or being actively over-exploited for many fish species. However, putting forward this perspective as a single explanation assumes that fishes are merely passive objects that must be found and 'harvested' (that is, the epistemic problem I referred to above). A different way of conceptualising the rise of aquaculture, taking into account animal resistance, is as follows. The human technical means for capturing wild fishes through mechanised hunting technologies have now reached their limit. The economics are poor in terms of trying to hunt the remaining fish who currently evade capture, and due to these hunting activities, fishes are not able to 'replenish' themselves through reproduction to respond to the continuing parasitic demand to capture value on the seas. (Certainly, we know that regulatory controls have had a limited effect in preventing wild fish exploitation on a global level.)[107] However, economic realities associated with trying to ensnare evasive animals who are scarce, depleting and evade capture must surely drive the viability of other utilisation options, including intensive farming. Thus more concentrated forms of utilisation, such as aquaculture, have become economically viable. In this sense, on a global scale, fish resistance has had a role to play in the development of aquaculture. Wild fishes are not just scarce because humans cannot find them; they are scarce because they evade capture. Aquaculture solves this problem by 'domesticating' fishes into enclosed 'farms'. Domestication is a solution to animal resistance that has been effectively applied to land animals over millennia.[108] It is now being applied in earnest to fishes.

In other words, the recent history of industrialised fisheries, from the mechanisation and massification of wild capture to the rise of industrial aquaculture, is a story of subsumption. I described the movement from 'formal' to 'real' subsumption in Chapter 4: the former relates to the capture of pre-existing processes of production within the logic of capitalist value; the latter refers to the full incorporation of labour within the production process, transforming the character of that labour to conform with the internal rhythms of capitalist production, in ways that mean the labour is often not recognisable outside of this historical context. This usefully describes the history of the relation between fishes and capital. The industrialisation of wild fisheries sought to capture the productivity and energy of fishes as generated within the 'commons' of the oceans.[109] This industrialised endeavour was by definition parasitic in nature: wild fish capture simply sought to draw in and suck the value of the existing labour of fishes to produce themselves within 'nature'. This represents a formal subsumption of the productive processes of fishes, in so far as the subsumed productivity of fishes appears as identical to that which exists in 'nature'. These animals are found as raw materials in the oceans; and they are transformed through capture and slaughter into consumption commodities which circulate as a means of subsistence for humans.[110]

However, the fish farm – the factory farm for fishes – obeys different contours. Aquaculture represents a real subsumption in so far as the whole life and death of these animals is brought into alignment with the rhythms of production, in such a way as the lives of these animals looks nothing like the lives of fishes in 'nature'. Just as in land-based intensive animal agriculture, fishes in aquaculture enter production as an amalgamation of raw material and labour, and will exit as a consumption commodity. The whole production environment is designed to enable and make efficient the labour of fishes upon themselves, in order to preserve and enhance the value of the raw material and allow for the transformation of these animals into a commodity with a new use value. Death will mark the end of this process in which the whole life of the fish is captured by production. Aquaculture thus represents a complete model of domination, where life itself is equivalent to the production cycle. It responds to the difficulties and frictions associated with the continual process of formally subsuming the labour of animals by bringing this production within the fold of capital: thus, resistance produces a response.

Despite the overwhelming sense of total domination, there is also a complex story of resistance and power that accompanies the development of techniques in aquaculture, including those oriented towards improved welfare.[111] Aquaculture holds the promise of mitigating the effects of fish resistance on a day-to-day level through concentrated forms of control. This is because, like other factory farms, aquaculture provides operators the opportunity to exert birth to death controls in order to enable a more refined management over the final product. Perhaps tellingly, one expert comments: 'the entire life cycle has been rigorously controlled. We know where it was born, where it died, and what it ate throughout its entire life.'[112] One area of innovation is being able to control for parasites and diseases through immunisation;[113] another is exerting more control over the size and quality of meat offered for sale,[114] enabling production of a more consistent, homogenised end product. In other words, and in line with the argument I have developed in this book, aquaculture offers the opportunity, through a subsumption of the lives of fishes within production, to control and optimise the processes by which these animals labour on themselves in order to be transformed into consumption commodities.

This does not mean that aquaculture fishes lack the capacity to resist this overwhelming system of control; on the contrary, aquaculture attempts to manage the movement of populations that are themselves elusive, and thus represents a concentrated attempt to deal with fish resistance in an ongoing way. As John Law has noted with respect to salmon farms, fishes within aquaculture environments, despite the intensity of the farming methods, defy systems of control and detection:

> The salmon in the pen are more or less invisible. Sometimes you can see what's going on, but most of the time you can't. Instead, all that you can see is a few dozen salmon out of 50,000. This is the paradox. Even though they are being controlled, the salmon are also dissolving themselves into invisibility. So this is the argument. If salmon are animals this is precisely because in relation to human beings they are also elusive. Down there in the water, so far as the people are concerned, they are also doing their own sweet salmon thing.[115]

This does not mean, like in other systems of animal-based production, that creative resistance cannot be captured. In line with the operaist view of resistance I have advanced above, we can also identify a range of techniques and technologies which capture and use the autonomy of fish themselves. Consider current experiments on the use of lights in aquaculture pens to control behaviour. Some intensively farmed fishes will exhibit fin damage as a result of inter-fish aggression and abrasion against surfaces; these are problems which might not occur in the wild. In some cases, this is a reflection of the relative 'stocking densities' within aquaculture environments.[116] The problem is exacerbated where fishes congregate together and do not spread out evenly within the available space in sea cages; such as in the case of salmon. Various researchers have experimented with the use of underwater lamps to influence the behaviour of salmon and prevent congregation, thus helping to mitigate the problems associated with high density.[117] These techniques work to shape the responsiveness of fishes to the environment of the sea cage. The light techniques capture fish responses – such as aversiveness to bright light – and channel behaviours to improve the efficiency of production techniques. Turn on a light, and some fishes will run away: this technique thus uses fish resistance and autonomy to prevent fishes congregating and improve the quality of the meat produced. Creativity and resistance are channelled to create docile bodies out of resistant bodies; that is, to mould fishes that use the production space in ways which do not compromise the quality of stock.

In some cases, intensive techniques use the processes of the body of the animal itself as a means to achieve goals in relation to production efficiency. Consider the routine use of starvation prior to transport and slaughter for farmed fishes.[118] In some cases, farmed fishes are denied food for several days or weeks prior to being slaughtered. Fishes are 'ectothermic' and thus have metabolic efficiency in relation to food consumption: many fishes routinely survive in the wild for long periods without food. Aquaculture producers will make use of this in starvation techniques, taking advantage of reduced metabolism and the fact that fishes will empty their guts and faeces, thus enabling a more desirable end product.[119] Of course, the 'welfare' picture here is not straightforward. Some argue that the diminished metabolism induced by starvation benefits welfare, for example by reducing aggressive behaviours.[120] However, in these cases we find again that the creative energies of fishes, including their own resistance – at least at the level of a will to survive – is captured by the production process and harnessed towards the ends of production. Production in this sense is a process of interaction between humans and fishes, of which innovation in relation to fish resistance drives innovation in production towards human ends.[121]

Yet everywhere we look within the aquaculture environment, and against the overt visible sense of victory over fish resistance, we find discord and contestation. In Chapter 5, I explored the politics of circulation within animal agriculture in the interaction of human and nonhuman labour within the processes of transportation of living commodities which enable the movement of value to market. The technical and economic problem of circulation also haunts production processes involving fishes, since these animals must be moved, and sometimes moved alive. But how do you move living fishes? Fishes evade capture. They cannot breathe in open air, and thus water must accompany these living animals, or be in close proximity, if they are to survive transfer.

Within the vast, repetitive exchanges of globalised fish production techniques, practices and technologies can be utilised to speed up and make flows more efficient, enabling faster production cycles and increased profitability. Here, as elsewhere within global capitalist networks, ruthless efficiencies drive reform of technologies. Typically, fishes within fish farms need to be transferred *en masse*. But this is logistically challenging since fishes evade capture, and manual netting of fishes is time intensive. One solution is the use of mechanical brail nets:

A metal hoop, about 1 m in diameter, has a net tube hung from it, with the free end attached to a rope which allows this end to be opened or closed. The hoop is suspended from a small crane, which is used to drag the net through the crowded fish, catching them. The net can then be swung to where the fish are required, the end is released using the rope and the fish flow out.[122]

Such mechanised forms of netting can be effective, but they carry risks of injury and mortality for fishes, which will impact the profitability of operations due to losses during 'fish harvesting'. This is because fishes do not want to be caught and they evade capture, which is in contradiction with the imperatives of aquaculture operators who need to capture fishes in order to realise value. The clash of wills between fishes who do not want to be caught and producers who desire to catch them produces an internal friction within production. This means that when aquaculture producers impose their will over fishes, death and injury will be part of the process, despite any claims made by producers that welfare considerations are taken into account. As David Robb frankly acknowledges:

> a number of actions are implemented which can or do affect welfare. Some are avoidable, but others are not. For instance, it could be regarded that actually killing the animal is the greatest insult to its welfare – but it is of course una-voidable in a harvest procedure.[123]

One area of innovation has been in the development of fish pumps. Instead of attempting to net vast numbers of animals who do not want to be caught, the fish pump promises a smooth and apparently frictionless absorption and transfer of large numbers of fishes from one point in production to another. Typically, these devices involve the use of a flexible hose connected to a large vacuum pump designed to suck animals, like a large vacuum cleaner, from one place to another within the production cycle.[124] At least one advantage of the fish pump is that it has strong 'labor saving potential'.[125] As I have stated above, manual brailing of fishes out of sea pens is highly intensive in relation to human labour time. The fish pump device replaces the messy antagonism of humans attempting to net struggling fishes from one place to another with an automated system that simply sucks animals towards desired points of production. Fishes are moved more smoothly, with greater speed, with less friction. Indeed, while there is a delicate balancing act between flow rates, pump pressure and fish mortality and injury,[126] the advantage of the fish pump is that it speeds the production cycle. Thus, developments in pump technologies reduce the need for human labour to transfer fishes, and potentially accelerate production and turnover times (that is, make animal labour time more efficient by countering resistance), improving the potential for profitability. We therefore find a similar relation between fixed capital and animal labour time to that I have described in Chapter 4: namely, machines are deployed to displace human labour time, replacing an antagonism between humans and animals and maximising animal labour time efficiency, including through reductions in circulation time.

Although the fish pump appears to nullify resistance, we should not pretend that it removes the friction of wills between fishes and aquaculture producers (or in this case, a friction between fishes and fixed capital). We still find conflict here: indeed, the point of the fish pump as a technology is to respond to this conflict through the deployment of a fixed capital that can more effectively overcome the resistance of fishes. Researchers have been interested in the mortality rates and behaviour of fishes within fish pumps. In part this research is driven by the need to reduce mortality and injury rates of fishes in the industry, and thus promote enhanced profitability. Here, I would like refer to one study conducted by Dutch researchers on the impact of pumping stations on fishes and eels.[127] The researchers looked at the mortality rates of fishes and eels based on different pressures, flow rates and animal sizes. They also used video imaging to capture the movement of fishes within the pumps, in an attempt to understand how the orientation of fish shaped injury rates. In this context, the researchers were surprised to observe the fishes swimming backwards: 'Fish were seen to resist pumping by swimming in an upstream direction, away from the pump. A number of fish succeeded to escape during tests ... and took shelter in the large container upstream of the shelter box.'[128] The researchers go on to observe:

> Although not anticipated, the video recordings provided very useful data as to the orientation and distribution of fish. . . . Previous studies either assumed the fish to be aligned with the flow ... or at an arbitrary orientation. . . . The video recordings in the current study showed that fish resisted pumping by swimming in an upstream direction . . .[129]

This study offers a useful description of mainstay human–animal relations within the context of industrial animal agriculture. These relations are 'co-shaping' and co-constitutive for both humans and animals. But they are marked by a continual tussle in which industrial production seeks to chase, pin down and bend the wills of animals in order to make them conform to the rhythms of production. And even where production systems evince peaceability, smoothness and lack of friction, there is within the works of capital hostility, antagonism and conflict.

We are also confronted by the unique antagonism that accompanies the relations between fixed capital and animals. As we discovered in Chapter 4, and as is highlighted here in looking at industrial fisheries, when fixed capital arrives, human labour time is displaced, and the confrontation between humans and animals is substituted with a hostility mediated by machines. Humans increasingly lose their jobs as the machines arrive; animals, on the other hand, are left behind to face down against capital.

Beyond a parasitic relation?

Acknowledging fish resistance inevitably involves rendering fishes as co-creators of the world we live in. Global mechanised fisheries, whether wild capture or aquaculture based, aim to capture parasitically the value generated by fishes through their own labour on themselves. Yet this production is itself a continual interaction with the resistance of fishes to this subsumption. Our systems of violence directed towards fishes – the long food supply chains that link ocean or fish farm to dinner plate – owe something to fish resistance, since industries and economies have been created out of countering this resistance. This is both a sobering and empowering way to conceptualise the problem of fish resistance. It is sobering because so much potential creativity – human and nonhuman – has been channelled into so much violence; violence that many animal advocates are increasingly arguing is unnecessary. It is, however, empowering to consider fish resistance in this way, because understanding that fishes might resist offers us a way to comprehend the immense contribution of nonhuman political agency to the world that we see around us. Our world would be unrecognisable without all the animals that have been willing and unwilling co-creators, labourers, in our pasts; and this simultaneously offers us a way to think about how much our world would change if we cultivated a different relationship with the animals in the future worlds we build. In a discussion on the value of considering resistance and its usefulness for thinking about political structure and change, Hardt and Negri state:

> Now, it is perfectly reasonably to ask if it is in fact true that resistance comes before power and that social struggle precede and prefigure capitalist restructuration. We have not offered an argument for it, really – precisely, we have treated it as an axiom. Our book tries to demonstrate that it is plausible to read the history from below, but that is really not a proof. What is more interesting, though, is the *political effect* of this axiom, that it highlights the power of resistance and the power of social struggles. . . . Today, when facing the forces of capitalist globalisation and our new world order, it is all too easy and all too common to feel ourselves and our social movements powerless. This method can work as a kind of antidote to that cynicism and sense of powerlessness. It is not a matter of pretending that we are powerful when we are not, but rather recognising the power we really have; the power that created the contemporary world and can create another.[130]

Animals create worlds we cannot understand; they defy our imagination. Our primary relationship with animals within the context of industrial capitalism is violent and parasitic. This is, as I have argued in this book, an example of a confrontation between fixed capital and animals to suck value from the latter. Through these relations, capitalism has quite literally fed off the creativity of animals for its own benefit. Recognising animal resistance could provide different ways to think about how humans might relate to animals beyond simply finding new ways to counter their resistance. What would our world look like if we worked with and supported the creativity of animals, rather than simply working against it? This, of course, leads us to think about what a post-anthropocentric, post-capitalist vision might entail. We turn to that question in the final chapter.

7   Dreams

> The only reality we know is that ruled by theft, capitalist alienation and the objectification of living labor, of its use value, of its creativity. To make all of that function according to the law of value, supposing it were possible, would modify nothing. Because there is no value without exploitation. Communism is thus the destruction at the same time of the law of value, of value itself, of its capitalist or socialist variants. Communism is the destruction of exploitation and the emancipation of living labor. *Of non-labor.* That and it is enough. Simply.
>
> Antonio Negri, *Marx Beyond Marx*[1]

An ambition of this book is to offer an analysis which will establish a useful basis for advancing our conceptual understanding of human–animal relations. This analysis, I hope, will inform the framing, tactics and goals of those working to make change for animals.[2] In highlighting the interconnections between animals and capital, the book provides a frame by which to understand the way in which animal advocacy might operate as an anti-capitalism, and simultaneously, highlight to movements on the left the under-theorised situation for animals under capitalism and the unique possibilities for system transformation.

We could summarise the findings of the book as follows.

1. *Food animals hold a unique structural position under capitalism.* The trillions of animals used annually for food occupy a distinct place within the circuits of capitalism. From a value perspective, animals within industrial agriculture appear as hybrids of constant and variable capital: raw materials that enter production and are asked to labour on themselves, leaving production as a consumption commodity. For capitalism, food animals are useful in two broad

senses. Firstly, as a labour force they are attractive because they are able to create surplus within the sphere of production; that is, they generate value during the production cycle that exceeds the reproduction costs of their labour. Secondly, as consumption commodities, they allow for the reproduction of human populations and their formal and informal labour within the totality of capitalism; that is, animals have been positioned within the present historical context as one of the important elements allowing for the reproduction of human life. Food animals sit at the meeting point of a hierarchical anthropocentrism and a capitalist value process. These beings are literally fabricated to appear as raw materials and commodities in ways which have multiple use values, not only as a means to a surplus and as 'good to eat', but also as a 'currency' within a symbolic economy which continually verifies human supremacy over other animals. This unique positioning of food animals under capitalism is suggestive that this labour force cannot be structurally assimilated with the human worker; as such, food animals might be regarded as a distinct economic class.

2. *Animals have different use values depending on whether they appear in the sphere of production or the sphere of consumption.* It is almost self-evident that an animal in a factory farm has a different value from meat to be purchased in a supermarket. One entity is 'alive', the other is 'dead'. Yet focusing on use value allows us to reveal more complexity here. When animals are raw materials and labour – that is, when they are alive – they appear as a use value for production, and productive processes will aim to subdue and contain these energies towards the creation of value, by generating a surplus that exceeds input and labour reproduction costs. When animals appear as consumption items – that is, when they are dead – they are 'abandoned' by production and become a means of subsistence, thus entering a radically different use value for capitalism and for the beings who consume these products. Importantly, as I have highlighted in Chapter 3, animal products interact with human wages within capitalism today in a perhaps historically unprecedented way. The wage appears in money form and represents an exploitative portion of the value produced by human workers in production. It is designed solely to enable the reproduction of human life and labour. Animal products are the objects of wages; and since the explosion in the availability of animal-sourced foods is tied to rising living standards – that is, either in the form of higher relative wages or cheaper food – a truly perplexing politics of freedom, identity and pleasure appears to accompany food consumption choices under capitalism, both producing avid defenders of animal-based foods and simultaneously generating a market for those who want to resist. This, as I shall discuss below, asks important critical questions of veganism as a political strategy.

3. *Recognising the value of animal labour power creates unexpected results in how we understand capitalist processes where they involve animals.* I have argued in this book that understanding the distinct value of animal labour power allows us to see capitalism in a different light, recognising an animal labour force as a constitutive pillar of the economic system. But this recognition also comes with results that disarm traditional Marxist analyses. One of these outcomes is a different perspective on the relationship between the rising technical composition of capital and labour time. In the traditional view, as machines, fixed capital and inputs to production increase, relative human labour time decreases, as this labour is made more efficient. This is certainly true of animal agriculture if we assume that only humans provide labour and that animals are mere raw materials. However, acknowledging animals as also representing labour time helps us to make sense of the way in which the drive to reduce animal labour time shaped the factory farm in a unique way. While human labour time is minimised, the mass of animal labour time has to be increased (since more animals arrive as raw materials and more animals leave as dead meat). But this does not stand in the way of the drive for labour time efficiency. The drive to promote efficiencies in animal labour time led to the shortening of these lives and the maximisation of their 'yield'. Thus, as humans leave the scene of production, animal labour time remains in place: it cannot be replaced, as animals are the labour and the product. However, dramatic steps are taken to make this animal labour time more efficient. This gives us some of the specific and unique coordinates of the factory farm, which simultaneously massifies animal lives as raw materials, and at the same time seeks to shorten these lives and increase growth rates, in order to speed turnover time and improve productivity. We also noticed another curiosity when we looked at the role of animal labour within the live animal transport industry. Circulation time was understood by Marx as disconnected from production time, since the movement of raw materials or finished commodities happened outside of the strict sphere of production. As such, the time spent moving raw materials and commodities from one site of production to another was time lost for production. However, as I discussed in Chapter 5, animals are required to labour on themselves to maintain their own value within the proliferating business of land, sea and air-based live transport. Conveniently, as if by divine intervention, these transported 'commodities', which would otherwise perish, arrive at the next phase of production ready for use. This is due to the metabolic labour of animals on themselves; if this labour was not provided, then it would not be possible to take advantage of the value realisation opportunities available through live animal transport. Thus, live animals in circulation have the capacity to continue production time.

4. *Food animals exist in a unique antagonistic relation with capital.* All work-ers, human or nonhuman, face capitalism in an antagonistic relation. Capitalism as an organism and mechanism seeks to suck and drain life away in order to amass value in the form of dead labour (surplus). Yet animals face capitalism in a unique way. As I have described, in an overt sense, capitalism seeks to coun-ter the resistance of animals to their own utilisation, and continually develops the technical means for this value capture. We thus find, as I have described, nightmarish mechanisms deployed everywhere, such as the chicken-harvesting machine described in Chapter 4 or the fish pumps described in Chapter 6. But this also highlights a unique relationality between animals and capitalism. Historically, mechanisation of production progressively displaced human labour. Thus, human workers existed in competition with machines which took their jobs (and, as a result, their means of survival). But the machine means some-thing different to animals within animal agriculture. Here, there is no sense that animals are being replaced by machines. If machines could replace this work, it would annually save billions of animals being brought into the world, fabricated in horrific, intensive processes and extinguished ruthlessly when profitable to do so. But machines do not save animals this labour. Instead, machines expand in number and so do animals, while humans vacate the scene of production. We are thus left with a confrontation that has been orchestrated under capitalism between animals and fixed capital. This is, in essence, the factory farm. This has a number of implications for theoretical understandings of human–animal rela-tions. At least one implication is that while there is a lot of work within animal studies on understanding entanglements between animals and humans within productive processes, this scholarship seems to miss that the main 'relationality' experienced by most animals who are utilised for food on the planet is a relation with fixed capital (that is, machines, instruments and enclosures). Automation of production only promises animals a seamless and uninterrupted relation with the machine, one that does not occur in the presence of humans. Secondly, against celebratory posthuman readings of the relations between animals and technologies, for example as advanced by Braidotti,[3] we are instead confronted by the sobering reality of a large-scale conflict orchestrated between technolo-gies and animals as a structural relation under capitalism. Today, most animals in relation with human societies confront fixed capital as the primary mode of 'entanglement'. This relationship is hostile, but paradoxically, structured to be 'value-producing'.

What do the above findings mean for how we move forward? Ideally, an anal-ysis such as I have provided in the book will elaborate a theoretical understand-ing of the political terrain, which will determine actions that might move us closer towards an agreed goal. As such, we might break down the implications of this study into the following three areas: framing, tactics and goals.

Framing

At the level of *framing*, this book has a number of implications for the task of animal advocacy. The first implication relates to advocacy itself. As discussed in Chapter 2, a reality of pro-animal movements is that they are 'advocacy' movements: that is, movements where humans are required to speak and act on behalf of animals. This marks out pro-animal movements as different from left movements that involve those who experience violence and oppression and are guided democratically by these constituents. The yardstick for the democracy within these movements is the involvement of the beneficiaries of the movements in decision-making. This does not mean that the social movements of the left only feature direct forms of democracy. There are of course social movements which include non-direct forms of democratic participation (ranging from formal representation and delegate structures to vanguardism), and there are many social movements, such as those representing people with disabilities[4] or children, where advocacy on behalf of others is more prominent. However, pro-animal movements are strongly marked by the need to speak on behalf of animals, since animals themselves do not have direct engagement with formal institutional political decision-making (as I have highlighted, the epistemic violence experienced by animals includes their 'silencing').[5] But this does not mean that animals are *not* political agents; indeed, as I have outlined, the form of capitalist production in animal agriculture corresponds directly with the need to subdue the corporate resistance of animals to their subjugation. Here in this resistance, animals express their political interests collectively, including challenging the presumption that they want to labour for humans and that they are happy to die.

This offers some ways to rethink animal advocacy and its purpose. In Chapter 1 I discussed the politics of animal welfare, which often has the goal of seeking to minimise 'unnecessary suffering'. One problem with this framing is that it has done little to reduce the volume of animals used and killed globally; thus, while welfarist approaches have arguably been very successful in the introduction of measures to reduce suffering – such as stunning techniques prior to slaughter, or 'free-range' systems that have relieved the intensity of close confinement – these approaches have been less successful in curbing the expansion in the use of animals for food, since they offer no particular political view on the continued instrumentalisation of animal life. Welfarism has had a worrying interrelationship with intensification, or as I have described it, the increased presence of fixed capital within animal agriculture. In some cases, developments that speed production processes come with the veneer of better 'welfare'. This is certainly the case for a device such as the fish pump, which does away with manual brailing of fish, potentially reducing injury and death. As such, because of the promise of the reduction of suffering, advocates can be drawn into supporting such welfare measures even though they will have the long-term effect of enabling an expanded production through increased efficiency (that is, increasing the numbers of animals used). While such advocacy reduces the volume of suffering, it does not respond in any way to the political demands of animals, expressed in their resistance; indeed, we can see examples where welfare effectively continues the epistemic erasure of the political resistance of animals. For instance, fishes resist the brail net because they do not want to be caught. The use of the fish pump addresses this friction, perhaps offering a reduction in injury and mortality; but this technology does so in a way that silences the political agency of fishes, which is expressed as resistance to capture. The vacuum so effectively whisks fishes away, and does so by hiding from sight the scene of struggling fishes, that it would appear almost as if the fishes wanted to be taken. Thus, the technology conspires with a prevailing knowledge system to produce an epistemic effect.

None of this means that advocates should be blocking demands for the reduction in suffering of animals through the application of welfare measures. However, recognising the continual resistance expressed by animals within capitalist agriculture, often in open confrontation with fixed capital – their continuing insubordination in relation to enclosures, fish hooks, cattle prods, fish pumps, chutes, stun guns, etc. – shapes how animal advocates could respond. The knowledge that the systemic imperative within capitalism is to speed production in order to expand surplus, and to use techniques and technologies to nullify the resistance of animals to achieve these ends, allows advocates to focus on the longer-term goals of ending the exploitative system itself, rather than providing a means for it to intensify. Importantly, this allows pro-animal movements to break free of the framing of animal welfare and its almost singular attachment to the reduction of suffering. The political interest of animals is not merely to suffer less in production but is also a demand to have lives back – that is, a life that is allowed to flourish without the constraint of the abrasive confinement system, a demand to not have shortened lives and a demand to not die. The resistance of animals, their continuing expression of this in acts of political insubordination, occurs in the context of their existence as a labour force, and the tenor of their demands corresponds to this reality. In other words, the demands of animals relate not just to the experience of suffering, but their life of activity within the context of animal agriculture; to their experience of labour, and the material reality of the subsumption of their labour within capitalism. I am here emphasising that thinking of animals as a labour force potentially moves animal advocacy away from 'protection', where the goal is simply to protect animals from harm. Certainly, animals do not want to die, nor do they want to suffer; but they also do not want the lives capitalist agriculture has made them endure as the only way they can live. Animal advocacy thus has the role of presenting the uncompromising demands of animals as labour power and using appropriate tactics to realise goals.

At the level of framing, there is another potential offered by this book; namely, a shift towards the politics of production. As I have outlined in Chapter 1, one curious dimension of the way animal liberation politics has developed is in the overinvestment in changing human consumption habits as a strategy, rather than the demand to end the production of animal products. This misses the centrality of animal-based production to the problem of the consumption of animal-sourced foods. Capitalist production seeks to take control of the reproduction of animals and proliferate them in order to extract the difference between the reproduction costs of the metabolic labour and the value this same labour produces. The overproduction of animal-sourced foods that follows integrates itself with the means of subsistence for human populations, allowing for the reproduction of formal and informal human labour; what I have described in this book as 'the reproduction of reproduction'. Capitalism leapt on animals because of their use value as both a means of surplus for production, and a means of subsistence for human populations. A focus only on the side of consumption fails to engage with the important role of production in the proliferation of animal-sourced foods, and fails to see the rationality for this proliferation (which is not solely about human desires but a drive to capture the value animals produce).

Animal advocates are certainly not alone in this overdetermination of consumption as the only site where political transformation is imagined possible. For example, while it has been encouraging to see advocacy by climate scientists who have stressed the impact of animal agriculture on the climate emergency, it is striking that reducing meat consumption – that is, encouraging consumers to change dietary practices – is often the main solution proposed, rather than diminishing or ending meat production itself.[6] This is odd given that almost all other realistic proposals to mitigate the effects of anthropogenic climate change rely on solutions that are structural and require change at the level of institutions and economies (such as enabling transitions to low-carbon-emitting energy production). This is because these large-scale changes cannot occur by waiting for consumers to adjust consumption habits: for example, relying on consumers to purchase solar panels or energy that is derived from 'green sources'. We face a similar problem with animal-sourced foods globally. Just like coal, the drivers for production do not relate solely to consumer demand for the end product, but the continuing value that can be derived from extraction and production. The analysis offered in this book provides one way of reframing the problem of animal-sourced foods, highlighting the importance of focusing on the drivers of production. Rather than imagining that the issue before policymakers is an unrelenting human demand for meat, this analysis highlights instead capitalism's structural addiction to the production of animals for food; an attachment that derives from the usefulness of animal labour power as a source of surplus, and their simultaneous usefulness as a means of subsistence to allow for the reproduction of human reproduction. I don't at all mean to imply that human desires and pleasures do not inform the fetishisation of animals as sources of food; this is clearly part of our peculiar contemporary hierarchical anthropocentrism.[7] But a focus on the problem of production offers a way for advocates to reframe and rethink how these desires and pleasures operate within the structural realities of capitalism as an economic system.

Tactics

The analysis presented in this book has implications for how we critically understand consumption strategies as mode of intervention towards change. And it is here that I move to look at the possibilities this book opens for the *tactics* engaged by pro-animal movements.

This book has taken a critical stance on the politics of veganism within capitalism. As I observed in Chapter 3, consumer veganism has arguably been shaped by the same forces which have shaped 'meat cultures':[8] that is, decisions over the means of subsistence are made in the sphere of consumption, and choice is determined in this context by the availability of wages (i.e., prevailing living standards). Despite the structural constraints within the consumption sphere which limit the impact of individual decision-making on production – including that wages are intended merely for human reproduction and are not a means to purchase capital – today the act of consumption is nevertheless saturated with narratives which are interconnected with ethics, politics and freedom. This places the politics of veganism in a challenging position under capitalism, as holding the promise for a structural change that it cannot deliver. Certainly, I don't mean to discount the reality that ethical decisions confront consumers and that these decisions should be taken seriously. However, understanding the limits of the politics of consumption helps to make sense of why at least some versions of vegan advocacy appear as merely a campaign directed at middle-class consumers on how their wages should be spent. As such, they likely do little to alter the structure of production.

In pointing out these structural limits, I am not arguing against the cultivation of veganism as a practice within pro-animal movements. On the contrary; building plant-based food cultures has a potentially important strategic role. This is because resisting animal-sourced foods directly shapes the imagination of a world without the utilisation of animals as a means of subsistence; decisions by movements to abstain from animal products produce a social imagination of a possible future. In this context, veganism serves as an important example of a collective form of 'counter-conduct' which challenges prevailing discourses and structures of violence.[9] From this standpoint, veganism might function as a political practice,[10] or perhaps praxis,[11] not only within pro-animal movements, but also within the context of anti-capitalist movements more broadly.

While there are certainly many examples of consumerist market-driven veganism today – from plant-based fast food, to alternative meat products, to cosmetics, to protein supplements – there are also examples of alternative vegan or plant-based ethics which work at cross purposes with the logics of capitalism. And many of these movements also take seriously the colonial foundations of capitalist economic relations, and thus are not merely campaigns for individuals to 'go vegan' by redirecting their wages to new consumer items, but instead are positioned towards potential system change. An example might be Indigenous plant-based food ethics and food sovereignty movements, as discussed by scholars such as Margret Robinson[12] and Kirsty Dunn.[13] Here, plant-based diets are articulated as a collective form of self-determination against colonising food cultures. Importantly, in so far as these movements represent acts of food sovereignty,[14] they potentially work against the subsumption of food supplies within the logics of capital. As Dunn explains:

> It is vital . . . in this context, that any kōrero regarding veganism, plant-based kai or 'kaimangatanga' and any challenges or conflicts that arise with regards to customary and contemporary practices involving nonhuman animals, must be conducted by and within Māori communities. Otherwise, the imposition of a vegan ethics without the knowledge, understanding, or respect Māori experiences, narratives, concepts, and knowledges, can only repeat the role of yet another colonial project.[15]

In this context veganism[16] shifts outside of being simply an individualistic 'ethical' consumer choice for those with wages to expend and becomes instead a collectively determined organising tactic which works against the hegemonic domination of food choices. The goal here is not simply creating more vegans, but responding to a structural problem that reproduces dispossession, oppression and violence.

Indigenous plant-based food movements highlight the interconnections between capitalist animal agriculture, animal-sourced foods, and movements against colonialism. However, we should not pretend that these locations for change are not also potentially sites of difference and contestation. Certainly, it is frequently observed that the traditions of some Indigenous peoples prominently include consumption of animal-sourced foods; and further, movements for self-determination by some Indigenous peoples can be fundamentally interconnected with demands to control food and food-related practices, including rights to subsistence hunting and artisanal animal agriculture.[17] In these contexts, demands by animal advocates for individuals to transition to plant-based foods potentially establish a 'zero-sum game' by placing aspirations for consumption 'ethics' in competition with Indigenous sovereignty claims. As such, as Claire Jean Kim discusses in an analysis of Makah whaling, some actions by advocates can explicitly utilise political framings where 'advancing animal and ecological concerns . . . manifestly trivialises concerns about tribal or racial justice'.[18]

However, tactical goals which aim at changing the structure of production provide different opportunities for alliances. And it is here that the politics of consumption must simultaneously keep the conditions of production in sight. Consider, for example, recent campaigning by social movements against kangaroo hunting in states and territories across Australia. Australian governments have endorsed a 'conservation' strategy to control kangaroo numbers through state-sanctioned 'culls' or elimination. This large-scale slaughter programme establishes quotas which have allowed for millions of kangaroos to be killed annually.[19] Further, this slaughter has been commercialised as an industry, allowing for a domestic and international trade in meat and hides. As such, kangaroo culls are not merely about 'conservation'; they represent the subsumption of this mass killing to transform it into a value-creating activity within the global flows of capital. In other words, the kangaroo cull – the world's 'largest annual commercial slaughter of a wild mammalian species'[20] – has metamorphosed into a modality of capitalist animal agriculture. The slaughter has, of course, been subject to much advocacy by animal advocates in relation to its cruelty,[21] and is also the target of substantial international controversy and opposition.[22]

In 2021, the New South Wales Government ordered an inquiry into the 'health and wellbeing' of kangaroos in the state, with a significant focus on issues arising as a result of the kangaroo slaughter. Numerous advocates and scientists were called as witnesses to provide evidence to the inquiry. Notable amongst these were the testimonies provided on 15 June 2021 by Aunty Ro Mudyin Godwin, a Palawa educator and writer, and that of Uncle Max Dulumunmun Harrison, an elder of the Yuin nation. In stark terms, Godwin and Harrison reflected on the political and cultural meaning of the commercial cull for Aboriginal communities. Godwin stated to parliament that 'it is colonialism that sees country as only something to gain a financial profit from – to be used, to be abused – and that sees kangaroos as a pest'.[23] Further, Harrison highlighted the important differences between the commercial cull and cultural uses of kangaroos for medicines and food:

> This powerful, soft-footed animal that shares our nation with us has been relegated last, replaced by the hard-hooved introduced animal species, creating displacement and desecration. Inside cultural practice, we only took whatever was needed for food and medicine. We never harvested meat or medicine for profit. It is not spiritual practice to kill our iconic animals for $80 million per annum. It was not an industry that drove the hunt. It was our ceremonial practice for food and medicine, and still is today.[24]

The hearings preceded a remarkable event on 24 October 2021, 'World Kangaroo Day'. A Yuin ceremony was held at a New South Wales kangaroo sanctuary, and a message stick was presented from Harrison to a member of parliament.[25] The message stick was the 'Yuin Declaration for Kangaroos': seven articles which proclaimed that kangaroos have 'sovereign rights above and beyond any human claims of dominion over them' and that 'kangaroos shall not be sold or subjected to any inhumane, cruel or degrading treatment'.[26]

I raise this example of the Yuin Declaration for Kangaroos in response to the commercial kangaroo cull to highlight the way in which alternative framings and goals create different conditions for alliance-building and shared objectives. The kangaroo cull represents the massification of killing as a capitalist industry. Animal-sourced products are an outcome of this production: that is, the industry produces items which are available for purchase by consumers, and now this trade is global in nature. Advocates could singly pursue a boycott of these consumer products as a way to protest the industry; there are certainly pressures on the industry from consumers in the United States and the European Union for such a ban to take place. However, such a strategy would be potentially fraught.

Given that some Indigenous people use kangaroos as a cultural practice for food and medicine, seeking a consumer ban as a mainstay tactic risks trivialising racial justice, precisely as Kim suggests. However, this does not mean alliance is not possible. Here, it is the site of production – rather than consumption – where unique shared goals reveal themselves. Clearly, the cultural relationship described by Harrison between some Indigenous people and kangaroos differs from that of the commercial kangaroo cull; the latter subsumes mass slaughter within the production cycles of capitalism: as Godwin described, 'their flesh and body parts are taken, cut up, shipped around the world and taken again'.[27] In order for more money to be created, kangaroos must be shot, taken apart and sold globally as commodities. In order for additional money to be made, the process must be repeated, again and again. M-C-M. The limit on making money is only dictated by the metabolic limits of kangaroos to reproduce their own lives, and the technical capacity of humans to incessantly take these lives and make body parts available on the market. This is a process of production we have seen repeated again and again throughout this book. In other words, capitalist agriculture is the problem. By focusing on the site of production rather than the site of consumption, it is possible for different sorts of alliances to develop; alliances that, we may note, work directly against the value structure of capitalist production, but that also simultaneously, in the case I have outlined above, take seriously the colonial relations underpinning value exchange today. This strategic approach to the interrelationship between consumption and production is certainly resonant with the work of the Mexican anti-speciesist organisation FaunAcción, which utilises plant-based foods as a means to challenge inequality and colonialism:

> the AR [Animal Rights] movement is moving more and more towards consumerism, and we need to tackle that now. . . . In the Molcajete (a food van project ran by FaunAcción) we travel around, especially in poor neighbourhoods, to share and talk about food. Our materials don't say 'Go Vegan' – they are about the defence of the corn, against Monsanto, and telling people we love their food: old, indigenous recipes. We want people to get over the shame of their traditional food.[28]

This example points towards the different ways in which a politics centred around consumption might be reconfigured towards the politics of production. Here veganism cannot be simply an expression of an individual consumer choice, nor operate in isolation from other social struggles; director of FaunAcción Gerardo (Watko) Tristan states: 'We can't just pick veganism to talk about, because we can only do that because of our privilege.'[29]

204 | ANIMALS AND CAPITAL

It is clear that focusing on consumption is not enough. As I have emphasised in this book, it is the site of production where I believe the most work needs to be done by animal advocates, and it is also the space where alliances are possible which have not yet been explored. One such site I have previously discussed[30] is the possibility of alliances between animal advocates and trade unions to intervene within production. There are here, naturally, a set of conflicts and antagonisms that must be overcome; as I shall discuss below, the fact that animals occupy a different structural position from human workers means that some demands may be irreconcilable. Nevertheless, there is much space for shared working. One example is the space of the slaughterhouse, and the continual demand from producers to increase line speeds within industrial production.[31] As this book highlights, this is a tendency within capitalism which seeks to make both human and animal labour more efficient. Increasing line speeds inevitably leads to an expansion in the number of animals killed. There is poorer welfare for the animals, who must be pushed through to slaughter more quickly,[32] and simultaneously there is increased harm and injury for human workers.[33] Here an obvious site of collaboration is in working with trade unions to slow line speeds.[34] Naturally, animal advocates have different goals from trade unions in this context: pro-animal movements want to reduce the number of animals killed, with a goal of ending meat production; trade unions, on the other hand, may also want to slow production, but have a different set of goals in providing safe working conditions and job security to workers. Nevertheless, at the level of tactics, there are significant opportunities for alliance around decreasing line speeds. Importantly, for animal advocates, building alliances serves many functions, not only in supporting other movements to resist the drive of capitalism towards continuing accelerated production, but also in working with the unique structural capacity of human trade unions to literally halt production. As I have previously explored, the 2015 general strikes in Iceland, which led to the closure of slaughterhouses and subsequent meat shortages, are a reminder of the capacity of human labour movements to deeply impact industrial animal agriculture in ways that cannot be replicated by pro-animal movements.[35]

A different site where collaborative action may be possible is in relation to industrial wild fish capture. As I have outlined in Chapter 6, wild capture fisheries, particularly in the Asia Pacific region, represent a social and environmental catastrophe that wreaks havoc on trillions of creatures. The growth of the global market for seafood has expanded wild capture fisheries to their limit. Human labour conditions are highly exploitative, with extensive use of low-wage and forced labour in supply chains.[36] The cost to animals is immense; as discussed in Chapter 6, trillions of fish are killed each year by wild capture fisheries, with an extraordinary incidence of 'by-catch' and many unwanted species of fish caught, killed and dumped annually. These animals are subsumed by industrial capitalism through processes of extraordinary violence, and their resistance demonstrates their opposition to this utilisation. There have, however, been a number of pressures exerted by social movements to reform wild capture fisheries. Globally there are a number of environmental and labour rights groups working to identify the use of forced labour in the industry and campaign for better wage conditions.[37] Arguably any attempt to raise the value of human labour within supply chains will have a dramatic effect on the financial viability of the global industry, adding pressure to slow down the violence wrought by global wild capture fisheries. Thus there is a strong case for animal advocates to work tactically to support labour advocates, in order to not only apply upward pressure on wages and impact the viability of fishing operations, but also to build solidarity and exchange with labour movements. Importantly, while there is no indication that labour and environmental groups share the aspirations of pro-animal advocates to end wild fish capture, such alliance work allows animal advocates to broaden awareness of the conditions faced by animals and promote a conception of structural change that includes consideration of non-human interests. Once again, radical pro-animal advocates and labour rights movements have potentially very different long-range goals; however, there remains much scope for partnership over transitional goals, including reducing the number of animals used, killed and made to suffer.

Perhaps more radically, this book points to different sites of tension which could be usefully exploited by advocates within the space of production. One site relates to the progressive tendency of industrial animal agriculture to curtail the life of animals in order to shorten production time. As I have suggested, welfarist approaches, in their focus on reducing 'unnecessary suffering', have not provided a counter-narrative to this intensification; and thus, while there have been improvements in the form of stunning practices and increased stall sizes for some animals, there has not been a strong public campaign challenging the shortening of animal lives that has been part and parcel of intensification. In this context, demanding that animals have the right to a full life, the ability to age, is a radical demand which corresponds to the demand from animals themselves to live rather than die. The demand for animals to live a full life is one that works directly against the logic of capital's relation with animals. It is both political and epistemic. Here, the political demand functions as a means to rupture logics; in this respect, it resonates with other campaigns such as 'wages for housework' which point towards a site of contradiction in order to highlight and mobilise counter-hegemonic truths, and end the imposition of labour.[38] Naturally, the demand must be qualitative and not merely quantitative: it is not clear that animals want an extended life within the hell of the factory farm. But we know that animals have a will to live, to endure against the horrors they experience; to pretend otherwise is to play into the same epistemic violence that pretends that animals have no interest in their own lives. To an extent we see examples of the demand for animals to live a full life within the repertoire of pro-animal movements: for example, in sanctuaries where animals have the possibility of living full lives;[39] or in artistic works which capture, almost unimaginably, images of ageing farm animals.[40] The demand for animals to live a full life works directly against the logic of capitalist production, in just the same way as the demand for the eight-hour day struck at the heart of the logic of capital and represented one of the important victories of labour movements in the twentieth century: 'In the place of the pompous catalogue of the "inalienable rights of man" there steps the modest Magna Carta of the legally limited working day, which at last makes clear "when the time which the worker sells is ended, and when his own begins".'[41] This connects with the demand for reduction in labour time and elimination of unnecessary labour: something I will explore more fully below.

A different, albeit connected, site of tension relates to the reproductive or gestational labour of animals. As I have discussed, feminist analysis has highlighted the way in which the reproductive work of animals is buttressed and reproduces patriarchal logics and the rationalities of gendered labour. This book has also highlighted the unique structural place of this labour within cycles of reproduction under capitalism: animals are forced to reproduce in order to create an animal labour force, who in turn are compelled to work on their bodies to become a means of subsistence to allow humans to reproduce themselves. The gestational labour of animals here is fundamental: it was a structuring element in the history of the domestication of animals, and today this labour sits at the core of industrial animal agriculture and its metabolic relation to human populations. Lewis's proposal for the end of forced gestational labour and the collectivisation of reproductive work has peculiar implications for animal agriculture. On one hand, as I have discussed, the gestational labour of animals has already been completely subsumed within the flows of capitalist production, and this has produced a reality where animals experience, by force, 'full surrogacy now'. On the flip side, the demand for animals to have the right to refuse gestational labour is radical in scope. If animals have the right to refuse the violence of forced insemination and the gestational work of reproducing the animal labour force of capitalism, then this is the end of animal agriculture. For this reason alone, the portion of the animal labour force who are compelled to perform gestational work have a highly unique and potentially powerful structural position within capitalist animal agriculture, one which animal advocates should leap upon as a site of organisation.

But all of the above opportunities for reframing and thinking tactically are meaningless if there is no agreement on where we are going. One of the important aims of this book was to understand the ways in which pro-animal advocacy might function as an anti-capitalism; that is, understand how the historically situated position of animals today conforms and interacts with the value structure of capitalism, and the unique opportunities available in this context for realising the end of violence against animals, by working to end capitalism. Yet I have simultaneously kept in sight the deep problems – the antagonisms – that structure the terrain before us, and potentially prevent agreement on goals. As I discussed in Chapter 2, Wilderson's thought experiment of the socialist slaughterhouse, while reminding readers of the unique political ontology of the Black subject and the inadequacy of the left project for offering liberation for this structural position, simultaneously offered the perspective that animals shared this structural isolation from the projects of the left:

> would it feel more like freedom to be slaughtered by a workers' collective where there was no exploitation, where the working day was not a minute longer than the time it took to reproduce workers' needs and pleasures, as opposed to being slaughtered in the exploitative context of that dreary old nine to five?[42]

How do we move beyond this structural dilemma? In this context, I turn to think about *goals*; in particular, the possibility of imagining a post-anthropocentric vision of the economic system that will replace capitalism.

Goals

Marx's *Critique of the Gotha Program* is known as one of the few short, but vaguely 'programmatic' explorations of what a communism might look like.[43] The short text is perhaps most famous for the oft-quoted line within it: 'From each according to his ability, to each according to his needs.' This itself would provide an interesting basis for a 'justice'[44] proposal for post-anthropocentric society that was structured towards the flourishing of both human and nonhuman beings. However, that assumes we can easily reconcile the flourishing of humans with that of animals; but as I have highlighted in this book, capitalism places these two flourishings in antagonistic relation with each other. In this context, a more interesting focus is the text that immediately follows Marx's famous pronouncement. For here Marx turns to question distributional models of justice: that is, views of justice that depend upon the 'fair distribution of the proceeds of labour'. Marx expresses his suspicion over what a fair distribution might look like, instead noting that distributions within the sphere of the means of consumption are symptomatically connected with the structure of the means of production:

> it was generally a mistake to make a fuss about so-called distribution, and put principle stress on it. Any distribution of the means of consumption is only a consequence of the distribution of the conditions of production. The latter distribution, however, is a feature of the mode of production itself. The capitalist mode of production, for example, rests on the fact that the material conditions of production are in the hands of non-workers in the form of property in capital and land, while the masses are only owners of the personal condition of production, of labour power. If the elements of production are so distributed, then the present-day distribution of the means of consumption results automatically. If the material conditions of production are the co-operative property of the workers themselves, then there likewise results a distribution of the means of consumption.[45]

This short section of *The Critique of the Gotha Program* is hugely productive for thinking about both the inherent antagonism between humans and animals under capitalism, *and* the possibilities for building a different vision for a society after capitalism. For humans, the difference is clear. Under capitalism, minority private ownership of the means of production in turn creates the conditions for an unfair distribution of the means of consumption to the majority (that is, the distribution of wages, their relative buying power, and the capacity for wage-earners to reproduce themselves and sustain social reproduction). Altering the ownership of the means of production will change this distribution of the means of consumption. Thus, in this view, if we want a 'just distribution' of the means of consumption, we must arrange ownership of the means of production in such a way as to ensure this just distribution. If the goal is an equitable distribution of the means of consumption (or perhaps something equating to 'from each according to their ability, to each according to their needs') then this cannot be achieved through minority ownership of the means of production (that is, the prevailing pattern of ownership of the means of production we find under capitalism).

For animals, however, we have a more complex story. The three 'lives' of animals I have described in this book – consumption commodity, raw material and labour – sit awkwardly against Marx's quick diagnosis of the difference between capitalism and the communism to come. Animals exist as a means of consumption. Animals who are transformed into consumption commodities thus represent the distribution – fair or unfair – of the means of subsistence within the sphere of consumption, and appear in a patterned and uneven way as the target of human wages. We encounter here at least one structural antagonism, in so far as human deliberation on the justice of the distribution of the means of consumption, including animals as a means of consumption – who gets what, and if so how much – does not have an interest in the question of whether animals *should* appear as a means of consumption. Certainly, if we imagine 'communism' as *only a human process* of ensuring a just distribution of the means of consumption, it is not clear that the interests of animals in not being a means of consumption will be taken into account.

But as Marx informs us, the distribution of the means of consumption exists symptomatically in relation to the mode of production itself. Here, we face another structural difference. Human workers appear under capitalism – workers who have only their labour – in an antagonistic relation with the money-owner who commands the means of production. The means of production is thus alienated from the human worker as a condition of their exploitation. Food animals, on the other hand, appear both as labour and as the means of production. Further, where the human worker is presumed to own their person and body, these animals are instead owned as a means of production. Thus, if communism represents cooperative human ownership of the means of production as a mechanism by which to ensure a fair distribution of the means of consumption, it is not clear that this means anything to animals as long as they remain a means of production (which under communism has been democratised) and as long as they remain a means of subsistence (which under communism has been fairly distributed). Marx was of course only thinking about human workers here. Nothing here directly implies that the human workers would share control over the conditions of production with the animal workers. Instead, after the revolution, cooperative control of the conditions of production by humans would include cooperative property in animals as a means of production. We thus arrive exactly where Wilderson predicted we would: animals cannot be saved by the left project, since they are positioned structurally in a different location from the human worker; indeed, they are the material base which allows the human worker to realise their 'liberation'. While the reduction of necessary human labour time – 'where the working day was not a minute longer than the time it took to reproduce workers' needs and pleasures' – holds the promise of reducing the number of animals killed, Wilderson points out that this should not be mistaken for freedom for those animals who are about to be killed.

The central issue is that animals are situated only as the means of production, rather than as political agents who are part of the collective transformative project to own the conditions of production. The essential question here is, who is the worker who might enjoy the conditions of production as their collective property? If we acknowledge animals as workers, albeit *not* proletarians, then what is their stake in collective ownership of the conditions of production?

How we understand communism, socialism, or some other economic system as an aspirational goal after capitalism is of course a complex question. It is contentious in part because of the nightmares of the totalitarian experiment of State socialism, which makes a conversation on 'communism' fraught as a result of this historical legacy.[46] Totalitarian states which took 'socialism' and 'communism' as labels are important for leftists to study; taking this history seriously places question marks over whether these same labels are useful for describing the post-capitalist societies that leftists dream of, which of necessity must be democratic to the core. A different problem, and one highlighted above, is exactly what 'ownership' of the means of production signifies. As discussed, any human democratisation of the means of production will mean little to the animals who are owned; they will simply have new masters, albeit comrades who have been freed from the shackles of wage labour. I note one other issue here which relates to the history of the 'means of production'. The original – *'ursprünglich'* – accumulation of capitalism comprised a history of violent expropriation. In societies based on forced labour, the means of production was established through racial slavery; indeed, slavery required the ownership of the slave as a means of production. This established wealth which was central to the rise of capitalism; as Robinson states:

> African labor power as slave labor was integrated into the organic composition of nineteenth-century manufacturing and industrial capitalism, thus sustaining the emergence of an extra-European world market within which the accumulation of capital was garnered for the further development of industrial production.[47]

In settler colonial contexts, the means of production represents the historic and ongoing theft of these means, and with it the subsumption of the economies that pre-existed this theft through a continuing process of absorption. As Patrick Wolfe highlights, for Indigenous people this meant a slow erasure of access to the means of production proportional to the continual capture of land and resources by the colonists:

> Economically, Native societies were reduced to generating subsistence from an ever-shrinking repository that, even within territory that remained unconquered, became subject to the depredations of an advance guard of settlement made up of frontier irregulars (with or without auxiliary subordinates), imported livestock, exotic predators, and more besides.[48]

I raise this to highlight that the ambition for a democratic control over the means of production immediately opens different questions over what constitutes a means of production, and who has a right to claim it. Certainly, in settler colonial contexts, democratisation of the means of production might imply democratising ownership rights to settlers; and thus, ignoring the historical injustice that founded the present distribution of the means of production. That is, ignoring the self-determination and sovereignty claims of Indigenous peoples. We thus confront foundational problems about the rationalities that would organise a post-capitalist society. A different vision might see a post-capitalist economy as one which democratises surplus value: thus, the decision on whether to produce a surplus, how much, and how it would be distributed becomes cooperative.[49] This approach has potential for a different framing of social goals; however, it remains difficult to disentangle from ownership, since the ownership of the means of production is interconnected with the production of surplus.

A different, and potentially more appealing post-capitalist demand relates to time. This demand is interconnected with the possibility of reducing necessary labour time and the abolition of work. It is here that I want to propose that if there is any possibility for imagining a shared version of a non-anthropocentric, post-capitalist society, then it is at the level of time that I believe such a unified vision might be possible. The reason I stress this is the importance of time for all labour forces, human and nonhuman. Capital commands time; this is a central pillar of capitalism's domination of life. While the accumulation of value is important as an economic 'law' under capitalism, time remains the measure by which the duration of life is modulated with respect to economy.[50] The production of commodities is always determined by temporality. The commodity enters production, leaving it transformed and with a new value attached; however, this metamorphosis can only occur after a discrete period of time. Despite the fantasies of capital for ever-accelerated processes, production can never be instantaneous. Processes of exchange – the endless transformation of commodities into money and money into commodities – also reveal capitalism's rhythmic power. The sale of commodities necessarily involves temporality: a movement from the space of production, to the space of circulation, to the point of exchange of commodity into money. Despite all the developments in just-in-time production processes and electronic transactions, this process cannot be instantaneous; it is instead dependent on real spacings of time, time when commodities leave one sphere of production and enter another, or time when commodities await the transfer and exchange for money at the point of sale. Time is of course central to the wage relation, since the wage is always a measure of time bought from the worker. And to an extent this conforms with at least one vector within Marx's understanding of the society to come; namely a society where unnecessary labour is eliminated:

> The worker must work surplus time in order to be allowed to objectify, to realize the labour time necessary for his reproduction. On the other side, the *capitalist's necessary labour time* is *free* time, not time required for direct subsistence. Since all *free time* is time for free development, the capitalist usurps the *free time* created by the workers for society.[51]

In a direct sense, under capitalism the material world as we know it has in part been established through the theft of free time, time that would otherwise have been available freely to those who have laboured to produce it.[52] The wage relation highlights the role capital has in structuring and ordering life in relation to time: not just the working day, but with it, the time available for other activities, the time for nutrition, relaxation, sexuality, relationality, 'kinship'. Capitalism intervenes into life, structuring and subsuming time as duration, turning lived moments into value-producing moments. In other words, capital seeks a thoroughly 'biopolitical' governance of life through the modulation of time. Is the domination of capital's time the only formation that seeks to regulate life and its normative rhythm? And is capital's time experienced differently by different collectivities? Certainly, as Jack Halberstam notes, time as a 'natural' duration is also constructed by intersecting relations of gender, race and sexuality: 'Reproductive time and family time are, above all, heteronormative time/space constructs . . . all kinds of people, especially in postmodernity, will and do opt to live outside of reproductive and familial time as well as on the edges of logics of labor and production.'[53] In a sense here, telling the story of capital's time is also telling the story of non-conformance with this time, and understanding the different forms of temporal asymmetries that shape collective resistances. As José Esteban Muñoz argues, displacement from a hegemonic conception of time is what perhaps marks the subjective experience of those who are outcast by a range of different modalities of domination. Responding to the work of Tavia Nyong'o,[54] Muñoz reflects:

> There is something black about waiting. And there is something queer, Latino and transgender about waiting. Furthermore there is something disabled, Indigenous, Asian, poor and so forth about waiting. . . The essential point here is that our temporalities are different and outside.[55]

As this book has highlighted, animals too are commanded by time within capital's circuits. Today, global animal agriculture constitutes an extraordinary proportion of global production. This intensive production requires a ruthless domination of the temporalities of animal lives, governing with absolute precision when and where animals are born, the parameters of the life they will live, and when they will die, in such a way that the whole life of the food animal represents capital's time. And animals must wait: their lives are structured by a demand that every moment of the lived duration will be commanded by capital's time, capital's presence which orders time.

The reason I suggest that time potentially offers a space for alliance between animal advocates and the left relates to the way that capital's time has come to dominate all life, in such a way that the demand to be free of labour now operates as a radical project for restructuring societies. Once again, I note that the starting point here is antagonism, and the reality that the project of the human workers differs from that of the animal; this means, *prima facie*, that the demands made by the human worker for liberation look nothing like the demands made by animals; animals indeed might simply exist as means (of production, of consumption) for human liberation. Animals resist this role by seeking to endure against productive circuits which seek eventually to make them die. This materialises for animals in a revolt against productivity itself; against work. Referring again to Wilderson's 'Gramsci's Black Marx':

> the slave makes a demand, which is in excess of the demand made by the worker. The worker demands that productivity be fair and democratic (Gramsci's new hegemony, Lenin's dictatorship of the proletariat), the slave, on the other hand, demands that production stop; stop without recourse to its ultimate democratisation. Work is not an organic principle for the slave.[56]

Recall that Wilderson connects by analogy the structural experience of the Black subject with the cow in the slaughterhouse. And certainly, in a direct sense, Wilderson, while demonstrating the structural antagonism between the slave and the free worker, here also illustrates the material reality for animals under capitalism: animals have no investment in production continuing; they want production to stop. Animals want the factory farm to stop: that is their political demand, to end their positioning under capitalism as raw material, consumption item and labour. The demand is uncompromising, and in no uncertain terms uncomfortable for humans whose surplus, living standards, livelihoods and sustenance are dependent on the continuation of industrial animal agriculture.

However, the end of work is not a demand that *only* animals make. Human social movements are now increasingly invested in this goal. And it is here that 'time' proves important as a space by which to frame shared political demands. We sit now at a curious point where perhaps there is a convergence of campaigning and thinking which appears to resonate with a radical demand to end work time. There are now numerous competing visions for post-capitalist solutions, in part driven as responses to anthropogenic climate change, which have attempted to imagine no-growth or negative-growth economies.[57] All of these proposals are premised on challenging logics of accumulation and with this, proposing reductions in labour time. Also bubbling in the background is scholarship, such as that of Paul Mason, which speculates on the potential of automation as a means for creating a society without work.[58] Simultaneously, we have autonomist or operaist Marxist approaches which have emphasised that the contestation with capitalism occurs not through the embrace of labour but through its negation; as Negri states:

> The content, the program of communism are a development of universal needs which have emerged on the collective but miserable basis of the organization of waged work, but which in a revolutionary way signify the abolition of work, its definitive death.[59]

Kathi Weeks, drawing energies from autonomist Marxism but supplementing this with socialist feminist approaches, also links the utopian future of post-capitalism with the politics of the refusal of work:

> The problem with work is not just that it monopolizes so much time and energy, but that it also dominates the social and political imaginaries. What might we name the variety of times and spaces outside waged work, and what might we wish to do with and in them? How might we conceive the content and parameters of our obligations to one another outside the currency of work?[60]

While there has been this undeniable convergence of perspectives on the problem of work, and resistance to work, as part of the imaginary for postcapitalist societies, these perspectives have remained focused on humans (and thus are anthropocentric). By implication they have assumed that while humans have the potential to create societies that reduce human labour time, animals will continue to work. We thus have a version of the continuing tendency we have observed in this book: as the technical composition of capitalism alters and humans leave production, animal labour time is not reduced. Indeed, as we observed in Chapter 4, developments in human productivity which reduce necessary human labour time may precisely rely on the expansion of animal labour time as a structural necessity. One suspects that many human visions of post-capitalism rely on the continued availability of animals as a means of production and a means of subsistence which will continue to be the foundation for human creativity: 'hunt in the morning, fish in the afternoon, rear cattle in the evening, criticise after dinner'.[61]

We have thus before us a question that we must ask of what our vision for post-capitalism might entail, and which beings are included in this utopia. The question arrives at just the point at which an expanded understanding of capitalism and its relation with the nonhuman has come into view. If, as many contemporary theorists have argued, the conditions of production today reflect a kind of enlarged, all-encompassing social production, where society and nature are necessarily entangled together in a collaborative activity to produce and reproduce for capitalism, what does collective ownership of the conditions of production mean from this standpoint? Or alternatively, if the vision we have before us is for a society which reduces necessary labour time, and eliminates unnecessary labour time, what does this mean for nonhuman life, which is necessarily entangled? Can we imagine societies freed from the drive to produce surplus, where labour time is reduced for all, humans and nonhumans? Is it possible to dream of societies where animals are freed from their structural role as raw material, commodity and labour, and allowed to flourish in ways not determined by capitalist value chains? Will post-capitalism continue the nightmare imposed by capitalism on animals, or are our visions for a different order of liberation?

Notes

1 Value

1. Karl Marx, *Grundrisse: Foundations of the Critique of Political Economy (Rough Draft)*, trans. Martin Nicolaus (London: Penguin, 1993), 614.
2. I use the term 'food animals' in this book, defined as animals required to deploy their own metabolic processes to convert themselves into the consumption commodity. My utilisation of the term 'food animals' is inspired by Paula Arcari's similar use. See Paula Arcari, *Making Sense of 'Food' Animals: A Critical Exploration of the Persistence of 'Meat'* (Singapore: Palgrave Macmillan, 2020), 10, n. 11.
3. Food and Agriculture Organization of the United Nations (FAO), *FAOSTAT Statistical Database*, 2020, www.fao.org/faostat/en/.
4. Hannah Ritchie and Mark Roser, 'Meat and Seafood Production and Consumption', *Our World in Data*, 2017, www.ourworldindata.org/meat-and-seafood-production-consumption#per-capita-milk-consumption.
5. FAO, *The State of World Fisheries and Aquaculture 2020: Sustainability in Action* (Rome: FAO, 2020), 3.
6. See OECD/FAO, *OECD-FAO Agricultural Outlook 2018–2027* (Paris: OECD Publishing, 2018), 163–301.
7. The OECD estimates 3 per cent per capita growth in meat and fish over the period 2018 to 2027. Note there are strong regional differences in consumption growth, but it is instructive that the OECD notes that 'for meat, per capita consumption will grow most strongly in absolute terms in the developed world (+2.9kg per person over the outlook period) facilitated by lower prices'. Per capita dairy consumption growth rates are substantially larger; the OECD suggests 2.2 per cent growth per year over 2018 to 2027, 'the highest growth rate among the commod-

ities covered in the *Agricultural Outlook*'. See OECD/FAO, *Agricultural Outlook*, 26–8.

8. See Tony Weis, *The Ecological Hoofprint: The Global Burden of Industrial Livestock* (London: Zed Books, 2013).

9. See Raj Patel and Jason W. Moore, *A History of the World in Seven Cheap Things: A Guide to Capitalism, Nature, and the Future of the Planet* (Oakland: University of California Press, 2017), 3–5.

10. Patel and Moore, *A History of the World in Seven Cheap Things*, 138.

11. See Juliet Clutton-Brock, *Animals as Domesticates: A Worldview Through History* (Ann Arbor: University of Michigan Press, 2012), 3.

12. On biopolitics and its applications to industrial animal agriculture, see Dinesh Joseph Wadiwel, 'Biopolitics', in *Critical Terms for Animal Studies*, ed. Lori Gruen (London: University of Chicago Press, 2018), 79–98.

13. See Gavin Corral et al., 'On Producing Estimates for NASS's Quarterly Hogs and Pigs Report', United States Department of Agriculture, 2019.

14. USDA, 'Quarterly Hogs and Pigs', United States Department of Agriculture, 27 June 2019, 1. The relationship between the stock of animals kept for breeding, their productivity, the survival of litters and the availability of markets to exchange these animals (and consumers to purchase) is vital for this whole process and requires in-depth monitoring of these population flows and characteristics. This quarterly report notes: 'The March–May 2019 pig crop, at 34.2 million head, was up 4 percent from 2018. This is the largest March–May pig crop since estimates began in 1970. Sows farrowed during this period totaled 3.11 million head, up slightly from 2018. The sows farrowed during this quarter represented 49 percent of the breeding herd. The average pigs saved per litter was a record high 11.00 for the March–May period, compared to 10.63 last year' (1).

15. See for example Carol J. Adams, *The Sexual Politics of Meat: A Feminist-Vegetarian Critical Theory* (New York: Continuum, 1990); Val Plumwood, *Feminism and the Mastery of Nature* (London: Routledge, 1993); Lori Gruen, 'Dismantling Oppression', in *Ecofeminism: Women, Animals Nature*, ed. Greta Gaard (Philadelphia: Temple University Press, 1993), 60–90; and Mackenzie L. April, 'Readying the Rape Rack: Feminism and the Exploitation of Non-Human Reproductive Systems', *Dissenting Voices* 8, no. 1 (2019).

16. Kathryn Gillespie, 'Sexualized Violence and the Gendered Commodification of the Animal Body in Pacific Northwest US Dairy Production', *Gender, Place & Culture* 21, no. 10 (2014), 1329.

17. Gillespie highlights the particular way in which dairy industries tie together productive logics with gender norms: 'The use of bovine bodies for breeding, milk, semen, and meat is highly gendered, based on the industry's assessment

of the animal's biological sex at birth and notions of biological sex as it is tied to reproduction. In so doing, the dairy industry reproduces binary ways of thinking about sex and reproductive capacity and reinforces gendered ideas about the body. Animals are framed in the industry, first, as being "female" or "male" at birth and, then, as being reproductively viable or not; the trajectory of their lives is organized around these logics.' See Kathryn Gillespie, *The Cow with Ear Tag #1389* (Chicago: University of Chicago Press, 2018), 17.

18. See Sophie Lewis, *Full Surrogacy Now: Feminism Against Family* (London: Verso, 2019).

19. Richard Twine, *Animals As Biotechnology: Ethics, Sustainability and Critical Animal Studies* (London: Earthscan, 2010), 94.

20. Dinesh Joseph Wadiwel, *The War against Animals* (Leiden: Brill/Rodopi, 2015).

21. Tithi Bhattacharya, 'Introduction: Mapping Social Reproduction Theory', in *Social Reproduction Theory: Remapping Class, Recentering Oppression*, ed. Tithi Bhattacharya (London: Pluto Press, 2017), 2.

22. Michael Hardt and Antonio Negri, *Empire* (Cambridge, MA: Harvard University Press, 2000), 29.

23. Marx has a somewhat convoluted approach to understanding a 'raw material', separating out those commodities that are 'spontaneously provided by nature' from 'raw materials': 'The land (and this, economically speaking, includes water) in its original state in which it supplies man with necessaries or means of subsistence ready to hand is available without any effort on his part as the universal material for human labour. All those things which labour merely separates from immediate connection with their environment are objects of labour spontaneously provided by nature, such as a fish caught and separated from their natural element, namely water, timber felled in virgin forests, and ores extracted from their veins. If, on the other hand, the object of labour has, so to speak, been filtered through previous labour, we call it raw material. For example, ore already extracted and ready for washing. All raw material is an object of labour, but not every object of labour is a raw material; the object of labour counts as raw material only when it has already undergone some alteration by means of labour.' Karl Marx, *Capital: A Critique of Political Economy*, vol. 1, trans. Ben Fowkes (London: Penguin, 1986), 284–5.

24. This is certainly illustrated in academic discussion on how taxation should be applied to animals as assets. See for example Alexander Fullarton and Dale Pinto, 'Tax Accounting for Livestock: Mother or Meat/Capital or Revenue?' *New Zealand Journal of Taxation Law and Policy* 27, no. 1 (2021).

25. Marco Maurizi, *Beyond Nature: Animal Liberation, Marxism, and Critical Theory* (Leiden: Brill, 2021), 4.

26. Tom Regan, *The Case for Animal Rights* (Berkeley: University of California Press, 1983), 151–4.

27. Regan, *The Case for Animal Rights*, 243.

28. Martha C. Nussbaum, *Frontiers of Justice: Disability, Nationality, Species Membership* (Cambridge, MA: Harvard University Press, 2006).

29. Nussbaum, *Frontiers of Justice*, 365.

30. The latter approach is perhaps most famously developed by Sue Donaldson and Will Kymlicka in *Zoopolis: A Political Theory of Animal Rights* (Oxford: Oxford University Press, 2011).

31. See Wadiwel, *The War against Animals*, 29–36.

32. A. J. F. Webster, 'Animal Welfare: The Five Freedoms and the Free Market', *BSAP Occasional Publication* 17 (1993), 45. See also John Webster, 'Farm Animal Welfare: The Five Freedoms and the Free Market', *Veterinary Journal* 161, no. 3 (2001).

33. See Gary L. Francione, *Animals, Property, and the Law* (Philadelphia: Temple University Press, 2007).

34. Francione, *Animals, Property, and the Law*, 17–32.

35. See Maurizi, *Beyond Nature*, 100.

36. Erica Fudge, 'The Animal Face of Early Modern England', *Theory, Culture & Society* 30, no. 7/8 (2013), 195. See also Erica Fudge, 'Farmyard Choreographies in Early Modern England', in *Renaissance Posthumanism, ed.* Joseph Campana and Scott Maisano (New York: Fordham University Press, 2016), 145–66.

37. Marx, *Capital*, vol. 1, 247–57.

38. Marx, *Capital*, vol. 1, 254.

39. See David Harvey and Daniel Denvir, 'Why Marx's Capital Still Matters', *Jacobin*, 12 July 2018, www.jacobinmag.com/2018/07/karl-marx-capital-david-harvey.

40. And certainly, this means that in many parts of the world, animals serve complex economic and social functions, including as a means of attaining credit and insurance value. See for example Faizal Adams et al., 'Economic Benefits of Livestock Management in Ghana', *Agricultural and Food Economics* 9, no. 17 (2021).

41. As Marx emphasises, and as I shall discuss below, 'value' is always a construction, an imposition of one commodity in place of another, a process of exchange that is distinct from the 'intrinsic' qualities of the object of commodification. This is laid out with clarity in Marx's discussion of 'fetishism': 'the commodity-form, and the value relation of the products of labour within which it appears, have absolutely no connection with the physical nature of the commodity and the material [*dinglich*] relations arising out of this. It is nothing but the definite social relation between men themselves which assumes here, for them, the fantastic form of a relation between things.' Marx, *Capital*, vol. 1, 164–5. On animals and commodity

fetishism see Wadiwel, *The War against Animals*, 168–73; see also Vasile Stănescu, 'Selling Eden: Environmentalism, Local Meat, and the Postcommodity Fetish', *American Behavioral Scientist* 63, no. 8 (2019).

42. As Ted Benton notes, once we cut away the problem of an apparent ontological difference between animals and humans (which is usually used to justify our treatment of them), we are left with the structural question of how the animal is constructed for our utilisation and by our utilisation as a productive entity (in the same way that capitalism might create the 'worker' as a subject within capitalist production). See Ted Benton, *Natural Relations: Ecology, Animal Rights and Social Justice* (London: Verso, 1993), 42.

43. David Nibert, *Animal Oppression and Human Violence: Domesecration, Capitalism, and Global Conflict* (New York: Columbia University Press, 2013), 68.

44. Danielle Taschereau Mamers, 'Human-Bison Relations as Sites of Settler Colonial Violence and Decolonial Resurgence', *Humanimalia: A Journal of Human-Animal Interface Studies* 10, no. 2 (2019), 13. See also Billy-Ray Belcourt, 'Animal Bodies, Colonial Subjects: (Re)Locating Animality in Decolonial Thought', *Societies* 5, no. 1 (2014).

45. See Patrick Wolfe, *Traces of History: Elementary Structures of Race* (London: Verso, 2016); see also Bruce Pascoe, *Dark Emu* (Broome: Magabala Books, 2018).

46. Irene Watson, *Aboriginal Peoples, Colonialism and International Law: Raw Law* (Abingdon: Routledge, 2015), 17.

47. See Kim TallBear, 'Caretaking Relations, Not American Dreaming', *Kalfou* 6, no. 1 (2019), 24–5. See also Kim TallBear, 'An Indigenous Reflection on Working Beyond the Human/Not Human', *GLQ: A Journal of Lesbian and Gay Studies* 21, no. 2–3 (2015), 234.

48. On the relation of capitalism to the violence of colonialism, see for example Cedric J. Robinson, *Black Marxism: The Making of the Black Radical Tradition* (Chapel Hill: University of North Carolina Press, 2000); Patrick Wolfe, *Traces of History: Elementary Structures of Race* (London: Verso, 2016), particularly the 'Introduction' on 'preaccumulation'; and Saidiya Hartman, 'The Belly of the World: A Note on Black Women's Labors', *Souls* 18, no. 1 (2016).

49. Tom Tyler, *CIFERAE: A Bestiary in Five Fingers* (Minneapolis: University of Minnesota Press, 2012), 20–1.

50. As Ariel Salleh comments, referring simultaneously to the gendered ordering of nature, 'the silent cooperation of animals has been indispensable to men in building civilisation'. Ariel Salleh, *Ecofeminism as Politics: Nature, Marx and the Postmodern*, 2nd ed. (London: Zed Books, 2017), 112.

51. For example, consider the following: Dom Phillips et al., 'Revealed: Rampant Deforestation of Amazon Driven by Global Greed for Meat', *Guardian*, 2 July 2019,

https://www.theguardian.com/environment/2019/jul/02/revealed-amazon-de forestation-driven-global-greed-meat-brazil.

52. Karl Marx, *Capital: A Critique of Political Economy*, vol. 2, trans. David Fernbach (London: Penguin, 1992), 199.

53. John Bellamy Foster, 'The Financialization of Accumulation', *Monthly Review: An Independent Socialist Magazine*, 1 October 2010, https://monthlyreview.org/2010 /10/01/the-financialization-of-accumulation/.

54. See, for example, Jan Dutkiewicz, 'Uncertain Hog Futures: Life, Death, and Arbitrage on the Factory Farm', *Journal of Cultural Economy* 13, no. 3 (2020).

55. Indeed, Michael Roberts argues that we must reckon with the reality that an argument for financialisation as the contemporary source of value within capitalism would require 'the abandonment of the labor theory of value, an erroneous understanding of modern capitalism's *modus operandi* and, I think, eventually to reformist politics'. See Michael Roberts, 'Owning Financialization', *Monthly Review: An Independent Socialist Magazine*, 1 April 2019, https://monthlyreview.org/2019/04 /01/owning-financialization/. See also Ben Fine, 'Financialization from a Marxist Perspective', *International Journal of Political Economy* 42, no. 4 (2013).

56. I have used the term 'communism' strictly to mean the democratic control over production, surplus and/or labour time. As I discuss in Chapter 7, the term 'communism' is certainly tainted by its use as a descriptor for totalitarian state socialism and/or state-controlled forms of capitalist economy. As I suggest, the left must understand this history and rearticulate the meaning of this concept.

57. I note here the growing scholarship that connects analysis of Marx and/or analysis of capitalism to animal agency and/or liberation. A non-exhaustive list might include: Maurizi, *Beyond Nature*; Nibert, *Animal Oppression and Human Violence*; David Nibert, ed., *Animal Oppression and Capitalism*, vols 1 and 2 (Santa Barbara: Praeger, 2017); Maan Barua, 'Lively Commodities and Encounter Value', *Environment and Planning D: Society and Space* 34, no. 4 (2016); Les Beldo, 'Metabolic Labor: Broiler Chickens and the Exploitation of Vitality', *Environmental Humanities* 9, no. 1 (2017); David Brooks, 'The Fallacies: Theory, Saturation Capitalism and the Animal', *Southerly* 73, no. 2 (2013); Benton, *Natural Relations*; Ryan Gunderson, 'Marx's Comments on Animal Welfare', *Rethinking Marxism* 23, no. 4 (2011); Jason Hribal, '"Animals are Part of the Working Class": A Challenge to Labor History', *Labor History* 44, no. 4 (2003); Barbara Noske, *Beyond Boundaries: Humans and Animals* (Montreal: Black Rose Books, 1997); Corinne Painter, 'Non-Human Animals within Contemporary Capitalism: A Marxist Account of Non-Human Animal Liberation', *Capital & Class* 40, no. 2 (2016); Katherine Perlo, 'Marxism and the Underdog', *Society & Animals* 10 (2002); Marcel Sebastian, 'Deadly Efficiency: The Impact of Capitalist Production on the "Meat" Industry,

Slaughterhouse Workers and Nonhuman Animals', in *Animal Oppression and Capitalism*, vol. 2, ed. Nibert, 167–83; Nicole Shukin, *Animal Capital: Rendering Life in Biopolitical Times* (Minneapolis: University of Minnesota Press, 2009); Dianna Stuart, Rebecca L. Schewe and Ryan Gunderson, 'Extending Social Theory to Farm Animals: Addressing Alienation in the Dairy Sector', *Sociologia Ruralis* 53, no. 2 (2013); Bob Torres, *Making a Killing: The Political Economy of Animal Rights* (Oakland: AK Press, 2007); *Beasts of Burden: Capitalism, Animals, Communism* (London: Antagonism Press, 1999); Eliza Littleton, *Animals in Capital: A Marxist Perspective on the Use of Other Animals in Capitalist Commodity Production*, honours thesis, University of Sydney, 1 October 2015, http://hdl.handle.net/21 23/14087; and Bündnis Marxismus und Tierbefreiung/Alliance for Marxism and Animal Liberation, '18 theses on Marxism and Animal Liberation', 28 August 2018, https://mronline.org/2018/08/28/18-theses-on-marxism-and-animal-liberation/.

58. Marx, *Capital*, vol. 1, 343. As Ryan Gunderson observes, the fact that Marx saw animal welfare as a bourgeois activity does not necessarily mean that animals should not be of concern to leftist politics; indeed it only demonstrates with certainty that Marx was suspicious of reformist politics driven by interests other than those of the working class. See Gunderson, 'Marx's Comments on Animal Welfare', 546.

59. See Karl Marx, 'Economic and Philosophic Manuscripts of 1844', in *The Marx-Engels Reader: Second Edition*, ed. Robert Tucker (New York: W. W. Norton & Company, 1978), 66–125. This view of animal labour is repeated even in relatively contemporary left scholarship; for example, in the classic 1974 text *Labor and Monopoly Capital*, Harry Braverman devotes substantial space to defending the view that humans labour in a way that is non-'instinctual', arguing that 'labor that transcends mere instinctual activity is thus the force which created humankind and the force by which humankind created the world as we know it'. See Harry Braverman, *Labor and Monopoly Capital: The Degradation of Work in the Twentieth Century* (New York: Monthly Review Press, 1974), 50. This perspective has been challenged by other scholars who point out that there is more than enough evidence to suggest that at least some animals labour in ways that might resemble the ways humans labour, including in accumulating stocks or reserves beyond necessity. See Benton, *Natural Relations*, and Noske, *Beyond Boundaries*.

60. See Marx, 'Economic and Philosophic Manuscripts of 1844'.

61. Benton, *Natural Relations*, 40–3.

62. Marx repeats this later in *Grundrisse*: 'Basically the appropriation of animals, land etc. cannot take place in a master-servant relation, although the animal provides service. The presupposition of the master-servant relation is the appropriation of

an alien *will*. Whatever has no will, e.g. the animal, may well provide a service, but does not thereby make its owner into a *master*' (500–1).

63. Marx, 'Economic and Philosophic Manuscripts of 1844', 74.

64. See Craig Browne's exploration of the concept of alienation within social theory, and its many forms during the twentieth century. Craig Browne, *Critical Social Theory* (London: Sage, 2017), 59–88.

65. Michel Foucault, *The Order of Things: An Archaeology of the Human Sciences* (New York: Vintage Books, 1994), 261.

66. See for example Maurizi, *Beyond Nature*, 105–8; and John Bellamy Foster and Brett Clark, 'Marx and Alienated Speciesism', *Monthly Review: An Independent Socialist Magazine*, 1 December 2018, https://monthlyreview.org/2018/12/01/marx-and-alienated-speciesism/.

67. Maurizi, *Beyond Nature*, 106.

68. See Will Kymlicka and Sue Donaldson, 'Animal Rights, Multiculturalism, and the Left', *Journal of Social Philosophy* 45 (2014), 116–35.

69. See Henry Salt, *The Logic of Vegetarianism: Essays and Dialogues*, 2nd ed. (London: George Bell and Sons, 1906).

70. John Sanbonmatsu, 'Introduction', in *Critical Theory and Animal Liberation*, ed. John Sanbonmatsu (Lanham: Rowman & Littlefield, 2011), 1–32 (13). Fahim Amir produces a similarly pithy summary of the problem: 'When it comes to animals, the left turns right.' See Fahim Amir, *Being and Swine: The End of Nature (As We Knew It)*, trans. Geoffrey C. Howes & Corvin Russell (Toronto: Between the Lines, 2021), 5. More expansively, Bob Torres observes: 'While the animal rights movement organizations themselves could alleviate some of these problems by actively thinking about their relations with the working class, people of color, and other movements on the political Left, at least some of this thinking stems from a form of human supremacy that needs to be seriously questioned within the Left, if Leftists and progressives are serious about overcoming domination and exploitation.' Torres, *Making a Killing*, 119.

71. For example, Colonel Richard Martin, the instigator of the pioneering English *Cruel Treatment of Cattle Act of 1822* and one of the initiators of the Society for the Prevention of Cruelty to Animals, could not be mistaken for anything but a member of the elite.

72. Paola Cavalieri, 'Introduction', in *Philosophy and the Politics of Animal Liberation*, ed. Paola Cavalieri (New York: Palgrave Macmillan, 2016), 1–13 (4).

73. See The Vegan Society, 'About the International Rights Network', 2019, https://www.vegansociety.com/get-involved/international-rights-network/about-international-rights-network. See also Jeanette Rowley, 'Human Rights are Animal Rights: The Implications of Ethical Veganism for Human Rights', in *Critical*

Perspectives on Veganism, ed. Jodey Castricano and Rasmus R. Simonsen (Basingstoke: Palgrave Macmillan, 2016), 67–92.

74. See Nancy Fraser, 'Social Justice in the Age of Identity Politics: Redistribution, Recognition and Participation', The Tanner Lectures on Human Values, Stanford University, 30 April–2 May 1996, 6–7, https://tannerlectures.utah.edu/_resources /documents/a-to-z/f/Fraser98.pdf.

75. It is of course not just in the space of food production that this total subsumption of animal life within the rhythms of capitalist production occurs. Global statistics on the use of animals for research remain inconsistent, though some measures suggest over 100 million animals a year (see Lush Prize, *A Global View of Animal Experiments*, 2014, http://www.lushprize.org/wp-content/uploads/Global_View _of-Animal_Experiments_2014.pdf). Certainly, there is evidence to suggest that there is growing use of animals in research, at least in some jurisdictions such as the European Union; see Kate Taylor and Laura Rego, 'EU Statistics on Animal Experiments for 2014', *ALTEX* 33 (2016).

76. Indeed, we might roughly characterise the contemporary animal movement as a symptomatic response to developments in capitalism and their relation to the structural position of animals. This would be reminiscent of a 'dialectical' approach to history, where material relations and knowledge move in relation to each other, and contradictions have the capacity to produce progressive changes in knowledge. Of course, such a characterisation of the history of animal advocacy is deterministic and potentially lacks subtlety. However, it seems difficult to escape the way in which capitalism as a relation shapes human–animal relations, and this gives contemporary animal movements a lens by which to view and problematise anthropocentrism as a contemporary material problem. Should we be surprised that the emergence of a contestation in relation to the utilisation of animals – that is, the beginning of the modern animal welfare movement in the Global North – is tied to a specific moment where capitalism seizes upon and massively over-exploits animals as a source and engine of wealth? For an example of such a 'dialectical' approach to thinking about human–animal relations in the context of capitalism, see Maurizi, *Beyond Nature*, 132–60.

77. It is not merely animals here that we may focus on, but the way in which animals interact with other constituents or 'factors' of production. It is certainly worth noting the interaction between children and animals in the histories of industrial capitalism. With respect to coal mining, it is curious to consider the way in which the experiences of children used in mines coalesce with those of draught animals, as illustrated by this passage from the 1842 report from the United Kingdom Commission into children's mine work: 'There are no rewards but they are often punished until they can scarcely stand. He has to draw as well as guide the corve

by the belt; has to often draw hard when the asses tire, and they have to start them again. He often had his hips ache and smart again when he got home, and often it galls him as the collar does a horse.' See Great Britain Commissioners for Inquiring into the Employment and Condition of Children in Mines and Manufactories, *The Condition and Treatment of the Children employed in the Mines and Colliers of the United Kingdom Carefully compiled from the appendix to the first report of the Commissioners: With copious extracts from the evidence, and illustrative engravings* (London: William Strange, 1842), 58, https://www.bl.uk/collection-items/report-on-child-labour-1842.

78. Silvia Federici, *Caliban and the Witch*: *Women, The Body and Primitive Accumulation* (Brooklyn: Autonomedia, 2004).

79. See Robinson, *Black Marxism*. On Robinson, and the significance of this work within US intellectual life and thought, see Brenda Gayle Plummer, 'On Cedric Robinson and Black Marxism: a view from the US academy', *Race & Class* 47, no. 2 (2005), 111–14.

80. Michael Oliver, *The Politics of Disablement* (Houndmills: Macmillan, 1990), 25–42. For more recent analysis of the relations between disability and capitalism, see also David T. Mitchell and Sharon L. Snyder, *The Biopolitics of Disability: Neoliberalism, Ablenationalism, and Peripheral Embodiment* (Ann Arbor: University of Michigan Press, 2015).

81. Dipesh Chakrabarty, 'The Climate of History: Four Theses', *Critical Inquiry* 35 (2009). See also Rosi Braidotti's discussion of Chakrabarty and the current challenge faced by classical humanism; Rosi Braidotti, *The Posthuman* (Cambridge: Polity, 2013), 83–4.

82. John Bellamy Foster, *Marx's Ecology: Materialism and Nature* (New York: Monthly Review Press, 2000).

83. Foster, *Marx's Ecology*, 141. Foster goes on to argue that this 'contradiction develops through the growth simultaneously of large-scale industry and large-scale agriculture under capitalism, with the former providing the latter with the means of the intensive exploitation of the soil. Like Liebig, Marx argued that long-distance trade in food and fiber for clothing made the problem of the alienation of the constituent elements of the soil that much more of an "irreparable rift"' (156). See also 155–6.

84. Foster and Clark, 'Marx and Alienated Speciesism'. See also Foster, *Marx's Ecology*, 148–9; 253; John Bellamy Foster, *Ecology Against Capitalism* (New York: Monthly Review Press, 2000), 163–6.

85. To an extent Maurizi advances a resonant argument: see for example Maurizi, *Beyond Nature*, 88–101, 105–8. However, Maurizi notes that 'I believe that a "Marxist" critique of Marxist anthropocentrism has already been elaborated by

the Frankfurt School in the 1940s' (18); this leads to a different historical critique, which suggests that 'Surely Marx could not imagine the alienating and destructive development that the domination of man over nature would bring in the twentieth century. Yet, Marx and Engels's unshakable belief in the goodness and rationality of such domination reveals an inability to conceive a *limit* in our appropriation of nature, a limit that would have forced them to accord nature the status of the *subject*' (151).

86. For resonant analysis, see Christian Stache, 'Conceptualising Animal Exploitation in Capitalism: Getting Terminology Straight', *Capital and Class* 44, no. 3 (2019).

87. See Jason W. Moore, *Capitalism in the Web of Life: Ecology and the Accumulation of Capital* (London: Verso, 2015).

88. See Moore, *Capitalism in the Web of Life*, 83–7.

89. Moore, *Capitalism in the Web of Life*, 25.

90. Moore, *Capitalism in the Web of Life*, 54.

91. Patel and Moore, *A History of the World in Seven Cheap Things*. See also Raj Patel and Jason W. Moore, 'How the Chicken Nugget Became the True Symbol of Our Era', *Guardian*, 8 May 2018, https://www.theguardian.com/news/2018/may/08/how-the-chicken-nugget-became-the-true-symbol-of-our-era.

92. Moore, *Capitalism in the Web of Life*, 232.

93. Moore, *Capitalism in the Web of Life*, 232.

94. Moore, *Capitalism in the Web of Life*, 65; 93 n. 9.

95. Salleh, *Ecofeminism as Politics*, 1.

96. Salleh defines ecofeminist politics as applying to a 'man or woman whose political actions support the premise that the domination of nature and domination of women are interconnected'. Salleh, *Ecofeminism as Politics*, 162.

97. Salleh argues that 'it is precisely this attempt to gain domination and control over nature that gives rise to class society, as men harness the labour power of Others to help subdue the wild'. Salleh, *Ecofeminism as Politics*, 114.

98. Salleh, *Ecofeminism as Politics*, 118.

99. Salleh, *Ecofeminism as Politics*, 91–2; see also 70 and 78.

100. See for example Salleh, *Ecofeminism as Politics*, 283.

101. Salleh, *Ecofeminism as Politics*, 282–3.

102. See J. K. Gibson-Graham, *The End of Capitalism (As We Knew It):A Feminist Critique of Political Economy* (Minneapolis: University of Minnesota Press, 2006), 5–11.

103. See Bertell Ollman, 'Marxism and the Philosophy of Internal Relations; or, How to Replace the Mysterious "Paradox" with "Contradictions" that can be Studied and Resolved', *Capital and Class* 39, no. 1 (2015). Ollman states: 'The philosophy of internal relations . . . [treats] its relational parts, when extended to their fur-

NOTES | 227

thest limits, as so many versions – albeit one-sided versions – of the whole. The one-sidedness is a product, of where one begins to examine the interactions and changes that go on, and its role in establishing the order, visibility and relative importance of the rest that comes into view' (10).

104. Marx, *Capital*, vol. 1, 280.

105. Indeed, Marx begins his *Capital* with the provocation that wealth 'appears' as a collection of commodities, however, value as relation sits behind this immediate 'appearance': 'the wealth of societies in which the capitalist mode of production prevails appears as an "immense collection of commodities"; the individual commodity appears as its elementary form' (125). See also Karl Marx, *Preface and Introduction to a Contribution to the Critique of Political Economy* (Peking: Foreign Languages Press, 1976). On 'appearance' ('*Erscheinung*') in Marx and its distinct function within Marx's epistemology, see Igor Hanzel, 'Mistranslations of "*Schein*" and "*Erscheinung*": The Structure of Chapter 1 of "Capital", Volume I', *Science & Society* 74, no. 4 (2010).

106. Louis Althusser, 'From Capital to Marx's Philosophy', in *Reading Capital: The Complete Edition*, ed. Louis Althusser et al. (London: Verso, 2015), 9–76 (27).

107. Althusser, *Reading Capital*, 21.

108. Althusser, *Reading Capital*, 22.

109. Note this question differs from the question 'Do animals labour?' Asking after the *value* of animal labour power moves us beyond understanding whether animals can labour and pushes us towards understanding the unique value role of animals for capitalism. The question I am asking here also differs from the question of what makes animals attractive as final saleable products (e.g., 'are animals good to eat?'), which deals only with the fetishisation of commodities in the consumption circulation of capital and not the production circulation.

110. See Louis Althusser, 'The Object of Capital', in *Reading Capital*, ed. Althusser et al., 215–355 (268–70). See also Louis Althusser, *For Marx* (London: New Left Books, 1977), 221–47. On antihumanism as a tendency, see Braidotti, *The Posthuman*, 16–25.

111. Marx, *Grundrisse*, 498. To an extent, Gilles Deleuze and Félix Guattari noticed this, reworking Marx's value theory by suggesting that science and technologies might independently produce value. See Gilles Deleuze and Félix Guattari, *Anti-Oedipus: Capitalism and Schizophrenia* (Minneapolis: University of Minnesota Press, 1994), 222–40. Jason Read highlights how this was an important development in how to read Marx: 'Deleuze and Guattari do not recognise the existence of anything like an anthropological constant underlying abstract labour, arguing that any idea of a standard amount of labour is itself the product of an arbitrary imposition. What Deleuze and Guattari focus on is not the equivalence underlying

abstract labour, the fact that the labour of one person is equal to that of others, but its abstraction, or, more properly, deterritorialisation, its indifference to object or subject. It is perhaps for this reason that in *Anti-Oedipus* Deleuze and Guattari also consider the role of machines, actual machines, in the production of surplus-value. If labour can be abstracted from particular forms of subjectivity, from the blacksmith or shoemaker as a particular kind of labourer, and from particular objects, from the land or industry, then why cannot it also be abstracted from humanity, from human hands and minds altogether? Abstract labour becomes part of the machine; not just in the sense that Marx might have argued, in which the pure motor force of the body is replaced by the machine, but in the sense that abstract subjective activity, including that of knowledge, can become part of the machine.' See Jason Read, 'The Fetish is Always Actual, Revolution is Always Virtual: From Noology to Noopolitics', *Deleuze Studies* 3 (2009), 90.

112. In a sense, this is precisely the approach of Moore: 'Marx's conception of value relations, in other words, provides a way of seeing the exploitation of labour power and the appropriation of unpaid work as a singular metabolism of many determinations. The exclusion of value-relations from the historical materialism of nature has the virtue of never specifying how capital works through nature . . .' Moore, *Capitalism in the Web of Life*, 81. However, in collapsing animals into unpaid appropriated work, Moore misses the explicit dynamics that circulate animals in formal production.

113. On 'multispecies justice', see Danielle Celermajer et al., 'Multispecies Justice: Theories, Challenges, and a Research Agenda for Environmental Politics', *Environmental Politics* 30, no. 1–2 (2021).

114. For an indication of the extent of this life, see Yinon Bar-On, Rob Phillips and Ron Milo, 'The Biomass Distribution on Earth', *Proceedings of the National Academy of Sciences* 115, no. 25 (2018); Kenneth Locey and Jay Lennon, 'Scaling Laws Predict Global Microbial Diversity', *Proceedings of the National Academy of Sciences* 113, no. 21 (2016).

115. See for example the Intergovernmental Panel on Climate Change (IPCC), 'Summary for Policymakers', in *Climate Change and Land: An IPCC Special Report on Climate Change, Desertification, Land Degradation, Sustainable Land Management, Food Security, and Greenhouse Gas Fluxes in Terrestrial Ecosystems* (Geneva, 2019); and Paul J. Crutzen, 'Geology of Mankind', *Nature* 415 (2000), 23.

116. See Wadiwel, *The War against Animals*, 65–124 and 178–220.

117. See for example Donaldson and Kymlicka, *Zoopolis*; Kimberley Smith, *Governing Animals: Animal Welfare and the Liberal State* (Oxford: Oxford University Press, 2012); and Gregory Smulewicz-Zucker, 'Bringing the State into Animal Rights

NOTES | 229

Politics', in *Philosophy and the Politics of Animal Liberation*, ed. Paola Cavalieri (New York: Palgrave Macmillan, 2016), 239–72.

118. Michael Hardt and Antonio Negri, 'Marx's Mole is Dead! Globalisation and Communication', *Eurozine*, 13 February 2002, https://www.eurozine.com/marxs -mole-is-dead-2/.

2 Material

1. Marx, *Capital*, vol. 1, 91.
2. Althusser, *Reading Capital*, 109.
3. Marx, *Critique of Political Economy*, 4.
4. Marx, *Preface and Introduction to a Contribution*, 4.
5. Antonio Gramsci, *Further Selections from the Prison Notebooks* (Minneapolis: University of Minnesota Press, 1995), 238.
6. See for example Stuart Hall, *The Hard Road to Renewal: Thatcherism and the Crisis of the Left* (London: Verso, 1988).
7. Foucault provides a short and clear critique of this Marxist notion of ideology in an interview: 'the notion of ideology appears to me to be difficult to make use of, for three reasons. The first is that, like it or not, it always stands in virtual opposition to something else which is supposed to count as truth. Now I believe that the problem does not consist in drawing the line between that in a discourse which falls under the category of scientificity or truth, and that which comes under some other category, but in seeing historically how effects of truth are produced within discourses which in themselves are neither true or false. The second drawback is that the concept of ideology refers, I think necessarily, to something of the order of the subject. Thirdly, ideology stands in a secondary position relative to something which functions as its infrastructure, as its material, economic determinant etc.' Michel Foucault, 'Truth and Power', in *Power/Knowledge: Selected Interviews & Other Writings, 1972–1977*, ed. Colid Gordon (New York: Pantheon Books, 1980), 109–33 (118).
8. Vicky Kirby, 'Matter out of Place: "New Materialism" in Review', in *What if Culture Was Nature all Along?*, ed. Vicky Kirby (Edinburgh: Edinburgh University Press, 2017), 1–25 (8).
9. Christopher N. Gamble, Joshua S. Hanan and Thomas Nail, 'What Is New Materialism?' *Angelaki* 24, no. 6 (2019), 118.
10. Simon Choat, 'Science, Agency and Ontology: A Historical-Materialist Response to New Materialism', *Political Studies* 66, no. 4 (2018), 1029.
11. Diana Coole and Samantha Frost, 'Introducing the New Materialisms', in *New Materialisms: Ontology, Agency, and Politics*, ed. Diana Coole and Samantha Frost (Durham, NC: Duke University Press, 2010), 1–43.

230 | ANIMALS AND CAPITAL

12. At least part of this involves a distancing from Judith Butler's understanding of the text, normative construction and power. It should be noted here that while it might be argued that Butler rehearses a view that human knowledge and signification systems shape the material, the argument put forward by Butler is arguably more interested in the way that regulatory norms relate to matter, including through processes of continual sedimentation or change, and is not strictly in this sense 'constructionist'. Butler states: 'What I would propose in place of these conceptions of construction is a return to the notion of matter, not as a site or surface, but as *a process of materialization that stabilizes over time to produce the effect of boundary, fixity, and surface we call matter.* That matter is always materialized has, I think, to be thought in relation to the productive, indeed materializing effects of regulatory power in the Foucaultian sense. Thus the question is no longer, How is gender constituted as and through a certain interpretation of sex? (a question that leaves the "matter" of sex untheorized), but rather, Through what regulatory norms is sex itself materialized? And how is it that treating the materiality of sex as given presupposes and consolidates the normative conditions of its own emergence?' Judith Butler, *Bodies That Matter* (London: Routledge, 1993), 9–10. For a discussion of Butler and responses to Butler relevant to new materialisms, see Sara Ahmed, 'Imaginary Prohibitions: Some Preliminary Remarks on the Founding Gestures of the "New Materialism"', *European Journal of Women's Studies* 15, no. 1 (2008), 33; and Jessica Cadwallader, 'How Judith Butler Matters', *Australian Feminist Studies* 24, no. 60 (2009).

13. Coole and Frost, 'Introducing the New Materialisms', 5.

14. Coole and Frost, 'Introducing the New Materialisms', 3.

15. Coole and Frost, 'Introducing the New Materialisms', 5. This has meant that at least some new materialist approaches function as a route to establish a method for humanities and social sciences researchers to approach and work with the natural sciences. Elizabeth A. Wilson, for example, notes that 'one thing feminist theory still needs, even after decades of feminist work on the life sciences, is a conceptual toolkit for reading biology'. Elizabeth A. Wilson, *Gut Feminism* (Durham, NC: Duke University Press, 2015), 3. For work that moves between the human and natural sciences, and questions the boundaries between, see Kirby, 'Matter out of Place'; Vicky Kirby, *Quantum Anthropologies: Life at Large* (Durham, NC: Duke University Press, 2011); and Karen Barad, *Meeting the Universe Halfway: Quantum Physics and the Entanglement of Matter and Meaning* (Durham, NC: Duke University Press, 2007).

16. Here I am associating 'old materialism' with Marx; though as Gamble, Hanan and Nail discuss, there is an ancient tradition of materialism that at least some

new materialism attempts to recover. See Gamble, Hanan and Nail, 'What Is New Materialism?' 113–15.

17. Coole and Frost, 'Introducing the New Materialisms', 30.

18. For more a more detailed discussion of new materialism in comparison to historical materialism, see Choat, 'Science, Agency and Ontology'; and Hanna Meißner, 'New Material Feminisms and Historical Materialism: A Diffractive Reading of Two (Ostensibly) Unrelated Perspectives', in *Mattering: Feminism, Science, and Materialism*, ed. Victoria Pitts-Taylor (New York: NYU Press, 2016), 43–57.

19. Meißner, 'New Material Feminisms and Historical Materialism', 53.

20. Choat, 'Science, Agency and Ontology', 1040.

21. Antonio Negri remarks of the *Grundrisse*: 'One last element of our starting hypotheses on the method in the *Grundrisse*: it is a question of the crisis of the law of value, that is to say of the summit of Marx's research. The hypothesis is that we have already entered into an advanced phase of the crisis of the law of value. Our Marxist method, materialist and dialectical, must take into account the resulting modifications and must change accordingly. It will not be enough to pose the question. We must also offer a response. Nothing is more central than this question.' Antonio Negri, *Marx Beyond Marx: Lessons on the Grundrisse*, trans. Harry Cleaver, Michael Ryan and Maurizio Viano (Brooklyn: Autonomedia, 1991), 14.

22. See Kim TallBear, 'Beyond the Life/Not-Life Binary: A Feminist-Indigenous Reading of Cryopreservation, Interspecies Thinking, and the New Materialisms', in *Cryopolitics: Frozen Life in a Melting World*, ed. Joanna Radin and Emma Kowal (Cambridge: MIT Press, 2017), 179–202 (193). Importantly, for TallBear, recognising Indigenous perspectives also means committing to the political movements of Indigenous people, including the material politics of distribution: 'Indigenous people, our movements and our voices are the others it seems the new materialists – indeed most of Western thought – cannot fully comprehend as living. They may hear us like ghosts go bump in the night. Once forced to see us, they may be terrified of the claims we make on their house' (198).

23. See Jason Edwards, 'The Materialism of Historical Materialism', in *New Materialisms*, ed. Coole and Frost, 281–92 (282). The problem of value does not appear as central to Edwards's understanding of Marx's capitalism. Edwards veers towards encouraging an analysis of the assemblage of material practices which make up capitalism and its reproduction. Value, and surplus value, are only mentioned briefly (see 283–4). Nevertheless, I believe Edwards's reworking of historical materialism is more or less compatible with the approach I have advanced in this book. The aim – precisely – is to situate animals within the contemporary logic of value with capitalism, in circulatory processes of production and reproduction.

24. Rick Dolphijn and Iris van der Tui, *New Materialism: Interviews & Cartographies* (Ann Arbor: Open Humanities Press, 2012), 119.

25. Braidotti, *The Posthuman*, 3.

26. Kirby, 'Matter out of Place', 16.

27. Although new materialisms draw ethical judgements from ontological, it is not self-apparent what the relation between ontology and ethics is. Erika Cudworth and Stephen Hobden state plainly of new materialisms that the 'claim that we exist in a condition of complexity is an ontological one, not an ethical one'. See Erika Cudworth and Stephen Hobden, 'Liberation for Straw Dogs? Old Materialism, New Materialism, and the Challenge of an Emancipatory Posthumanism', *Globalizations* 12, no. 1 (2015). For a different discussion of the politics of new materialism, see Stephanie Clare, 'On the Politics of "New Feminist Materialisms"', in *Mattering*, ed. Pitts-Taylor, 58–72.

28. See for example Bruno Latour, 'The Powers of Association', in *Power, Action and Belief: A New Sociology of Knowledge?*, ed. John Law (London: Routledge and Kegan Paul, 1986), 264–80, and Bruno Latour, *We Have Never Been Modern* (Cambridge, MA: Harvard University Press, 1993).

29. Jane Bennett, *Vibrant Matter: A Political Ecology of Things* (Durham, NC: Duke University Press, 2010), 36. Latour produces a similar delegated and diffused model of power, comparing political power to the movement of a ball in a football game. See Latour, 'The Powers of Association', 267–8.

30. Bennett, *Vibrant Matter*, 38.

31. Bennett, *Vibrant Matter*, 38. Thomas Lemke offers an alternative to Bennett's flattening of ontology in the form of Foucault's 'government of things'. See Thomas Lemke, 'New Materialisms: Foucault and the "Government of Things"', *Theory, Culture & Society* 32, no. 4 (2015).

32. As Ferenc Feber observed, 'European modernity came armed with a particular form of political monism in the shape of an absolute faith in an orientalising conception of human progress and technology; and a different and interconnected political monism arrives post 1989 into the single story of the "triumph of capitalism".' Ferenc Feher, '1989 and the Deconstruction of Political Monism', *Thesis Eleven* 42, no. 1 (1995), 94–5.

33. Rosi Braidotti, 'Anthropos Redux: A Defence of Monism in the Anthropocene Epoch', *Frame: A Journal of Literary Studies* 29, no. 2 (2016), 40.

34. See Pheng Cheah, 'Non-Dialectical Materialism', in *New Materialisms*, ed. Coole and Frost, 70–91.

35. Jacques Derrida makes this dynamic clear when thinking of law and its relation to justice. The point of justice is that the just decision is not self-apparent. It emerges through a process that is fraught and always open to subsequent re-inquiry or, in

Derrida's sense, 'deconstruction': 'The undecidable is not merely the oscillation or the tension between two decisions; it is the experience of that which, though heterogeneous, foreign to the order of the calculable and the rule, is still obliged – it is of obligation that we must speak – to give itself up to the impossible decision, while taking account of law and rules. A decision that didn't go through the ordeal of the undecidable would not be a free decision, it would only be the programmable application or unfolding of a calculable process. It might be legal; it would not be just. But in the moment of suspense of the undecidable, it is not just either, for only a decision is just (in order to maintain the proposition "only a decision is just", one need not refer decision to the structure of a subject or to the propositional form of a judgment). And once the ordeal of the undecidable is past (if that is possible), the decision has again followed a rule or given itself a rule, invented it or reinvented, reaffirmed it, it is no longer presently just, fully just. There is apparently no moment in which a decision can be called presently and fully just: either it has not yet been made according to a rule, and nothing allows us to call it just, or, it has already followed a rule – whether received, confirmed, conserved or reinvented – which in its turn is not absolutely guaranteed by anything; and, moreover, if it were guaranteed, the decision would be reduced to calculation and we couldn't call it just.' Jacques Derrida, 'Force of Law: The Mystical Foundation of Authority', in *Deconstruction and the Possibility of Justice*, ed. Drucilla Cornell, Michel Rosenfeld and David Gray Carlson (New York: Routledge, 1992), 3–67 (24). Note, and highly relevant to this discussion, Derrida observes the way that the politics of justice includes the politics of who is admitted as a subject of violence, and therefore owed justice: 'In the space in which I'm situating these remarks or reconstituting this discourse one would not speak of injustice or violence toward an animal, even less toward a vegetable or a stone. An animal can be made to suffer, but we would never say, in a sense considered proper, that it is a wronged subject, the victim of a crime, of a murder, of a rape or a theft, of a perjury – and this is true a fortiori, we think, for what we call vegetable or mineral or intermediate species like the sponge. There have been, there are still, many "subjects" among mankind who are not recognized as subjects and who receive this animal treatment (this is the whole unfinished history I briefly alluded to a moment ago). What we confusedly call "animal", the living thing as living and nothing else, is not a subject of the law or of law (*droit*). The opposition between just and unjust has no meaning in this case. As for trials for animals (there have been some) or lawsuits against those who inflict certain kinds of suffering on animals (legislation in certain Western countries provides for this and speaks not only of the rights of man but also of the rights of animals in general), these are considered to be either archaisms or still marginal and rare phenomena not constitutive of our culture.

In our culture, carnivorous sacrifice is fundamental, dominant, regulated by the highest industrial technology, as is biological experimentation on animals – so vital to our modernity' (18).

36. And this is perhaps why Joanna Oksala has argued that ontologies should be considered from the domain of politics. See Joanna Oksala, 'Foucault's Politicization of Ontology', *Continental Philosophy Review* 43 (2010). See also Kelly Struthers Montford and Chloë Taylor, 'Beyond Edibility: Towards a Nonspeciesist, Decolonial Food Ontology', in *Colonialism and Animality: Anti-Colonial Perspectives in Critical Animal Studies*, ed. Kelly Struthers Montford and Chloë Taylor (New York: Routledge, 2020), 129–56.

37. Mario Tronti, *Workers and Capital* (London: Verso, 2019), 202. As I shall discuss in Chapter 6, this view of capital as a relation between domination and resistance is central to the autonomist or 'operaist' account of capitalism; Negri observes that 'the totality of this process is permanently shaped by the fundamental antagonism and carries the mark of exploitation. In other words, the dynamic unity of the process of surplus-value does not, in any way, eliminate the separation of the subjects (wage labor and capital), but rather continually pushes each mediation (value form, money, forms of work or exchange, etc.) to its point of contradiction and its supercession.' See Negri, *Marx Beyond Marx*, 9.

38. Frank B. Wilderson III, *Red, White & Black: Cinema and the Structure of US Antagonisms* (Durham, NC: Duke University Press, 2010), 35–53.

39. Wilderson makes this point with reference to Indigenous sovereignty, which he argues operates at least partially through a framework of conflict rather than antagonism: 'But these differences do not cancel each other out. That is, they are not differences with an antagonistic structure, but differences with a conflictual structure, because articulation, rather than a void, makes the differences legible.' Wilderson, *Red, White & Black*, 45. Note Wilderson stresses this is 'partial' because of the operation of genocidal logics in the settler project, which were necessarily antagonistic: 'Clearly, the coherence of Whiteness as a structural position in modernity depends on the capacity to be free from genocide, perhaps not as a historical experience, but at least as a positioning modality. This embodied capacity (genocidal immunity) of Whiteness jettisons the White/Red relation from that of a conflict and marks it as an antagonism: it stains it with irreconcilability. Here, the Indian comes into being and is positioned by an a priori violence of genocide' (49).

40. Wilderson, *Red, White & Black*, 52.

41. Michiel van Ingen, 'Beyond The Nature/Culture Divide? The Contradictions of Rosi Braidotti's *The Posthuman*', *Journal of Critical Realism* 15, no. 5 (2016).

42. On feminist Indigenous standpoint theory, see Aileen Moreton-Robinson, 'Towards an Australian Indigenous Women's Standpoint Theory', *Australian*

Feminist Studies 28, no. 78 (2013). See also Kim TallBear, 'Standing with and Speaking as Faith: A Feminist-Indigenous Approach to Inquiry', *Journal of Research Practice* 10, no. 2 (2014); and Donna Haraway, 'Situated Knowledges: The Science Question in Feminism and the Privilege of Partial Perspective', *Feminist Studies* 14, no. 3 (1988).

43. Zakiyyah Iman Jackson, 'Outer Worlds: The Persistence of Race in Movement "Beyond the Human"', *GLQ: A Journal of Lesbian and Gay Studies* 21, no. 2/3 (2015). See also Diana Leong, 'The Mattering of Black Lives: Octavia Butler's Hyperempathy and the Promise of the New Materialisms', *Catalyst: Feminism, Theory, Technoscience* 2, no. 2 (2016); and Armond R. Towns, 'Black "Matter" Lives', *Women's Studies in Communication* 41, no. 4 (2018).

44. See for example Alexander G. Weheliye, *Habeas Viscus: Racializing Assemblages, Biopolitics, and Black Feminist Theories of the Human* (Durham, NC: Duke University Press, 2014), 2–3.

45. Eva Haifa Giraud, *What Comes after Entanglement? Activism, Anthropocentrism, and an Ethics of Exclusion* (Durham, NC: Duke University Press, 2019), 4.

46. Giraud, *What Comes after Entanglement?*, 172.

47. Giraud, *What Comes after Entanglement?*, 180.

48. Or as Giraud observes: 'A focus on specific relations or encounters in themselves, for instance, can mask asymmetrical distributions of agency that not only constrain what ways of being are possible in a given situation but, in doing so, inhibit possibilities for future transformation.' Giraud, *What Comes after Entanglement?*, 177.

49. It is precisely this liberal fantasy which Charles Mills targets in *The Racial Contract*, in arguing that the social contract was in fact a domination contract; 'producing the ironic outcome that whites will in general be unable to understand the world they themselves have made. Part of what it means to be constructed as "white" . . . is a cognitive model that precludes self-transparency and genuine understanding of social realities. To a significant extent, then, white signatories will live in an invented delusional world, a racial fantasy land.' Charles W. Mills, *The Racial Contract* (Ithaca: Cornell University Press, 1999), 18.

50. Jared Sexton, 'The Resentment of (Black) Politics', *Alienocene, Strata IV* (2019), https://alienocene.com/2019/03/01/the-resentment-of-black-politics/amp/.

51. Frantz Fanon, *The Wretched of the Earth* (London: Penguin, 2003), 33–4.

52. See Claire Jean Kim, *Dangerous Crossings: Race, Species and Nature in a Multicultural Age* (New York: Cambridge University Press, 2015), 24–60. See also Claire Jean Kim, 'Murder and Mattering in Harambe's House', *Politics and Animals* 3 (2017). In line with this, Syl Ko remarks that 'what condemns us to our inferior status, even before we speak or act, is not merely our racial category

but *that* our racial category is marked *the most* by animality'. See Syl Ko, 'We've Reclaimed Blackness Now It's Time to Reclaim "The Animal"', in Aph Ko and Syl Ko, *Aphro-ism: Essays on Pop Culture, Feminism, and Black Veganism from Two Sisters* (New York: Lantern Books, 2017), 63–9 (67).

53. See for example Adams, *The Sexual Politics of Meat*; Greta Gaard, 'Toward a Postcolonial Feminist Milk Studies', *American Quarterly* 65, no. 3 (2013); Yamini Narayanan, '"Cow is a Mother, Mothers Can Do Anything for Their Children!" Gaushalas as Landscapes of Anthropatriarchy and Hindu Patriarchy', *Hypatia* 34, no. 2 (2019); Plumwood, *Feminism and the Mastery of Nature*; and Lori Gruen, *Entangled Empathy: A New Ethic for our Relationships with Animals* (New York: Lantern Books, 2015).

54. Gillespie, *The Cow with Ear Tag #1389*, 17.

55. Sunaura Taylor, *Beasts of Burden: Animal and Disability Liberation* (New York: New Press, 2017).

56. On the potential expansiveness of the concept of intersectionality, see Sumi Cho, Kimberlé Williams Crenshaw and Leslie McCall, 'Toward a Field of Intersectionality Studies: Theory, Applications, and Praxis', *Signs* 38, no. 4 (2013). I note here Jennifer C. Nash's argument that in a sense 'intersectionality' reflects the central project of feminism. Nash argues that 'studying the field's engagement with intersectionality allows a window into the discipline's longer and fraught relationship with black feminist studies, and with black feminists'. See Jennifer C. Nash, *Black Feminism Reimagined: After Intersectionality* (Durham, NC: Duke University Press, 2019), 2.

57. Kimberlé Crenshaw, 'Mapping the Margins: Intersectionality, Identity Politics, and Violence against Women of Color', *Stanford Law Review* 43, no. 6 (1991). See also Kimberlé Crenshaw, 'Demarginalizing the Intersection of Race and Sex: A Black Feminist Critique of Antidiscrimination Doctrine, Feminist Theory and Antiracist Politics', *University of Chicago Legal Forum* 1989, no. 1 (1989). For a reimagining of intersectionality theory, drawing from new materialist as well as assemblage theory, see Jasbir K. Puar, '"I Would Rather Be a Cyborg Than a Goddess": Becoming-Intersectional in Assemblage Theory', *philoSOPHIA* 2, no. 1 (2012).

58. Note here the 'topological' nature of Crenshaw's approach, which was always about locating, mapping, positioning, etc.; 'intersectionality' is concerned with finding the edge of a structural form of subordination, noting how this met other forms of subordination, and then observing what effects this had for those located within a terrain of power structured by these oppressions. Crenshaw, 'Mapping the Margins', 1265. This is perhaps why Puar stresses that the analysis of intersections should focus on the 'event' rather than the static identity. See Puar, '"I Would Rather Be a Cyborg Than a Goddess"', 59–60.

59. Crenshaw, 'Mapping the Margins', 1282.

60. Note that of course this methodological approach has been built on by others, including prominently within animal studies by Claire Jean Kim, who takes a similar approach using 'optics' to locate the position of the political subject or political demand. See Kim, *Dangerous Crossings*.

61. Crenshaw states: 'Although collective opposition to racist practice has been and continues to be crucially important in protecting Black interests, an empowered Black feminist sensibility would require that the terms of unity no longer reflect priorities premised upon the continued marginalization of Black women.' Crenshaw, 'Mapping the Margins', 1295.

62. Crenshaw, 'Mapping the Margins', 1299.

63. Crenshaw states that 'the location of women of color at the intersection of race and gender makes our actual experience of domestic violence, rape and remedial reform qualitatively different than that of white women'. Crenshaw, 'Mapping the Margins', 1245.

64. Crenshaw, 'Mapping the Margins', 1250. Crenshaw goes on: 'When reform efforts undertaken on behalf of women neglect this fact, women of color are less likely to have their needs met than women who are racially privileged.' Elsewhere Crenshaw makes this explicit: 'To bring this back to a non-metaphorical level, I am suggesting that Black women can experience discrimination in ways that are both similar to and different from those experienced by white women and Black men. Black women sometimes experience discrimination in ways similar to white women's experiences; sometimes they share very similar experiences with Black men. Yet often they experience double-discrimination – the combined effects of practices which discriminate on the basis of race, and on the basis of sex. And sometimes, they experience discrimination as Black women – not the sum of race and sex discrimination, but as Black women.' See Crenshaw, 'Demarginalizing the Intersection of Race and Sex', 149.

65. Gayatri Chakravorty Spivak, 'Can the Subaltern Speak?', in *Marxism and the Interpretation of Culture*, ed. Cary Nelson and Lawrence Grossberg (Basingstoke: Macmillan Education, 1988), 271–313.

66. Hortense J. Spillers, 'Mama's Baby, Papa's Maybe: An American Grammar Book', *Diacritics* 17, no. 2 (1987).

67. Frank B. Wilderson III, 'Gramsci's Black Marx: Whither the Slave in Civil Society?' *Social Identities* 9, no. 2 (2003).

68. Wilderson's essay has attracted commentary from some within animal studies and posthumanism. See for example Jishnu Guha-Majumdar, 'Slavery, Social Death, and Animal Labor', *Politics and Animals* 8 (2022).

238 | ANIMALS AND CAPITAL

69. The essay predates Wilderson's later book, which argued that modernity itself depends upon the continual articulation of the Black subject as a political ontology. See Wilderson, *Red, White & Black*, 20–1.

70. Wilderson, 'Gramsci's Black Marx', 235.

71. Wilderson, 'Gramsci's Black Marx', 231.

72. Wilderson, 'Gramsci's Black Marx', 229.

73. Wilderson, 'Gramsci's Black Marx', 233–4.

74. On 'common sense', see for example Antonio Gramsci, *Selections from the Prison Notebooks of Antonio Gramsci* (New York: International Publishers, 1980), 406. See also Kate Crehan, *Gramsci's Common Sense: Inequality and its Narratives* (Durham, NC: Duke University Press, 2016).

75. Wilderson, 'Gramsci's Black Marx', 238.

76. Wilderson, *Red, White & Black*, 53.

77. See Esther Alloun, '"That's the Beauty of it, it's Very Simple!" Animal Rights and Settler Colonialism in Palestine–Israel', *Settler Colonial Studies* 8, no. 4 (2018).

78. See Ko and Ko, *Aphro-ism*; A. Breeze Harper, ed., *Sistah Vegan: Black Female Vegans Speak on Food, Identity, Health and Society* (New York: Lantern Books, 2010). See also Julia Feliz Bruek, ed., *Veganism in an Oppressive World: A Vegans of Color Community Project* (Sanctuary Publishers, 2017).

79. See Wadiwel, *The War against Animals*, 23–4.

80. Marx, *Capital*, vol. 1, 342. See also Marx, *Grundrisse*, 646. In this context, see Mark Neocleous, 'The Political Economy of the Dead Marx's Vampires', *History of Political Thought* 24, no. 3 (2003); and Amedeo Policante, 'Vampires of Capital: Gothic Reflections between Horror and Hope', *Cultural Logic* 3, no. 1 (2011).

81. Marx, *Capital*, vol. 1, 375–6. Note that Ben Fowkes chooses to translate this section as 'insatiable appetite for surplus-labour'. The German text reads 'Wehrwolfs-Heisshunger nach Mehrarbeit': that is, a 'werewolf's voracious hunger for surplus labour'. On the werewolf hunger of capitalism, see Robert McKay, 'A Vegetarian Diet for the Were-wolf Hunger of Capital: Leftist and Pro-animal Thought in Guy Endore's *The Werewolf of Paris*', in *Werewolves, Wolves and the Gothic*, ed. Robert McKay and John Miller (Cardiff: University of Wales Press, 2017), 177–202.

82. In this context, it is not surprising that Negri observes that 'capital appears as a force of expansion, as production and reproduction, and always as command'. Negri, *Marx Beyond Marx*, 76.

83. See Marx, *Grundrisse*, 470.

84. Deleuze and Guattari, *Anti-Oedipus*.

85. Deleuze and Guattari, *Anti-Oedipus*, 25. Deleuze and Guattari note: 'To a certain degree, the traditional logic of desire is all wrong from the very outset: from the very first step that the Platonic logic of desire forces us to take, making us choose

NOTES | 239

between *production* and *acquisition*. From the moment we place desire on the side of acquisition, we make desire an idealistic (dialectical, nihilistic) conception, which causes us to look upon it as primarily a lack; a lack of object, a lack of the real object' (25).

86. Deleuze and Guattari, *Anti-Oedipus*, 25. Deleuze and Guattari go on: 'The real is the end product, the result of the passive synthesis of desire as autoproduction of the unconscious. Desire does not lack anything; it does not lack its object. It is, rather, the *subject* that is missing in desire, or desire that lacks a fixed subject; there is no fixed subject unless there is repression' (26).

87. To an extent, Deleuze and Guattari are continuing and refining Wilhelm Reich's critique of ideology: as Reich states, 'when an "ideology has a repercussive effect upon the economic process", this means it has become a material force'. Wilhelm Reich, *The Mass Psychology of Fascism* (Harmondsworth: Penguin Books, 1978), 51.

88. Aidan Tynan observes: 'Capital is constantly deterritorialising, finding new, exotic markets and innovative practices of decoding at its periphery, but as part of the same movement it must reterritorialise, rediscovering within its centre zones of archaism and lack which check this expansion. Without subjects ready and willing to occupy, to live, this interior limit, capitalism itself would not be possible since it would be unable to legitimate its periods of crisis. Capitalism, then, must constitute a subjectivity based on hostility towards codes, but it must also produce subjects unwilling to follow decoding all the way beyond the social relations which condition the production of the decoded flows themselves. The psychoanalytic subject discovers "desire in the abstract", a free floating desire (libido) which, however, is only free to the extent that it is tied to a social order that denies it satisfaction (prohibition of incest).' Aidan Tynan, 'The Marx of Anti-Oedipus', *Deleuze Studies* 3 (2009), 41.

89. Deleuze and Guattari note that despite the different use values which capitalism presents to the owner of money versus the owner of labour, there is here a solidarity at the level of desire: 'in this manner it is indeed the global object of an investment in desire. The wage earner's desire, the capitalist's desire, everything moves to the rhythm of one and the same desire, founded *on the differential relation of flows having no assignable exterior limit, and where capitalism reproduces its immanent limits on an ever widening and more comprehensive scale.'* Deleuze and Guattari, *Anti-Oedipus*, 239.

90. Tynan, 'The Marx of Anti-Oedipus', 44.

91. Barad, *Meeting the Universe Halfway*, 244. Note further, how close Barad's reading of the relation of materialism and discourse is to Butler. See Butler, *Bodies that Matter*, xviii–xix.

240 | ANIMALS AND CAPITAL

92. Gilles Deleuze, *Negotiations* (New York: Columbia University Press, 1995), 171.

93. Deleuze, *Negotiations*, 173.

94. Félix Guattari and Toni Negri, *Communists Like Us: New Spaces of Liberty, New Lines of Alliance* (New York: Semiotext(e), 1990).

95. Robinson, *Black Marxism*, 28.

96. Robinson, *Black Marxism*, 66.

97. Robinson, *Black Marxism*, 10.

98. See Kim, 'Murder and Mattering in Harambe's House'.

99. As I discuss in Chapter 3, I use 'fabrication' in a specific way to describe the transformation of the living commodity into the (dead) consumption commodity. I note the resonance here with the so-called 'fabrication of corpses' which Martin Heidegger and Hannah Arendt used at different times to describe the Holocaust. Heidegger in particular described this fabrication as akin to other rationalised modalities of production, including industrial agriculture, equated as the 'motorized food industry'. See Peter Trawny's discussion of the problems with Heidegger's utilisation of this phrase: Peter Trawny, 'Heidegger and the Shoah', in *Reading Heidegger's Black Notebooks, 1931–1941*, ed. Ingo Farin and Jeff Malpas (London: MIT Press, 2016), 169–79. See also Bruce Heinly, Peter E. Gordon, 'Heidegger & the Gas Chambers', *New York Review of Books*, 4 December 2014, https://www.nybooks.com/articles/2014/12/04/heidegger-and-gas-chambers/. Gordon challenges Heidegger for making a comparison between industrial agriculture and the Holocaust, using the following grounds: 'Heidegger may have believed that all differences of technological production dissolve into the generalized phenomenon of "machination" or *Machenschaft*. (This is a term that recurs with some frequency in the black notebooks he wrote between 1931 and 1941.) But a philosopher should draw clear distinctions. The comparison to industrial farming is morally obtuse not least because scientifically managed agricultural production keeps alive millions of individuals across the globe who would otherwise have died of starvation. The passage erases this distinction; it equates technologies of sustenance with technologies of murder.' While I agree there are deep problems with comparisons between the Holocaust and contemporary forms of industrial animal agriculture, the description of scientifically managed agricultural production as a 'technology of sustenance', simply because it produces a means of subsistence for human populations, misses that animal agriculture also functions as a technology of torture and murder, or more specifically, scientifically managed mass violence aimed at enabling mass human sustenance. But this highlights why comparisons between animal agriculture and human forms of mass violence towards other humans lack sophistication, since the Holocaust aimed at a terrorising mass erasure of human life; animal agriculture puts animal death in sacrificial service of human life. My

NOTES | 241

use of 'fabrication' might be compared to Nicole Shukin's focus on 'rendering' as both an artistic production and 'the industrial boiling down and recycling of animal remains'. Shukin, *Animal Capital*, 20; see also 49–86.

100. This view that capitalism is merely a system of domination resonates partially with my previous work. In my book *The War against Animals*, I argue that humans subject animals to large-scale systematic violence, and this violence is a materialisation of a self-declared human sovereignty over nonhuman animals. In this view, hierarchically anthropocentric claims to domination arise after humans have conquered animals with large-scale violence; the sovereignty humans gain through this domination is then rationalised through proclamations of self-superiority.

3 Commodity

1. Marx, *Grundrisse*, 93.
2. Marx: 'The taste of porridge does not tell us who grew the oats, and the process we have presented does not reveal the conditions under which it takes place, whether it is happening under the slave-owner's brutal lash or the anxious eye of the capitalist, whether Cincinnatus undertakes it in tilling his couple of acres, or a savage, when he lays low a wild beast with a stone.' Marx, *Capital*, vol. 1, 290–1. On the characterisation of 'savage' labour relations to property, see Fiona Nicoll, 'The White Possessive Against and Within the Neoliberal University', *Kalfou* 6, no. 1 (2019), 56–7.
3. I am reframing here the argument that Marx puts forward to conceptualise equivalent value between linen and a coat. See Marx, *Capital*, vol. 1, 147. In this context, note Adam Smith's discussion of the linen shirt in Book 1 of Adam Smith, *An Inquiry into the Nature and Causes of the Wealth of Nations* (Indianapolis: Liberty Press, 1981). Note that Marx himself demonstrates awareness that the identification of use value and its conversion to exchange value is far from a neat process: see particularly Marx, *Capital*, vol. 1, 131. In this regard, see Gayatri Chakravorty Spivak, *An Aesthetic Education on the Era of Globalization* (Cambridge, MA: Harvard University Press, 2012), 193–6.
4. Marx, *Capital*, vol. 1, 147.
5. Marx, *Capital*, vol. 1, 148.
6. Joan Robinson's somewhat scathing attack on Marx's theory of value appears to bypass this philosophical discussion of the commodity and its relation to value. While Robinson notes the 'metaphysical' nature of value, and I think correctly observes the difficult problem of how to translate Marx's concept of 'value' to prices (exchange values), there is a failure to relay the full depth of the philosophical point Marx is making about how a good or relation becomes 'valuable'

within a social context, even without a system of currency in operation. For Robinson's discussion of Marx and value, see Joan Robinson, *Economic Philosophy* (Harmondsworth: Pelican Books, 1968), 29–47.

7. Marx, *Capital*, vol. 1, 148. Earlier Marx states: 'In order to inform us that its sublime objectivity as a value differs from its stiff and starchy existence as a body, it says that value has the appearance of a coat, and therefore that in so far as the linen itself is an object of value [*Wertding*], it and the coat are as like as two peas' (144).

8. Marx was of course fully aware of the classical understanding of *oikonomia*, and the narrowing of this concept in the modern utilisation of 'economics'. On Marx and *oikonomia* see Angela Mitropoulos, 'Oikonomia', *Philosophy Today* 63, no. 4 (2019).

9. Marx, *Capital*, vol. 1, 144 n. 19.

10. Jacques Lacan, 'The Mirror Stage as Formative of the *I* Function as Revealed in Psychoanalytic Experience', *écrits* (New York: W. W. Norton & Company, 2006), 75–81 (76).

11. We might further speculate that the use of the name 'Peter', 'Paul', and now as I have introduced it, 'Mary', reminds us that this equivalent value is established within the racialised terrain of the Judeo-Christian imaginary. Would Peter recognize himself in Dinesh, see himself as equivalent and replaceable by Dinesh? And even if this equivalence of value were possible, the equivalence of male homosociality across race and culture boundaries, might this equivalence hold across gender difference? Would Peter recognise himself in Sushila; could Sushila be a mirror? Indeed, how would a Peter, someone who identifies as male, confront another, Dash, who is gender non-conforming; would self-recognition be possible?

12. See 'The Chapter on Money' in Marx, *Grundrisse*, 115–238.

13. Marx, *Grundrisse*, 190.

14. Marx, *Capital*, vol. 1, 204.

15. At the time of writing, Poultry Australia suggests that 'day old chicks can be found ranging in price from $3.00 to $15.00 each [AUD]'. See Poultry Australia, 'Buying Live Poultry', https://www.poultryaustralia.com.au/buying-live-poultry. Meat and Livestock Australia suggest a per head price of approximately $2000 to $3200 for Cows, Heifers, Steers and Bulls sold in May 2022 at the Armidale, News South Wales, saleyard. See Meat and Livestock Australia, 'Cattle Physical Report: Saleyard: Armidale', 26 May 2022, https://www.mla.com.au/prices-markets/cattlephysicalreport/.

16. Luce Irigaray, 'Women on the Market', *This Sex Which is Not One* (Ithaca: Cornell University Press, 1985), 170–91.

17. Irigaray, 'Women on the Market', 187. See also in the same volume the essay 'Commodities Among Themselves'. Irigaray states: 'The exchanges upon which

patriarchal societies are based take place exclusively among men. . . . Thus the labor force and its products, including those of mother earth, are the objects of transactions among men and men alone.' Luce Irigaray, 'Commodities among Themselves', in *This Sex Which is Not One*, 192–7 (192).

18. Note that the concept of an 'intrinsic' use value – a use value that precedes the social relations that determine value – is highly contested. As Gayatri Chakravorty Spivak observes, 'in the value-form, use as well as exchange suffers abstraction'. See Spivak, *An Aesthetic Education*, 193–6.

19. Of course, this is the point Gayle Rubin makes in the classic essay 'The Traffic in Women'. Rubin states that '"Exchange of women" is a shorthand for expressing that the social relations of kinship system specify that men have certain rights in their female kin, and that women do not have the same rights either to themselves or to their male kin. In this sense, the exchange of women is a profound perception of a system in which women do not have full rights to themselves.' See Gayle Rubin, 'The Traffic in Women', in *Toward an Anthropology of Women*, ed. Rayna Reiter (New York: Monthly Review Press, 1975), 157–209 (177).

20. Luce Irigaray, *Speculum of the Other Woman* (Ithaca: Cornell University Press, 1994), 133–4, 147–51 and 308–10.

21. Irigaray, 'Women on the Market', 187.

22. Irigaray, 'Women on the Market', 187–8.

23. Irigaray states: 'Her value-invested form amounts to what man inscribes in and on its matter; that is, her body.' Irigaray, 'Women on the Market', 187.

24. I use the term 'epistemic violence' here in the way in which it is described by Spivak in her essay 'Can the Subaltern Speak?' See also Wadiwel, *The War against Animals*, 33–6.

25. Adams, *The Sexual Politics of Meat*, 47.

26. Adams, *The Sexual Politics of Meat*, 41–2.

27. Orlando Patterson, *Slavery and Social Death: A Comparative Study* (Cambridge, MA: Harvard University Press, 1982), 148–71. On slaves as money, see 167–9.

28. Patterson, *Slavery and Social Death*, 169.

29. On the libidinal economy of anti-Blackness see Wilderson, 'Gramsci's Black Marx', 239, n. 4. See also Guha-Majumdar, 'Slavery, Social Death, and Animal Labor'.

30. Wilderson, *Red, White & Black*, 20–1.

31. I don't have space here to expand upon the 'biopolitical' aspect of species value; however, it is certainly worth noting that Michel Foucault's original formulation of biopolitics, and revitalisations from scholars such as Giorgio Agamben and Roberto Esposito, offer significant material for exploring the biopolitics of animal commodification. On biopolitics, see Michel Foucault, *The Will to Knowledge: The History of Sexuality*, vol. 1 (London: Penguin Books, 1998); Michel Foucault,

244 | ANIMALS AND CAPITAL

Society Must Be Defended: Lectures at the College de France, 1975–76 (London: Penguin Books, 2004); Giorgio Agamben, *Homo Sacer: Sovereign Power and Bare Life* (Stanford: Stanford University Press, 1998); and Giorgio Agamben, *The Open: Man and Animal* (Stanford: Stanford University Press, 2004).

32. Jacques Derrida, 'White Mythology: Metaphor in the Text of Philosophy', in *Margins of Philosophy* (Chicago: Chicago University Press, 1982), 207–29. Beyond this essay, there are numerous places we can look within Derrida's work to find resonant arguments relevant to how we might read Marx on commodification. For example, Derrida's critique in *Politics of Friendship* of an incarnation of democracy as based on fraternal homosociality – as an alliance between brothers – might serve as an extension of Marx's remarkable footnote. See Jacques Derrida, *Politics of Friendship* (London: Verso, 2000), particularly 227–308. We might also find a reverberation in Derrida's *Beast and Sovereign* lectures, where the philosopher draws issue with an ethics that is based upon the recognition of similarity in the Other (the relation, we might say, between Peter and Paul): 'The 'unrecognizable' [*méconnaissable*], I shall say in a somewhat elliptical way, is the beginning of ethics, of the Law, and not of the human. So long as there is recognisability and fellow, ethics is dormant. It is sleeping a dogmatic slumber.' See Jacques Derrida, *The Beast and the Sovereign*, vol. 1 (Chicago: University of Chicago Press, 2009), 108. And although Derrida seems to hurry past an analysis of commodification itself towards a discussion of commodity fetishism in *Specters of Marx*, we still find here echoes that remind us of a certain resonance between Marx's project and that of Derrida in understanding value, at least in so far as the surplus, the gift, the remainder, that which exceeds and cannot be captured by applied worth in the context of exchange, continues to haunt value. See for example Jacques Derrida, *Specters of Marx: The State of Debt, the Work of Mourning and the New International* (New York: Routledge, 1994), 189–9. Derrida's examination of exchange and surplus in relation to the gift and generosity in *Given Time* is also potentially useful. See Jacques Derrida, *Given Time: I. Counterfeit Money* (Chicago: University of Chicago Press, 1994).

33. Anatole France, *The Garden of Epicurus* (New York: Dodd, Mead, 1922).

34. See also Derrida's essay 'Plato's Pharmacy' in Jacques Derrida, *Dissemination* (London: Continuum, 2004).

35. Derrida, 'White Mythology', 211.

36. Derrida, 'White Mythology', 270. We might note here the difference Derrida offers from Carol J. Adams in understanding the metaphor. For Adams, the absent referent betrays its violence by removing the point of origin for the metaphor; thus, for example, the cow is erased when the metaphor 'beef' is applied. For Derrida, there is a distancing from the origin, however the nature of the process of

language is one which seeks meaning in a lost origin. In this sense the 'trace' of the animal signified remains and always challenges (undermines) the meaning of the metaphor.

37. Derrida, 'White Mythology', 231.
38. Derrida quotes Aristotle: 'Metaphor consists in giving the thing a name that belongs to something else, the transference being either from genus to species, or from species to genus, or from species to species, or the grounds of analogy.' Aristotle qtd in Derrida, 'White Mythology', 231.
39. Aristotle, *Logic*, in *The Works of Aristotle*, vol. 1, ed. R. Hutchins (Chicago: Encyclopaedia Britannica, 1952), 3–253 (40) [25a].
40. Derrida, 'White Mythology', 236.
41. Derrida, 'White Mythology', 236.
42. Derrida, 'White Mythology', 237.
43. Note the resonances here with Foucault's understanding of epistemology. See Oksala, 'Foucault's Politicization of Ontology'.
44. Derrida, 'White Mythology', 237. In some respects, Derrida's concept of the 'anthropophysics' and the alignment of power and reason correlates very strongly with his later identification of sovereignty with *Gewalt*. See Jacques Derrida, *The Beast and the Sovereign*, vol. 2 (Chicago: University of Chicago Press, 2011), 258–90.
45. This is perhaps the shared nature that Peter recognises in Paul as species-typical; Peter commodifies Paul to find his own species-typical characteristic, which happens to be the capacity to commodify; that is, the capacity to apply value to an object by making it equivalent to an object which it is not.
46. Marx, *Grundrisse*, 202.
47. In this regard see Bill Winders and David Nibert, 'Consuming the Surplus: Expanding "Meat" Consumption and Animal Oppression', *International Journal of Sociology & Social Policy* 24, no. 9 (2004).
48. In this sense, this reflects the 'stupidity' that Derrida identifies in his late lectures as characteristic of sovereign decision-making. See Jacques Derrida, *The Beast and the Sovereign*, vol. 1, 149.
49. See Wadiwel, *The War against Animals*.
50. On the signification of meat see Robert McKay, 'Read Meat', in *Animal Remains*, ed. Sarah Bezan and Robert McKay (New York: Routledge, 2022), 129–57.
51. This historical process is evolving, so that even today, with the emergence of digital forms of currency (the ultimate form of currency that is pure and can never be eroded) and cryptocurrencies (which do not have sovereign authorisation), there is an ongoing mystery to unpack in relation to what money is and the relationship between its form and its value.

52. Marx, *Grundrisse*, 166; see also 192. As Francione reminds us, the etymological origins of the word 'capital' arises from 'cattle'. See Francione, *Animals, Property and the Law*, 35. Note also Cheryl I. Harris's discussion of the use of slaves as currency in Cheryl I. Harris, 'Whiteness as Property', *Harvard Law Review* 106, no. 8 (1993), 1720. Today animals can still operate as potential stores of wealth in some economies, particularly for small-scale farming. See FAO, *World Livestock 2011: Livestock in Food Security* (Rome: FAO, 2011), 23.

53. Marx states: 'The precious metals uniform in their qualities, so that equal quantities of them should be so far identical as to present no ground for preferring this one to others. Not the case, for example, with equal numbers of cattle and equal quantities of grain.' Marx, *Grundrisse*, 174.

54. Marx, *Grundrisse*, 166.

55. Marx, *Grundrisse*, 231.

56. 'To accumulate grain requires special stores etc. Accumulating sheep does not make one into a shepherd; to accumulate slaves or land requires relations of domination and subordination etc. Money as the *general* representative of wealth absolves me of all this.' Marx, *Grundrisse*, 233.

57. Marx, *Grundrisse*, 211–12.

58. As discussed, Irigaray observes that women also bear this transformation not simply as a symbolic erasure but as a material effect of objectification: 'her value-invested form amounts to what man inscribes in and on its matter; that is, her body'. This process is of course not without resistance or failure. In this sense, we might interpret Judith Butler's suggestion that drag performance might be an 'effect that resists calculation' as the resistance to calculation of an exchange value within a gendered economy. See Judith Butler, 'Critically Queer', *GLQ: Journal of Lesbian and Gay Studies* 1 (1993), 29. See also Judith Butler, *Gender Trouble* (New York: Routledge, 2006), 186–7.

59. As Alex Blanchette observes, this homogenisation is crucial for enabling the kind of automation within the factory farm that will reduce human labour time (an interplay we will return to in Chapter 4): 'Standardized life can reduce labor costs by enabling more machine-driven automation in slaughterhouses; its outputs can fetch higher prices on global wholesale markets; it generates biochemically consistent animals to build more commodities from their bodies; and it promises to serve as a model for replication elsewhere.' Alex Blanchette, *Porkopolis: American Animality, Standardized Life, and the Factory Farm* (Durham, NC: Duke University Press, 2020), 17.

60. Jan Dutkiewicz, '"Postmodernism", Politics, and Pigs', *PhaenEx* 8, no. 2 (2013), 301–2.

61. Marx, *Grundrisse*, 202. See also the Preface to the first edition of Capital: 'We suffer not only from the living but also from the dead.' Marx, *Capital*, vol. 1, 91.

62. With his tongue firmly pressed against his cheek, Marx characterises the free market at the close of chapter 6 with the following words: 'The sphere of circulation or commodity exchange, within whose boundaries the sale and purchase of labour power goes on, is in fact a very Eden of the innate rights of man. There alone rule Freedom, Equality, Property and Bentham.' Marx, *Capital*, vol. 1, 280. See also Marx, *Grundrisse*, 163–4.

63. Marx, *Capital*, vol. 1, 280.

64. See for example Marx, *Capital*, vol. 1, 204; 425 ('It is not the capitalist whose skin he tans'); 608 ('the caprice of the capitalist, who, in this industry . . . risks nothing by a stoppage of work but the skin of the worker himself'); 780 ('old capital . . . sheds its skin'); 874 ('Thus it came to pass that the former sort accumulated wealth, and the latter sort finally had nothing to sell except their own skins'). See also Marx, *Grundrisse*, 240 ('cast off their old skin').

65. Elaine Scarry, in her famous study of torture, calls Marx to account for the use of this metaphor, pointing out that a tanning is no laughing matter and cannot be regarded as a 'joke'. Elaine Scarry, *The Body in Pain: The Making and Unmaking of the World* (New York: Oxford University Press, 1985), 366 n. 89.

66. I note that removing the skin from the living functioned as a routine punishment in the long history of tortures and indignities that have characterized human violence. See my own writing on the whip as a mode of biopolitical violence: Dinesh Joseph Wadiwel, 'The Sovereign Whip: Flogging, Biopolitics and the Frictional Community', *Journal of Australian Studies* 76 (2003), 117–25; Dinesh Joseph Wadiwel, 'Thick Hides: Whipping, Biopolitics and the White Soul of Power', *Social Semiotics* 19, no. 1 (2009), 47–57; and Dinesh Joseph Wadiwel, 'Whipping to Win: Measured Violence, Delegated Sovereignty and the Privatised Domination of Non-Human Life', in *Law and the Question of the Animal: A Critical Jurisprudence*, ed. Yoriko Otomo and Edward Mussawir (New York: Routledge, 2013), 116–32.

67. Irigaray, 'Women on the Market', 176–7.

68. Thus, Gillespie notes, with reference to the dairy industry, commodification obscures the possibility of knowledge which troubles the value relation established by the commodity. Gillespie, *The Cow with Ear Tag #1389*, 23.

69. Accounts of live skinning do occur, at least sporadically, within the context of animal agriculture. For example, in February 2012, Animal Liberation in New South Wales Australia released footage from the Hawkesbury Valley Meat Processors at Wilberforce, which showed sheep 'being hung up and skinned while apparently still conscious'. See Jen Rosenberg and Ben Cubby, 'Covert Evidence of Cruelty Halts Abattoir', *Sydney Morning Herald*, 10 February 2012, https://www.smh.com.au/en

248 | ANIMALS AND CAPITAL

vironment/conservation/covert-evidence-of-cruelty-halts-abattoir-20120209-1rx
7w.html.

70. Timothy Pachirat, *Every Twelve Seconds: Industrialized Slaughter and the Politics of Sight* (New Haven: Yale University Press, 2011), 61.

71. Pachirat, *Every Twelve Seconds*, 63.

72. Pachirat, *Every Twelve Seconds*, 65.

73. Marx, *Capital*, vol. 1, 342.

74. Marx, *Capital*, vol. 1, 376.

75. As I shall discuss in Chapter 4, there are forms of metabolic labour performed by humans that position the labourer as both means and object of production. See for example Catherine Waldby and Melinda Cooper's work: Melinda Cooper and Catherine Waldby, *Clinical Labor: Tissue Donors and Research Subjects in the Global Bioeconomy* (Durham, NC: Duke University Press, 2014); and Catherine Waldby and Melinda Cooper, 'From Reproductive Work to Regenerative Labour: The Female Body and the Stem Cell Industries', *Feminist Theory* 11, no. 1 (2010), 3–22. However, as I argue in this book, the fact that animals will become the 'product' – for example, 'meat' – shapes these productive processes in different ways.

76. Marx, *Capital*, vol. 2, 468–564 (471). See also Rosa Luxemburg's summary of this process: Rosa Luxemburg, *The Accumulation of Capital* (London: Routledge, 2003), 48–64.

77. That is, an economy 'where the whole surplus value is unproductively consumed'. Marx, *Capital*, vol. 2, 473.

78. Luxemburg summarises: 'The essential difference between enlarged reproduction and simple reproduction consists in the fact that in the latter the capitalist class and its hangers-on consume the entire surplus value, whereas in the former a part of the surplus value is set aside from the personal consumption of its owners, not for the purpose of hoarding, but in order to increase the active capital, i.e. for capitalisation.' Luxemburg, *The Accumulation of Capital*, 84.

79. See Anwar Shaikh, 'Marx's Theory of Value and the "Transformation Problem"', in *The Subtle Anatomy of Capitalism*, ed. J. Schwarz (Santa Monica: Goodyear, 1977), 106–39.

80. Marx, *Capital*, vol. 2, 113.

81. Marx, *Capital*, vol. 2, 515.

82. Marx, *Capital*, vol. 2, 115. See also 457.

83. Ernest Mandel, 'Introduction', in Marx, *Capital*, vol. 2, 11–79 (27).

84. Though a different definition of 'capital' is advanced, Thomas Piketty's *Capital in the Twenty-First Century* has powerfully highlighted this reality. The structure of capitalism means that all countries maintain deeply unequal distributions in wealth, and this produces a world where those who rely on wage incomes

effectively live in a different world from the small elite who do not rely on wages to survive. See particularly Thomas Piketty, *Capital in the Twenty-First Century*, trans. Arthur Goldhammer (Cambridge, MA: Harvard University Press, 2014), 377–429.

85. Marx, *Capital*, vol. 1, 272–3.

86. See for example Government of India, *NSS Report No. 558: Household Consumption of Various Goods and Services in India, 2011–12* (National Sample Survey Office, 2014). Migration and remittances also shape rural consumption patterns. See Jajati K. Parida, Sanjay K. Mohanty and K. Ravi Raman, 'Remittances, Household Expenditure and Investment in Rural India: Evidence from NSS Data', *Indian Economic Review* 50, no. 1 (2015).

87. Marx: 'in this connection it is quite immaterial whether a product such as tobacco, for example, is from the physiological point of view a necessary means of consumption or not; it suffices that it is such a means of consumption by custom'. Marx, *Capital*, vol. 2, 479.

88. Certainly, this is one axis of the critique advanced by Cedric Robinson of Marx: namely that the primary site of conflict under capitalism is between the worker and the capitalist. Robinson states that 'perhaps the most obvious of the ideological constructs that appear in the work of Marx and Engels (and most of the Marxists who have followed them) are the notions of the proletariat as the revolutionary subject, and the class struggle between the proletariat and the bourgeoisie'. Robinson, *Black Marxism*, 43.

89. Marx, *Capital*, vol. 1, 718.

90. There is certainly also variance between humans and their status as wage-earners that follow the contours of race, gender, reproductive capacity, ability and disability. The monetary wage, as described above, appears to represent a kind of distinct and much-loved 'freedom' – the freedom to consent to the sale of labour power, the freedom to spend wages on the means of subsistence – and as such, there is a tendency to venerate waged labour and misunderstand the value role of non-waged or low-wage labour. Stepping away from this veneration of monetary wages allows us to pay attention to the ways in which the wage – including its level and its security – are deployed as one technology (and only one technology) for the extraction of surplus.

91. Foucault, *The Will to Knowledge*, 135–8.

92. Foucault, *The Will to Knowledge*, 138.

93. On state racism and the governance of biological populations, see respectively Foucault, *Society Must Be Defended*, and Michel Foucault, *Security, Territory, Population: Lectures at the Collège de France, 1977–78* (London: Palgrave Macmillan, 2007).

250 | ANIMALS AND CAPITAL

94. Foucault, *The Will to Knowledge*, 140–1. See also 125–7, where Foucault refers to one of Marx's more overtly 'biopolitical' chapters in Capital, 'The Working Day'. I shall discuss this further below in Chapter 4. In the above I have blurred the distinction between 'biopower' and 'biopolitics', though Foucault originally intended a difference: biopower was initially used to describe the emergence of an anatamopolitics (that is, disciplinary power focused on the body) with biopolitics; the two marking the shift in contemporary rationalities of power. However, in later work from Foucault, it is not clear if the distinction between biopolitics and biopower is consistent. See my discussion on the differences in Wadiwel, 'Biopolitics'. See also Thomas Lemke, *Biopolitics: An Advanced Introduction* (New York: New York University Press, 2011), 34.

95. Thus, as Jemima Repo observes, control over gender, and the erasure of gender 'abnormality', became aligned with the reproductive aims of capitalism. See Jemima Repo, *The Biopolitics of Gender* (Oxford: Oxford University Press, 2015).

96. There has been more recently an expansion of scholarship which has attempted to correct Foucault's oversight. See particularly Matthew Chrulew and Dinesh Joseph Wadiwel, eds, *Foucault and Animals* (Leiden: Brill, 2016). See also my own works, particularly Wadiwel, *The War against Animals*; Wadiwel, 'Biopolitics'. See also Matthew Chrulew, 'Animals in Biopolitical Theory: Between Agamben and Negri', *New Formations* 76 (2012); Cary Wolfe, *Before the Law: Humans and Other Animals in a Biopolitical Frame* (Chicago: University of Chicago Press, 2013); Matthew Cole, 'From "Animal Machines" to "Happy Meat"? Foucault's Ideas of Disciplinary and Pastoral Power Applied to "Animal-Centred" Welfare Discourse', *Animals* 1, no. 2 (2011); Lewis Holloway et al., 'Biopower, Genetics and Livestock Breeding: (Re)constituting Animal Populations and Heterogeneous Biosocial Collectivities', *Transactions of the Institute of British Geographers* 34 (2009); Krithika Srinivasan, 'The Biopolitics of Animal Being and Welfare: Dog Control and Care in the UK and India', *Transactions of the Institute of British Geographers* 38 (2013); and James Stanescu, 'Beyond Biopolitics: Animal Studies, Factory Farms, and the Advent of Deading Life', *PhaenEx* 8, no. 2 (2013).

97. See Wadiwel, 'Biopolitics'.

98. Patel and Moore, *A History of the World in Seven Cheap Things*, 138.

99. Thus, globally animals are often seen as simply a use object for food 'security'. The FAO puts this plainly: 'even in small amounts, food of animal origin can play an important role in improving the nutritional status of low income households by addressing micro- and macronutrient deficiencies, particularly of children and pregnant and lactating women'. FAO, *World Livestock 2011*, 10.

100. To an extent, these contradictions are mirrored in the repertoire of animal rights theory, which often starts from these sites of contradiction. See for example Gary

L. Francione, *Introduction to Animal Rights: Your Child or the Dog?* (Philadelphia: Temple University Press, 2000); or Melanie Joy, *Why We Love Dogs, Eat Pigs, and Wear Cows: An Introduction to Carnism* (San Francisco: Conari Press, 2010). On contradictory attitudes and morality, see James Serpell, *In the Company of Animals: A Study of Human–Animal Relationships* (Cambridge: Cambridge University Press, 1996).

101. Indeed international agencies, governments and others frequently remind us of these two fronts when they pronounce the importance of livestock production, or global fishing, for the economic wellbeing of producers while simultaneously they extol the need to feed the planet, or emphasise the irreplaceability of animals as a source of protein. The FAO captures this perfectly with the claim that 'livestock have an important part to play, as they provide high-quality protein to consumers and regular income to producers'. FAO, *World Livestock 2011*, ix.

102. Marx, *Grundrisse*, 289.

103. See for example Jonathan Watts, 'Argentinians React to Report Linking Meat to Cancer: "I'd Rather Die than Give it Up."' *Guardian*, 27 October 2015.

104. At least within European history, this might explain why meat becomes valued as reflective of attained living standards. Reflecting on the medieval European peasant diet, Bridget Ann Henisch observes: 'The basic foodstuff was grain of one kind or another: wheat, rye, barley, oats, or some combination of these, depending on local conditions. This was supplemented with peas and beans, either fresh or dried. Monotony and blandness could be countered with fruits and vegetables, grown on a private plot, harvested on a larger scale, bought at a market, or found in the wild. Milk and cream, cheese and butter were all readily obtainable in the spring and summer months. Eggs were not scarce, because it was easy to keep a cock and some hens contented in a small garden. The one item conspicuous by its absence is meat. That absence was deeply regretted, and bitterly resented because, quite apart from any nutritional value it might have been thought to possess, meat had an undisputed place at the very top of the medieval prestige pyramid. The dinner tables of the powerful were laden with meat dishes of every kind; on fast days fish, the accepted substitute, was offered in the same variety and abundance. However . . . while animals themselves were familiar figures in the peasant's landscape, their meat was in frustratingly short supply.' Bridget Ann Henisch, *Medieval Cook* (Woodbridge: Boydell Press, 2013), 58.

105. See Patel and Moore, *A History of the World in Seven Cheap Things*.

106. Elspeth Probyn, 'An Ethos with a Bite: Queer Appetites from Sex to Food', *Sexualities* 2, no. 4 (1999), 429. See also Chloë Taylor, 'Foucault and the Ethics of Eating', *Foucault Studies* 9 (2010); and John Coveney, *Food, Morals, and Meaning: The Pleasure and Anxiety of Eating* (London: Routledge, 2006).

107. Thus as Emiko Fukase and Will Martin observe, 'per capita demand growth is likely to be a more important driver of food demand than population growth between now and 2050'. See Emiko Fukase and Will Martin, *Economic Growth, Convergence, and World Food Demand and Supply*, World Bank Policy Research Working Paper 8257, November 2017.

108. In the context of overproduction, this drives consumption in a moving tension: 'Since capital's purpose is not the satisfaction of needs but the production of profit, and since it attains this purpose only by methods that determine the mass of production by reference exclusively to the yardstick of production, and not the reverse, there must be a constant tension between the restricted dimensions of consumption on the capitalist basis, and a production that is constantly striving to overcome these immanent barriers. Moreover, capital consists of commodities, and hence overproduction of capital involves overproduction of commodities.' Karl Marx, *Capital: A Critique of Political Economy*, vol. 3, trans. David Fernbach (London: Penguin, 1991), 365.

109. And what would freedom look like for vegans if we did not treat food as a site of freedom? How does this obsession with food restrict us, and produce subjectivities that invest anxiety, pleasures, distastes, self-hatred, ethics, political freedom in food choices? These are all hugely difficult questions. And I ask these questions not with any intention of leaving aside veganism as a strategy, but seeking to develop it, improve it, refine it. And perhaps ask the difficult question: 'What would an anti-capitalist veganism look like?'

110. David Harvey announced no less than seventeen contradictions in a recent book. See David Harvey, *Seventeen Contradictions and The End of Capitalism* (London: Profile Books, 2014). On contradiction and Marx's philosophy, see Lawrence Crocker, 'Marx's Use of Contradiction', *Philosophy and Phenomenological Research* 40, no. 4 (1980). As Crocker observes, Marx's sense of contradiction in material conditions is, at least at first glance, at odds with a contradiction in logic: for example, it might be illogical for capitalism to destroy its own foundations (for example, climate change), but this does not stop this contradiction materially playing out. However, as Crocker observes, the two views of contradiction unite where we understand Marx as observing material processes and their trajectories: 'A and B are contradictory if and only if (1) A and B are both processes (2) A and B have natural paths of development (3) The natural path of development of A and the natural path of development of B cannot be jointly realized' (560).

111. See Marx, *Capital*, vol. 2, 349–75.

112. See Luxemburg, *The Accumulation of Capital*, 338.

113. James O'Connor, 'On the Two Contradictions of Capitalism', *Capitalism Nature Socialism* 2, no. 3 (1991). See also Martin Spence, 'Capital Against Nature: James

O'Connor's Theory of the Second Contradiction of Capitalism', *Capital & Class* 24, no. 3 (2000).

114. James O'Connor, 'Capitalism, Nature, Socialism: A Theoretical Introduction', *Capitalism Nature Socialism* 1, no. 1 (1988), 25.

115. See Moore, *Capitalism in the Web of Life*, 91–109.

116. For example, in *Capital* vol. 3 Marx states: 'The contradiction between the general social power into which capital has developed and the private power of the individual capitalists over these social conditions of production develops ever more blatantly, while this development also contains the solution to this situation, in that it simultaneously raises the conditions of production into general, communal, social conditions. This transformation is brought about by the development of the productive forces under capitalist production and by the manner and form in which this development is accomplished.' Marx, *Capital*, vol. 3, 373.

117. See for example Jeffrey Kluger, 'Sorry Vegans: Here's How Meat-Eating Made Us Human', *Time*, 9 March 2016, https://time.com/4252373/meat-eating-veganism-evolution/.

118. Meat-eating is one site of intense friction in relation to cultural and national identity. One contemporary example is India, where both vegetarianism, driven by Hindu nationalism, and beef-eating as a form of resistance play out within Indian cultural politics. See for example C. Sathyamala, 'Meat-Eating in India: Whose Food, Whose Politics, and Whose Rights?' *Policy Futures in Education* 17, no. 7 (2018).

119. This was the view put forward by Jeremy Bentham in his famous footnote, which in turn shaped the argument in Singer's *Animal Liberation*: 'If the being eaten were all, there is very good reason why we should be suffered to eat such of them as we like to eat: we are the better for it, and they are never the worse. They have none of those long-protracted anticipations of future misery which we have. The death they suffer in our hands commonly is, and always may be, a speedier, and by that means a less painful one, than that which would await them in the inevitable course of nature. If the being killed were all, there is very good reason why we should be suffered to kill such as molest us: we should be the worse for their living, and they are never the worse for being dead.' Jeremy Bentham, *An Introduction to the Principles of Morals and Legislation* (New York: Dover, 2007), chapter XIX, Note §.

120. Chase Purdy, 'Being Vegan Isn't as Good for Humanity as You Think', *Quartz*, 4 August 2016, https://qz.com/749443/being-vegan-isnt-as-environmentally-friendly-as-you-think/.

121. Mike Archer, 'Ordering the Vegetarian Meal? There's More Animal Blood on Your Hands', *Insight*, 23 April 2019, https://www.sbs.com.au/news/insight/ordering-the-vegetarian-meal-there-s-more-animal-blood-on-your-hands.

254 | ANIMALS AND CAPITAL

122. See OECD/FAO, *OECD-FAO Agricultural Outlook 2019–2028* (Paris: OECD Publishing, 2019), 30–3.

123. OECD/FAO, *OECD-FAO Agricultural Outlook 2019–2028*, 32.

124. See Hannah Ritchie, 'Which Countries Eat the Most Meat?' *BBC News*, 4 February 2019, https://www.bbc.com/news/health-47057341. Per capita meat consumption figures globally are potentially misleading because of the arbitrary separation between land-based 'meat' and 'seafood' in reporting. Combining per capita meat and seafood consumption produces somewhat different results: for example, against the view that rich countries have stabilised in relation to per capita 'meat' consumption, we find instead that if we add in seafood consumption, in countries like Australia per capita meat consumption has steadily increased since the 1980s (my own calculation from FAO data suggests that Australia's per capita meat consumption – including seafood – sits around 140kg per person per year). You could also factor dairy consumption per capita to get a full picture of consumption of animal-sourced foods. For countries like India this would again change the picture, since per capita consumption of dairy products is high, and consumption of seafood products significant.

125. See FAO, *Rome Declaration on World Food Security* (Rome: FAO, 1996).

126. See FAO, 'Key facts on food loss and waste you should know!', https://twosides.in fo/includes/files/upload/files/UK/Myths_and_Facts_2016_Sources/18-19/Key_fa cts_on_food_loss_and_waste_you_should_know-FAO_2016.pdf.

127. See Steven Van Passel, 'Food Miles to Assess Sustainability: A Revision', *Sustainable Development* 21, no. 1 (2013).

128. Industrialisation has also progressively eliminated the need to use animals as draught power for industries; indeed, arguably it is only preventable poverty which means that animals remain in use in the Global South for this purpose. The picture here is not necessarily straightforward. Recently FAO and other international organisations have been singing the praises of draught animals as a new environmentally friendly solution to the poverty of smallhold farmers in Asia and sub-Saharan Africa. FAO has argued that there are benefits to expanding the use of draught animals in these areas: 'Animal power is a renewable energy source that is particularly suited to family-level farming and to local transport. Animal power is generally affordable and accessible to the smallholder farmers, who are responsible for much of the world's food production. The availability of animal power allows women and men to increase their efficiency and reduce their drudgery, compared with manual alternatives.' (See FAO, *Draught Animal Power and Overview*, 2010, 2–3). A similar approach has been taken in relation to 'innovation' in sustainable energy generation using animals: the 'equipment is emission free, low cost and has long life. Also this equipment needs less maintenance and any

person can run either skilled or unskilled.' See Sharad Kumar Chandrakar et al., 'Experimental Study of Micro Industry of Animal Powered Mechanical Device for Battery Charging', *Procedia Technology* 14 (2014). Notice that reducing human drudgery here relies upon increasing animal drudgery. Indeed, animals here are required to address poverty, when other solutions to addressing poverty, such as a fair distribution of global resources – solutions that might avoid animal labour – are not considered. I note that despite these pressures to use animals as labourers, the overall trend seems to be towards reduction. The FAO actively acknowledges this; see for example FAO, *State of Livestock*, 2009, 29.

129. IPCC, 'Summary for Policymakers', in *Climate Change 2022: Mitigation of Climate Change. Contribution of Working Group III to the Sixth Assessment Report of the Intergovernmental Panel on Climate Change*, ed. P. R. Shukla et al. (Cambridge: Cambridge University Press, 2022), 37 n. 61.

130. See Vasile Stănescu, 'New Weapons: "Humane Farming", Biopolitics, and the Post-Commodity Fetish', in *Animal Oppression and Capitalism*, vol. 1, ed. Nibert, 209–28.

4 Labour

1. Tronti, *Workers and Capital*, 162.

2. Smith, *The Wealth of Nations*, 363–4. The missing section of the above quote reads: 'The most important operations of agriculture seem intended, not so much to increase, though they do that too, as to direct the fertility of nature towards the production of the plants most profitable to man. A field overgrown with briars and brambles may frequently produce as great a quantity of vegetables as the best cultivated vineyard or corn field. Planting and tillage frequently regulate more than they animate the active fertility of nature; and after all their labour, a great part of the work always remains to be done by her.'

3. See Marx, 'Economic and Philosophic Manuscripts of 1844', 76. See also Elizabeth R. Johnson, 'At the Limits of Species Being: Sensing the Anthropocene', *South Atlantic Quarterly* 116, no. 2 (2017).

4. John Bellamy Foster, 'Marx's Theory of Metabolic Rift: Classical Foundations for Environmental Sociology', *American Journal of Sociology* 105, no. 2 (1999), 387.

5. Foster and Clark, 'Marx and Alienated Speciesism'.

6. Foster and Clark present a compelling argument that Marx was aware of the moral problems with intensification of animal agriculture. See Foster and Clark, 'Marx and Alienated Speciesism'.

7. Smith, *The Wealth of Nations*, 68.

8. Marx, *Capital*, vol. 2, 449 n. 6; see also 278–9.

9. In *Capital* vol.1, Marx describes the domestication of animals as an outcome of human labour: 'In the earliest period of human history, domesticated animals, i.e. animals that have undergone modification by means of labour, that have been bred specially, play the chief part as instruments of labour along with stones, wood, bones and shells, which have also had work done on them. The use and construction of instruments of labour, although present in germ among certain species of animals, is characteristic of the specifically human labour process, and Franklin therefore defines man as "a tool making animal".' Marx, *Capital*, vol 1, 285–6; see also 287–8. Luxemburg repeats Marx's critique of Smith, chastising him for attributing 'to animal as well as human labour the faculty of creating value'. See Luxemburg, *The Accumulation of Capital*, 39. Luxemburg's reasoning is that Smith conflates the capacity for labour in nature with the historically specific understanding of labour within the capitalist relation (see 40).

10. Commenting on this exchange between Marx and Smith, Jason Hribal observes that: 'True value came from those humans who managed the operations of plowing the fields or transporting the goods. Animals did not work. This difference between Smith and Marx in how they saw other animals is not a matter of semantics. Rather it is of central importance to our discussion.' Jason Hribal, 'Animals are Part of the Working Class Reviewed', *Borderlands e-Journal* 11, no. 2 (2012).

11. See Benton, *Natural Relations*.

12. See for example Noske, *Beyond Boundaries*, 12–21; see also Painter, 'Non-Human Animals within Contemporary Capitalism'; and Stuart, Schewe and Gunderson, 'Extending Social Theory to Farm Animals'.

13. Hribal, '"Animals are Part of the Working Class"'; and Perlo, 'Marxism and the Underdog', 306–7.

14. Kendra Coulter, *Animals, Work, and the Promise of Interspecies Solidarity* (New York: Palgrave Macmillan, 2016); and Alasdair Cochrane, 'Labour Rights for Animals', in *The Political Turn in Animal Ethics*, ed. Robert Garner and Siobhan O'Sullivan (London: Rowman & Littlefield, 2016), 15–32.

15. Coulter, *Animals, Work, and the Promise of Interspecies Solidarity*, 90.

16. Coulter, *Animals, Work, and the Promise of Interspecies Solidarity*, 31–2.

17. See for example Bob Torres, *Making a Killing*, 38 and 60; Painter, 'Non-Human Animals within Contemporary Capitalism', 8; and Rosemary-Claire Collard and Jessica Dempsey, 'Life for Sale? The Politics of Lively Commodities', *Environment and Planning A* 45, no. 11 (2013), 2686.

18. See for example Marjorie Spiegel, *The Dreaded Comparison: Human and Animal Slavery* (New York: Mirror Books, 1996); and Francione, *Animals, Property and the Law*, 110–11.

19. See Wilderson, *Red, White & Black*, 22–3; Jared Sexton, 'People-of-Color-Blindness: Notes on the Afterlife of Slavery', *Social Text* 28, no. 2 (2010); and Jared Sexton, 'The Social Life of Social Death: On Afro-Pessimism and Black Optimism', *InTensions Journal* 5 (2011). See also Guha-Majumdar, 'Slavery, Social Death, and Animal Labor'.

20. Zakiyyah Iman Jackson, 'Losing Manhood: Animality and Plasticity in the (Neo) Slave Narrative', *Qui Parle: Critical Humanities and Social Sciences* 25, no. 1–2 (2016), 108. See also Kim, 'Murder and Mattering in Harambe's House', 46–7.

21. See Gerhard Feiner, *Meat Products Handbook: Practical Science and Technology* (Cambridge: Woodhead Publishing, 2006), 47–50.

22. See N. Čobanović et al., 'The Influence of Pre-Mortem Conditions on Pale, Soft and Exudative (PSE) and Dark, Firm and Dry (DFD) Pork Meat', *Acta Veterinaria* 66, no. 2 (2016).

23. Patterson, *Slavery and Social Death*, 7.

24. See Patterson, *Slavery and Social Death*, 2–13.

25. Patterson, *Slavery and Social Death*, 10.

26. And this implies an indignity that is central to human treatment of animals, not because something intrinsic in animals is disrespected, but that within human–animal relations the devaluing of the moral status of animals is a fundamental characteristic of this relationality. On animal 'dignity' as a relational concept, see Lori Gruen, 'Dignity, Captivity, and an Ethics of Sight', in *The Ethics of Captivity* (Oxford: Oxford University Press, 2014), 231–47; Will Kymlicka, 'Human Rights without Human Supremacism', *Canadian Journal of Philosophy* 48, no. 6 (2018); and Dinesh Joseph Wadiwel, 'Cruel Indignities: Animality and Torture', *Borderlands e-journal* 13, no. 1 (2014).

27. Patterson states: 'more tragic than the victim's outward acceptance of blame as part of the dynamics of interaction with the master was his tendency to express psychological violence against himself: the outward show of self-hatred in the presence of the master, which was prompted by the pervasive indignity and underlying physical violence of the relationship'. Patterson, *Slavery and Social Death*, 12.

28. On these interconnections, see particularly Kim, *Dangerous Crossings*; see also Ko and Ko, *Aphro-Ism*.

29. Here intensities of pain are essential to the terror they inflict; thus in historical accounts whipping is accompanied by rituals such as the rubbing of salt, pepper and vinegar into wounds to scarify the body and intensify suffering. Here whipping functions within a biopolitics which aims to keep the body alive, while exerting a maximum of suffering. See Wadiwel, 'The Sovereign Whip'; and Wadiwel, 'Thick Hides'. Referring to one Virginia slaveowner, William A. Link observes

258 | ANIMALS AND CAPITAL

that: 'Eppes saw few alternatives to corporal discipline. "Let it once be known that the plantation master will not whip" he commented in his diary, and there would be "an end to all management".' William A. Link, *Roots of Secession: Slavery and Politics in Antebellum Virginia* (Chapel Hill: University of North Carolina Press, 2003), 41. Note, and relevant to my analysis here, there are many accounts of slaves being whipped to death. This highlights the reality that the economy of racialised violence did not need to protect the body in the same way as the economy of violence which circulates animal agriculture does.

30. Reviewing slave abuse cases in Virginia, South Carolina, North Carolina, Georgia, Mississippi and Alabama, Andrew Fede observes that 'juries apparently legitimized all killings but those among the most brutal and extreme cases in recorded human history; these cases were examples of the most gratuitous and sadistic killings imaginable'. Andrew Fede, 'Legitimized Violent Slave Abuse in the American South, 1619–1865: A Case Study of Law and Social Change in Six Southern States', *American Journal of Legal History* 29, no. 2 (1985), 121. On the North Carolina slave courts, see Alan D. Watson, 'North Carolina Slave Courts, 1715–1785', *North Carolina Historical Review* 60, no. 1 (1983), 24–36.

31. Saidiya V. Hartman, *Scenes of Subjection: Terror, Slavery and Self-Making in Nineteenth-Century America* (New York: Oxford University Press, 1997), 8.

32. Hence in the logic of animal welfare, the goal is to limit 'unnecessary suffering': that is, justification is provided for suffering that is a necessary and unavoidable feature of the object of production – in the case of animal agriculture, the production of the consumption commodity. This means that, at least prima facie, reductions in suffering are always possible where these do not interfere with the object of producing these consumption commodities, or if the promotion of welfare enhances the consumption commodity.

33. Indeed, in some cases the State has moved towards criminalisation of those who expose the inner workings of animal agriculture, through so called 'ag-gag' laws. See Will Potter, 'Ag-Gag Laws: Corporate Attempts to Keep Consumers in the Dark', *Griffith Journal of Law and Human Dignity* 5, no. 7 (2017).

34. Timothy Pachirat, *Every Twelve Seconds*.

35. Donna J. Haraway, *When Species Meet* (Minneapolis: University of Minnesota Press, 2008), 46.

36. Haraway, *When Species Meet*, 46.

37. On Haraway and the problems with how labour is understood, see Wadiwel, *The War against Animals*, 209–20.

38. Maan Barua, 'Nonhuman Labour, Encounter Value, Spectacular Accumulation: The Geographies of a Lively Commodity', *Transactions of the Institute of British Geographers* 42, no. 2 (2017), 284. See also Barua's excellent summary of

recent work which has evolved the concept of labour: Maan Barua, 'Animating Capital: Work, Commodities, Circulation', *Progress in Human Geography* 43, no. 4 (2019).

39. Barua, 'Lively Commodities and Encounter Value', 728.

40. Barua, 'Nonhuman Labour, Encounter Value, Spectacular Accumulation'.

41. Collard and Dempsey, 'Life for Sale?', 2684. See also Rosemary-Claire Collard, *Animal Traffic: Lively Capital in the Global Exotic Pet Trade* (Durham, NC: Duke University Press, 2020).

42. Rosemary-Claire Collard, 'Putting Animals Back Together, Taking Commodities Apart', *Annals of the Association of American Geographers* 104, no. 1 (2014), 152.

43. See Agamben, *Homo Sacer*; see also Wadiwel, *The War against Animals*, 70–80.

44. Melinda Cooper, *Life as Surplus: Biotechnology and Capitalism in the Neoliberal Era* (Seattle: University of Washington Press, 2008), 148. See also Cooper and Waldby, *Clinical Labor*, 230–1, n. 10.

45. Beldo, 'Metabolic Labor'.

46. Beldo, 'Metabolic Labor', 119.

47. Beldo, 'Metabolic Labor', 110.

48. Beldo, 'Metabolic Labor', 110.

49. Beldo, 'Metabolic Labor', 124–5.

50. Gillespie, 'Sexualized Violence and the Gendered Commodification of the Animal Body', 1326–7. Gillespie notes that the cow arrives in production with a body already formed by a historical process of production: 'Assuming the cow with ear tag #1389 had a typical life on a small or industrial scale dairy farm, she, herself, would be the result of a long line of genetic selection of dairy breeding chosen over generations to select for qualities like volume of milk production (10 times the normal amount needed to sustain a calf), milk taste, temperament. In other words, her body, to begin with, would be the result of human interference, breeding, and selection for traits deemed desirable and profitable for commodity production' (1326).

51. Marx states, notably ignoring the capacity for animal labour, that 'a particular product may be used as both instrument of labour and raw material in the same process. Take, for instance, the fattening of cattle, where the animal is raw material, and at the same time an instrument for the production of manure.' Marx, *Capital*, vol. 1, 288.

52. See for example Kelly Oliver, 'Marxism and Surrogacy', *Hypatia* 4, no. 3 (1989); Rashné Limki, 'On the Coloniality of Work: Commercial Surrogacy in India', *Gender, Work & Organization* 25, no. 4 (2018); Amrita Pande, 'Global Reproductive Inequalities, Neo-Eugenics and Commercial Surrogacy in India', *Current Sociology* 64, no. 2 (2016); and Lewis, *Full Surrogacy Now*.

260 | ANIMALS AND CAPITAL

53. Arlie Russell Hochschild, *The Managed Heart: Commercialization of Human Feeling* (Berkeley: University of California Press, 2012).

54. See Rachel Lara Cohen, Kate Hardy, Teela Sanders and Carol Wolkowitz, 'The Body/Sex/Work Nexus: A Critical Perspective on Body Work and Sex Work', in *Body/Sex/Work: Intimate, Embodied and Sexualised Labour*, ed. Carol Wolkowitz et al. (Basingstoke: Palgrave Macmillan, 2013), 3–27.

55. See Lewis, *Full Surrogacy Now*, 19.

56. Amrita Pande, *Wombs in Labor: Transnational Commercial Surrogacy in India* (New York: Columbia University Press, 2014), 90.

57. Pande, *Wombs in Labor*, 91.

58. Pande, *Wombs in Labor*, 135.

59. Lewis, *Full Surrogacy Now*. Lewis states: 'Pregnancy is not something society as a whole tends to question. Surrogacy, on the other hand, is hotly contested. Yet we can readily perceive that all that really separates the two is the possibility of a wage' (44). See also Sophie Lewis, 'International Solidarity in Reproductive Justice: Surrogacy and Gender-Inclusive Polymaternalism', *Gender, Place & Culture* 25, no. 2 (2018).

60. See Lewis, *Full Surrogacy Now*, 7–8.

61. Lewis, *Full Surrogacy Now*, 56.

62. Lewis, *Full Surrogacy Now*, 168.

63. While Lewis does much work to de-link gestational labour from gender, this labour is not de-linked from its connection to the human (see 22–6). This is perhaps due to the claim, early in the book, that human gestational labour, 'unlike almost all other animals' (1) is unique in form. Lewis states, 'mammals whose placentae don't "breach the walls of the womb" in this way can simply abort or reabsorb unwanted fetuses at any stage of pregnancy. . . . Conversely, a human cannot rip away a placenta in the event of a change of heart – or, say, a sudden drought or outbreak of war – without risk of lethal hemorrhage. Our embryo hugely enlarges and paralyzes the wider arterial system supplying it, while at the same time elevating (hormonally) the blood pressure and sugar supply' (2). See also Suzanne Sadedin, 'War in the Womb: A Ferocious Biological Struggle Between Mother and Baby Belies any Sentimental Ideas We Might Have About Pregnancy', *Aeon*, 4 August 2014, https://aeon.co/essays/why-pregnancy-is-a-biological-war-between-mother-and-baby. Note Sadedin discusses other species: primates, mice and hyenas.

64. I certainly don't mean to imply that Lewis's analysis *should* have included a focus on animals; rather that a compelling and relevant case study of mass forced gestational labour was missed in both *Full Surrogacy Now*, and other relevant work that sits on the border of the human–animal relation: see for example Sophie

Lewis, 'Do Electric Sheep Dream of Water Babies?' *Logic* 8, 3 August 2019, https://logicmag.io/bodies/do-electric-sheep-dream-of-water-babies/.

65. See Gillespie on the mourning of cows who lose their calves: Gillespie, 'Sexualized Violence and the Gendered Commodification of the Animal Body', 1326. See also Melissa Boyde, 'The Dairy Issue: "Practicing the Art of War"', *Animal Studies Journal* 7, no. 2 (2018). Boyde states: 'The separation of mothers from their calves is standard operating procedure in the dairy industry – in fact the industry can only exist because of this separation. Even the farmer who lives near me and who doesn't appear to care reveals that they are aware of the stress caused to the mothers when they say things such as "they'll get over it"' (11).

66. Marx, *Capital*, vol. 1, 314–15. Note the remarkable resonance between this section of Marx and the following from G. W. F. Hegel: 'what first appeared as the object sinks for consciousness to the level of its way of knowledge it, and since the in-itself becomes a *being-for-consciousness* of the in-itself, the latter is now the new object. Herewith a new pattern of consciousness comes to the scene as well, for which the essence is something different from what it was at the preceding stage. It is this fact that guides the entire series of the patterns of consciousness in their necessary sequence. But it is just this necessity itself, or the *origination* of the new object, that presents itself to consciousness without its understanding how this happens, which proceeds for us, as it were, behind the back of consciousness. For it, what has thus arisen exists only as an object; for us, it appears at the same time as movement and a process of becoming.' See G. W. F. Hegel, *The Phenomenology of Spirit* (Oxford: Oxford University Press, 1977), 56 (§87). The two sections, when placed side by side, usefully describe the difference between the dialectical approach of Hegel and that of Marx; for the former, change occurs within the space of ideas and consciousness, for the latter, this same change is material.

67. Marx, *Capital*, vol. 1, 316.

68. Marx, *Capital*, vol. 1, 317.

69. Marx, *Capital*, vol. 1, 317.

70. And to an extent, it is useful to note that Marx himself recognised that animals could at least serve the different functions of constant and circulating capital depending on their position with respect to production: 'here the distinction between means of labour and object of labour which is based in the nature of the labour process itself is reflected in new form of the distinction between fixed capital and circulating capital. It is only in this way that a thing that functions as a means of labour becomes fixed capital. If its material properties allow it to serve for other functions than that of means of labour, then whether it is fixed capital or not depends on these various functions. Cattle as draught animals are fixed capital; when being fattened for slaughter they are a raw material that eventually

passes into circulation as a product, and so not fixed but circulating capital.' Marx, *Capital*, vol. 2, 241; see also 279.

71. Although, it should be noted that perhaps a properly 'post-human' analysis of capital might force us to reconsider the value terms of the whole production process. If we treat all nonhuman actors, including non-sentient objects, as providing energy or 'labour', then the hard division between capital and labour time is threatened with redundancy.

72. Including systems of transhumance where the capacity for mobility of animals allows for their movement to take advantage of new elements of production: 'a form of pastoralism which allows people engaged in agriculture in specific ecological zones to use seasonally productive pastures in other areas'. See Eugene Costello and Eva Svensson, 'Transhumant Pastoralism in Historic Landscapes: Beginning a European Perspective', in *Historical Archaeologies of Transhumance across Europe*, ed. Eugene Costello and Eva Svensson (London: Routledge, 2018), 1–13 (3).

73. Speaking of ancient Vedic animal agriculture, Purushottam Chandra Jain summarises: 'the main duty of the herdsmen was to take the cattle to pasture for grazing in the morning and bring them back home safely at sunset. . . . The main quality of a herdsman was that under his keen vigilance, cattle are seldom lost.' Purushottam Chandra Jain, *Labour in Ancient India (from the Vedic period up to the Gupta Period)* (New Dehli: Motilal Banarsidass, 1971), 37.

74. Haraway, *When Species Meet*, 73.

75. See Lewis Holloway, Christopher Bear and Katy Wilkinson, 'Robotic Milking Technologies and Renegotiating Situated Ethical Relationships on UK Dairy Farms', *Agriculture and Human Values* 31, no. 2 (2014).

76. See C. F. Costa et al., 'Automated Sorting for Size, Sex and Skeletal Anomalies of Cultured Seabass using External Shape Analysis', *Aquacultural Engineering* 52 (2013).

77. Marx, *Capital*, vol. 1, 762–81.

78. These circulating commodities which are consumed by animals reflect a 'productive consumption' in so far as they contribute towards the generation of surplus value. Marx states: 'It is only in so far as consumption is productive consumption of this kind that it falls within the actual circuit of capital; the condition for consumption to occur is that surplus-value is made by means of the commodities thus consumed.' See Marx, *Capital*, vol. 2, 155. On the explosion of what is described by Weis as a 'grain-oil seed – livestock complex' see Weis, *The Ecological Hoofprint*, 93–128.

79. Marx, *Capital*, vol. 1, 78.

80. By definition this is true, if we assume no production losses and that each labouring animal becomes one product.

NOTES | 263

81. For example, as Gillespie describes: 'fewer cows are producing more milk on fewer farms than ever before'. See Gillespie, *The Cow with Ear Tag #1389*, 19.

82. Marx, *Capital*, vol. 1, 323. This section includes the following footnote from Marx: 'What Lucretius says is self-evident: "nil posse creari de nihilo", out of nothing, nothing can be created. "Creation of value" is the transposition of labour-power into labour. Labour-power itself is, above all else, the material of nature transposed into a human organism [*menschlichen Organismus*].' See Marx, *Capital*, vol. 1, 323 n. 2. It is worth comparing the section above quoted from *Capital*, vol. 1, with the following from *Capital*, vol. 2, where Marx applies the same 'fluidic' notion of labour power adding value to a material in a discussion of animals for food: 'Fattening cattle function in the production process as a raw material, not as an instrument like draught cattle. They therefore enter the product as substance, and their entire value enters the product, just as that of the ancillary materials – their fodder. This is why they are the fluid part of productive capital, and not because the product sold, the fattened cattle, has here the same natural form as the raw material, the not yet fattened cattle. That is a mere accident.' Marx, *Capital*, vol. 2, 279.

83. Note that in the German version of the quote above, Marx makes mention of cotton and iron as examples of raw materials to which capitalism is relatively indifferent: 'Die Natur dieses Stoffes is daher auch gleichgültig, ob Baumwolle oder Eisen' (177).

84. See Gibson-Graham, *The End of Capitalism (As We Knew It)*, 5–11.

85. Gibson-Graham, *The End of Capitalism (As We Knew It)*, 6.

86. Gibson-Graham, *The End of Capitalism (As We Knew It)*, 13.

87. Lynne Pettinger, *What's Wrong With Work* (Bristol: Policy Press, 2019), 17.

88. See my extended discussion of Marx's chapter 'The Working Day' for thinking about animal labour. Dinesh Joseph Wadiwel, 'The Working Day: Animals, Capitalism and Surplus Time', in *Animal Labour: A New Frontier of Interspecies Justice?*, ed. Charlotte Blattner, Kendra Coulter and Will Kymlicka (Oxford: Oxford University Press, 2019), 181–206.

89. Marx, *Capital*, vol. 1, 432.

90. Marx, *Capital*, vol. 1, 375–6.

91. Collard and Dempsey, 'Life for Sale?', 2684.

92. Dutkiewicz, '"Postmodernism", Politics, and Pigs', 303.

93. Tronti states: 'even before the transformation of money into capital and even before the birth of a specific form of the capitalist relation of production, the class relation sees the workers one side and, on the opposite side, the social conditions of labour as a power over them. In other words, on the one side is a mass of isolated individuals who are necessarily united by their common situation as sellers of labour-power,

94 | ANIMALS AND CAPITAL

and on the other side the pure and simple constancy of the objective conditions that deserve the title "dead labour".' Tronti, *Workers and Capital*, 171.

94. Siegfried Giedion, *Mechanization Takes Command: A Contribution to Anonymous History* (New York: Oxford University Press, 1948), 246. See also Amir, *Being and Swine*, 63–92.

95. Marx, *Capital*, vol. 1, 340–4.

96. Marx, *Capital*, vol. 2, 314–15. See also Foster and Clark, 'Marx and Alienated Speciesism'.

97. See M. Petracci et al., 'Meat Quality in Fast-Growing Broiler Chickens', *World's Poultry Science Journal* 71, no. 2 (2015), 364; and Craig W. Tallentire, Ilkka Leinonen and Ilias Kyriazakis, 'Breeding for Efficiency in the Broiler Chicken: A Review', *Agronomy for Sustainable Development* 36 (2016). See also Moore, *Capitalism in the Web of Life*, 232.

98. Indeed, at least one reading of this situation is that while there are normative limits on the expansion of the working day and the shortening of lives placed on much human labour, the same is not true for animal labour. All available time is expanded for production purposes for animals in intensive animal agriculture, and life is shortened to realise value quicker through faster turnover times. In some respects this is produced as an effect of the introduction of fixed capital: as I have discussed, the introduction of fixed capital reduces human labour time but expands animal labour; indeed the expansion of the mass of animal labour and the simultaneous condensation of animal labour time (shortening of animal life) is the additional free gift that expanding fixed capital offers (aside, that is from reduced human labour time). On the length of the working day and turnover time, see Marx, *Capital*, vol. 3, 170.

99. See Giedion, *Mechanization Takes Command*, 209–46; see also 248–51.

100. Thus, Weis describes a somewhat circular process of development: 'Although the higher value of livestock products relative to grains and oilseeds makes it profitable to burn large volumes of usable nutrition in the metabolism of animals, there remains an inexorable pressure to increase levels of labor productivity and enhance the rates at which feed is converted to flesh, eggs, and milk. These have propelled the rising density of animal populations within highly automated spaces, which reduce both infrastructure and labor costs per animal. Corporate-led livestock science has also vigorously pursued selective breeding to: make animals grow, reach sexual maturity, reproduce, and lactate faster; become more uniform; and augment the relative size of more valuable body parts, such as poultry breasts. Just as with crops, this process of genetic enhancement has driven a radical narrowing of animal breeds.' Weis, *The Ecological Hoofprint*, 95.

101. Twine, *Animals as Biotechnology*, 93–4.

102. See for example C. R. Pierozan et al., 'Factors Affecting the Daily Feed Intake and Feed Conversion Ratio of Pigs in Grow-Finishing Units: The Case of a Company', *Porcine Health Management* 2, no. 7 (2016); K. R. Perryman, H. Olanrewaju and W. A. Dozier, 'Growth Performance and Meat Yields of Broiler Chickens Fed Diets Containing Low and Ultra-Low Oligosaccharide Soybean Meals During a 6-week Production Period', *Poultry Science* 92, no. 5 (2013).

103. Pierozan et al., 'Pigs in Grow-Finishing Units', 2.

104. Roberto Sainz, 'Modeling Feed Efficiency', in *Feed Efficiency in the Beef Industry*, ed. Rodney A. Hill (Iowa: John Wiley & Sons, 2012), 284.

105. For an example of the relationship between the feed conversion ratio and profit, see Luciano F. Montenegro et al., 'Effects of Stocking Density on Productive Performance, Economic Profit and Muscle Chemical Composition of Pacu (Piaractus Mesopotamicus H) Cultured in Floating Cages', *Aquaculture Research* 53, no. 9 (2022), 3380–1.

106. See Marx, *Capital*, vol. 1, 324–9.

107. Marx, *Capital*, vol. 1, 276.

108. Marx, *Capital*, vol. 1, 276.

109. It is no surprise that precise calculations are developed to understand 'maintenance energy' requirements, and attention is paid to animal selection to improve feed conversion ratios. See for example Jason K. Ahola and Rodney A. Hill, 'Input Factors Affecting Profitability: A Changing Paradigm and a Challenging Time', in *Feed Efficiency in the Beef Industry*, ed. Hill, 7–19; and L. F. Dong et al., 'Comparison of Maintenance Energy Requirement and Energetic Efficiency Between Lactating Holstein-Friesian and Other Groups of Dairy Cows', *Journal of Dairy Science* 98, no. 2 (2015).

110. Karl Marx, 'Results of the Direct Production Process', *Economic Works of Karl Marx 1861–1864*, 2002, https://www.marxists.org/archive/marx/works/1864/eco nomic/index.htm (the parenthesis is Marx's); see also Shukin, *Animal Capital*, 69–70.

111. See Wadiwel, *The War against Animals*, 65–86. See also Wadiwel, 'Biopolitics'.

112. See G. T. Tabler, I. L. Berry and A. M. Mendenhall, 'Mortality Patterns Associated with Commercial Broiler Production', 13 December 2004, http://www.thepoul trysite.com/articles/253/mortality-patterns-associated-with-commercial-broiler -production/; see also N. M. Stokholm et al., 'Causes of Mortality in Commercial Organic Layers in Denmark', *Avian Diseases* 54, no. 4 (2010).

113. Leonie Jacobs et al., 'Broiler Chickens Dead on Arrival: Associated Risk Factors and Welfare Indicators', *Poultry Science* 96, no. 2 (2017); see also Claire A. Weeks, 'Poultry Handling and Transport', in *Livestock Handling and Transport*, ed. Temple Grandin (Wallingford: CAB Publishers, 2007), 295–311.

266 | ANIMALS AND CAPITAL

114. Achille Mbembe, 'Necropolitics', *Public Culture* 15 (2003). See also Stanescu, 'Beyond Biopolitics'; and Wadiwel, *The War against Animals*, 87–96.

115. Marx, *Capital*, vol. 1, 558–9.

116. Marx, *Grundrisse*, 704.

117. Marx, *Capital*, vol. 1, 557.

118. Marx, *Grundrisse*, 695.

119. I shall discuss the word 'harvest' in the context of fish capture in Chapter 6.

120. As a result, the resistance of chickens necessitates the deployment of tactics and subterfuge to counter it: hence the need for human workers to work in collectives and use dimmed lighting. A 2017 expose in the *New Yorker* documents this intersection between low paid human labour and chickens in this production stage: 'At night, when the chickens are sleeping, crews of chicken catchers round them up, grabbing four in each hand and caging them as the birds peck and scratch and defecate. Workers told me that they are paid around $2.25 for every thousand chickens. Two crews of nine catchers can bring in about seventy-five thousand chickens a night.' See Michael Grabell, 'Exploitation and Abuse at the Chicken Plant', *New Yorker*, 8 May 2017, http://www.newyorker.com/magazine/2017/05/08/exploitation-and-abuse-at-the-chicken-plant.

121. See Nina Langkabel et al., 'Influence of Two Catching Methods on the Occurrence of Lesions in Broilers', *Poultry Science* 94, no. 8 (2015).

122. E. Nijdam et al., 'Factors Influencing Bruises and Mortality of Broilers During Catching, Transport, and Lairage', *Poultry Science* 83, no. 9 (2004).

123. See Sara A. Quandt et al., '3-D Jobs and Health Disparities: The Health Implications of Latino Chicken Catchers' Working Conditions', *American Journal of Industrial Medicine* 56, no. 2 (2012); Human Rights Watch, *Blood, Sweat and Fear: Worker's Rights in US Meat and Poultry Plants* (New York: Human Rights Watch, 2004); and Angela Stuesse, *Scratching out a Living: Latinos, Race, and Work in the Deep South* (Berkeley: University of California Press, 2016), 120–46.

124. M. W. Schilling et al., 'The Effects of Chicken Catching on Broiler Breast Meat Quality', *Meat Science* 79, no. 1 (2008), 163–4.

125. Taija Kaarlenkask, taking a new materialist approach to examining the introduction of milking machines, makes such an argument: 'If the agency of cows was interpreted merely as resistance, it would be minor or at least temporary in the accounts describing the introduction of the milking machine. However, animal agency as active assenting becomes visible here.' See Taija Kaarlenkask. '"Machine Milking is More Manly than Hand Milking": Multispecies Agencies and Gendered Practices in Finnish Cattle Tending from the 1950s to the 1970s', *Animal Studies Journal* 7, no. 2 (2018), 91. On the introduction of milking machines and the problem of resistance see Richie Nimmo, 'The Mechanical Calf: On the Making

of a Multispecies Machine', in *Making Milk: The Past, Present and Future of Our Primary Food*, ed. Mathilde Cohen and Yoriko Otomo (London: Bloomsbury, 2017), particularly 97.

126. On animals and epistemic violence, see Wadiwel, *The War against Animals*, 29–36.

127. The movements of cows are thus regulated with the system: 'Pneumatically powered gates open or shut after identifying each animal by their livestock identification ear tag. Early lactating cows travel around the system generally better, with shorter milking permission times [greater access to the dairy] as the lactation progresses, milking permission is lengthened allowing late lactation cows longer grazing intervals. The flexibility afforded by the robot allows cows to milk anytime of day or night.' Jamie Brown, 'Robot Dairy Replaces Subjectivity with Data', *The Land*, 1 December 2017, https://www.theland.com.au/story/5074127/robotic-dairy-makes-a-surprising-discovery/.

128. One of the interviewees in a study by Lewis Holloway and Christopher Bear states that 'milking is ideally suited to robot technology. I mean, it's a poor use of somebody's time, it's a difficult job, but it's a job that's done by a robot much better than a human could do it if it's done well.' Lewis Holloway and Christopher Bear, 'Bovine and Human Becomings in Histories of Dairy Technologies: Robotic Milking Systems and Remaking Animal and Human Subjectivity', *BJHS Themes* 2 (2017), 228.

129. An Australian dairy a claimed 25 per cent increase in productivity followed introduction of automated milking. See Anthony Scully, 'Robotic Dairy Delivers Increased Milk Production and Training Challenges for Electrical Apprentices', *ABC News*, 2 December 2016, https://www.abc.net.au/news/rural/2016-12-02/robotic-dairy-delivers-increased-milk-production/8082764.

130. Dairy Australia, 'Technology on Dairy Farms: Robotic Milking', 2019, https://www.dairy.edu.au/information/technology-on-dairy-farms.

131. Holloway and Bear, 'Bovine and Human Becomings in Histories of Dairy Technologies', 228.

132. Holloway and Bear state: 'Particular kinds of cow body might be chosen, and indeed selectively bred, to suit the robot. For example, the robot finds it easier to milk cows with certain udder shapes and teat sizes, and the whole system is better suited to high-yielding cows who will visit the robot several times per day.' Holloway and Bear, 'Bovine and Human Becomings in Histories of Dairy Technologies', 228. Blanchette also notes this homogenisation in pork which facilitates that arrival of automation. See Blanchette, *Porkopolis*, 17.

133. An industry guidance document certainly confirms this reality: 'Avoid placing too much emphasis on a strong central ligament when selecting sires for udder

conformation. Robots will have difficulty attaching cups to cows with crossed over rear teats. Teat placement at the bottom of the lobes of the udder is ideal. It would be helpful to be able to breed for a high level of motivation for voluntary cow movement around the farm, but we don't know how to categorise for that yet. There is some anecdotal evidence that some breeds or cross-bred cows may be more hardy and more motivated for voluntary movement. When making sire selections, you may also wish to consider animal efficiency. For example, milking speed may be more important when you consider the impact that it can have on throughput potential (the number of milkings the robots can conduct each day). In a conventional dairy, cutting the average milking time by 30 seconds would have virtually no impact on a milking session. In a single-box AMS [Automatic Milking System], cutting the average milking time by 30 seconds would allow an additional 10 milkings per day (that is you could milk an extra five cows, twice a day, or an extra three cows, three times a day). Similarly, you could milk more cows through an AMS if you had a herd of cows that can cope with average milking intervals of say 18 hours (instead of 12) without decreasing milk production.' Kendra Kerrisk and Lee-Ann Monks, 'Raising Cows for Large Herd Automatic Milking Systems', 2016, http://futuredairy.com.au/wp-content/uploads/2016/02 /Raising_cows_for_AMS.pdf.

134. Dairy Australia makes this clear: 'Many farmers use powerful computer databases to monitor paddocks and fertiliser use and to store detailed health, milk production and breeding information on each cow, work out how much to feed the cows and calculate how much it will cost. This information is often fed directly into the milking process to increase the efficiency of the milking shed.' See Dairy Australia, 'Technology on Dairy Farms'.

135. On epistemic violence, see Wadiwel, *The War against Animals*, 29–36.

136. Haraway, *When Species Meet*, 205–46.

137. Haraway, *When Species Meet*, 216.

138. Mary Louise Pratt, 'Arts of the Contact Zone', *Profession* 91 (1991), 34.

139. Mary Louise Pratt, *Imperial Eyes: Travel Writing and Transculturation* (London: Routledge, 2008), 8.

140. Pratt, *Imperial Eyes*, 8.

141. Haraway, *When Species Meet*, 205.

142. See Wadiwel, *The War against Animals*, 202–20.

5 Circulation

1. Marx, *Grundrisse*, 635.

2. Marx, *Capital*, vol. 2, 326. On circulation time, see 200–6; 326–33.

3. See Juliet Clutton-Brock, ed., *The Walking Larder: Patterns of Domestication, Pastoralism, and Predation* (London: Unwin Hyman, 1989). The use of animals as a household-level asset continues today in various forms, often as an insurance against risk; see for example Dee Von Bailey et al., *Livestock Markets and Risk Management among East African Pastoralists: A Review and Research Agenda*, GL-CRSP Pastoral Risk Management Project Technical Report No. 03/99 (Logan: Utah State University, 1999); and G. Gryseels, 'The Role of Livestock in the Generation of Smallholder Farm Income in Two Vertisol Areas of the Central Ethiopian Highlands', in *Management of Vertisols in Sub-Saharan Africa*, ed. S. C. Jutzi et al. (Addis Ababa: Conference Proceedings, 1988), 345–58.

4. For a history of live animal transport see Jean Blancou and Ian Parsonson, 'Historical Perspectives on Long Distance Transport of Animals', *Veterinaria Italiana* 44, no. 1 (2008), 19–30.

5. See Amy J. Fitzgerald, 'A Social History of the Slaughterhouse: From Inception to Contemporary Implications', *Human Ecology Review* 17, no. 1 (2010), 58–69 and Paula Young Lee, 'Siting the Slaughterhouse: From Shed to Factory,'in *Meat, Modernity, and the Rise of the Slaughterhouse*, ed. Paula Young Lee (Lebanon: New Hampshire Press), 46–70.

6. One estimate suggests that on average chickens will be transported twice in their lives; see D. M. Broom, 'The Welfare of Livestock During Road Transport', in *Long Distance Transport and Welfare of Farm Animals*, ed. M. C. Appleby, V. Cussen and L. Garcés (Oxfordshire: CABI International, 2008), 157–81 (158). Assuming this is correct, then the expected transport journeys for chickens in 2020 would be 140 billion.

7. Cooperatives form part of the structure of many meat industry value chains, often in very different contexts. See Onno-Frank van Bekkum, *Cooperative Models and Farm Policy Reform: Exploring Patterns in Structure-Strategy Matches of Dairy Cooperatives in Regulated vs. Liberalized Markets* (Assen: Van Gorcum, 2001).

8. On this sort of production, see for example Tsedeke Kochoa et al., 'Marketing Value-Chain of Smallholder Sheep and Goats in Crop-Livestock Mixed Farming System of Alaba, Southern Ethiopia', *Small Ruminant Research* 96, no. 2–3 (2011); Kefyalew Alemayehu, 'Value Chain Assessment of Beef Cattle Production and Marketing in Ethiopia: Challenges and Opportunities of Linking Smallholder Farmers to the Markets', *Livestock Research for Rural Development* 23, Art. 255 (2011), http://www.lrrd.org/lrrd23/12/alem23255.htm; and Zekarias Bassa and Teshale Woldeamanuel, *Value Chain Analysis of the Cattle Trade in Moyale, Southern Ethiopia: An Economic Assessment in Oromiya Regional State*, IIED Country Report (London: IIED, 2015).

9. This phrase – 'from squeal to meal' – is attributed to Lewis Little, president of Smithfield Packing Company, one of the largest meat packing companies in the world ('We like to say that vertical integration gives us control over our pork products from squeal to meal'). See Smithfield Foods, *Annual Report* (Smithfield, 2001), 9. Note this contrasts with meat processing operations which specialise in dealing with the body of the animal post mortem. These have been characterised by Margaret Pacey as 'everything but the moo'. See Margaret Pacey quoted in Joel Novek, 'Peripheralizing Core Labour Markets? The Case of the Canadian Meat Packing Industry', *Work, Employment & Society* 3, no. 2 (1989), 159. On integration in the pork industry, see Jeffrey J. Reimer, 'Vertical Integration in the Pork Industry', *American Journal of Agricultural Economics* 88, no. 1 (2006); and Catalina Perez, Rodolfo de Castro Vila and Maria Font i Furnols, 'The Pork Industry: A Supply Chain Perspective', *British Food Journal* 111, no. 3 (2009). See also Margaret Walsh, *The Rise of the Midwestern Meat Packing Industry* (Lexington: University of Kentucky Press, 1982).

10. Novek, 'Peripheralizing Core Labour Markets?' 159.

11. See Ian MacLachlan, *Kill and Chill: Restructuring Canada's Beef Commodity Chain* (Toronto: University of Toronto Press, 2001), 28.

12. Marcy Lowe and Gary Gereffi, *A Value Chain Analysis of the US Pork Industry*, Report for Environmental Defense Fund, 3 October 2008, 11–14.

13. Lowe and Gereffi, *A Value Chain Analysis of the US Pork Industry*, 10.

14. Dermot J. Hayes, Daniel M. Otto and John D. Lawrence, 'Pork Production in Iowa: An Industry at a Crossroads', CARD Briefing Papers 37 (1996), 2.

15. This may be in part due to the intense capital costs associated with beef production. See Lowe and Gereffi, *A Value Chain Analysis of the US Beef and Dairy Industries*, 20.

16. See Vasile Stănescu, '"Green" Eggs and Ham? The Myth of Sustainable Meat and the Danger of the Local', *Journal for Critical Animal Studies* 8, no. 1/2 (2010).

17. Bernadette Logozar, 'Adding Value for Greater Profitability in Meat Products', *St Lawrence County Agricultural News* 10, no. 4 (2012).

18. See for example Nicolette Hahn Niman, *Defending Beef: The Case for Sustainable Meat Production* (White River Junction: Chelsea Green Publishing, 2014). In this context, see Cole, 'From "Animal Machines" to "Happy Meat"?'

19. Chenjun Pan and Jean Kinsey, 'The Supply Management of Pork: US and China', Working Paper 02-01, University of Minnesota, http://ageconsearch.umn.edu/bit stream/14300/1/tr02-01.pdf, 6. On the new characteristics of meat supply chains in China see Philip C. C. Huang, 'China's New-Age Small Farms and Their Vertical Integration: Agribusiness or Co-ops?' *Modern China* 37, no. 2 (2011).

20. Scott Waldron, Colin Brown and John Longworth, 'A Critique of High-Value Supply Chains as a Means of Modernising Agriculture in China: The Case of the Beef Industry', *Food Policy* 35, no. 3 (2010), 479–80. See also Allan N. Rae and Xiaohui Zhang, 'China's Booming Livestock Industry: Household Income, Specialization, and Exit', *Agricultural Economics* 40 (2009).

21. See Waldron, Brown and Longworth, 'A Critique of High-Value Supply Chains'.

22. Huang, 'China's New-Age Small Farms and Their Vertical Integration', 119.

23. Marx, *Capital*, vol. 1, 463.

24. See Marnie Hunter, 'World's First Luxury Animal Terminal Under Construction at JFK Airport', *CNN*, 21 July 2015, http://edition.cnn.com/2015/07/20/travel/ark-luxury-pet-terminal-jfk-feat/.

25. See Shelley Clarke, *Understanding China's Fish Trade and Traceability Systems* (Hong Kong: The Wildlife Trade Monitoring Network, 2009), http://www.traffic.org/home/2009/8/17/chinas-fisheries-must-adapt-to-meet-new-eu-regulations.html.

26. Even though in many contexts road-based transportation of live animals is predominant, the development of national rail systems in the late nineteenth and early twentieth centuries is linked to the demand to move live animals. Referring to the case of Canada, Ian MacLachlan notes that 'Live cattle were among the earliest western commodities to be carried on Canadian railways.' See MacLachlan, *Kill and Chill*, 96; see also 97–100.

27. P. G. Chambers et al., *Guidelines for Humane Handling, Transport and Slaughter of Livestock* (FAO, RAP Publication, 2001), 33, https://www.fao.org/3/x6909e/x6909e.pdf. We should note that technologies have existed for a long time to transport live animals. For example, in Jean Blancou and Ian Parsonson's short history of live animal transport, they note that the transport of animals such as elephants and lions to Rome in antiquity, often for display in menageries, would have involved combinations of land and sea transport often at great risk to the cargo: 'in a letter written in 394AD to his friend Aurelius, the Roman statesman, Symmachus, deplored the deaths of a large number of bears during a shipwreck and asked to be reimbursed'. Blancou and Parsonson, 'Historical Perspectives on Long Distance Transport of Animals', 20.

28. See 'MV Ocean Drover', *Wellard*, http://www.wellard.com.au/home/shipping/shipping-fleet/mv-ocean-drover.html. See also Rob Almeida, 'World's Largest Livestock Carrier Catches Fire in Fremantle', *G-Captain*, 9 October 2014, http://gcaptain.com/worlds-largest-livestock-carrier-catches-fire-fremantle/.

29. See MI News Network, 'MV Becrux: The Largest Livestock Carrier in the World', *Marine Insight*, 18 August 2011, http://www.marineinsight.com/marine/types-of-ships-marine/mv-becrux-the-largest-livestock-carrier-in-the-world/.

272 | ANIMALS AND CAPITAL

30. See James Nason, 'Live Export Leviathan Sets Sail for Egypt', *Beef Central*, 3 July 2012, http://www.beefcentral.com/live-export/other-markets/live-export-leviathan-sets-sail-for-egypt/.

31. 'First Livestock Carrier in the World', Chengxi Shipyard Co., http://chengxi.cssc .net.cn/cms_chengxi_en/compay_mod_file/news_detail.php?cart=3&id=178.

32. The impetus for these developments was partly driven by European Union regulation. See Willy Baltussen, Girma Gebrenset and Kees de Roest, *Study on the Impact of Regulation (EC) No 1/2005 on the Protection of Animals During Transport* (Brussels: European Commission, 2011). Note that tracking systems are also an essential reality for effective logistics planning and 'just in time' processes. See G. C. Miranda-de la Lama, M. Villarroel and G. A. Maria, 'Livestock Transport from the Perspective of the Pre-Slaughter Logistic Chain: A Review', *Meat Science* 98 (2014). See also Paolo Dalla Villa et al., 'Quality Management for the Road Transportation of Livestock', *Veterinaria Italiana* 44, no. 1 (2008). In relation to watering systems and the failure of much land-based live animal transport to include basic welfare amenity such as access to fresh water, see Ashifa Kassam, 'Judge Dismisses Case of Woman Who Gave Water to Pigs Headed to Slaughter', *Guardian*, 5 May 2017, https://www.theguardian.com/world/2017/may/04/canada-anita-krajnc-pigs-water-case-dismissed.

33. Developments have included seven-deck triple road trains, capable of carrying 1,000 animals, and operated over long distances, such as the over 1,600km run between Perth and Port Hedland. See Jason Nason, 'How Seven-Deck Road Trains Came to the North', *Beef Central*, 15 December 2013, http:// www.beefcentral.com/features/how-seven-deck-road-trains-came-to-the-north/. See also Peter M. Thornber and David B. Adams, 'How Scientific Evidence is Used in Australia to Inform Public Policy on the Long Distance Transportation of Animals', *Veterinaria Italiana* 44, no. 1 (2008). The Australian government-funded scientific agency, the Commonwealth Scientific and Industrial Research Organisation (CSIRO), has been involved in developing a tool for tracking transport and developing logistics solutions for industry; this tool has been used to model potential innovations in the supply chain to reduce transport costs, including where ideal locations for new industrialised slaughter facilities might be located. See 'New Tool Cuts Cattle Transport Costs with Maths', CSIRO, 5 May 2015, http://www.csiro.au/en/News/News-releases/2015/New-tool-cuts-cattle-transport-costs-with-maths. In this context, see also Akshit Singh et al., 'Cloud Computing Technology: Reducing Carbon Footprint in Beef Supply Chain', *International Journal of Production Economics* 164 (2015).

34. See 'Wellard Sets New Live Cattle Ship Record – Again', *Wellard* (2011), http:// www.wellard.com.au/home/corporate/media-and-publications/media-releases

/media-releases-archive/2011-media-releases/wellard-sets-new-live-cattle-ship-record-again.html. Wellard also promoted its 'record-breaking' business in 2015, claiming to have 'shipped 389,327 head of cattle in 2014/15, helped by a record month in April when 54,314 cattle were transported on the company's vessels; the MV Ocean Outback, the MV Ocean Swagman, the MV Ocean Drover and the MV Ocean Ute'. See 'Wellard Breaks its Shipping Record for Live Cattle Exports', *ABC Rural*, 30 June 2015, http://www.abc.net.au/news/2015-06-30/wellard-cattle-shipping-record/6584628. Note that Wellard has named its animal transport ships within the tradition of the Australian nationalist vernacular ('Outback', 'Swagman', 'Ocean Drover', 'Ute'). When Wellard acquired MV *Ocean Ute*, a media release, written in a way that can only be intended to distract from the violent context of its intended operation, stated: 'Like any Australian rural-based business, we recognised the value of owning a ute and quite frankly I wish we had been able to buy this ute sooner given the huge number of uses for it.' (A 'ute' in an Australian context is a utility land vehicle with a tray back for loading equipment, resources and animals.) See 'Wellard Buys a Ute', *Wellard* (13 January 2015), http://www.wellard.com.au/home/corporate/media-and-publications/media-releases/wellard-buys-a-ute.html. In 2015 Wellard announced that it was building a new ship – the MV *Kelpie* – named after an Australian sheep dog. See 'Wellard Celebrates Start Of MV Ocean Kelpie Construction', *Wellard* (24 November 2015), http://www.wellard.com.au/home/corporate/media-and-publications/media-releases/wellard-buys-a-ute.html. The project was reportedly abandoned in 2018.

35. Clive Phillips notes that the processes of transfer for live export animals means that they must undergo a number of transitions: 'the stock will be handled at least a further five or six times and the whole process is likely to last between 1 and 2 months'. This includes mustering animals at the start of their journey, restricting food and water prior to journey, road or rail transport to a depot, loading and unloading, further transport to a port, and loading and unloading on to the ship. See C. J. C. Phillips, 'The Welfare of Livestock During Sea Transport', in *Long Distance Transport and Welfare of Farm Animals*, ed. Appleby, Cussen and Garcés, 137–56 (139–41).

36. D. Ljungberg, G. Gebresenbet and S. Aradom, 'Logistics Chain of Animal Transport and Abattoir Operations', *Biosystems Engineering* 96, no. 2 (2007), 277. See also M. Winter, C. Fry and S. P. Carruthers, 'European Agricultural Policy and Farm Animal Welfare', *Food Policy* 23, no. 3/4 (1998), 310–11.

37. See Jonathan Cowie, *The Economics of Transport: A Theoretical and Applied Perspective* (London: Routledge, 2010), 207–8. The continuous supply of feed is crucial to the economic sustainability of the industrial process, and thus creates a ferocious logistical challenge as animals are utilised on a large sale: 'Pig feed

consumption cannot be disrupted because continuous feeding is crucial for pig growth.' See Kullapapruk Piewthongngam, Supachai Pathumnakul and Suphakan Homkhampad, 'An Interactive Approach to Optimize Production–Distribution Planning for an Integrated Feed Swine Company', *International Journal of Production Economics* 142, no. 2 (2013).

38. See Miranda-de la Lama, Villarroel and Maria, 'Livestock Transport', 11; and Ljungberg, Gebresenbet and Aradom, 'Logistics Chain of Animal Transport and Abattoir Operations'. See also David Simons and David Taylor, 'Lean Thinking in the UK Red Meat Industry: A Systems and Contingency Approach', *International Journal of Production Economics* 106, no. 1 (2007).

39. A. Zugarramurdi et al., 'Investment and Production Costs for Fishmeal Plants in Developing and Developed Countries', *International Journal of Production Economics* 76 (2002), 56.

40. See Jonathan Swan and Lisa Cox, 'Crimea Tensions Behind Russia's Ban of Australian Beef Imports, says Barnaby Joyce', *Sydney Morning Herald*, 3 April 2014, http://www.smh.com.au/federal-politics/political-news/crimea-tensions-behind-russias-ban-of-australian-beef-imports-says-barnaby-joyce-20140402-zqpyw.html#ixzz3swBcjX2d.

41. Sue Neals, 'Big Shipment to Beef Up Exports to Russia', *The Australian*, 25 April 2015, https://www.theaustralian.com.au/business/big-shipment-to-beef-up-exports-to-russia/news-story/0b2271bb7301ed750e4102d9c834eedb.

42. One area in which this change is occurring is in relation to dairy industries. Recent reports suggest that a new 100,000-dairy-cow-capacity facility has been constructed in Mudanjiang City, north-east China, ostensibly to serve Chinese and Russian markets. See Jonathan Riley, 'China Building 100,000-Cow Dairy Unit to Supply Russian Market', *Farmers Weekly*, 6 July 2015, http://www.fwi.co.uk/livestock/china-building-100000-cow-dairy-unit-to-supply-russian-market.htm.

43. See for example Joseph Stiglitz, *Globalization and its Discontents* (New York: W. W. Norton & Company, 2003).

44. See particularly Saskia Sassen's influential work: Saskia Sassen, *The Mobility of Capital and Labor: A Study in International Investment and Labor Flow* (Cambridge: Cambridge University Press, 1988); and Saskia Sassen, *The Global City: New York, London, Tokyo* (Princeton: Princeton University Press, 2001). See also William I. Robinson, 'Saskia Sassen and the Sociology of Globalization: A Critical Appraisal', *Sociological Analysis* 3, no. 1 (2009).

45. See William I. Robinson, 'Theories of Globalization', in *The Blackwell Companion to Globalization*, ed. George Ritzer (Oxford: Blackwell, 2007), 125–43. On history and globalisation see William R. Nester, *Globalization: A Short History of the Modern World* (New York: Palgrave Macmillan, 2010). See also David Held et

al., *Global Transformations: Politics, Economics and Culture* (Stanford: Stanford University Press, 1999). On world systems, see for example Giovanni Arrighi, *Adam Smith in Beijing: Lineages of the Twenty-First Century* (London: Verso, 2007).

46. See for example Frank J. Garcia, 'Globalization and the Theory of International Law', *International Legal Theory* 11 (2005); W. Twining, *General Jurisprudence: Understanding Law from a Global Perspective* (Cambridge: Cambridge University Press, 2009); Ralf Michaels, 'Globalization and Law: Law Beyond the State', in *Law and Social Theory*, ed. Reza Banakar and Max Travers (Oxford: Hart Publishing, 2013), 287–304; P. G. Cerny, 'Globalization and the Erosion of Democracy', *European Journal of Political Research* 36 (1999); F. Felice, 'The Viability of the United Nations Approach to Economic and Social Human Rights in a Globalized Economy', *International Affairs* 75 (1999); Richard Fairbrother and Robert McCorquodale, 'Globalization and Human Rights', *Human Rights Quarterly* 21, no. 3 (1999).

47. See Manuel Castells, *The Rise of the Network Society. Vol. I of The Information Age: Economy, Society, Culture* (Oxford: Blackwell, 1996).

48. See for example Robert Cox, *Production, Power, and World Order: Social Forces in the Making of History* (New York: Columbia University Press, 1987); and William I. Robinson, *A Theory of Global Capitalism: Production, Class and State in a Transnational World* (Baltimore: Johns Hopkins University Press, 2004).

49. Hardt and Negri, *Empire*. In many respects Hardt and Negri offer a unified critique of globalisation that takes into account economy, culture, technology and sovereignty. See John Hutnyk's discussion: John Hutnyk, *Bad Marxism: Capitalism and Cultural Studies* (London: Pluto Press, 2004), 115–38.

50. On the effect of this in the European Union, see Baltussen, Gebrenset and de Roest, *Study on the Impact of Regulation (EC) No 1/2005*.

51. Thus, the delays on the movements of money which would have been routine in Marx's day seem absurd to us today: 'Say the commodity is sent to India. This takes maybe four months. Let us take the selling time as zero, i.e. assume that the commodity is shipped to order and paid for on delivery to the producer's agent. A further four months is required to send back the money (the form in which it is remitted is immaterial here). It is thus altogether eight months before the same capital can function once again as productive capital, and can be used to renew the same operation.' Marx, *Capital*, vol. 2, 329.

52. See Phil McManus, Glenn Albrecht and Raewyn Graham, *The Global Horseracing Industry: Social, Economic, Environmental and Ethical Perspectives* (New York: Routledge, 2013), 59–72. On the global wildlife trade, see Collard, *Animal Traffic*.

53. L. Manning and R. N. Baines, 'Globalisation: A Study of the Poultry-Meat Supply Chain', *British Food Journal* 106, no. 10 (2004), 833. See also D. Quirke et al., *Effects of Globalisation and Economic Development on the Asian Livestock Sector* (Canberra: Australian Centre for International Agricultural Research, 2003).

54. See Margaret E. Derry, *Masterminding Nature: The Breading of Animals, 1750–2010* (Toronto: University of Toronto Press, 2015). See also Phillip K. Thornton, 'Livestock Production: Recent Trends, Future Prospects', *Philosophical Transactions B of the Royal Society* 365, no. 1554 (2010).

55. See Twine, *Animals as Biotechnology.*

56. See for example D. A. Funk, 'Major Advances in Globalization and Consolidation of the Artificial Insemination Industry', *Journal of Dairy Science* 89, no. 4 (2006). It is worth noting the links between the development of the international trade in bull semen and the later development of the trade for human semen. See Bronwyn Parry, 'A Bull Market? Devices of Qualification and Singularisation in the International Marketing of US Sperm', in *Bodies Across Borders: The Global Circulation of Body Parts, Medical Tourists and Professionals*, ed. Bronwyn Parry et al. (Surrey: Ashgate, 2015), 53–72. See also Gillespie, *The Cow with Ear Tag #1389.*

57. In a sense this is not any radical departure from Marx's understanding of machinery and its relationship to production processes. The initial incentive for the introduction of a machine is to reduce the socially necessary labour time required to produce a thing, but maintain the length of the working day in order to generate additional surplus value. However, as Marx notes, this process is attended by all sorts of contradictions. See Marx, *Capital*, vol. 1, 526–33.

58. See T. P. Robinson et al., *Global Livestock Production Systems* (Rome: FAO and ILRI, 152, 2011), 43–59. This intensification of course has implications in relation to environmental impact. See for example Gowri Koneswaran and Danielle Nierenberg, 'Global Farm Animal Production and Global Warming: Impacting and Mitigating Climate Change', *Environmental Health Perspectives* 116, no. 5 (2008); A. E. Latawiec et al., 'Intensification of Cattle Ranching Production Systems: Socioeconomic and Environmental Synergies and Risks in Brazil', *Animal* 8, no. 8 (2014).

59. See for example World Organization for Animal Health (OIE), *Health Standards, Terrestial Animals, Terrestial Animal Health Code 2006*, WHO 2006, http://www.oie.int/eng/normes/mcode/en_index.htm. On stunning, see Fiona Probyn-Rapsey, 'Stunning Australia', *Humanimalia* 4, no. 2 (2013), 87. As Probyn-Rapsey observes, within the global geopolitics of animal welfare, failures of some nation states or cultures to uphold perceived welfare norms or practices (stunning techniques, eating dogs, killing whales) become sites of intense public friction. In these cases technology-facilitated killing is invested with ethical norms that are increasingly international in scope.

60. We should not necessarily be surprised by this development, as some of these processes have been understood by others for a long time. In a paragraph in *Capital* that could be a summary of the global meat industry, Marx states: 'The immediate result of machinery is to augment surplus-value and the mass of products in which surplus-vale is embodied. It also increases the quantity of substances for the capitalists and their dependants to consume, and therefore the size of these social strata themselves. Their growing wealth, and the relatively diminished number of workers required to produce the means of subsistence, begets both new luxury requirements and the means of satisfying them. A larger proportion of the social product is converted into surplus product, and a larger proportion of the surplus product is reproduced and consumed in a multitude of refined shapes. In other words, the production of luxuries increases. The products are also made more refined and more varied by the new world market relations created by large-scale industry. Not only are greater quantities of foreign luxury articles exchanged for home products, but a greater mass of foreign raw materials, ingredients and half-finished articles are used as means of production in the home industries. Owing to these relations within the world market, the demand for labour increases in the transport industry, and splits the latter into numerous extra subdivisions.' Marx, *Capital*, vol. 1, 572–3.

61. See FAO, *FAOSTAT*. This UN-derived figure includes a combination of the following animals: chickens, ducks, turkeys, pigeons and other birds; rabbits and hares; asses, buffaloes, camels, cattle, goats, horses, mules, pigs and sheep.

62. International Trade Centre, *Trade Map*, https://www.trademap.org/.

63. International Trade Centre, *Trade Map*.

64. It is claimed that Brazil beef industry exports grew by 731 per cent between 1995 and 2010. See Jamie-Lee Oldfield, 'The Brazilian Beef Industry's Slow Climb Could be a Nightmare for Australia', *Weekly Times*, 29 March 2016, https://www.weeklyt imesnow.com.au/agribusiness/decisionag/the-brazilian-beef-industrys-slow-climb-could-be-a-nightmare-for-australia/news-story/89557e992a11ff036ca0812 fa4b6a8be.

65. See Yacob Aklilu and Andy Catley, *Livestock Exports from the Horn of Africa: An Analysis of Benefits by Pastoralists Wealth Group and Policy Implications* (Boston: Feinstein International Center, 2009); and Sintayehu GebreMariam et al., *Study of the Ethiopian Live Cattle and Beef Value Chain*, ILRI Discussion Paper 23 (Nairobi: International Livestock Research Institute, 2013).

66. IGAD, *The Contribution of Livestock to The Ethiopian Economy*, IGAD Centre for Pastoral Areas and Livestock Development, 2013, Policy Brief: ICPALD 5/CLE/8/2013.

67. United States Agency for International Development (USAID), *Agricultural Growth Project – Livestock Market Development – Value Chain Analysis for Ethiopia: Meat and Live Animals; Hides, Skins and Leather; Dairy* (Washington: United States Agency for International Development, 2013), 9.

68. The implication here is that Ethiopian agriculture has failed to adequately realise the capital value of their assets: 'In Ethiopia, many producers only sell their livestock when they need the money or when a drought hits. As a result, most farmers do not consider the livestock trade as a profitable endeavour and ignore husbandry practices that could increase their livestock's market value, such as providing adequate and proper nourishment during the years of growth and development, preventing scarring, and do not consider the timing of sale designed to maximize sales price. Large numbers of animals are held for five to seven years or more to supply draught power and milk for the family in the highland areas. Animals this old do not produce the best meat and their hides are usually so worn that they have limited value to the leather industry.' USAID, *Value Chain Analysis for Ethiopia*, 12. See also Mohammad Jabbar et al., 'Market Institutions and Transaction Costs Influencing Trader Performance in Live Animal Marketing in Rural Ethiopian Markets', *Journal of African Economies* 17, no. 5 (2008).

69. USAID, *Value Chain Analysis for Ethiopia*, 13. See also Getachew Legese et al., *Live Animal and Meat Export Value Chains for Selected Areas in Ethiopia*, ILRI Discussion Paper 12 (Nairobi: International Livestock Research Institute), 2008.

70. See USAID, *Value Chain Analysis for Ethiopia*, 11. See also Jemimah Njuki and Pascal C. Sanginga, eds., *Women, Livestock Ownership and Markets: Bridging the Gender Gap in Eastern and Southern Africa* (Abingdon: Routledge, 2013).

71. See Council Regulation (EC) No 1/2005 of 22 December 2004 on the protection of animals during transport and related operations and amending Directives 64/432/EEC and 93/119/EC and Regulation (EC) No 1255/97.

72. See Baltussen, Gebrenset and de Roest, *Study on the Impact of Regulation (EC) No 1/2005*, 15. See also European Commission, *Report from the Commission to the European Parliament and the Council on the Impact of Council Regulation (EC) No 1/2005 on the Protection of Animals During Transport* (Brussels: European Commission, 2011); Elena Ares, Christopher Watson and Rachael Harker, 'Export of Live Animals within the European Union', Commons Briefing Papers SN06504, United Kingdom House of Commons, 23 July 2013, http://researchbriefings.parlia ment.uk/ResearchBriefing/Summary/SN06504; and EFSA Panel on Animal Health and Welfare (AHAW), 'Scientific Opinion Concerning the Welfare of Animals During Transport', *EFSA Journal* 9, no. 1 (2011), 1966.

73. Baltussen, Gebrenset and de Roest, *Study on the Impact of Regulation (EC) No 1/2005*, 14.

NOTES | 279

74. Baltussen, Gebrenset and de Roest, *Study on the Impact of Regulation (EC) No 1/2005*, 94.

75. Indeed a complicating factor in the implementation of the EU regulation was its inconsistent implementation and policing, and the incentivisation of trade with providers who had successfully structured their business to avoid being impacted by the regulation: 'The lack of increase in prices is mainly due to "unfair" competition of transporters that travel at lower prices because they do not comply with the regulations in force both for animal welfare during transport (observing of journey times and rest periods of the animal with any stop at control posts, absence or inadequate adjustment of the vehicle, etc.) and for daily driving times (not respecting daily journey times, forgery of instrumentation on board, etc.). Control activities of the competent authorities should arrest this phenomenon more vigorously; otherwise the transport companies that travel in compliance with the rules will have unsustainable costs compared to the market price made by those who travel not complying the rules and the law.' Baltussen, Gebrenset and de Roest, *Study on the Impact of Regulation (EC) No 1/2005*, 95. It seems odd that the main injury noted by evaluators here is to hallowed principles of 'fair competition' rather than the violent effects for animal and human labour. Arguably animal lives and human labour are the variable components here.

76. At first glance there appear to be strong parallels which might be made between the brute economics of ship-based live animal transport and historic accounts of the middle passage of the transatlantic slave trade. Certainly, there is evidence that voyage duration and 'stocking' densities were drivers of mortality rates in the slave trade. See for example Nicholas J. Duquette, 'Revealing the Relationship Between Ship Crowding and Slave Mortality', *Journal of Economic History* 74, no. 2 (2014). Christina Sharpe describes one example of this brute economics: 'Built to hold approximately 220 African men, women, and children; the Zong sailed with twice that many; there were 442 (or 470) captive Africans on board. When the ship set out for Jamaica on August 18, 1781, it had provisions for three months and the knowledge that there were a number of ports in the Caribbean where it could stop to replenish if it ran short of water and food. Records show that due to navigational errors the ship overshot Jamaica. Records show that the captain and crew reported that they decided to jettison some of the enslaved in order to "save the rest of the cargo".' Christina Sharpe, *In the Wake: On Blackness and Being* (Durham, NC: Duke University Press, 2016), 35. As discussed in Chapter 4, while there are apparent similarities between transport within the live animal trade and the slave trade, similarities that might prompt us to make all-too-quick comparisons, a focus on the value structure pushes us to exercise more caution. As I have discussed, chattel slavery existed within different economies, including that which

related to the project of racialisation. Further, the fact that animals transported will become consumption items shapes practices: as I discuss below, the use of lairage post transport and prior to slaughter is an example of one practice that is utilised with animals in order to safeguard the quality of meat by minimising stress before slaughter. This same commitment to 'welfare' did not appear to accompany racial slavery.

77. Phillips, 'The Welfare of Livestock During Sea Transport', 145.

78. Phillips, 'The Welfare of Livestock During Sea Transport', 145.

79. These same conditions apply to the welfare of humans in the production process, too: the conditions of human labour are not relevant unless they threaten the value process. Thus, it is tolerable for extreme low-wage labour or debt bondage to be part of a global supply chain, such as in the case of fisheries, as long as this does not compromise the process of valorisation (indeed, as I shall discuss in Chapter 6, in the case of wild capture fisheries this sort of exploitative labour is essential from a value chain perspective, and hence difficult to eliminate). It is true that animals and humans are treated differently within meat production industries. However, these rationalities circulating the protection of value rule. This rule seems to dominate, whether we examine the condition of industrially confined battery hens, or low-wage garment workers in fire-prone factories in the subcontinent.

80. Although recently there has been a lot of focus on sea transport, bad publicity for live animal transport practices has not been centred on this mode alone; high mortality rates can also affect high-value live animal transport. For example, Tim Harris describes mortality rates as high as 80 per cent for primates transported for medical research by air in the 1950s; as Harris describes, the industry responded not by ending what might otherwise have been understood as a spectacularly cruel practice, but by seeking to improve welfare (or at least its public perception) in order to maintain trade. See Tim Harris, 'Welfare Aspects of the Long Distance Transportation of Animals: The Animal Transportation Association', *Veterinaria Italiana* 44, no. 1 (2008), 31.

81. Leah Garcés, Victoria Cussen and Hugh Wirth, 'Viewpoint of Animal Welfare Organisations on the Long Distance Transportation of Farm Animals', *Veterinaria Italiana* 44, no. 1 (2008), 62. See also Phillips, 'The Welfare of Livestock During Sea Transport'.

82. See Calla Wahlquist, 'Live Exporter Charged with Animal Cruelty over Deadly Awassi Shipment', *Guardian*, 31 July 2019, https://www.theguardian.com/austra lia-news/2019/jul/31/live-exporter-charged-with-sheep-cruelty-over-deadly-awassi-shipment.

83. Australian Government, *Australian Standards for the Export of Livestock*, Version 2.3, April 2011, 107, http://www.agriculture.gov.au/SiteCollectionDocuments

/animal-plant/animal-welfare/standards/version2-3/australian-standards-v2
.3.pdf. Very recently, after much heated public pressure, the Australian government
reduced the acceptable mortality rate for sheep and goats to 1 per cent. However,
it should be noted that even where mortality rates are exceeded, action by government to ensure compliance is almost non-existent. See Nick Evershed and Calla
Wahlquist, 'Live Exports: Mass Animal Deaths Going Unpunished as Holes in
System Revealed', *Guardian*, 10 April 2018, https://www.theguardian.com/world
/2018/apr/10/live-exports-mass-deaths-going-unpunished-as-holes-in-system-re
vealed.

84. Note that the sheep mortality rate in Australian live animal sea transport was
recorded at 0.99 per cent in 2003, or 60,000 animals. See Phillips, 'The Welfare of
Livestock During Sea Transport', 143.

85. C. A. Weeks et al., 'Levels of Mortality in Hens by End of Lay on Farm and in
Transit to Slaughter in Great Britain', *Veterinary Record* 170, no. 25 (2012), 647.

86. Bidda Jones and Julian Davis note that in 2014, 15,889 sheep died in Australian
export voyages. See Bidda Jones and Julian Davis, *Backlash: Australia's Conflict of
Values Over Live Exports* (Braidwood: Finlay Lloyd, 2016), 49; see also 48.

87. See Broom, 'The Welfare of Livestock During Road Transport', 168. See also
G. C. Miranda-de la Lama et al., 'Critical Points in the Pre-Slaughter Logistic
Chain of Lambs in Spain that May Compromise the Animal's Welfare', *Small
Ruminant Research* 90, no. 1 (2010), 176. For a summary of mortality rates and
rates of animals that are non-ambulatory post transport within the context of
the pork industry, see M. J. Ritter et al., 'Transport Losses in Market Weight
Pigs: I. A Review of Definitions, Incidence and Economic Impact', *Professional
Animal Scientist* 25, no. 4 (2009). I note that mortality statistics are often only
available where data is available and there is regulatory oversight. There is reason
to believe that there is poor regulatory oversight and potentially problems with
reporting in the case of much live animal transport globally. See Garcés, Cussen
and Wirth, 'Viewpoint of Animal Welfare Organisations on the Long Distance
Transportation of Farm Animals', 62.

88. See Temple Grandin, 'Engineering and Design of Holding Yards, Loading Ramps
and Handling Facilities for Land and Sea Transport of Livestock', *Veterinaria
Italiana* 44, no. 1 (2008), 243–4.

89. C. Chauvin et al., 'Factors Associated with Mortality of Broilers During Transport
to Slaughterhouse', *Animal* 5, no. 2 (2011), 292.

90. Broom, 'The Welfare of Livestock During Road Transport', 161. The conditions
of production which subsume animals and mould their productivity to fit their
evolving use value also create conditions by which they are more likely to be
harmed by the transport process. Broom notes: 'If animals are kept in such a way

that they are very vulnerable to injury when handled and transported, this must be taken into account when transporting them or the rearing conditions must be changed. A notable example of such an effect is the osteopenia and vulnerability to broken bones, which is twice as high in hens in battery cages than in hens which are able to flap their wings and walk around' (169).

91. Phillips, 'The Welfare of Livestock During Sea Transport', 140. See also B. Earley, A. D. Fisher and E. G. O'Riordan, 'Effects of Pre-transport Fasting on the Physiological Responses of Young Cattle to 8-hour Road Transport', *Irish Journal of Agricultural and Food Research* 45, no. 1 (2006), 51–60. Note that starvation during transport is at least one of the routine forms of deprivation animals experience during their transfer between locations; in many cases this starvation is cumulative, in that animals are not fed prior to transport, nor when they disembark and are awaiting slaughter. One Chilean study, for example, tells us that 'the animals' mean waiting time on the farm before they were loaded was two hours, the mean duration of the journey was 24 hours and the mean period in lairage at the slaughterhouse was 29 hours, adding up to a total of 55 hours without food'. See C. Gallo, G. Lizondo and T. G. Knowles, 'Effects of Journey and Lairage Time on Steers Transported to Slaughter in Chile', *Veterinary Record* 152, no. 12 (2003), 362.

92. P. N. Grigor et al., 'Pre-Transport Loading of Farmed Red Deer: Effects of Previous Overnight Housing Environment, Vehicle Illumination and Shape of Loading Race', *Veterinary Record* 142, no. 11 (1998), 265.

93. Bert Driessen et al., 'Practical Handling Skills During Road Transport of Fattening Pigs from Farm to Slaughterhouse: A Brief Review', *Agricultural Sciences* 4, no. 12 (2013), 757.

94. See J. A. Correa et al., 'Effects of Different Moving Devices at Loading on Stress Response and Meat Quality in Pigs', *Journal of Animal Science* 88, no. 12 (2014).

95. One Indian study describes some of the methods used to incentivise animals that are resistant to loading: 'Nervous animals were blindfolded before being dragged into the truck and this technique was quite effective in reducing nervousness. Animals, that offered stiff resistance to being moved were handled cruelly. Two types of cruelty, namely thrusting a stick into the vagina or rectum or poking a stick in the udder or testes were inflicted.' B. S. Chandra and N. Das, 'The Handling and Short-haul Road Transportation of Spent Buffaloes in Relation to Bruising and Animal Welfare', *Tropical Animal Health and Production* 33 (2001), 161.

96. See for example S. P. Ndou, V. Muchenje and M. Chimonyo, 'Animal Welfare in Multipurpose Cattle Production Systems and its Implications on Beef Quality', *African Journal of Biotechnology* 10, no. 7 (2011), 1054; or historically in the con-

text of small-scale farming, see MacLachlan, *Kill and Chill*, 124. See also Wadiwel, 'Whipping to Win'.

97. In this sense these techniques conform precisely to what Darius Rejali has described as 'clean torture': that is, forms of applied suffering which leave no scars or trace. See Darius Rejali, *Torture and Democracy* (Princeton: Princeton University Press, 2007), 4. Pursuing clean techniques of domination under the guise of welfare demobilises the political efficacy of pro-animal advocacy: 'appropriate handling weakens arguments by animal rightists/welfarists that those in the production and packing sectors do not have a caring attitude about the animals in their charge'. Gary Smith et al., 'Effect of Transport on Meat Quality and Animal Welfare of Cattle, Pigs, Sheep, Horses, Deer, and Poultry', 2004, http://www.grandin.com/behaviour/effect.of.transport.html.

98. See Wadiwel, *The War against Animals*, 10–16. In this context, forms of domestication which utilise 'gentle' techniques to acculturate animals and prevent aversive reactions to the more overt forms of control and domination that are part of production might also be understood as forms of productivity which have subsumed and responded to resistance. In one article on animal fear, for example, it is noted that: 'Regular gentle handling, particularly from a young age, can help overcome the negative effects of those aversive procedures that are a necessary part of animal husbandry, as well as reducing general fearfulness.' See Jeffrey Rushen, Allison A. Taylor and Anne Marie de Passillé, 'Domestic Animals' Fear of Humans and its Effect on their Welfare', *Applied Animal Behaviour Science* 65 (1999), 299. Given that fear-inducing handling effects reduce 'productivity' (288) and the simultaneous reality that the mechanised forms of transport and slaughter necessary for large-scale production generate fear, the strategy of acculturating animals to prepare them for the horrors to come in such a way that these horrors will not present as aversive appears to make good business sense. On animal emotion in animal agriculture, from birth to slaughter, see Elodie F. Briefer et al., 'Classification of Pig Calls Produced from Birth to Slaughter According to Their Emotional Valence and Context of Production', *Nature: Scientific Reports* 12, no. 1 (2022), 3409C.

99. 'One of the cruellest things that the author has observed was the tying of a chain to a fallen animal on a truck. The old emaciated dairy cow crashed to the ground when the truck drove away.' Grandin, 'Engineering and Design of Holding Yards', 243. See also Animals' Angels, 'Summary of the Abuse of "Downer" Animals During Transport and Related Operations', *Report for European Commission Directorate-General for Health and Consumers* (*DG SANCO*), 22 November 2006, http://www.animals-angels.com/publications/recent-documentations/2005-2011/animal-transports.html.

284 | ANIMALS AND CAPITAL

100. However, it is not the only reason. Another explanatory factor is that transport remains one of the few sites of visibility for animals within production chains. Under classic vertically integrated models, animals have been produced under conditions of secrecy, with corporate interests legally protected by governments who have sought to secure the interests of meat industries. Within this context, the transfer of animals from one phase of production to another becomes one of the few sites where animals become publicly visible: hence the tactical opportunity exploited by some animal advocates, such as the Save Movement, to target transport. On the question of visibility in general, see Pachirat, *Every Twelve Seconds*, 233–56.

101. See for example Fufa Sorri Bulitta, Samuel Aradom and Girma Gebresenbet, 'Effect of Transport Time of up to 12 Hours on Welfare of Cows and Bulls', *Journal of Service Science and Management* 8 (2015).

102. See for example I. Wikner, G. Gebresenbet and C. Nilsson, 'Assessment of Air Quality in Commercial Cattle Transport Vehicle in Swedish Summer and Winter Conditions', *German Veterinary Journal* 110 (2003); Genaro C. Miranda-de la Lama et al., 'Effects of Road Type During Transport on Lamb Welfare and Meat Quality in Dry Hot Climates', *Tropical Animal Health and Production* 43, no. 5 (2011); M. A. Mitchell and P. J. Kettlewell, 'Engineering and Design of Vehicles for Long Distance Road Transport of Livestock (Ruminants, Pigs and Poultry)', *Veterinaria Italiana* 44, no. 1 (2008); and Phillips, 'The Welfare of Livestock During Sea Transport'.

103. See for example S. D. M. Jones et al., 'The Effects of Withholding Feed and Water on Carcass Shrinkage and Meat Quality in Beef Cattle', *Meat Science* 28 (1990).

104. See for example M. S. Cockram et al., 'Effect of Driver Behaviour, Driving Events and Road Type on the Stability and Resting Behaviour of Sheep in Transit', *Animal Science* 79, no. 1 (2004).

105. See for example S. Buijs et al., 'Stocking Density Effects on Broiler Welfare: Identifying Sensitive Ranges for Different Indicators', *Poultry Science* 88, no. 8 (2009); P. V. Tarrant et al., 'Long Distance Transportation of Steers to Slaughter: Effect of Stocking Density on Physiology, Behaviour and Carcass Quality', *Livestock Production Science* 30, no. 3 (1992); Smith et al., 'Effect of Transport on Meat Quality and Animal Welfare'; R. Palme et al., 'Transport Stress in Cattle as Reflected by an Increase in Faecal Cortisol Metabolite Concentrations', *Veterinary Record* 146, no. 4 (2000); and Phillips, 'The Welfare of Livestock During Sea Transport', 147–9.

106. Broom, 'The Welfare of Livestock During Road Transport', 176. See also S. Aradom et al., 'Effect of Transport Times on Welfare of Pigs', *Journal of Agricultural Science and Technology A* 2 (2012); and Marianne Werner et al., 'Effects of a Long Distance

Transport and Subsequent Recovery in Recently Weaned Crossbred Beef Calves in Southern Chile', *Livestock Science* 152, no.1 (2007). See also Christine Hafner and Julia Havenstein, *Animal Suffering Is Inherent in Long Distance Transports: Lisbon Treaty Necessitates Ban of Long Distance Transports* (Frankfurt: Animals' Angels, 2012).

107. John W. Lapworth, 'Engineering and Design of Vehicles for Long Distance Road Transport of Livestock: The Example of Cattle Transport in Northern Australia', *Veterinaria Italiana* 44, no. 1 (2008), 216. These long-distance freight transports are not exclusive to animal industry zones such as Australia or North America, but also extend to interstate trade in Europe. See for example T. G. Knowles et al., 'Long Distance Transport of Export Lambs', *Veterinary Record* 134 (1994), 134.

108. Phillips, 'The Welfare of Livestock During Sea Transport', 141.

109. Phillips, 'The Welfare of Livestock During Sea Transport', 146. Phillips states: 'Normally, a hard pad is formed, which makes a suitable lying surface for the sheep. However, in very humid conditions, the slurry is formed, which will probably reduce the welfare of the sheep.'

110. Phillips, 'The Welfare of Livestock During Sea Transport', 145–6; 149–51.

111. Thus, as Clive Phillips observes in a frank summary of the regulation of sea-based live animal transport: 'The standards which have evolved over more than 20 years of experience are those that lead to maximum financial gain for the exporter and not optimum welfare of the stock.' Phillips, 'The Welfare of Livestock During Sea Transport', 154.

112. See for example P. D. Warriss et al., 'The Effect of Stocking Density in Transit on the Carcass Quality and Welfare of Slaughter Pigs: 2. Results from the Analysis of Blood and Meat Samples', *Meat Science* 50, no. 4 (1998); P. V. Tarrant, F. J. Kenny and D. Harrington, 'The Effect of Stocking Density During 4-Hour Transport to Slaughter on Behaviour, Blood Constituents and Carcass Bruising in Friesian Steers', *Meat Science* 24 (1988), 209–22; and H. J. Guise and R. H. C. Penny, 'Factors Influencing the Welfare and Carcass and Meat Quality of Pigs: The Effects of Stocking Density in Transport and the Use of Electric Goads', *Animal Production* 49 (1999).

113. Phillips, 'The Welfare of Livestock During Sea Transport'.

114. See Baltussen, Gebrenset and de Roest, *Study on the Impact of Regulation (EC) No 1/2005*.

115. Baltussen, Gebrenset and de Roest, *Study on the Impact of Regulation (EC) No 1/2005*, 94–5.

116. See Grandin, 'Engineering and Design of Holding Yards', 242.

117. Model guidelines, such as Australian codes which aim for fewer than 25 per cent of animals to be coerced using goads, only indicate the extraordinary prevalence

of these methods, and the pressure placed on workers to make transfers of animals happen faster than animals may actually want to be transferred. On Australian guidelines, see John L. Barnett, Michelle K. Edge and Paul H. Hemsworth, 'The Place of Quality Assurance in Managing Animal Welfare During Long Distance Transport', *Veterinaria Italiana* 44, no. 1 (2008), 125–8.

118. For animals there is evidence of a direct correlation between loading times and rates of injury. One study finds that 'an increase in the average loading time per pig reduced the risk of mortality during the journey, particularly when the levels of recorded injuries were high and the pigs had not been fasted'. See X. Averos et al., 'Factors Affecting the Mortality of Pigs Being Transported to Slaughter', *Veterinary Record* 163, no. 13 (2008), 388.

119. On the inevitable role of human labour in meat-packing industries – 'because no two animals are alike, much of the work is still butcher's work to be done by hand' – see Novek, 'Peripheralizing Core Labour Markets?' 168.

120. Novek, 'Peripheralizing Core Labour Markets?' 158.

121. Phillips, 'The Welfare of Livestock During Sea Transport', 151.

122. There is now a lot of documentation on the high rates of injury experienced by workers within meat-packing industries. The United States Government's Accountability Office finds that 'the work environment in slaughterhouses poses risks greater than those faced by workers in many other manufacturing operations'. See Humane Society of the United States, *Human Health Implications of Live Hang of Chickens and Turkeys on Slaughterhouse Workers* (Humane Society Institute for Science and Policy, 2006), http://animalstudiesrepository.org/hsus _reps_environment_and_human_health/10/. In Australia, animal agriculture has the second-highest rate of workplace-related mortality, with fifty-three recorded fatalities in 2012. Inga Ting, 'Ag Workers in the Line of Fire', *The Land*, 21 October 2014, http://www.theland.com.au/news/agriculture/general/healthcare/ag-worke rs-in-the-line-of-fire/2715459.aspx.

123. The Australian government had proposed to dismantle the Road Safety Remuneration Tribunal, a regulatory body which has sought to impose minimum pay rates on industry, including small contractors. Naturally, the imposition of flexibility in pay rates by removing minimum conditions will apply downward pressure on pay rates and lead to unsafe practices, such as long shifts: 'Truck drivers are under pressure to speed, drive long hours, skip mandatory rest breaks and skip maintenance on their vehicles because of the financial squeeze placed on them by major clients.' Tony Sheldon, quoted in Paul Karp, 'Union Anger Over Delay of Minimum Pay Rates for Truck Owner-Drivers', *Guardian*, 5 April 2016, http://www.theguardian.com/australia-news/2016/apr/05/union-anger-over-de lay-of-minimum-pay-rates-for-truck-owner-drivers.

NOTES | 287

124. Jennifer Woods and Temple Grandin, 'Fatigue: A Major Cause of Commercial Livestock Truck Accidents', *Veterinaria Italiana* 44, no. 1 (2008), 262. See also Thornber and Adams, 'How Scientific Evidence is Used', 108–9.

125. Thornber and Adams, 'How Scientific Evidence is Used', 109.

126. Phillips, 'The Welfare of Livestock During Sea Transport', 146.

127. Marx, *Capital*, vol. 1, 314–15.

128. Marx, *Capital*, vol. 1, 316.

129. Perhaps understood as: 'modes of autonomous, self-directed movement'. See Mike Featherstone, 'Automobilities: An Introduction', *Theory, Culture and Society* 21, no. 4–5 (2004), 1–24.

130. See Marx, *Capital*, vol. 1, 323.

131. Phillips notes in relation to sea journeys that: 'The biggest contributor to sheep mortality is persistent failure to eat (inappetence), which accounts for nearly half of all deaths, and/or salmonellosis (about a fifth of all deaths).' See Phillips, 'The Welfare of Livestock During Sea Transport', 144. See also Anne Barnes et al., *Inanition of Sheep: Literature Review*, Meat and Livestock Australia, June 2008, https://www.mla.com.au/contentassets/f30d216d1b3c4ee99d80e326c3db7246 /b.liv.0243_final_report.pdf.

132. Marx, *Capital*, vol. 2, 225–6.

133. Marx, *Capital*, vol. 2, 209 n.

134. See for example A. N. Bailey and J. A. Fortune, 'The Response of Merino Wethers to Feedlotting and Subsequent Sea Transport', *Applied Animal Behaviour Science* 35, no. 2 (1992); and L. A. González et al., 'Factors Affecting Body Weight Loss During Commercial Long Haul Transport of Cattle in North America', *Journal of Animal Science* 90, no. 10 (2012).

135. Thus, Marx draws a line between the production process and the circulation process, even if circulation is productive of use values: 'the transport industry forms on the one hand an independent branch of production, and hence a particular sphere for the investment of productive capital. On the other hand it is distinguished by its appearance as the continuation of a productive process *within* the circulation process and *for* the circulation process.' See Marx, *Capital*, vol. 2, 229.

136. Marx, *Capital*, vol. 2, 226–7.

137. M. Keogh, M. Henry and N. Day, *Enhancing the Competitiveness of the Australian Livestock Export Industry*, Research report by the Australian Farm Institute, August 2016. See 'Executive Summary'.

138. Hence the argument in favour of live export, which has suggested that live export is necessary to secure animal welfare. Chris Back, a former senator in the Australian parliament, provided this view: 'Senator Back said the trade should be resumed immediately to the six big abattoirs in Indonesia that currently exceeded

288 | ANIMALS AND CAPITAL

international standards. That would cater for about half of the 13,000 cattle now on Australian wharves. He said that, unless exports were resumed, within three to four weeks more than 150,000 cattle would be too heavy to be exported and too underweight to be brought south to domestic abattoirs. Unless they were to be shot they would have to be set loose on the rangelands of northern Australia, he said, which would be an "animal welfare disaster". "We will see starvation of animals on an unprecedented scale and an environmental catastrophe on the rangelands that will take 100 years to recover from," Senator Back told the meeting.' See AAP, 'Export Ban Risks Starvation "On An Unprecedented Scale"', *Sydney Morning Herald*, 14 June 2011, https://www.smh.com.au/environment/conserv ation/export-ban-risks-starvation-on-an-unprecedented-scale-20110614-1g1d5 .html.

139. And thus producers are presented with a window by which they can make available animals when values can be maximised. See Keogh, Henry and Day, *Enhancing the Competitiveness of the Australian Livestock Export Industry*, 71.

140. Anna Krien, 'Live Animal Exports a Struggle to the Death', *The Age*, 8 May 2013, http://www.theage.com.au/comment/live-animal-exports-a-struggle-to-the-dea th-20130507-2j5oz.html. Krien compares the question of stocking densities to the economics of slave transport: 'On the long journeys, some of the shackled slaves – unable to jump overboard – begged others to strangle them or refused to eat. Is it too much to connect this to what live animal exporters call "shy-feeding"?'

141. Phillips makes this clear in the case of sheep who are transported by sea: 'The adverse effects of high stocking densities do not just relate to agonistic behaviour. Sheep will be initially reluctant to lie down if stocking densities are too high, a phenomenon that I have observed on board ship. This may be in part because of a fear of being trampled.' See Phillips, 'The Welfare of Livestock During Sea Transport', 147.

142. Bulitta, Aradom and Gebresenbet, 'Effect of Transport Time of up to 12 Hours on Welfare of Cows and Bulls', 179.

143. See Phillips, 'The Welfare of Livestock During Sea Transport', 147.

144. See J. L. Ruiz-De-La-Torre et al., 'Effects of Vehicle Movements During Transport on the Stress Responses and Meat Quality of Sheep', *Veterinary Record 148, no. 8* (2001).

145. Bulitta, Aradom and Gebresenbet, 'Effect of Transport Time', 179.

6 Resistance

1. Marx, *Capital*, vol. 1, 178.

2. Hribal, '"Animals are Part of the Working Class"', 449.

NOTES | 289

3. FAO, 'Trade in Fish and Fishery Products', *Trade Policy Briefs* no. 28, October 2017, http://www.fao.org/3/a-i8003e.pdf. I use the terms 'fish' and 'fishes' extraordinarily loosely in this chapter to describe 'sea animals'. In keeping with my broad conceptual questions, I will suspend discussion of taxonomic classification of sea animals, and whether these variations suggest differences in how we might understand resistance.

4. Daniel Pauly and Dirk Zeller, 'Catch Reconstructions Reveal that Global Marine Fisheries Catches are Higher than Reported and Declining', *Nature Communications* 7 (2016).

5. Crutzen, 'Geology of Mankind', 23. See also P. J. Crutzen and E. F. Stoermer, 'The "Anthropocene"', *Global Change Newsletter (IGBP)* 41 (2000).

6. This has led to some headlines suggesting that the world is 'running out of fish'. See Gaia Vince, 'How the World's Oceans Could Be Running Out of Fish', *BBC*, 21 September 2012, http://www.bbc.com/future/story/20120920-are-we-running-out-of-fish. As discussed in Chapter 1, on average humans are eating more fish per person than ever before. See FAO, *The State of World Fisheries and Aquaculture, 2014* (Rome: FAO, 2014), 3.

7. Pauly and Zeller, 'Catch Reconstructions', 5.

8. Pauly and Zeller, 'Catch Reconstructions', 5. In May 2016 a team of University of Auckland researchers built on the Pauly and Zeller research to focus specifically on the results for New Zealand. What they found was that the actual numbers of fish captured in New Zealand's fisheries over the 1950 to 2010 period were approximately 2.7 times the official reported statistics. Glenn Simmons et al., 'Reconstruction of Marine Fisheries Catches for New Zealand (1950–2010)', *Sea Around Us*, Global Fisheries Cluster, Institute for the Oceans and Fisheries, University of British Columbia, http://www.seaaroundus.org/doc/PageContent/OtherWPContent/Simmons+et+al+2016+-+NZ+Catch+Reconstruction+-+May+11.pdf.

9. Collard and Dempsey, 'Capitalist Natures in Five Orientations', 79.

10. Kathryn Gillespie, 'The Afterlives of the Lively Commodity: Life-Worlds, Death-Worlds, Rotting-Worlds', *Environment and Planning A* 53, no.2 (2021), 282.

11. Gillespie, 'The Afterlives of the Lively Commodity', 289–91.

12. FAO, *The State of World Fisheries and Aquaculture, 2014*, 6.

13. FAO, *The State of World Fisheries and Aquaculture, 2016* (Rome: FAO, 2016), 2.

14. Michael Marshall, 'Farmed Fish Overtakes Farmed Beef for First Time', *New Scientist*, 19 June 2013, http://www.newscientist.com/article/dn23719-farmed-fish-overtakes-farmed-beef-for-first-time.html.

15. See for example FAO, *FAOSTAT*, 2010 data.

16. Alison Mood, *Worse Things Happen at Sea: The Welfare of Wild-Caught Fish*, fishcount.org.uk, 2010, 71. Fishcount.org.uk have since revised down their estimate for 2007–16, suggesting that the number of wild-caught fish for this period was between 0.79 and 2.3 trillion fish a year. See 'Numbers of Fish Caught from the Wild Each Year', 2019, http://fishcount.org.uk/fish-count-estimates-2/numbers-of-fish-caught-from-the-wild-each-year.

17. 'Numbers of Farmed Fish Slaughtered Each Year', 2019, http://fishcount.org.uk/fish-count-estimates-2/numbers-of-farmed-fish-slaughtered-each-year. See also Alison Mood and Phil Brooke, 'Estimating the Number of Farmed Fish Killed in Global Aquaculture Each Year', fishcount.org.uk, 2012, 1.

18. See Celeste Black's excellent summary: Celeste Black, 'The Conundrum of Fish Welfare', in *Animal Law in Australasia: Continuing the Dialogue*, 2nd ed., ed. Peter Sankoff, Steven White and Celeste Black (Sydney: Federation Press, 2012), 245–63.

19. See for example FSBI (Fisheries Society of the British Isles), *Fish Welfare*, Briefing Report 2, 2002; Animals Australia, 'Fishing', *Animals Australia*, http://www.animalsaustralia.org/issues/fishing.php; P. J. Ashley, 'Fish Welfare: Current Issues in Aquaculture', *Applied Animal Behaviour Science* 104 (2007); Mood, *Worse Things Happen at Sea*; Australian Animal Welfare Strategy, *Commercial Capture Fishing Guidelines*, http://www.australiananimalwelfare.com.au/content/aquatic-animals/commercial-capture-fishing-guidelines2.

20. B. M. Poli et al., 'Fish Welfare and Quality as Affected by Pre-Slaughter and Slaughter Management', *Aquaculture International* 13 (2005), 37.

21. Poli et al., 'Fish Welfare and Quality', 38. These are all observed stunning periods, however there is great variation, and a wealth of anecdotal information suggesting some fish endure many hours of asphyxiation.

22. 'Humane Slaughter', http://fishcount.org.uk/fish-welfare-in-commercial-fishing/humane-slaughter.

23. Poli et al., 'Fish Welfare and Quality', 39.

24. Poli et al., 'Fish Welfare and Quality', 38.

25. Ashley, 'Fish Welfare'.

26. See Black, 'The Conundrum of Fish Welfare'.

27. In the case of Australia, this includes state-based legislation such as the NSW Prevention of Cruelty to Animals Act 1979, and the Australian Animal Welfare Strategy. As discussed in Chapter 1, animal welfare is shaped by a prerogative to attain human use value, rather than any inherent commitment to animal flourishing. As Malcolm Caulfield notes, 'killing an animal is not *per se* a cruel act'. See Malcolm Caulfield, *Handbook of Australian Animal Cruelty Law*, Animals Australia, 2008, 139.

NOTES | 291

28. This is the utilitarian balancing act that is central to welfare considerations. See Webster, 'Farm Animal Welfare'.

29. Animals Australia's web page on fishing is one example of this. Animals Australia states: 'Fishing is considered a recreational pastime among most Australians and Australia has a large commercial fishing fleet. Any animal protection group that raises the issue of fish welfare in this country is instantly derided. Having to acknowledge that fish feel pain and distress is not something that those who enjoy fishing, or those whose income is generated through fishing, want to know about. As an animal protection organisation, Animals Australia's role is to present facts that will allow the community to make informed choices – whether they be fishermen (or women) or those who eat fish –knowing that many members of the community if informed, will make personal choices that do not cause harm to others. Therefore, the fact that fish feel pain and distress is just another inconvenient truth that needs to be told.' See 'Fishing: Can They Suffer? Do They Feel Pain? Understanding the Creatures of the Marine Kingdom', http://www.animalsaustralia.org/issues/fishing.php.

30. Lynne U. Sneddon, 'The Evidence for Pain in Fish: The Use of Morphine as an Analgesic', *Applied Animal Behaviour Science* 83, no. 2 (2003). See also L. U. Sneddon, V. A. Braithwaite and M. J. Gentle, 'Do Fish Have Nociceptors? Evidence for the Evolution of a Vertebrate Sensory System', *Proceedings of the Royal Society London Series B* 270, no. 1520 (2003); and V. A. Braithwaite and F. A. Huntingford, 'Fish and Welfare: Can Fish Perceive Pain and Suffering?' *Animal Welfare* 13 (2004). I have left aside here emerging research on fish emotion and intelligence. See for example Culum Brown, 'Fish Intelligence, Sentience and Ethics', *Animal Cognition* 18, no. 1 (2015), 1–17.

31. V. A. Braithwaite, *Do Fish Feel Pain?* (Oxford: Oxford University Press, 2010). See also Culum Brown and Catherine Dorey, 'Pain and Emotion in Fishes: Fish Welfare Implications for Fisheries and Aquaculture', *Animal Studies Journal* 8, no. 2 (2019).

32. See John Cottingham, 'A Brute to the Brutes? Descartes' Treatment of Animals', *Philosophy* 53 (1978).

33. Notably, James D. Rose and his fellow researchers in 2012 contested the view that fish could experience pain in the way that humans do. The researchers argued: 'even if fishes were conscious, it is unwarranted to assume that they possess a human-like capacity for pain. Overall, the behavioural and neurobiological evidence reviewed shows fish responses to nociceptive stimuli are limited and fishes are unlikely to experience pain.' J. D. Rose et al., 'Can Fish Really Feel Pain?' *Fish and Fisheries* 15, no. 1 (2014). Arguably there is approaching scientific consensus on the issue of pain in fish, even if this has not produced any material change in

292 | ANIMALS AND CAPITAL

institutional practices. It is possible to get a sense of this consensus by examining the 2016 open peer review debate that has occurred, as hosted by the journal *Animal Sentience*. See Brian Key's article and the large volume of responses from the scientific community: Brian Key, 'Why Fish Do Not Feel Pain', *Animal Sentience* 3, no. 1 (2016). See also Lynne U. Sneddon, David C. C. Wolfenden, Matthew C. Leach, Ana M. Valentim, Peter J. Steenbergen, Nabila Bardine, Donald M. Broom and Culum Brown, 'Ample Evidence for Fish Sentience and Pain', *Animal Sentience* 21, no. 17 (2018).

34. Singer, *Animal Liberation*. See also Peter Singer, 'Speciesism and Moral Status', *Metaphilosophy* 40, no. 3–4 (2009).

35. Regan, *The Case for Animal Rights*.

36. See Nussbaum, *Frontiers of Justice*.

37. Foucault, *The Will to Knowledge*, 93. I note further that Foucault amends his view of resistance, or at least offers different perspectives on resistance, particularly in the context of his later work. It would be incorrect to say that resistance does not matter in his late work; on the contrary we find the problem of resistance revisited in different forms. For example, Foucault has a lengthy discussion of the concept of 'counter-conduct', a mode of resistance against governmental regimes, in his 1977–8 lectures. See Foucault, *Security, Territory, Population*, 194–5.

38. Foucault, *The Will to Knowledge*, 96.

39. See Dinesh Joseph Wadiwel, 'Lubricative Power', *Theory and Event* 12, no. 4 (2009).

40. In this chapter, I explicitly build on the conceptualisation of epistemic violence and resistance that I offer in my book *The War against Animals*.

41. See Foucault's famous closing paragraphs in *The Order of Things*, 386–7.

42. Foucault, *The Order of Things*, xxii.

43. See Dinesh Joseph Wadiwel, 'Fish and Pain: The Politics of Doubt', *Animal Sentience* 1, no. 3 (2016). I have treated this as an epistemological problem, but it may be an ontological problem, depending on how 'ontology' is understood. See Oksala, 'Foucault's Politicization of Ontology'.

44. Rose et al., 'Can Fish Really Feel Pain?' 123.

45. Rose et al. state: 'A justification for restrictive welfare policies is exemplified by the "benefit of the doubt" dogma. This brand of logic peculiar to welfare biology is, in effect, an admission that the fish pain issue is not resolved (hence the doubt), but the consequence is to mandate policy as if the matter actually was resolved in favor of fish pain interpretations. This is a social-political manoeuvre that effectively exempts valid science from policy.' Rose et al., 'Can Fish Really Feel Pain?', 123–4.

46. I note the latter question is not scientific in nature, but ethical and political, but equally relates to how we understand and respond to truth. I am deliber-

ately playing with Jeremy Bentham here, and his famous footnote, which proved influential for pro-animal discourse, at least in Peter Singer's foundational text *Animal Liberation*. See Bentham, *An Introduction to the Principles of Morals and Legislation*, chapter XIX, note §.

47. On this politics, see Wendy Brown, *States of Injury: Power and Freedom in Late Modernity* (Princeton: Princeton University Press, 1995); and Wendy Brown, 'Suffering Rights as Paradoxes', *Constellations* 7, no. 2 (2000).

48. This should not seem strange to those who have engaged in a variety of other social justice struggles. Feminists have, for example, fought for decades to have domestic and sexual violence recognised in domestic and international law as violence worthy of attention from the law. This is an epistemic problem, in so far as the law, and by extension patriarchy, have systematically failed to see acts of domestic and sexual violence as constituting violence, have failed to recognise perpetrators as wielding violence (so, for example, men are configured as unlucky, or unwitting, or victims themselves) and finally have situated subjects of gender-based violence as not having a subjecthood that can be violated, or are open to violation without protection of the law under particular circumstances (such as in the home).

49. Spivak, 'Can the Subaltern Speak?'

50. On the international gender politics of 'customary practice' see Dicle Kogacioglu, 'The Tradition Effect: Framing Honor Crimes in Turkey', *differences: A Journal of Feminist Cultural Studies* 15, no. 2 (2004).

51. Spivak, 'Can the Subaltern Speak?', 293.

52. Brown, 'Suffering Rights as Paradoxes', 231.

53. See for example Francione's critique of animal welfare; Francione, *Animals, Property and the Law*. See also Peter Sankoff, 'The Welfare Paradigm: Making the World a Better Place for Animals?' in *Animal Law in Australasia: A New Dialogue*, ed. Peter Sankoff and Steven White (Sydney: The Federation Press, 2009).

54. See for example Adam Shriver, 'Knocking Out Pain in Livestock: Can Technology Succeed Where Morality has Stalled?' *Neuroethics* 2, no. 3 (2009). See also Twine, *Animals as Biotechnology*.

55. One example of this sort of argument is Christie Wilcox, 'Bambi or Bessie: Are Wild Animals Happier?' *Scientific American*, 12 April 2011, http://blogs.scientificameri can.com/guest-blog/2011/04/12/bambi-or-bessie-are-wild-animals-happier/.

56. Culum Brown states: 'We "harvest" fish much the same way as we would a field of wheat. Rather than referring to fish populations, they are "stocks" to be traded like other commodities. The way we quantify commercial catches and aquaculture production [is] by weight rather than by counting individual fish. We can only guess how many individual fish are killed each year for human consumption

and other purposes.' See Culum Brown, 'Sentience Politics: A Fishy Perspective', *Animal Sentience* 31, no. 4 (2022), 1.

57. A prominent critique of making this assumption is that it relies on a 'sentimental anthropomorphism'. We see elements of this critique advanced in Elspeth Probyn's work on fishing, which, in its care not to employ anthropocentric views on what fish may want, fails to engage with the welfare issues that might attend the use of fish for food, and the violence of this use. Probyn states: 'In terms of our own areas of study, the complex and vexed questions of eating and human and non-human relations cannot be reduced to which species is most anthropomorphically endowed. If we are truly to advance a program of research, and of ethics, in eating we need to attend to both the singularity of species as well as our mutuality. This is a tough call, but necessary if we are to attend to the material conditions of what makes for emotional geographies and for whom. As researchers we are compelled to pay close attention to the faceted aspects of life, recognizing the multiplicity of what makes things feel. We may not like that the tuna men are businessmen, but they are also complex people with ties to places, fish, families, and communities and of course the sea. We do not know what tuna feel, and to speculate on that risks drawing us into the false security of sentimental comfort.' Elspeth Probyn, 'Swimming with Tuna: Human–Ocean Entanglements', *Australian Humanities Review* 51 (2011). Probyn is attempting to avoid a kind of epistemic violence that arises from sentimentality; however, I think there is a 'sentimental comfort' in assuming that 'the fish actually wanted to die'. This is surely a central and comfortable assumption that allows mainstay violent practices against animals to continue.

58. To an extent, I would argue that the same logic sits behind Spivak's questions such as 'Can the subaltern speak?' or 'How does one critique what one cannot not want?' These questions are aimed at breaking apart an order of truth.

59. See Hribal, '"Animals Are Part of the Working Class"', and Jason Hribal, *Fear of the Animal Planet: The Hidden History of Animal Resistance* (Oakland: AK Press/ Counter Punch Books, 2010).

60. See also Sarat Colling, *Animal Resistance in the Global Capitalist Era* (East Lansing: Michigan State University Press, 2020).

61. Hribal, *Fear of the Animal Planet*, 'Epilogue: When Orcas Resist'.

62. Gabriela Cowperthwaite, *Blackfish* (Dogwoof, 2013).

63. Herman Melville, *Moby-Dick* (Mineola: Dover Publications, 2003).

64. Ernest Hemingway, *The Old Man and the Sea* (New York: Scribner, 1952).

65. See Dinesh Joseph Wadiwel, '"Fishing for Fun": The Politics of Recreational Fishing', *Animal Studies Journal* 8, no. 2 (2019).

66. See Dinesh Joseph Wadiwel, 'The Will for Self-Preservation: Locke and Derrida on Dominion, Property and Animals', *SubStance* 43, no. 2 (2014).

67. In this regard, see Adrian Franklin's discussion of trout fishing and the contesting agencies between fish and anglers. See Adrian Stephen Franklin, 'Performing Acclimatisation: The Agency of Trout Fishing in Postcolonial Australia', *Ethnos: Journal of Anthropology* 76, no. 1 (2011).

68. Agnieszka Kowalczyk, 'Mapping Non-Human Resistance in the Age of Biocapital', in *The Rise of Critical Animal Studies: From Margins to Centre*, ed. Nik Taylor and Richard Twine (London: Routledge, 2014), 183–200 (194). In relation to fish agency and Kantian ethics, see Frederike Kaldewaij, 'Does Fish Welfare Matter? On the Moral Relevance of Agency', *Journal of Agricultural Environmental Ethics* 26 (2013).

69. Clare A. Palmer, 'Taming the Wild Profusion of Existing Things? A Study of Foucault, Power and Human/Animal Relationships', *Environmental Ethics* 23, no. 4 (2001). Palmer argues that there is no means for animals caught within intensive systems of domination to effect power relations: 'There is no relationship. . . . All spontaneity and almost all communication is removed from our brutal encounter. Thus it cannot be a power relationship' (354). See also Jonathan L. Clark on animal resistance in Jonathan L. Clark, 'Labourers or Lab Tools? Rethinking the Role of Lab Animals in Clinical Trials', in *The Rise of Critical Animal Studies*, ed. Taylor and Twine, 139–64.

70. See my discussion in Wadiwel, *The War against Animals*, 10–16.

71. For one summary of the operaist tendency, see Sandro Mezzadra, 'Italy, Operaism and Post-Operaism', in *International Encyclopedia of Revolution and Protest*, ed. Immanuel Ness (Oxford: Blackwell Publishing, 2009), 1841–5.

72. See, for example, Fahim Amir, *Schwein und Zeit: Tiere, Politik, Revolte* (Hamburg: Nautilus, 2018). For a discussion of the relationship of pigeons to the city, see also Fahim Amir, '1000 Tauben: Vom Folgen und Fliehen, Aneignen, Stören und Besetzen', *Eurozine*, May 2013, https://www.eurozine.com/1000-tauben/. The final lines read: 'Wo es Stadt gibt, da gibt es auch Stadttauben. Und wo es Stadttauben gibt, da gibt es auch Widerstand. [Where pigeons are present, where cities are present, and where this interaction occurs, there is resistance to the actions by cities to quell the presence of pigeons.]'

73. See Noske's discussion of domestication as a case of social parasitism in *Beyond Boundaries*, 4–5.

74. See Hardt and Negri, *Empire*, 272–6. See also Melissa Gregg, 'Learning to (Love) Labour: Production Cultures and the Affective Turn', *Communication and Critical/Cultural Studies* 6, no. 2 (2009).

75. Mario Tronti, 'Our Operaismo', *New Left Review* 73 (2012).

76. See, for example, Temple Grandin, 'Race System for Cattle Slaughter Plants with 1.5m Radius Curves', *Applied Animal Behaviour Science* 13, no. 3 (1985).

77. Grandin, 'Race System for Cattle Slaughter Plants with 1.5m Radius Curves', 295.
78. Hardt and Negri, *Empire*, 32.
79. See for example John Law, 'Notes on Fish, Ponds and Theory', *Norsk Antropologisk Tidskrift* 23, no. 3–4 (2012); Haraway, *When Species Meet*; and Elspeth Probyn, 'The Cultural Politics of Fish and Humans: A More-Than-Human Habitus of Consumption', *Cultural Politics* 10, no. 3 (2014).
80. See Sue O'Connor, Rintaro Ono and Chris Clarkson, 'Pelagic Fishing at 42,000 Years Before the Present and the Maritime Skills of Modern Humans', *Science* 334, no. 6059 (2011).
81. Describing evidence of 100,000-year-old human remains at the Klasies River Mouth caves, Richard Klein and Blake Edgar observe that it is probable that these people avoided confrontation and risky hunting practices: 'the people tended to avoid confrontations with the more common – and more dangerous – buffalo to pursue a more docile and less common antelope, the eland. Both buffalo and eland are very large animals, but buffalo stand and resist potential predators, while eland panic and flee at signs of danger.' Richard Klein and Blake Edgar, *The Dawn of Human Culture* (New York: John Wiley and Sons, 2002), 18.
82. Klein and Edgar, *The Dawn of Human Culture*, 20. See also Andres Von Brandt, *Fish Catching Methods of the World* (Farnham: Fishing News Book, 1984), 1.
83. See my discussion of John Locke, the 'commons' and property relationships in animals. See Wadiwel, 'The Will for Self-Preservation'.
84. David M. Ewalt, 'The Twenty Most Important Tools Ever', *Forbes*, 15 March 2006, http://www.forbes.com/2006/03/14/technology-tools-history_cx_de_06toolsland .html.
85. The hook is primarily a catch device, however it is involved in killing even where fish practices (such as 'catch and release') aim to avoid death. One study for example suggests an 18 per cent mortality rate for catch and release fish, and, noting the difficulty of gaining a full picture of mortality rates, observes that 'many reported mortality estimates probably underestimate actual mortality, at least for marine species, because they rarely include predation during capture and after release, or consider cumulative mortality from multiple releases'. See Aaron Bartholomew and James A. Bohnsack, 'A Review of Catch-and-Release Angling Mortality with Implications for No-Take Reserves', *Reviews in Fish Biology and Fisheries* 15 (2005), 143–4.
86. Scarry, *The Body in Pain*, 47.
87. See Jeffrey A. Steina et al., 'The Influence of Hook Size, Type, and Location on Hook Retention and Survival of Angled Bonefish (*Albula vulpes*)', *Fisheries Research* 113 (2012).

NOTES | 297

88. For one summary of research in this area, see Matt Barwick, 'Are Barbless Hooks Really Better?' Australian Government Fisheries Research and Development Corporation, 2012, http://recfishingresearch.org/wp-content/uploads/2012/11 /AreBarblessHooksBetter.pdf.

89. See Wadiwel, '"Fishing for Fun"'.

90. Sea Grant Florida, 'Circle Hooks', *Sea Grant Florida*, SGEF, 170, http://nsgl.gso.uri .edu/flsgp/flsgpg08003.pdf. See also S. J. Cooke and C. D. Suski, 'Are Circle Hooks an Effective Tool for Conserving Marine and Freshwater Recreational Catch-and-Release Fisheries?' *Aquatic Conservation: Marine Freshwater Ecosystems* 14 (2004).

91. Sea Grant Florida, 'Circle Hooks', 2.

92. The Marine Stewardship Council offers the following description of this practice: 'When a school of target fish is located, water is sprayed from the back of the fishing vessel and small bait fish (e.g. sardines) are scattered onto the surface of the water, creating the illusion of an active school of prey fish. This process, known as chumming, sends the target fish into a feeding frenzy during which they will bite anything they see. Fishers line up along the back of the boat each with a hand-held wooden or fibreglass pole with a short line and barbless hook attached. Once a fish is hooked it is flicked up and over the head of the fisher and onto the deck.' See Marine Stewardship Council, 'Pole and Line', https://www.msc.org/what-we-are -doing/our-approach/fishing-methods-and-gear-types/pole-and-line.

93. Kevin T. Fitzgerald, 'Longline Fishing (How What You Don't Know Can Hurt You)', *Topics in Companion Animal Medicine* 28, no. 4 (2013), 152.

94. Alexia Morgan and Tom Pickerall, *Best Practices for Reducing Bycatch in Longline Tuna Fisheries* (Sustainable Fisheries Partnership, 2015), 5.

95. Fitzgerald, 'Longline Fishing', 152.

96. See Von Brandt, *Fish Catching Methods of the World*.

97. See for example Paul K. Dayton et al., 'Environmental Effects of Marine Fishing', *Aquatic Conservation: Marine and Freshwater Ecosystems* 5, no. 3 (1995); J. B. Jones, 'Environmental Impact of Trawling on the Seabed: A Review', *New Zealand Journal of Marine and Freshwater Research* 26, no. 1 (1992); FAO, *A Global Assessment of Fisheries Bycatch and Discards*, FAO Fisheries Technical Paper No.339 (Rome: FAO, 1996); Rebecca L. Lewison et al., 'Understanding Impacts of Fisheries Bycatch on Marine Megafauna', *Trends in Ecology and Evolution* 19, no. 11 (2004); Clifford H. Ryer, 'Trawl Stress and Escapee Vulnerability to Predation in Juvenile Walleye Pollock: Is There an Unobserved Bycatch of Behaviorally Impaired Escapees?' *Marine Ecology* 232 (2002); R. W. D. Davies et al., 'Defining and Estimating Global Marine Fisheries Bycatch', *Marine Policy* 33, no. 4 (2009); and Monin J. Amandè et al., 'Precision in Bycatch Estimates:

The Case of Tuna Purse-Seine Fisheries in the Indian Ocean', *ICES Journal of Maritime Science* 69, no. 8 (2012).

98. See Mood, *Worse Things Happen at Sea*, 26–31.

99. For a variety of studies on the sustainability and impact of purse seine fishing see for example Trond Bjørndal and Jon M. Conrad, 'The Dynamics of an Open Access Fishery', *Canadian Journal of Economics/Revue canadienne d'Economique* 20, no. 1 (1987); A. Ménard et al., 'Exploitation of Small Tunas by a Purse-Seine Fishery with Fish Aggregating Devices and their Feeding Ecology in an Eastern Tropical Atlantic Ecosystem', *ICES Journal of Maritime Science* 57, no. 3 (2000); Amandè et al., 'Precision in Bycatch Estimates'; Dennis O'Connell, 'Tuna, Dolphins, and Purse Seine Fishing in the Eastern Tropical Pacific: The Controversy Continues', *UCLA Journal of Environmental Law and Policy* 23, no. 1 (2005); Amandè et al., 'Bycatch of the European Purse Seine Tuna Fishery in the Atlantic Ocean for the 2003–2007 Period', *Aquatic Living Resources* 23 (2010); H. F. Campbell, R. B. Nicholl and G. Meyer, 'Search Behavior in the Purse Seine Tuna Fishery', *Natural Resource Modeling* 7, no. 1 (1993); and A. Murillas-Maza, 'Spatial and Inter-temporal Economic Sustainability Assessment: A Case Study of the Open Oceans Basque Purse-Seine Fleets', *Proceedings of the 1st World Sustainability Forum*, 1–30 November 2011 (Sciforum Electronic Conference Series, 1, 2011).

100. See Tim K. Davies, Chris C. Mees and E. J. Milner-Gulland, 'The Past, Present and Future Use of Drifting Fish Aggregating Devices (FADs) in the Indian Ocean', *Marine Policy* 45 (2014).

101. Martin Hall and Marlon Roman, *Bycatch and Non-Tuna Catch in the Tropical Tuna Purse Seine Fisheries of the World* (FAO Fisheries and Aquaculture Technical Paper, 568, 2013), 10.

102. See Aud Vold, Jostein Saltskar and Irene Huse, 'Crowding in Purse Seine Can Kill Half the Catch of North Sea Herring', *Marine Research*, Institute of Marine Research, Working Paper, 6, 2010; S. J. Lockwood, M. G. Pawson and D. R. Eaton, 'The Effects of Crowding on Mackerel (Scomber Scombrus): Physical Conditions and Mortality', *Fisheries Research* 2 (1983); and Maria Tenningen, Aud Vold and Rolf Erik Olsen, 'The Response of Herring to High Crowding Densities in Purse-Seines: Survival and Stress Reaction', *ICES Journal of Marine Science* 69, no. 8 (2012). Conversely, where fish are needed to be kept alive, such as when capturing fish for aquaculture, then the purse will be 'stopped half way'. See Hall and Roman, *Bycatch and Non-Tuna Catch*, 13.

103. For a visual outline of the purse seine set process, see Cambria Bold, 'One Way to Catch Salmon in Alaska: Onboard the Purse Seine Owyhee', *The Kitchn*, 15 August 2013, http://www.thekitchn.com/this-is-one-way-to-catch-salmon-in-alaska-19 3566.

NOTES | 299

104. See P. G. Schmidt, 'The Puretic Power Block and its Effect on Modern Purse Seining', in *Modern Fishing Gear of the World*, ed. Hilmar Kristjansson (Rome: FAO, 1959), 400–14.

105. See Von Brandt, *Fish Catching Methods of the World*, 2–3.

106. FAO, *The State of World Fisheries and Aquaculture*, 2014, 3–10.

107. See Q. Hanich and Y. Ota, 'Moving Beyond Rights-Based Management: A Transparent Approach to Distributing the Conservation Burden in Tuna Fisheries', *International Journal of Marine and Coastal Law* (2013), 28; and Q. Hanich et al., 'Research into Fisheries Equity and Fairness – Addressing Conservation Burden Concerns in Transboundary Fisheries', *Marine Policy* 51 (2015).

108. For some different perspectives on this long history of domination, see Tim Ingold, *The Perception of the Environment: Essays on Livelihood, Dwelling and Skill* (London: Routledge, 2000); Nibert, *Animal Oppression and Human Violence*; and Fudge, 'The Animal Face of Early Modern England'.

109. John Locke, of course, described the seas as the last commons. See John Locke, *Two Treatises of Government* (Cambridge: Cambridge University Press, 2009), 289. See also Wadiwel, *The War against Animals*, 147–56.

110. Note Marx's footnote in *Capital*: 'It appears paradoxical to assert that uncaught fish, for instance, are a means of production in the fishing industry. But hitherto no one has discovered the art of catching fish in waters that contain none.' Marx, *Capital*, vol. 1, 287 n. 7.

111. The rise of aquaculture need not produce poorer outcomes for fish welfare. Certainly, it is conceivable that 'welfare' provisions could improve as a result. For example, there is more scope to use relatively 'quick' stun and kill methods, such as individually stunning fish with a blow or spike, or using new techniques such as electrocution. In so far as health outcomes are considered important for welfare, aquaculture provides opportunities to prevent disease and injury through concentrated management.

112. 'Aquaculture Is Needed to Satisfy Global Demand for Fish', 18 October 2006, http://knowledge.wharton.upenn.edu/article/aquaculture-is-needed-to-satisfy-global-demand-for-fish/.

113. M. Krkošek et al., 'Impact of Parasites on Salmon Recruitment in the Northeast Atlantic Ocean', *Proceedings of the Royal Society of London, B: Biological Sciences* 280, no. 1750 (2013); Samantha Bui et al., 'Modifying Atlantic Salmon Behaviour with Light or Feed Stimuli May Improve Parasite Control Techniques', *Aquaculture Environmental Interactions* 3, no. 2 (2013); Law, 'Notes on Fish, Ponds and Theory', 2–3.

114. See for example Sigurd O. Handelanda, Albert K. Imslanda and Sigurd O. Stefanssona, 'The Effect of Temperature and Fish Size on Growth, Feed Intake,

Food Conversion Efficiency and Stomach Evacuation Rate of Atlantic Salmon Post-Smolts', *Aquaculture* 283, no. 1–4 (2008).

115. Law, 'Notes on Fish, Ponds and Theory', 9.

116. Ashley, 'Fish Welfare', 211–13.

117. Ashley, 'Fish Welfare', 214. See also Bui et al., 'Modifying Atlantic Salmon Behaviour'.

118. Ashley, 'Fish Welfare', 208–9.

119. Ashley, 'Fish Welfare', 208. See also David H. F. Robb, 'Welfare of Fish at Harvest', in *Fish Welfare*, ed. Edward J. Branson (Oxford: Blackwell, 2008), 217–42.

120. See Jenny Bergqvist and Stefan Gunnarsson, 'Finfish Aquaculture: Animal Welfare, the Environment, and Ethical Implications', *Journal of Agricultural and Environmental Ethics* 26 (2013), 82–3.

121. See Law, 'Notes on Fish, Ponds and Theory'.

122. Robb, 'Welfare of Fish at Harvest', 226.

123. Robb, 'Welfare of Fish at Harvest', 217.

124. These devices appear to have been developed in the 1970s. 'Pollution-Free Fish Pump', *Marine Pollution Bulletin* 7, no. 6 (1976).

125. John M. Grizzle et al., 'Skin Injuries and Serum Enzyme Activities of Channel Catfish (*Ictalurus punctatus*) Harvested by Fish Pumps', *Aquaculture* 107 (1992), 334.

126. See A. Thompson et al., 'Mortality in Juvenile Salmonids Passed Through an Agricultural Hidrostal Pump', *Fisheries Management and Ecology* 18, no. 4 (2011). See also Hanne Digre et al., 'Pumping of Mackerel (*Scomber Scombrus*) Onboard Purse Seiners, the Effect on Mortality, Catch Damage and Fillet Quality', *Fisheries Research* 176 (2016).

127. B. P. M. van Esch and I. L. Y. Spierts, 'Validation of a Model to Predict Fish Passage Mortality in Pumping Stations', *Canadian Journal of Fisheries and Aquatic Sciences* 71 (2014).

128. Van Esch and Spierts, 'Validation of a Model', 1920.

129. Van Esch and Spierts, 'Validation of a Model', 1919.

130. Hardt and Negri, 'Marx's Mole is Dead!'

7 Dreams

1. Negri, *Marx Beyond Marx*, 83.

2. Tronti states: 'the dissociation between theory and politics is only a consequence of the contradiction between strategy and tactics. Both have their material basis in the still slowly developing process by which the class and the historical organisations of class – the "working class" and the "workers' movement" – divide and

then counterpose one other. What does this discourse mean in concrete terms, and where will it take us? Right away, it is worth saying that the objective to be achieved is the solid recomposition of a politically appropriate relationship between the two moments.' Tronti, *Workers and Capital*, 69.

3. See for example Braidotti, *The Posthuman*, 75. Here Braidotti rejects approaches to animal rights that attempt to rescue animals by reinstating them within humanistic categories. Instead, Braidotti implies that the alteration of the condition of animals by contemporary technologies should be embraced because it leads to the generation of new hybrid identities, such as the cloned sheep Dolly: 'In the universe that I inhabit as a postindustrial subject of so-called advanced capitalism, there is a great deal of familiarity and hence much in common in the way of embodied and embedded locations, between female humans, oncomouse and the cloned sheep Dolly. I owe as much to the genetically engineered members of the former animal kingdom, as to humanistic ideals of the uniqueness of my species. Similarly, my situated position as a female of the species makes me structurally serviceable and thus closer to the organisms that are willing or unwilling providers of organs or cells than to any notion of the inviolability and integrity of the human species' (80).

4. There is of course much contestation on the role of advocacy with respect to disability movements. See for example Leanne Dowse, 'Contesting Practices, Challenging Codes: Self Advocacy, Disability Politics and the Social Model', *Disability & Society* 16, no. 1 (2001); and Petri Gabor, Julie Beadle-Brown and Jill Bradshaw, '"More Honoured in the Breach than in the Observance": Self-Advocacy and Human Rights', *Law* 6, no. 4 (2017).

5. On animal speech and democratic process, see Eva Meijer, *When Animals Speak: Toward an Interspecies Democracy* (New York: New York University Press, 2019).

6. Consider a public statement published in *Bioscience*, signed by no less than 11,000 scientists, calling for urgent action on anthropogenic climate change. The statement lays out six steps towards addressing the climate emergency, including changes to economies, a reduction in land clearing, transitioning towards low-carbon renewables, and reductions in population growth. Most of these changes require significant change at the production end of capitalism, or at least, in the case of the population growth reductions, a strong commitment by government to policies which will shape human population growth. The glaring exception is the demand to change food practices by reducing meat consumption. Here the solution is framed as a demand for consumers to change their individual dietary practices, rather than for capitalism to alter its food production system. See William J Ripple et al., 'World Scientists' Warning of a Climate Emergency', *BioScience* 70, no. 1 (2020). See also Damian Carrington, 'Climate

Crisis: 11,000 Scientists Warn of "untold suffering"', *Guardian*, 6 November 2019, https://www.theguardian.com/environment/2019/nov/05/climate-crisis-11000-scientists-warn-of-untold-suffering. Carrington's summary of this demand is: 'Eat mostly plants and less meat, and reduce food waste.'

7. See Wadiwel, *The War against Animals*, 22–4; 168–9.

8. See Annie Potts, 'What is Meat Culture?' in *Meat Culture*, ed. Annie Potts (Leiden: Brill, 2016), 1–30.

9. See Dinesh Joseph Wadiwel, 'Counter-Conduct and Truce', in *Philosophy and the Politics of Animal Liberation*, ed. Paola Cavalieri (New York: Palgrave Macmillan, 2016), 187–237.

10. On the understanding of veganism as practice, see Wadiwel, 'Counter-Conduct and Truce'; C. Lou Hamilton, *Veganism, Sex and Politics: Tales of Danger and Pleasure* (Bristol: HammerOn Press, 2019); and Eva Haifa Giraud, *Veganism: Politics, Practice, and Theory* (London: Bloomsbury, 2021).

11. See Jonathan Dickstein et al., 'Veganism as Left Praxis', *Capitalism, Nature, Socialism* (2020).

12. Margret Robinson, 'Veganism and Mi'kmaq Legends', *Canadian Journal of Native Studies* 33, no. 1 (2013); and Margret Robinson, 'Is the Moose Still My Brother if We Don't Eat Him?' in *Critical Perspectives on Veganism*, ed. J. Castricano and R. Simonsen (Cham: Palgrave Macmillan, 2016), 261–84.

13. Kirsty Dunn, 'Kaimangatanga: Māori Perspectives on Veganism and Plant-Based Kai', *Animal Studies Journal* 8, no. 1 (2019), 56.

14. See Charlotte Coté, '"Indigenizing" Food Sovereignty: Revitalizing Indigenous Food Practices and Ecological Knowledges in Canada and the United States', *Humanities* 5, no. 3 (2016).

15. Dunn, 'Kaimangatanga', 56.

16. Note that Dunn carefully notes an uncertainty with the word 'veganism', observing that this does not necessarily have equivalence with the concept of 'kaimangatanga' being traced in this article. Dunn states: 'I would add that there are Indigenous veganisms too, and that kaimangatanga is but one iteration of these, with its own variations or branches. Some might even choose to refrain from using the "vegan" label entirely: this is my reason for refraining from presenting "veganism" and "kaimangatanga" as simple equivalents. Whilst some may see the word, "kaimangatanga", for example, as a translation of the word "veganism" or "vegetarianism", others, including myself, assert that kaimangatanga stands on its own as a decolonial food ethic. Whilst there will indeed be similarities between veganism and kaimangatanga, it is my view that the latter term can accommodate a more nuanced approach towards kai-related practices and the creation and preservation of taonga, and one that can adapt and change where needed. That some of us may

choose to name this way of being and relating to the world in our own language makes it, for me, a powerfully decolonial act: an act of tino rangatiratanga. This also helps us to kōrero with others in our own whānau, hapū, iwi, and in our own homes, communities, and wharekai, and to continue forging our own responses to the exploitation of animals and the environment, and the ramifications of intensive animal agriculture in Aotearoa and beyond.' Dunn, 'Kaimangatanga', 56–7.

17. See Claire Jean Kim, 'Makah Whaling and the (Non) Ecological Indian', in *Colonialism and Animality*, ed. Montford and Taylor, 50–103.

18. Kim, 'Makah Whaling and the (Non) Ecological Indian', 83.

19. L. Boronyak et al., *Kanganomics: A Socio-Economic Assessment of the Commercial Kangaroo Industry* (Report by the Centre for Compassionate Conservation, University of Technology, Sydney, 2013), 10.

20. David Brooks, 'Re-Thinking Kangaroos: The Ethics of the Slaughter of a Species', *ABC News*, 7 June 2021, https://www.abc.net.au/religion/david-brooks-rethinking -kangaroos-ethics-of-slaughter/13376542.

21. 'Understanding the Issues: Kangaroo Shooting', 7 December 2021, https:// animalsaustralia.org/latest-news/kangaroo-shooting/.

22. See for example Josh Becker and Hannah Palmer, 'US Congress to Consider Ban on Kangaroo Skin and Meat, Putting Australian Industry at Risk', *ABC News*, 12 February 2021, https://www.abc.net.au/news/rural/2021-02-12/us-considers- ban-on-kangaroo-products/13148454.

23. NSW Legislative Council, *Report on Proceedings Before Portfolio Committee No.7 – Planning and Environment: Health and Wellbeing of Kangaroos and Other Macropods in New South Wales*, 15 June 2021, 12.

24. NSW Legislative Council, *Report on Proceedings Before Portfolio Committee No.7*, 13.

25. The message stick was presented to a member of the Animal Justice Party, the Honourable Mark Pearson MLC. See 'Gallery: World Kangaroo Day 2021 and the Yuin Declaration for Kangaroos', https://markpearson.org.au/gallery-world- kangaroo-day-2021-and-the-yuin-declaration-for-kangaroos/.

26. See Kangaroos Alive, 'Yuin Declaration for Kangaroos', 24 October 2024, https://x.facebook.com/KANGAROOSALIVE/photos/a.805529609877090/ 1296843284079051/?type=3&source=48. See also Koori Mail, 'Declaration is a Call to Protect Our Kangaroos', *Koori Mail*, https://koorimail.com/declaration-is- a-call-to-protect-our-kangaroos/.

27. NSW Legislative Council, *Report on Proceedings Before Portfolio Committee No. 7*, 12. This section of Godwin's powerful testimony reads as follows: 'It was not enough that the invaders of this once-pristine country mass-slaughtered Indigenous peoples – my family, my ancestors. It was not enough that they

took body parts of Indigenous peoples, our tools, our artwork and the bones of those they slaughtered to the other side of the world as trophies. No, that was not enough. It is never enough as that behaviour pattern, that mindset, continues today. No lessons have been learned. In fact that very mindset and those behaviours repeat themselves ad nauseam and without any care, daily, via the behaviours of the government-sanctioned commercial kangaroo killing industry. These sacred totem animals, their spirits are never able to rest as they are gunned down. Their flesh and body parts are taken, cut up, shipped around the world and taken again. Their internal organs, their heads, are severed and tossed aside like garbage as they are killed. If kangaroo joeys are not legally bludgeoned to death by shooters those surviving little babies – little joeys – will ultimately die lingering deaths alone as they call to their slaughtered mothers. A lucky few will find their way to the arms of wildlife rescue, and we are so thankful for them' (12).

28. Gerardo (Watko) Tristan, quoted in Palestinian Animal League, 'Don't say GO VEGAN. Respond to the Local Context and Challenges of Your People', *Palestinian Animal League*, 28 November 2018, https://pal.ps/en/2018/11/28/dont-say-go-vegan-respond-to-the-local-context-and-challenges-of-your-people/. On Tristan, see Hamilton, *Veganism, Sex and Politics.*

29. Tristan, quoted in Palestinian Animal League, 'Don't say GO VEGAN'.

30. See Wadiwel, 'Counter-Conduct and Truce'.

31. See Julie Creswell, 'How Many Hogs Can Be Slaughtered Per Hour? Pork Industry Wants More', *New York Times*, 9 August 2019, https://www.nytimes.com/2019/08/09/business/pork-factory-regulations.html.

32. One example is the increased use of cattle prods to incentivise animals to move forward to their deaths: 'Pre-stunning handling facilities are of primary importance, given the need to handle pigs faster, so as to follow the speed of the slaughter-line. The combination of higher speeds . . . poorly designed handling systems and large groups is detrimental to animal welfare and pork quality as it increases the use of electric prods without necessarily speeding up the flow of pigs to the stunner.' See L. Faucitano, 'Invited Review: Effects of Lairage and Slaughter Conditions on Animal Welfare and Pork Quality', *Canadian Journal Of Animal Science* 90, no. 4 (2010), 464.

33. Israel Cook, 'How Fast Is Too Fast? OSHA's Regulation of the Meat Industry's Line Speed and the Price Paid by Humans and Animals', *Sustainable Development Law & Policy* 18, no. 1 (2018).

34. This would be resonant with the working-class-led approach to transformation advocated by Matthew T. Huber. See Matthew T. Huber, *Climate Change as Class War: Building Socialism on a Warming Planet* (London: Verso, 2022).

35. See Wadiwel, 'Counter-Conduct and Truce'. See also Dinesh Joseph Wadiwel, 'Can We Stop the Slaughterhouse for at Least One Day? Exploring Alliances with Labour Movements', *Animal Liberation Currents*, 4 January 2017, https://animalliberationcurrents.com/can-we-stop-the-slaughterhouse/.

36. For a careful commentary on some of these claims, and the difficulty of enduring success in countering these issues, see Peter Vandergeest, Olivia Tran and Melissa Marschke, 'Modern Day Slavery in Thai Fisheries: Academic Critique, Practical Action', *Critical Asian Studies* 49, no. 3 (2017).

37. See EJF, *Blood and Water: Human Rights Abuse in the Global Seafood Industry* (London: Environmental Justice Foundation, 2019).

38. Silvia Federici has made the point that this campaign did not necessarily set out to achieve its goal of wages, but to point out the value logic of capital and create the basis for the refusal of this work: 'To ask for wages for housework will by itself undermine the expectations society has of us, since these expectations – the essence of our socialisation – are all functional to our wageless condition in the home. . . . It should be clear, however, that when we struggle for a wage we do not struggle to enter capitalist relations, because we have never been out of them. We struggle to break capital's plan for women, which is an essential moment of that planned division of labour and social power within the working class, through which capital has been able to maintain its power. Wages for housework, then, is a revolutionary demand not because by itself it destroys capital, but because it attacks capital and forces it to restructure social relations in terms more favourable to us and consequently more favourable to the unity of the class. In fact, to demand wages for housework does not mean to say that if we are paid we will continue to do it. It means precisely the opposite. To say that we want money for housework is the first step towards refusing to do it, because the demand for a wage makes our work visible, which is the most indispensable condition to begin to struggle against it, both in its immediate aspect as housework and its more insidious character as femininity.' See Silvia Federici, *Wages Against Housework* (Bristol: Falling Wall Press, 1975).

39. Melissa Boyde, for example, discusses her own rescued cows, which include perhaps the oldest cows in Australia. See Melissa Boyde, '"Peace and Quiet and Open Air": The Old Cow Project', in *Meat Culture*, ed. Potts, 129–48. On sanctuaries, see Elan Abrell, 'Introduction: Interrogating Captive Freedom: The Possibilities and Limits of Animal Sanctuaries', *Animal Studies Journal* 6, no. 2 (2017); and Elan Abrell, *Saving Animals: Multispecies Ecologies of Rescue and Care* (Minneapolis: University of Minnesota Press, 2021).

40. See Sara Barnes, 'Powerful Portraits of Rescued Farm Animals Who Were Allowed to Grow Old', *My Modern Met*, 18 June 2019, https://mymodernmet.com/isa-leshko-farm-animal-photos/.

306 | ANIMALS AND CAPITAL

41. Marx, *Capital*, vol. 1, 416.

42. Wilderson, 'Gramsci's Black Marx', 234–5.

43. Karl Marx, 'Critique of the Gotha Program,'in *The Marx-Engels Reader*, ed. Robert C. Tucker (New York: W. W. Norton & Company, 1978), 525–41.

44. On Marx and social justice, see Norman Geras, 'The Controversy about Marx and Justice', in *Marxist Theory*, ed. Alex Callinicos (Oxford: Oxford University Press, 1989), 211–68.

45. Marx, 'Critique of the Gotha Program', 531.

46. One example is the media response to a *BuzzFeed* editor's call for 'full communism now', which immediately aligned this demand with the project of totalitarian states, including Cambodia's Khmer Rouge regime. Certainly, as Jodi Dean argues, there is every reason for the left to interrogate its own history and potentially rearticulate what 'communism' means as a goal or 'horizon'. See Jodi Dean, *The Communist Horizon* (London: Verso, 2012).

47. Robinson, *Black Marxism*, 113. Thomas Piketty provides a calculation of the capital value of slavery in the south of the United States, arriving at extraordinary observation: 'In the American South, the total value of slaves ranged between two and a half and three years of national income, so that the combined value of farmland and slaves exceeded four years of national income. All told, southern slave owners in the New World controlled more wealth than the landlords of old Europe. Their farmland was not worth very much, but since they had the bright idea of owning not just the land but also the labor force needed to work that land, their total capital was even greater.' See Piketty, *Capital in the Twenty-First Century*, 160.

48. Wolfe, *Traces of History*.

49. See Spivak, *An Aesthetic Education*, 192.

50. In this respect, 'economy' is precisely about the management of time. Marx states: 'On the basis of communal production, the determination of time remains, of course, essential. The less time the society requires to produce wheat, cattle etc., the more time it wins for other production, material or mental. Just as in the case of an individual, the multiplicity of its development, its enjoyment and its activity depends on the economization of time. Economy of time, to this all economy reproduces itself.' Marx, *Grundrisse*, 173.

51. Marx, *Grundrisse*, 634.

52. See Derrida's analysis of Madame de Maintenon's statement: 'The King takes all my time; I give the rest to Saint-Cyr, to whom I would like to give all.' See Jacques Derrida, *Given Time: 1. Counterfeit Money* (Chicago: University of Chicago Press, 1994), 1–5.

53. Jack Halberstam, *In a Queer Time and Place: Transgender Bodies, Subcultural Lives* (New York: New York University Press, 2005), 10.

NOTES | 307

54. Muñoz refers to a conference presentation Nyong'o made in 2008. See José Esteban Muñoz, *Cruising Utopia: The Then and There of Queer Futurity* (New York: New York University Press, 2009), 206 n. 12. However, the context of the citation, I believe, can be found in a later published paper, where Nyong'o asks: 'Is there anything black about waiting? It is certainly familiar enough, even in an era whose enigma is the arrival of the first US black president. The pedagogic time of the nation imposes a different imperative upon black freedom dreams than those available from radical traditions of black performativity.' See Tavia Nyong'o, 'Brown Punk: Kalup Linzy's Musical Anticipations', *Drama Review* 54, no. 3 (2010), 83.

55. Muñoz, *Cruising Utopia*, 182–3.

56. Wilderson, 'Gramsci's Black Marx', 230.

57. See for example Frederik Berend Blauwhof, 'Overcoming Accumulation: Is a Capitalist Steady-State Economy Possible?' *Ecological Economics* 84 (2012); and Peter Custers, 'The Tasks of Keynesianism Today: Green New Deals as Transition towards a Zero Growth Economy?' *New Political Science* 32, no. 2 (2010). See also John De Graaf, David Wann and Thomas H. Naylo, *Affluenza: The All-Consuming Epidemic*, 2nd ed. (San Francisco: Berrett-Koehler, 2005); and Clive Hamilton and Richard Denniss, *Affluenza: When Too Much Is Never Enough* (Crows Nest: Allen & Unwin, 2005). See also R. J. White and C. C. Williams, 'Anarchist Economic Practices in a "Capitalist" Society: Some Implications for Organisation and the Future of Work', *Ephemera: Theory and Politics in Organization* 14, no. 4 (2014).

58. Paul Mason, *PostCapitalism: A Guide to Our Future* (London: Penguin, 2016).

59. Negri, *Marx Beyond Marx*, 160.

60. Kathi Weeks, *The Problem with Work: Feminism, Marxism, Anti-Work Politics and Postwork Imaginaries* (Durham, NC: Duke University Press, 2011), 36. See also Robert E. Goodin et al., *Discretionary Time: A New Measure of Freedom* (Cambridge: Cambridge University Press, 2008).

61. It is not clear that in Marx's vision for communism described in *The German Ideology* we have an articulated plan for what communism should look like; instead, Marx rhetorically describes this array of activities to show how the division of labour which applies in other economic systems might not need to apply within communism: 'For as soon as the distribution of labour comes into being, each man has a particular, exclusive sphere of activity, which is forced upon him and from which he cannot escape. He is a hunter, a fisherman, a herdsman, or a critical critic, and must remain so if he does not want to lose his means of livelihood; while in communist society, where nobody has one exclusive sphere of activity but each can become accomplished in any branch he wishes, society regulates the general production and thus makes it possible for me to do one thing today and

another tomorrow, to hunt in the morning, fish in the afternoon, rear cattle in the evening, criticise after dinner, just as I have a mind, without ever becoming hunter, fisherman, herdsman or critic. This fixation of social activity, this consolidation of what we ourselves produce into an objective power above us, growing out of our control, thwarting our expectations, bringing to naught our calculations, is one of the chief factors in historical development up till now.' Karl Marx, *The German Ideology*, Part 1, https://www.marxists.org/archive/marx/works/1845/german-ideology/ch01a.htm.

Index

Page numbers for Figures appear in *italics*. The suffix n signifies an endnote.

Adams, Carol J., 66, 244n36
Agamben, Giorgio, 243n31
air transport, 137–8, 280n80
Althusser, Louis, 27–9, 35, 40, 174, 227n109
Amir, Fahim, 176, 195n72, 223n70
animal advocacy *see* pro-animal movements
animal dignity, 257n26
animal export figures, 142–3, 277n64
animal feed, 121–2, 264n100, 265n105/109
animal labour, 91–129
  overview, 12–14
  definitional problem of, 94–5
  formal and real subsumption, 122–4
  gestational labour, 3, 101–7, 163, 206–7
  metabolic labour, 95, 100–3, 107–12, 114–15, 121: and domestication, 123; and feed conversion rates, 122; and live animal transport, 155–60; and wild fishes, 163, 166, 181
  racial slavery compared, 95–7, 213–14, 257n27/29, 258n30, 279n76
  and reproductive costs, 81, 122
  resistance to mechanised processes, 124–9
  right to refuse, 206–7
  theory of labour value, 21–30

and time, 117–19, 204–6, 213–15
in value context, 21–30, 98–101, 107–17, 117–22
within live animal transport, 153–60
animal resistance, 161–91
  and animal labour time, 112, 125–7, 159–60
  conceptualisation of, 174–8
  to mechanised processes, 124–9
  operaist view, 176–8
  and value production, 99, 161–2
  see also fishes: fish resistance
animal rights movements *see* pro-animal movements
animal rights theory
  capabilities, 6
  and contradictory roles of animals, 83–4, 250n100
  focus on consumption, 18–19
  on intrinsic value of animals, 6
animal sourced foods
  consumption, 2–3, 88–9
  overproduction, 198–9
animal welfare approaches
  and capitalism, 7–8
  and intrinsic value, 6–7
  and production, 144–51, 177–8, 187, 196–8, 290n27
animals as property, 8, 12, 269n3

310 | ANIMALS AND CAPITAL

Animals Australia, 291n29
antagonism *see* structural antagonism
anthropocentrism *see* hierarchical
anthropocentrism
aquaculture, 112–13, 165, 183–9, 293n56,
299n111
Aradom, Samuel, 159 (quotes)
Arcari, Paula, 216n2
Arendt, Hannah, 240n99
Aristotle, 68–9, 245n38
artificial insemination, 3, 102, 141, 276n56
Australia
human working conditions, 286n122–3
live animal exports, 139–40, 146–7,
149, 157–8, 281n84/86, 285n117,
287n138
Averos, X., 286n118
Awassi Express (ship), 146

Back, Chris, 287n138
Barad, Karen, 56
Barua, Maan, 99, 258n18
Bear, Christopher, 127, 267n128/132
MV *Becrux see* MV *Ocean Drover*
beef production, 75, 135, 136, 242n15,
270n15
Beldo, Les, 100–1
Bennett, Jane, 42–3
Bentham, Jeremy, 253n119, 292n46
Benton, Ted, 16, 220n42
Bhattacharya, Tithi, 4
biopolitics
of animal production, 3, 82–3, 100,
106, 118–19, 123–4, 217n12, 243n31,
250n96
of human social reproduction, 3–4,
81–3, 250n94–6/99
Black, Celeste, 290n18
Blanchette, Alex, 246n59
Blancou, Jean, 271n27
Boyde, Melissa, 261n65, 305n39
Braidotti, Rosi, 42, 43–4, 195, 301n3
Braithwaite, Victoria, 167
Braverman, Harry, 222n59
Brazil beef industry exports, 277n64
Broom, D. M., 149 (quote), 269n6, 281n90
Brown, Culum, 293n56
Brown, Wendy, 172
Browne, Craig, 223n64

Bulitta, Fufa Sorri, 159 (quotes)
Butler, Judith, 230n12, 246n58

capital
circulating, 29, 92, 109–14, 261–2n70,
262n78
constant and variable, 108–9, 154,
192–3
fixed, viii–ix, 19–20, 124–9, 153, 162,
179, 195, 197, 261n70
lively, 98–100
origins of word, 246n52
variable, 108–13
capitalism
and animal welfare, 7–8
and 'capitalocentrism', 26, 116–17
colonialism and animals, 10–12
defined, vii, 8–9
and financialisation, 14
parasitism, 184, 190–1
racial, 56–7, 210–11
wastage, 164–5
cattle *see* beef production; dairy
production
Caulfield, Malcolm, 290n27
Cavalieri, Paola, 18
Celermajer, Danielle, 228n113
Chakrabarty, Dipesh, 22
cheap food, 2–3, 23–4, 83
chicken production
as central achievement of capitalism,
2–3
chicken-catching process, 125–6,
266n120
labour time of chickens, 120
metabolic labour of chickens, 100–1
numbers killed for human
consumption, 2
osteopenia, 281n90
price of poultry, 242n15
transportation, 147, 269n6
China, 136, 138
Choat, Simon, 37
circulation
and fishes, 187
and production time, 156–8
turnover time, 131
see also live animal transport
Clark, Brett, 93, 255n6

INDEX | 311

climate change, 31, 89–90, 198–9, 301n6
Collard, Rosemary-Claire, 99–100, 119, 164
colonialism *see* settler colonial contexts
commercial surrogacy, 103–6, 260n59/63–4
commodification of animals *see* consumption commodities; raw material
communism
  conceptualising, 207–11
  and Marx, 307n61
  use of term, 221n56
companion animals, 31, 83–4, 250n100
Concentrated Animal Feeding Operations (CAFOs), 139, 273n37
consumption commodities, animals as, 2–5, 59–60, 77–90
contradiction, 7, 87, 89, 252n110, 253n116
Coole, Diana, 37–9
Cooper, Melinda, 100
MV *Cormo Express*, 146
Coulter, Kendra, 95
Crenshaw, Kimberlé, 49, 236n58, 237n61/63–4
Crocker, Lawrence, 252n110
Crutzen, Paul, 163
Cudworth, Erika, 232n27

Dairy Australia, 127, 268n134
dairy production
  animal labour, 114
  artificial insemination processes, 3, 102, 141, 276n56
  discarded animals, 164
  high-capacity facilities, 274n42
  milking machines, 112–13, 127–8, 266n125, 267n127–9/132–3
  as reproductive labour, 102–3
  robotic (automated) dairy farms, 127–8
Dean, Jodi, 306n46
Deleuze, Gilles, 55–6, 227n111, 238n85, 239n86–7/89
Dempsey, Jessica, 99–100, 119, 164
Derrida, Jacques, 67–9, 232n35, 244n32/36, 245n38/44/48, 306n52
Descartes, René, 167
disability, 21, 48, 301n4
draught animals, 94, 254n128

Driessen, Bert, 148 (quote)
Dunn, Kirsty, 200, 302n16
Dutkiewicz, Jan, 72–3

ecofeminism *see* feminism and feminist theory
Edgar, Blake, 296n81
Edwards, Jason, 41, 231n23
Engels, Friedrich, 93
epistemic violence, 171–4
epistemology, 169–71
Esch, B. P. M. van, 189 (quote)
Esposito, Roberto, 243n31
Ethiopia, live animal exports, 143, 278n68
European Union regulations, 144, 151, 279n75
experimental animals, 83–4, 224n75, 280n80

fabrication, 69, 72, 74, 240n99, 246n59
factory farms
  absence of human–animal relation, 120–1, 195, 246n59, 264n98
  functions and roles within capitalism, vii–ix
  and labour value process, 112–14
  pro-animal movements and, 19–20
  as sites of hostility, 97–8
  within green Marxist and ecofeminist theory, 22–6
Fanon, Frantz, 47
FaunAcción, 203
Feber, Ferenc, 232n32
Fede, Andrew, 258n30
Federici, Sylvia, 21, 305n38
feminism and feminist theory
  on animal reproduction and gender relations, 3, 48
  and biopolitics, 250n95
  on capitalism's relation to nature, 24–6
  on commercial surrogacy, 103–6, 260n59/63–4
  on commodification of women, 65–6, 242n17, 243n19/23, 246n58
  ecofeminist politics, defined, 226n96
  and gender-based violence, 293n48
  Indigenous standpoint theory, 234n42
  intersectionality, 48–50

312 | ANIMALS AND CAPITAL

feminism and feminist theory (*cont.*)
  and life sciences, 230n15
  readings of capitalism, 21
  readings of Marx, 24–6, 65–6
  on silent cooperation of animals,
    220n50
  on work, 205, 214, 305n38
financialisation, 14, 221n55
Fishcount.org.uk, 165, 290n16
fishes
  capacity for suffering, 167–8, 170–1,
    291n29/33, 292n45
  fish consumption per capita, 2, 216n7,
    254n124
  fish meal production, 139
  fish resistance, 168–74, 175–6, 178–89,
    190, 294n57–8
  and pain, 167
  use of term, 289n3
  see also aquaculture; recreational
    fishing; wild fish capture fisheries
Fitzgerald, Kevin T., 180–1 (quote)
food animals
  defined, 216n2
  as economic class, 1, 14, 192–3
Foster, John Bellamy, 14, 22–3, 24, 25–6,
    92–3, 225n83, 255n6
Foucault, Michel, 16, 36, 81–2, 85, 168,
    169–70, 229n7, 232n31, 243n31,
    250n94, 292n37
Fowkes, Ben, 238n81
France, Anatole, 67–8
Francione, Gary, 8, 246n52
Fraser, Nancy, 19
Frost, Samantha, 37–9
Fudge, Erica, 8
Fukase, Emiko, 252n107

Gamble, Christopher, 37, 230n16
Gebresenbet, Girma, 159 (quotes)
genetically engineered animals, 301n3
Gibson-Graham, J. K., 116
Gillespie, Kathryn, 3, 48, 102–3, 164,
    217n17, 247n68, 259n50, 261n65,
    263n81
Giraud, Eva Haifa, 46, 235n48
globalisation, 140–4
Godwin, Aunty Ro Mudyin, 202, 203,
    303n27

Gordon, Peter E., 240n99
Gramsci, Antonio, 36
Grandin, Temple, 152, 283n99
Gruen, Lori, 257n26
Guattari, Félix, 55–6, 227n111, 238n85,
    239n86–7/89
Gunderson, Ryan, 222n58

Halberstam, Jack, 212
Hall, Stuart, 36
Hanan, Joshua, 37, 230n16
Haraway, Donna J., 98–9, 111–12, 128
Hardt, Michael, 4, 177, 178, 190, 275n49
Harris, Cheryl I., 246n52
Harris, Tim, 280n80
Harrison, Uncle Max Dulumunmun,
    202–3
Hartman, Saidiya V., 97
Harvey, David, 9, 252n110
Hegel, G. W. F., 261n66
Heidegger, Martin, 240n99
Henisch, Bridget Ann, 251n104
hierarchical anthropocentrism
  and anti-Blackness, 57, 97
  and capitalism, 9, 26
  and colonialism, 171–2
  and communism, 14
  defined, vii, 12, 241n100
  and epistemic violence, 6
  and Marx, 17–18, 93
  and new materialism, 42
  and value, 69–70, 193
  and the working day, 120
Hobden, Stephen, 232n27
Holloway, Lewis, 127, 267n128/132
Holocaust, 240n99
Hribal, Jason, 161, 174, 256n10
Huber, Matthew T., 304n34
human labour
  alienated nature of, 16–17, 76, 92
  function of the wage, 78–81, 84–5,
    249n90
  and live animal transport, 145, 151–3
  in meat-packing industries,
    286n119/122
  welfare conditions, 280n79
  see also commercial surrogacy; racial
    slavery
Hutnyk, John, 275n49

Iceland, 2015 general strikes, 204
ideology, 35–6
Indigenous cultures
  cultural significance of kangaroos,
    202–3, 303n27
  feminist Indigenous standpoint theory,
    234n42
  knowledge systems, 41, 231n22
  marginalisation by settler colonialism,
    10–11, 210–11
  plant-based food cultures, 200–1,
    302n16
  sovereignty, 234n39
Ingen, Michiel van, 45
internal relations, philosophy of, 26,
  226n103
intersectionality, 48–50, 52–3, 236n56/58,
  237n60–1/63–4
Irigaray, Luce, 65–6, 242n17, 243n19,
  246n58

Jackson, Zakiyyah Iman, 45–6, 96
Jain, Purushottam Chandra, 262n73
John F. Kennedy Airport, 138
justice
  and Derrida, 232n35
  and factory farms, ix
  and Marx, 207–9, 306n44
  racial, 201–3

Kaarlenkask, Taija, 266n125
kangaroo commercial cull, 201–3
Kim, Claire Jean, 48, 57, 201, 203,
  237n60
Kirby, Vicky, 37, 42
Klein, Richard, 296n81
Ko, Syl, 235n52
Kowalczyk, Agnieszka, 175
Krien, Anna, 288n140

labour value process, 1, 21–30, 107–17,
  122–3, 154, 228n112, 263n82–3; see
  also animal labour; human labour
Lacan, Jacques, 62–3
Latour, Bruno, 232n29
Law, John, 185–6
Lemke, Thomas, 232n31
Lewis, Sophie, 3, 104–6, 206,
  260n59/63–4

Link, William A., 257n29
Little, Lewis, 270n9
live animal transport, 128–60
  animal labour, 153–60
  in antiquity, 271n27
  cost drivers, 144
  geopolitical factors, 139–40
  impact of globalisation, 140–4
  interrelation with production systems,
    139
  loading, 147–8
  mortality rates, 146–7, 280n83–4/87,
    287n131
  and rearing conditions, 281n90
  semen trade, 141–2
  size of carriers, 138–9
  treatment during, 147–9, 282n91,
    282n95, 283n97–9, 285n109/117
  and value transfer, 132–8
  visibility during, 284n100
  see also air transport; rail transport;
    road transport; sea transport
Locke, John, 299n109
Luxemburg, Rosa, 87, 248n76/78, 256n9

machines
  chicken harvesting machine, 125–6
  fish pump, 188–9
  mechanical brail net, 187–8
  mechanisation of animal transport,
    138–40
  Puretic Power Block, 183
  robotic dairy farms, 127–8
  skinning machine, 75–7
  see also capital: fixed
McKay, Robert, 238n81, 245n50
MacLachlan, Ian, 271n26
Mandel, Ernest, 79
Martin, Richard, 223n71
Martin, Will, 252n107
Marx, Karl
  on absolute and relative surplus value,
    117–19
  on alienation of labour, 15–17, 76
  and animal labour, 15–17, 27–30, 92–4,
    222n62, 227n111, 228n112, 255n6,
    256n9–10, 259n51, 261n70, 262n78,
    263n82–3
  on animal welfare, 15, 222n58

314 | ANIMALS AND CAPITAL

Marx, Karl (*cont.*)
anthropocentrism, 17–18, 21–6, 29, 93–4, 113–14, 225n85
anti-humanism, 29–30, 81
approach in *Capital*, 227n105
on capitalist animal agriculture, 120
on circulation, 130, 131, 137, 156–7, 194, 287n135
on commodification, 61–4, 67, 70, 73–4, 219n41, 241n2–3/6, 242n7, 244n32
concept of metabolic rift, 22–3, 225n83
on contradictions in capitalism, 87, 89, 252n110, 253n116
Critique of the Gotha Program, 207–8
definition of capitalism, 9
on delays on movement of money, 275n51
on distributional models of justice, 207–10
on economy of time, 306n50
on the free market, 247n62
on free time, 212
function of the wage, 79, 80–1, 84–5, 249n87
Hegel compared, 261n66
labour process, 107–8
on machinery, 125, 276n57, 277n60
mode of reading, 27
on money, 63–4, 71–2, 246n53/56
and *oikonomia*, 242n8
'old' materialism, 35–6, 38–41, 231n21, 231n23
on overproduction, vii, 78, 86–7, 90, 158, 164, 252n108
philosophy of internal relations, 26, 226n103
on production and consumption, 59
on resistance by commodities, 161
skin removal as metaphor, 74, 247n64–5
structural position of the worker, 26–7
symptomatic reading of, 27–30
two department model of reproduction, 77–8, 248n77
on uncaught fish, 299n110
understanding of raw material, 218n23
use of names, 242n11
on value of labour power, 1, 27–8, 29–30, 107–14, 122–3, 154, 194, 228n112, 263n82–3
value theory, 98–9
vantage point, 26–7
vision for communism, 207–8, 307n61
werewolves and vampires, 54–8
on the working day, 117–19, 206
Mason, Paul, 214
Maurizi, Marco, 5, 224n76, 225n85
Mbembe, Achille, 124
meat consumption per capita, 2, 88–9, 216n7, 254n124
meat production value chains
disintegrated model, 136–7, *137*
simple model, 132–3, *133*, 269n8
vertically integrated model, 133–6, *135*, 270n9
'meatification', 2
Meijer, Eva, 301n5
Meißner, Hanna, 40
milk *see* dairy production
Mills, Charles, 235n49
money
as medium of anthropocentrism, 65–7
metallic currency, 71, 245n51
as mode of exchange, 9, 63–5, 70, 71–2, 245n51
see also wage
monism, 45–7
Mood, Alison, 165
Moore, Jason W., 2–3, 23–4, 25–6, 83, 85, 87, 228n112
Moreton-Robinson, Aileen, 234n42
Muñoz, José Esteban, 212–13, 307n54

MV *NADA*, 138, 140, 147
Nail, Thomas, 37, 230n16
Nash, Jennifer C., 236n56
Negri, Antonio, 4, 56, 177, 178, 190, 192, 214, 231n21, 234n37, 238n82, 275n49
new materialisms, 37–47, 232n27
Nibert, David, 10
Nietzsche, Friedrich, 46
Novek, Joel, 286n119
Nussbaum, Martha, 6, 168
Nyong'o, Tavia, 213, 307n54

MV *Ocean Drover* (formerly *Becrux*), 138–9, 146–7

O'Connor, James, 87
Oksala, Joanna, 234n36
old materialism, 35–6, 38–41, 231n21, 231n23
Oliver, Michael, 21
Ollman, Bertell, 26, 226n103
ontology, 15–16, 45–7
operaist view of resistance, 176–7

Pacey, Margaret, 270n9
Pachirat, Timothy, 75, 98
Palmer, Clare A., 176, 295n69
Pande, Amrita, 103–4
Parsonson, Ian, 271n27
Patel, Raj, 2–3, 23, 83, 85
Patterson, Orlando, 66, 96, 257n27
Pauly, Daniel, 162–3, 164, 289n8
Pettinger, Lynne, 116
Phillips, Clive, 146, 154–5, 273n35, 285n109/111, 287n131
pigs *see* pork production
Piketty, Thomas, 248n84, 306n47
plant-based foods, 88–9, 200–1, 302n16; *see also* veganism
pork production
  continuous feeding of pigs, 273n37
  pre-stunning handling facilities, 304n32
  reproduction of pigs, 3, 217n14
  smallholder production, 136
  transportation of pigs, 147–8, 281n87, 286n118
  treatment during, 286n118
Potter, Will, 258n33
Pratt, Mary Louise, 128
pro-animal movements
  attitude of the left, 17–18, 20–1
  goals, 207–15
  and politics of consumption, 18–19
  and politics of production, 19–21, 224n76–7
  reframing of, 196–9
  tactics, 199–207
Probyn, Elspeth, 85, 294n57
Probyn-Rapsey, Fiona, 276n59

race and racism
  anti-Blackness, 50–2
  and gender, 49–50, 237n64
  interaction with capitalism, 56–7

structural antagonism, 44–7, 50–3, 235n48–9
  and waiting, 212–13, 307n54
racehorse industry, 141
racial slavery
  animal labour compared, 95–7, 213–14, 257n27/29, 258n30, 279n76
  capital value in American South, 306n47
  and commodification, 66–7
  as means of production, 210, 306n47
  and structural antagonism, 46–7, 50–2, 213–14, 235n48–9
  transportation parallels, 279n76, 288n140
rail transport, 271n26
raw material
  animals as, 5–12, 59–60, 64–71, 72–7
  versus consumption commodities, 59–60
  Marx's understanding of, 61–4, 71–2, 76, 77, 218n23
Read, Jason, 227n111
recreational fishing, 166, 175, 180
Regan, Tom, 6, 168
Reich, Wilhelm, 239n87
Rejali, Darius, 283n97
Repo, Jemima, 250n95
research animals *see* experimental animals
resistance *see* animal resistance
road transport, 138, 152–3, 272n32–3, 282n91, 285n107, 286n123
Robb, David H. F., 187 (quote), 188
Roberts, Michael, 221n55
Robinson, Cedric J., 21, 56–7, 210, 249n88
Robinson, Joan, 241n6
Robinson, Margret, 200
Rose, James D., 291n33, 292n45
Rubin, Gayle, 243n19
Russia, beef imports, 139–40

Sadedin, Suzanne, 260n63
Salleh, Ariel, 24–6, 220n50, 226n96–7
Salt, Henry, 17
Sanbonmatsu, John, 17–18
Scarry, Elaine, 179, 247n65
sea transport, 138–9, 146–7, 149, 153, 272n34, 273n35, 279n76, 281n84, 285n109/111, 287n131, 288n140/141

316 | ANIMALS AND CAPITAL

settler colonial contexts, 10–11, 47, 48, 171–2, 210–11
Sexton, Jared, 46–7
Sharpe, Christina, 279n76
sheep, transportation of, 149, 280n83, 281n84/86, 285n109
Sheldon, Tony, 286n123
Shukin, Nicole, 241n99
Simmons, Glenn, 289n8
Singer, Peter, 18, 19–20, 168, 253n119
skinning, 64, 71–7, 247n64–5, 247n66, 247n69
slaughterhouses
    death as value producing, 72–3
    line speeds, 204
    partitions within, 75
    stunning of animals, 142, 177–8, 276n59, 304n32
    Wilderson's analogy of, 51–2, 207
    working environment, 286n122
slavery see racial slavery
Smith, Adam, 91, 93, 122, 255n2, 256n9/10
Sneddon, Lynne, 167
social reproduction, 4–5, 80, 83
speciesism, vi, 66
Spierts, I. L. Y., 189 (quote)
Spillers, Hortense J., 49–50
Spivak, Gayatri Chakravorty, 49, 171–2, 173, 243n18, 294n58
Stache, Christian, 226n86
the State, 32
structural antagonism, 44–7, 50–4, 235n48–9
stunning of animals, 142, 177–8, 276n59, 304n32
subsumption, 122–4, 163–4, 184–5
surplus value
    absolute and relative, defined, 117
    and shortening of animal lives, 119–21, 205–6, 264n98
    and yield, 121–2

TallBear, Kim, 11, 41, 231n22
Taschereau Mamers, Danielle, 10
Taylor, Sunaura, 48
Torres, Bob, 223n70
trade unions, 204
Tristan, Gerardo (Watko), 203
Tronti, Mario, 44, 91, 177, 263n93, 300n2

Twine, Richard, 4, 121
Tyler, Tom, 12
Tynan, Aidan, 55, 239n88

UN Food and Agriculture Organization, 163, 165, 173
USAID, 143

value
    animal labour theory, 21–30, 107–14
    encounter value, 98–9
    exchange value, 63–4, 78–9
    use value, 28–30, 193–4
value chain models, 132–7, *133, 135, 137*
veganism
    anti-colonial, 53, 200–3
    and consumption, 19, 53, 86–7, 90, 199–203, 252n109, 302n10/16
    as political tactic, 200, 302n10

wage, function of, 78–81, 84–5, 249n90
wastage, and capitalism, 164–5
Webster, John, 7–8, 10
Weeks, Kathi, 214
Weis, Tony, 2, 264n100
Wellard (live export company), 272n34
Wen's Food Group, 136
wild fish capture fisheries
    discards, 164–5
    formal and real subsumption, 163–4, 184–5
    global crisis in, 163
    the hook, 179–81, 296n85/92
    parasitism, 184, 190–1
    pole and line, 180–1, 296n92
    possible collaborative action, 204–5
    purse seines, 181–3
    quantification of catches, 165, 293n56
    slaughter practices, 166–7, 290n21
    uncaught fish, Marx on, 299n110
    and welfare, 166–7
Wilderson, Frank B., III, 44–5, 50–3, 66–7, 76, 95–6, 207, 209–10, 213–14, 234n39, 237n68, 238n69
Wilson, Elizabeth A., 230n15
Wolfe, Patrick, 210–11
Woods, Jennifer, 152

Zeller, Dirk, 162–3, 164, 289n8